D1025150

TENNESSEE WILLIAMS

ALSO BY DAKIN WILLIAMS
The Bar Bizarre
Nails of Protest

ALSO BY SHEPHERD MEAD

NOVELS

The Carefully Considered Rape of the World
The Magnificent MacInnes
Tessie, the Hound of Channel One
The Big Ball of Wax
The Admen
The Four-Window Girl
*"Dudley, There Is No Tomorrow!" "Then How About This After-
noon?"*
How to Succeed at Business Spying by Trying
*'Er, the Brassbound Beauty, the Bearded Bicyclist, and the Gold-
Colored Teen-age Grandfather*

HUMOR

How to Succeed in Business without Really Trying
How to Get Rich in TV without Really Trying
How to Succeed with Women without Really Trying
How to Live Like a Lord without Really Trying
How to Stay Medium-Young Practically Forever without Really Trying
Free the Male Man! The Manifesto of the Men's Liberation Movement
How to Succeed in Tennis without Really Trying

FACT

How to Get to the Future Before It Gets to You

TENNESSEE WILLIAMS

An Intimate Biography

by
DAKIN WILLIAMS
and
SHEPHERD MEAD

ARBOR HOUSE
New York

Library of Congress Catalogue Card Number: 82-74062

ISBN: 0-87795-488-7

Manufactured in the United States of America
10 9 8 7 6 5 4 3 2 1

This book is printed on acid free paper. The paper in this book meets the guidelines for permanence and durability of the Committee on Production Guidelines for Book Longevity of the Council on Library Resources.

ACKNOWLEDGMENTS

The authors wish to acknowledge the following list of sources:

My Brother's Keeper, unpublished manuscript by Dakin Williams;

Remember Me to Tom, by Edwina Williams with Lucy Freeman, New York, G. P. Putnam's Sons, 1973;

Close Up, by John Gruen, The Viking Press, New York, 1968; Playboy, April 1973, interview with Robert Jennings;

The Atlantic Monthly, November 1970, article by Tom Buckley;

Tennessee Williams and Friends, by Gilbert Maxwell, World Publishing Company, Cleveland, 1965;

Tennessee Williams' Letters to Donald Windham, 1940–1965, Holt, Rinehart & Winston, New York, 1977;

Without Stopping, by Paul Bowles, G. P. Putnam's Sons, New York, 1972;

New York Review of Books, February 5, 1976, article by Gore Vidal;

Theatre Book of the Year, edited by George Jean Nathan, Alfred A. Knopf, New York, 1945;

Laurette, by Marguerite Courtney, Rinehart & Company, New York, 1955;

Curtains, by Kenneth Tynan, Longmans, London, 1961;

Esquire, September 1971, interview with Rex Reed;

Kazan on Kazan, Interviews with Michael Ciment, Secker and Warburg, London, 1973;

A Look at Tennessee Williams, by Mike Steen, Hawthorn Books, New York, 1969;

John Gielgud, by Ronald Hayman, Heineman, London, 1971;

Gertrude Lawrence as Mrs. A., by Richard Aldrich, Greystone Press, New York, 1954;

The Hero Continues, by Donald Windham, T. Y. Crowell, New York, 1960;

Miss Tallulah Bankhead, by Lee Israel, W. H. Allen, London, 1972;

The Theatre in Spite of Itself, by Walter Kerr, New York, 1963, Simon & Schuster;

The Nation, March 14, 1966;

The World of Tennessee Williams, by Richard Leavitt, New York, G. P. Putnam's Sons, 1978;

Tennessee Williams: A Collection of Critical Essays, edited by Stephen S. Stanton, Prentice-Hall, Englewood Cliffs, New Jersey, 1977.

Special gratitude is owed to the many people who submitted to interviews, and most of all to those who gave us long statements on tape, such as Paul Bigelow, Margaret Foresman and Bill Glavin. The assistance given by the Humanities Research Center of the University of Texas at Austin, whose Tennessee Williams collection includes a thousand volumes and twenty thousand manuscript pages, was simply boundless.

TO JOYCE AND TO ANNABELLE

INTRODUCTION
How Do Two People Write One Book?

O ne way is for one person, who knows the facts, to tell another, who acts as a writer, or ghost-writer. A second way is for two collaborators to work together on common material. The third way, our way, is for two writers to collaborate, but each from a different vantage point. This happened by accident, but with luck it could, like two stereophonic sound tracks or two stereoscopic pictures, help to create a third dimension.

The accident is improbable because the two writers live four thousand miles apart, one in Collinsville, Illinois, the other in London, England.

Dakin Williams, a lawyer and a writer, had been making notes and collecting material about his brother all his life. Dakin was born in St. Louis just after the family had come up from Mississippi along with eight-year-old Tennessee, then known as Tom.

Shepherd Mead, younger than Tom and older than Dakin, was born and lived for his first twenty-two years in a house in a suburb of St. Louis, about a mile from the one where the Williams family lived longest—on opposite sides of the campus of Washington University, which all three attended, and where all three took the playwriting course.

As editor of the university magazine, Mead published some of Tom's first poems, all signed Thomas Lanier Williams, which was his real name.

Dakin went on to Washington University Law School, and served, during World War II and the Korean War, as a legal officer in the air force.

Tom and Mead, both determined to become playwrights, studied in New York under the same teacher, John Gassner, at the New School. Both also spent a year in Hollywood writing scripts, at about the same time, before either was known. Both had the same play agent, Audrey Wood. Mead even helped to beat Tom, then called Tennessee, out of his third Pulitzer Prize, with Mead's first (and only) shared one, in 1962. Tennessee's *Night of the Iguana* won his fourth New York Drama Critics' Circle Award that year for best play, while *How to Succeed in Business Without Really Trying* won the Critics' Award for musicals, and also the Pulitzer.

Meanwhile Dakin came back from the wars to establish a private law practice and enter Illinois politics as a Democratic candidate for governor and senator.

Tennessee, having established himself, by general consensus, as America's greatest living playwright (a term he detested), refused to rest on his laurels and was working harder and more compulsively than ever. In 1969 he had a serious nervous breakdown in Key West. Dakin dropped everything, flew down there and either saved Tennessee's life, as we believe, by bringing him to a hospital in St. Louis; or, as Tennessee believed—the controversy is still not resolved, and is given considerable attention in this volume.

After spending a few months in what he called "the looney bin," much improved, Tennessee wrote his bestselling *Memoirs*, and it was this that started our project. Mead read the book, was puzzled by the fact that Tennessee's year at Washington University had been completely wiped out of his life. Mead was also curious. What traumatic horror had obliterated that Washington year? He did a bit of literary detective work, wrote a number of letters, especially to members of the playwriting class, among them the biographer A. E. Hotchner, whom Mead had known at Washington. The whole shocking truth was revealed in an article for the university magazine, "The Secret Year of Tennessee Williams," the main facts of which are included in this book.

Dakin read the article, was amused and sent a factual correction to the magazine. Dakin also decided to put things right, and persuaded Tennessee and the university to stage a reunion and reconciliation. Tennessee was invited to pay a visit. He came, made a triumphant appearance in the university chapel, was mobbed by cheering students, gave a press conference and had his beaming face all over the St. Louis newspapers: Williams radiant, Washington University forgiven, a happy ending.

Correspondence followed between Dakin and Mead, who had never met, and the decision to collaborate on a biography. There would be equal voices, equal billing and equal rewards.

Mead spent nearly a year writing the first draft, incorporating some of Dakin's unpublished memoirs, *My Brother's Keeper*, and a mass of private letters, documents and other material never before published. Now Dakin is the only surviving member of the family, except for sister Rose, whose memory had been destroyed by lobotomy.

Then the two authors met in Florida and drove to Key West to see Tennessee, whom Mead, in spite of their parallel lives, had never met. The night meeting was a traumatic experience, recounted in this book.

Dakin and Mead then toured the country together, interviewing dozens of people, and making about twenty hours of tapes, some with Tennessee's closest former companions. Dakin brought Mead to visit their mother, "Miss Edwina," at a nursing home in St. Louis. Dakin did this almost every day, driving across the Mississippi River from Collinsville, to help feed her and speak a few words to her. She was then ninety-four; she died the following year.

Mead went through the vast Tennessee Williams Archives at the University of Texas, in Austin, and spent another year putting it all together in London.

The manuscript was then sent to Tennessee, asking him to refute or correct any statement. The results of this were indeed strange. But then, we are getting ahead of our story.

CHAPTER 1

Thomas Lanier Williams was born on March 26, 1911, in Columbus, Mississippi, on the opposite side of the state from the Mississippi River, a few miles from the Alabama border and about one hundred miles from Tennessee. It was no doubt within the boundaries of William Faulkner's mythical Yoknapatawpha County, since Oxford, Mississippi, and New Albany (where Faulkner was actually born) are less than one hundred miles to the northwest.

Thus two of the South's most famous writers were born within a short ride of each other.

Williams's speech still has the deep-down sound of Mississippi, even though his family left there when he was eight. He spent most of his youth in Missouri, mainly in St. Louis, yet he does not have the Midwestern accent of Missouri at all. But somehow the imprint of those eight Mississippi years was so indelible that he kept on going back to the deep South for most of his richest material.

So why isn't he Mississippi Williams, or even Missouri Williams? Actually he comes by his Tennessee writing name honestly, even though he spent little time there. His family's main roots are there. The first Thomas Lanier Williams was the first chancellor of the Southwest Territory before Tennessee was a state. Tennessee's first senator was John Williams, the hero of King's Mountain, and another paternal ancestor with the resounding name of Nollichucky Jack Sevier was the first governor of Tennessee. The playwright's grandfather, Thomas Lanier Williams II, spent most of the family fortune trying unsuccessfully to be governor. It was the cost of this struggle that left Tennessee's father stranded financially, and even emotionally. This had a profound effect on the life as well as the plays of Tennessee Williams.

Far back, the family name Sevier traces through the centuries to St. Francis Xavier. The Catholic side of the family kept the name Xavier, and the Huguenot branch changed theirs to Sevier when they fled to England after the St. Bartholomew's Day Massacre.

The main influences on the playwright's life came from his mother's side. And in spite of "Miss Edwina's" airs, this side was not as illustrious as the Lanier-Sevier-Williams ancestry of the paternal line.

The one person who had the strongest influence of all was his maternal grandmother, Rose, always called "Grand." Rosina Maria Francesca Otte was born of German-American parents who, though they were Lutheran, sent her to a Roman Catholic convent near Cincinnati. This was evidently for education rather than religious instruction, because they pulled her out quickly when they discovered she was secretly wearing a rosary under her clothes.

Rose wanted to escape from her stern parents, and at sixteen married one of the first eligible bachelors she met, an ambitious young man of Norman-English descent named Walter Edwin Dakin. A small and courteous gentleman, he was trained as an accountant, but he had a secret ambition.

Rose said, later, "I would never have married him if he had told me about his intended vocation."

Walter Dakin, the accountant, was determined to become an Episcopal minister, and Rose, so young and so small (she weighed only ninety-eight pounds) helped him to succeed, in spite of everything. Nothing stopped Rose. A favorite family story tells how Rose, shortly after the wedding, was thrown from a runaway horse and buggy. Hanging down, with her feet pinned under the seat, she would have been crushed if the wheel had passed over her body. She seized a spoke of one wheel and kept it from turning until the buggy finally stopped, after moving about a hundred feet.

Rose practiced every day on the piano and the violin, and for most of her life gave lessons in both instruments. The money she made from her music lessons helped to support her grandson during his long years in the theatrical wilderness.

Rose was beautiful, and so was their only child, Edwina, who did indeed (as Amanda said in *The Glass Menagerie*) have many gentlemen callers. One of these was Cornelius Coffin Williams, whose family tree must have impressed her, and whom she married.

Cornelius had had a miserable childhood. His mother, Isabel Coffin Williams, was also very beautiful. She died at twenty-eight from tuberculosis. Cornelius's father, Thomas Lanier Williams II, seemed to care mainly for other women and for his relentless and futile pursuit of the governorship of Tennessee. His high-water mark was to be appointed state railroad commissioner.

Cornelius was sent off to Bellbuckle Military Academy, where he spent much of his time in the guardhouse, eating turnips. Later he studied law at the University of Tennessee. But before he could win a degree he was shipped off to the Spanish-American War, where he caught typhoid fever and lost all his hair. He was bald the rest of his life. Nevertheless, Edwina claimed he was handsome until he began drinking heavily, and his later photographs show the puffy face of a dedicated drinker. He lost the sight of one eye from a fall.

Cornelius was fired from one of his early jobs as a telephone exchange manager in Gulfport, Mississippi, for reasons he never revealed. He became a traveling salesman, driving his car full of samples around the South. Often he would be gone a week or two at a time. Edwina lived with her father and mother at the Episcopal rectory in Columbus.

Their first child was named Rose, after her grandmother, and she too was beautiful, with blue eyes and lovely auburn curls. Though Rose was to become the prototype for Laura, the lame and painfully shy young woman of *The Glass Menagerie*, she was not lame; her mother claimed in her memoirs that Rose was certainly not shy in her early years. In fact, "she was the ringleader in games and very spirited."

Two years later Tom was born, and on the morning the Reverend Mr. Dakin and his congregation were celebrating Palm Sunday. Edwina was close by, in a small private hospital built by her doctor. "We barely made it," she said. Young Tom was in a hurry.

Tom's early years were happy and uncomplicated. By his own account, written while very young and saved by Edwina, he spent these years surrounded almost entirely by women. His father often traveled for weeks at a time.

He played with Rose, sailing paper boats, keeping white rabbits, cutting paper dolls out of mail order catalogues and collecting colored glass from broken bottles.

He was very fond of a pretty black nurse named Ozzie, who would sit beside their beds in the evening and tell wonderful stories about bears and foxes and rabbits. They all talked like Ozzie.

Edwina was worried that he might start talking like Ozzie, too, in a plantation dialect. His mother always wanted him to chew his food thoroughly, so Ozzie would say, "Chaw, honey, chaw!" And when Ozzie would give him a bath, Tom would chase the little celluloid fish around the tub and shout, "I kotch him, Ozzie, see, I kotch him!"

Ozzie had been virtually left on the family's doorstep by her older brothers, who were sharecroppers on one of the large plantations. Though she was then about sixteen, she was illiterate, and the Williams women taught her to read and write.

Giving Rose and Tom a bath was a major job for Ozzie. The water first had to be pumped out of the well and then heated on the wood-burning stove in the kitchen, which was, along with the toilet facilities, separate from the house. Then she had to carry the water in buckets into the house and upstairs to the oval-shaped corrugated metal tub.

There was nothing in these early years to suggest that Rose would have serious mental problems. Edwina wrote, "Rose was always faster than Tom in acquiring knowledge in the little classes I conducted at home. Sometimes we would hear her scream and Tom would be pulling her hair angrily and saying, 'She's too proud of herself.'"

When Tom was three the family moved to Nashville for the only year they were to spend in Tennessee. Tom went to kindergarten. Edwina writes: "He enjoyed himself sculpting in clay, usually forming elephants, as long as I stayed with him. The moment I left the room he would throw himself on the floor and scream, refusing to stop despite all bribery. I had to sit next to him the entire time; fortunately the session lasted only half a day."

Somehow Tom forgot that phase when he wrote a little poem about "Kindy Garden." He remembered only playing with frames of colored beads, thinking wistfully how Rose could rattle off the entire multiplication tables.

He began telling stories when he was very young, whenever he could overcome his shyness. His favorite characters were animals. On one occasion the hero, Tom, being chased by progressively bigger and wilder animals, finally cried out, "It's gettin' so scary I'm scared myself!"

Tom was already seeing some of the seamier sides of life at an early age. He followed his grandfather, whom he called "Grandfads," around town on his calls to sick and troubled parishioners. Young Tom called them his "visits to deathbeds," though his mother thought they were rarely as dramatic as that.

The bishop moved the Reverend Mr. Dakin back to Mississippi, this time to the western side of the state, Clarksdale, a town of three rivers, the Sunflower, the Tallahatchie and the great Mississippi, into which the two little rivers flowed.

Edwina and the children followed. Ozzie, who had been picking cotton with her brothers, failed to return. No one knew why. This left all the child raising to Edwina. Cornelius was drifting farther and farther away, driving his Model T Ford over mud roads, selling shoes. "One summer," Edwina wrote, "I did not see my husband at all."

Soon after they arrived in Clarksdale, Tom nearly died of a disease Edwina thought was diphtheria. He was then five years old. Since there was no hospital nearby, Edwina cared for him herself, keeping him with her in bed for nine nights, and changing ice packs on his throat. The doctors told her she had saved his life.

"On the ninth day," Edwina wrote, "I looked down his throat and noticed that his tonsils, which had become enlarged by his illness, had completely disappeared. I called the doctor in panic. He came over, examined Tom and said he must have swallowed his tonsils."

Edwina always stuck to this story, though it seems to be medically impossible. She attributed many of Tom's later physical problems to this miraculous occurrence.

The diphtheria, if that's what it was, affected Tom's kidneys and paralyzed both his legs. The doctor then told Edwina he was suffering from Bright's disease. Years later, in an interview with John Gruen, he said he thought both diagnoses had been wrong. No one is sure what diseases he had, but Tom said that he was so weak he had to push himself along the floor. He couldn't walk at all.

His eyesight was damaged, and was to remain poor all his life. For almost two years he could scarcely use his legs, and moved around outdoors on an "Irish Mail," a kind of toy handcar.

The psychological effect of the illness kept him from playing normally with other children and, according to Edwina, seems to have changed his whole personality.

"Tom had always been a very active child. Mothers would come to the house complaining he had beaten up their sons, little boys twice his size... That disease was a fearful thing. It took all the belligerency out of Tom."

He confirmed this in his *Memoirs*, saying that the disease changed his whole nature, which he, too, thought had been aggressive and bullying. He amused himself with quiet, lonely games, and his imagination was already working overtime. Not content with the ordinary game of solitaire, he invented one of his own. He had been reading, at this early age, *The Iliad*, and began fighting the Trojan War with cards, one side black and the other red.

Most important, he believed at this time that his mother helped change his nature by being too solicitous. He believed she was making him into a sissy, even a "hybrid."

Rose, too, suffered the "diphtheria," if that's what it was, but it was only a mild attack.

As Tom was recovering, something happened that was to change, probably for the worse, the lives of all the family. Cornelius had been so successful—he had won three solid-gold watches as the company's best salesman—that he was made sales manager of the Friedman-Shelby branch of the International Shoe Company. In a short, sympathetic play, *The Last of My Solid Gold Watches*, we can see what the older, mellowed Tom thought of his father, and how he might have ended if he kept on as a salesman.

Cornelius was now assigned to St. Louis to work in an office. And for the first time he and Edwina would have to make a home of their own, away from Grand and the Reverend Mr. Dakin.

Most important, Cornelius would be living with the family all the time. Tom had written, long before his *Memoirs*, that life under soft-spoken and gentle "Grandfads" had been quiet and peaceful. It was only when Cornelius came home on weekends that the tranquility was broken, with his heavy footsteps, doors slammed, furniture banged and his father's voice sounding like thunder.

For the first time they would be living north of the Mason-Dixon line, and they would be bringing the thunder of Cornelius with them—not just on weekends, but every evening. The first years in St. Louis were to seem so dreadful to Edwina and Tom that they were called "nine years in limbo."

CHAPTER 2

Tom and his mother arrived at Union Station in downtown St. Louis on a blazing hot day in July 1918, the last summer of the war. Rose was still back in Mississippi with her grandparents.

They were met by Cornelius, who had gone on ahead. Tom's main memory of that day was that they passed a fruit stand on the way out of the station and he plucked a grape. His father gave him a stinging slap on the hand, shouting that he must never steal again. For all his other faults, Cornelius was absolutely honest, and always truthful.

St. Louis was flooded with war workers and it was not easy to find an apartment. They went first to a boarding house run by a Miss Florence, on Lindell Boulevard, which Edwina described as "fashionable." At least, Lindell was a fashionable street. With Edwina all things seemed to mature, like wine, with the years, and became more fashionable. But a boarding house seemed a good idea at the time because Edwina had never actually cooked a meal. She said she could make angel food cake, and that was all.

The boarding-house period didn't last long. Edwina saw an advertisement for an apartment to be rented to anyone who would buy all the furniture. This sounded perfect because they had none of their own. And it was in Westminster Place, which was then a truly fashionable address, though it would not remain so much longer. It would later become part of the central city slum as the gentry with their new automobiles moved out west of Skinker Road and Forest Park. In 1918 the decay was already setting in.

Edwina found a sad young man sitting in the midst of his nice furniture. His wife had left him, and he didn't want any of it again. Edwina bought it all, some of which she kept for more than half a century.

The apartment at 4633 Westminster Place, six rooms and a bath, is noteworthy because it was, with some artistic license, the setting of *The Glass Menagerie*. It was probably much less fashionable than Edwina's remembrance (she did say it was dark) and somewhat less frightful than Tom's and Dakin's, as reported to him by Tom. Dakin was there, in a manner of speaking, but couldn't see out. Edwina was pregnant when they moved in, and Dakin was born a few months later.

To Tom the apartment was dismal, with walls the color of dried blood and mustard. The center apartment of three on the first floor, it had no windows except in the front and rear. The back ones looked out on a dark alley where cats were frequently cornered and disemboweled by dogs. Cornelius was happy with his large leather morris chair—but would use it less and less as time went on.

Some of the St. Louis elite still lived in Westminster Place, and Tom and Rose had their children as playmates. This was a mixed blessing, since the Williams children were attending Eugene Field public school, whereas most of the other children went to private schools, the most socially acceptable of which were Mary Institute for girls and Country Day for boys. This, together with the Williams's southern accents, so foreign sounding in St. Louis, made them seem like poor immigrants, whereas in Mississippi, as the grandchildren of the Episcopal minister, they were used to being among the best people in town. The haughty children, whom they met only at Sunday school, treated them like white trash. They would throw Tom's cap out the window when the teacher wasn't looking, and they gave Rose the silent treatment. "The girl snubbed me," she told her mother. The result was that Tom and Rose would stop at Masserang's drugstore across from the Sunday school and spend their time, as well as their offering money of twenty-five cents, at the soda fountain.

On February 21, 1919, Tom and Rose were brought to St. Anthony's Hospital, where they found their mother holding a small bundle, a baby brother named Walter Dakin Williams, after Edwina's father. He was to be Edwina's last child, though she later had a miscarriage. She would nurse him, for a time, as she had the others. The Reverend Mr. Dakin came up from Clarksdale, Mississippi, to baptize him.

The artificially rigged social barriers of St. Louis were frightful for the Williams family, but in spite of them Tom made friends with two Mary Institute girls, Mary Louise Aide and Hazel Kramer. Hazel, a plump redheaded girl, remained Tom's close friend for years. In his *Memoirs* he wrote that she was, outside the family, the greatest love of his life, even greater than his later homosexual loves.

In one of Tom's short stories, "Three Players of a Summer Game," there is a fine self-portrait as a very young boy with a girl like Hazel. The daughter of one of the three players is called Mary Louise (the name of Hazel's real-life girl friend), but it is also a fine portrait of the plump Hazel. In the story she spends a great deal of time waiting in an electric car while her mother makes love. The story has elements that were later to develop into parts of *Cat on a Hot Tin Roof*.

Edwina then committed a grave offense against the tribal customs of fashionable St. Louis. All she wanted was to get out of that dark apartment and into a bit of sunshine. They moved from Westminster Place to a brighter apartment at 3 South Taylor.

There was no plague at South Taylor, and no curse on it, but the people who lived on Westminster Place did not speak to the people on South Taylor.

Tom wrote that they were dropped immediately by all their friends. All but Hazel, anyway. And because they were left alone, Tom and Rose grew closer together, "aliens in an alien world," as Edwina wrote.

Tom, who could now walk but not run, was no good at team games, and since at grade school the pecking order was based on that, he was bullied. One day he came home with his ankles all black and blue. He had been sitting on a bench watching the game, and each boy who went by had kicked him on the ankles.

Life wasn't all bad. Edwina was learning to cook, to make sandwiches and deviled eggs, and would take the children for picnics into beautiful Forest Park, which still had lagoons and ponds and pagodas left over from the St. Louis World's Fair of 1904. They also spent hours at the famous St. Louis Zoo and at Shaw's Botanical Garden. Tom and Rose often swam at the Lorelei Pool. Swimming would later become Tom's favorite exercise.

But the marriage, never idyllic, was heading for more and more trouble. Since Cornelius wrote no memoirs, there is only Edwina's side of it, and by her account she was long-suffering and brave. Her friends, she wrote, bragged about having their husbands bring them coffee in bed, but not Edwina. She rose at six to cook Cornelius a big breakfast, and "no matter how difficult the drudgery all day, I always took a bath in the evening and changed to a dainty dress for dinner, as did Rose."

The trouble, according to Edwina, was Cornelius. She thought he was becoming a monster. But he did have a real problem. For the first time he was fenced in. The free-ranging salesman now had an office and an apartment. And in the office he was the dread sales manager who had to hire and fire salesmen. Sometimes that makes a man want to take a drink.

"Before we arrived in St. Louis," Edwina said, "I saw only the charming, gallant, cheerful side of Cornelius. For a while he tried to keep the Mr. Hyde from me. But he could hardly hold secret his excessive drinking, not when he would come home emitting fumes of alcohol, and in a cross and ugly mood."

At first Cornelius had his cronies in for poker, and Edwina said the game sometimes lasted "the whole weekend." She told him to take his games elsewhere. He would go off to his club or to hotels, often for the whole weekend. But he always made it to the office on time on Monday mornings.

Throughout all this Tom was having a very bad time. His father saw him as a delicate, nonathletic sissy, and called him "Miss Nancy." Tom's mother did not approve of Hazel, and in fact thought all the girls were too "common" for him. And the boys, she thought, were all "too rough" for her delicate son.

Edwina felt the same about Rose's girl friends. They were all a "bad moral influence." So Rose, too, was lonely, and she and Tom moved closer together emotionally. But something came between them, and he told about this years later in a sensitive and beautiful short story called "The Resemblance Between a Violin Case and a Coffin." What happened was that Rose became a woman. He told how she came down to breakfast one morning after her first menstruation, and how his mother and grandmother helped her gently to the table, and handed everything to her that she could not reach.

But the other side of the story was that he, too, was beginning to have feelings he could not understand. In the story his sister and a young man were practicing for a piano-violin duet, and he would bring his violin to their house. The "I" of the story, representing Tom, watched them as they played, through an opening of his bedroom door; he found himself watching not his sister but Richard, the young man, and this troubled him. To him, Richard seemed beautiful, as the sunlight shone through the sheer white cloth of his shirt, revealing his torso and the nipples on his chest. "I" was falling in love with Richard, and at the time the real Tom didn't know what the word *homosexual* meant.

And his mother would not have told him. In Edwina's entire vocabulary the word never appears, nor is the subject ever mentioned. In those days the word *sex* was simply taboo to most well-bred women. They never admitted that it existed at all.

In the case of the fictional Richard, nothing happened. "I" just watched. But in the story, Rose broke down at the recital and failed, though Richard was able to cover up partly for her. It was, for the narrator, the first indication that something was wrong with his sister. On the way back home she seemed to withdraw into herself.

The story is fiction, and the chronology is somewhat changed from actual fact, but the essential bits are true. The Sunflower River of the story does really flow through Clarksdale, but he and Rose left there when they were seven and nine respectively.

When Tom was eleven, Edwina took ten dollars out of the household money and bought him a second-hand typewriter. She said, "It was large and clumsy and sounded like a threshing machine, but Tom was delighted with it. I could hear him hitting the keys for hours." Tom said, "I forgot to write longhand after that." Much later, after he graduated from high school, he took a typing course. No hunt-and-peck man, he has always been a first-class typist. His letters and the *Memoirs* are full of anecdotes of renting, buying, borrowing and hauling typewriters, usually manual port-ables.

His first known composition, preserved by Dakin, was a contest entry, for a flour company, signed with his mother's name. An ode to crisp, brown muffins, it could scarcely have been better written, but the Jenny Wren flour company was not impressed and no prize money was forthcoming.

Edwina says he was twelve when he wrote his first literary piece. The teacher, he said, told the students to look around the classroom at the framed pictures on the wall, and to pick out a subject for a theme. He chose the Lady of Shalott, drifting down the river on a boat. He read the theme in front of the class, "and it had a very good reception. From that time on I knew I was going to be a writer."

His first known published works are two poems written for the junior high school paper, one called "Nature's Thanksgiving," about the woods in autumn, and the other titled "Old Things," about the lovely old contents of an attic. They are signed "Thomas Williams, 9th Gr." and are quite extraordinary for a fourteen-year-old. Poetry was always his first love, and he has written it all his life, in addition to the poetry that runs through his plays.

The situation between Edwina and Cornelius continued to deteriorate, but they were still appearing together at company gatherings. They would attend the annual picnics of the International Shoe Company, often with Paul Jamison, head of their division, and his wife Ida. They would travel out to Crève Coeur (locally pronounced "creeve cur") Lake, which was then out in the country, at the end of the electric trolley-car line. There, among the dogwoods and the lilacs and the daffodils, they would enjoy a fine day of near beer (no alcohol) and lemonade and boat rides—and, of course, company politics.

Many of the company people were from Tennessee, and at first Cornelius and Edwina were very popular with them. All the signs pointed toward great success and riches for the young sales manager.

But all that was to end; a strong contributing factor was the crumbling marriage of Edwina and Cornelius. They had slept in separate bedrooms for a long time and relations between them had probably stopped, Dakin believes, after Edwina's miscarriage in 1921.

Both sons remember violent arguments, usually about money, and his drinking. Edwina recalls one time when she did not have enough money to buy food for the weekend. Cornelius, who was making $7,500 a year, good money for those days, threw $6 on the kitchen table and said, "There, take it all and go to hell!"

Cornelius, she said, liked no living thing except Dakin and their Boston bull, Jiggs, whom he'd bought with his winnings at a poker game. The only time she ever saw him cry was the day Jiggs died. In Cornelius's room was a cartoon of a dog with the caption, "A friend's a friend who knows your faults and doesn't gave a damn."

The marital problems of Edwina and Cornelius might not have affected his career if they had not helped create a public explosion, the first of the two big Cornelius scandals.

On one of C.C.'s (his usual nickname) many weekends away from home, he and two of his younger cronies from International Shoe arranged a supper party. They rented a room in a downtown hotel, brought in bootleg booze, set up a green-topped table with cards and poker chips, and also brought in a couple of what Tom would have called "light ladies."

It probably was not the first time that such an exercise had taken place, but at this party one of the ladies was infected with a social disease, which one of the young salesmen caught and then passed on to his wife. She was, of course, highly displeased, and went straight to Paul Jamison, the boss, a man of strict morals. Jamison called C.C. and the two salesmen on the carpet. The two young men denied everything. C.C., always truthful, admitted it.

The two young men were fired; C.C. was kept on as sales manager because of his honesty—and perhaps also because he was so good at his job. But he and Edwina no longer met socially with the Jamisons, and his upward progress at International Shoe was almost finished.

This destroyed whatever was left of the marriage. Edwina was very ill and had two major operations, including a hysterectomy.

The effects of this destructive home life on the children must have been traumatic. Tom, already a neurotic and introverted child, was having all kinds of psychological problems. He was even terrified to go to sleep at night, because he thought sleep was similar to death.

As he grew into his teens he became almost pathologically shy. He said he blushed when anyone looked him in the eye. It was particularly bad when women looked at him, even his own girl friend, Hazel Kramer, who was his companion for eleven years.

This disturbed Hazel, who told him she would certainly never say anything to hurt him. He and Hazel were in love, and her mother, "Miss Florence," regarded him almost as a son. All three would drive around St. Louis, often in the evening, sometimes to the places where couples parked and "necked"—like the top of Art Hill (near the equestrian statue of St. Louis) and in a low, woodsy road called Lovers Lane.

If this mild voyeurism was intended to suggest anything to Tom, it apparently didn't work. He wrote that he liked being shocked. Some of the couples would not go "all the way." The activity often lasted an hour or so, and usually included the mutual handling of genitals, ending with orgasm and messy clothes. But no babies.

There is no indication that Tom and Hazel did this. Apparently he was most attracted to her shoulders, and his first "genital stirring" was when he saw them, bare, in the West End Lyric movie house on Delmar Boulevard. Later they went on the Mississippi River on the excursion steamer *J.S.* On the top deck, in the dark, he put his arm around her "delicious" shoulders and ejaculated in his white flannels. It was his first recorded orgasm with a girl, but not the last. He was very embarrassed, and Hazel decided they'd better not dance any more after that.

In his *Memoirs*, Tom suggests that there were already conflicting temptations. In the summer of 1928 he went with his grandfather to Europe. The Reverend Mr. Dakin was shepherding a group of Episcopalians on the grand tour. On the boat there was dancing, and Tom sometimes waltzed with a dancing teacher, a woman of about twenty-seven, who was having a flirtation with a man who was much older than Tom. He remembered a conversation the three of them had in the ship's bar. They were talking about him, and seemed to be sure what his future would be. The man was quite certain, but the woman said it was too early to tell, at seventeen. Tom concluded later, when he wrote his *Memoirs*, that they were talking about whether he was heterosexual or homosexual, though at the time he was totally mystified. So perhaps, even then, some people thought they could tell.

While he was in Europe, Tom had an odd psychological crisis apparently having little to do with the trip or his companions. It was a kind of wide-awake nightmare so intense that it left him shaking and drenched with sweat. He was terrified by the thought of thought, by the concept of the process of human thinking, as a mystery in human life, and it made him think he was going mad.

The panic struck him while he was walking in Paris (though it had nothing to do with Paris), followed him down the Rhine and was partially resolved by an experience that he thought was religious, almost supernatural. He was kneeling in prayer in the cathedral of Cologne, which he thought was the most beautiful he had ever seen.

Though he said that normally he does not believe in miracles, he felt that while he was kneeling an unseen hand had been placed on his head and suddenly his phobia was lifted away. He was sure then, at seventeen, that it was the hand of Jesus that had done it.

The phobia returned again, briefly, and this time he cured it himself, in Amsterdam, by a less supernatural method: he wrote a poem, a lovely one about strangers passing in the street. It made him recognize he was not alone but a part of humanity. The phobia left him for good.

In 1928 he returned to University City Public High School for his final semester and wrote an account of his travels for the school paper. It was serialized in many issues, but he made no mention of the phobia.

He remained the most bashful boy in school, so shy that he could not even answer questions aloud in class. But he *was* something special. He was the only one who had been abroad.

No matter what was happening, or where he was, Tom was always writing, every kind of thing. He entered many advertising contests. He won his first writing prize at sixteen. Smart Set magazine held a contest: "Can a Good Wife be a Good Sport?" The fact that Tom had never had a wife, good or bad, didn't stop him. With a straight face he recounted his own marital adventures, and told how, after their third wedding anniversary, he discovered his wife was unfaithful and how, unhappily, they were divorced a year later. Being a good sport was not necessarily a good thing. Competing with thousands of people who knew what they were talking about, Tom won third prize—five dollars.

The following year he sold his first short story to *Weird Tales*, a pulp magazine, called "The Vengeance of Nitocris." Nitocris was an Egyptian queen who rated only a paragraph or two in Herodotus, but Tom expanded her story into a minor epic, telling how Nitocris avenged the death of her brother by luring his murderers into an underground chamber, which she then flooded, drowning them all. After that, knowing she would be doomed, she went into a smoke-filled room and suffocated herself. His heroines would always have problems like that. He made thirty-five dollars for it, his first big writing money.

The smoke-filled ending may have been suggested by the fact that he had just won five dollars in a contest sponsored by the St. Louis Citizens

Smoke Abatement League, whose slogan was SMOKE MUST GO. Tom compared the smoke to a dragon engulfing the city. And in those days St. Louis was certainly engulfed. Sometimes in winter you couldn't see across the street.

Tom wrote his first play long before the "Tennessee" pen name was invented. Stopping at nothing, he decided to take on Shakespeare and improve him. The Williamses were spending a vacation at a YMCA camp at a lake near Springfield, Missouri. For amateur night Tom contributed a play, the first draft of which had already been roughed out by Shakespeare and was called *Romeo and Juliet*. Tom noticed that W.S. had not taken the trouble to rhyme the poetry, and decided to do it up right. Dakin, who played the part of Paris, can still recite many of the ringing couplets. Compared with the teen-age Tom Williams, Bowdler was an upstart.

Dakin was continually being bamboozled by his older brother. On drives through the country Tom would explain the animals. "Now that, Dakin," Tom would say, pointing to a pig, "is a cow." "So what is that?" Dakin would ask, pointing to a cow. "That is a pig, Dakin."

Tom was reading all the time. Edwina says he spent "endless hours" at the library, and continually brought home books. However, the only one of these she mentions is D.H. Lawrence's *Lady Chatterley's Lover*. She opened that at one of the really sexy bits. ("Tom said I had a veritable genius for opening always to the most lurid pages.") She thereupon "marched Tom and the book to the library, where I gave the librarian a piece of my mind."

From then on, Edwina crossed Lawrence off her list, and resolutely refused ever to see or read Tom's one-act play *I Rise in Flame, Cried the Phoenix*, his youthful (1941) poetic account of the death of Lawrence. Tom remained an admirer of Lawrence's work all his life.

In the last months of 1928, before his January graduation from high school, he was trying to make plans to enter a university. About Thanksgiving time he wrote a long letter to his grandfather, saying that he might even take a bit of postgraduate Latin to build up his credits to enter Washington University. He was reading a life of Shelley and was fascinated that the poet had been wild, passionate and dissolute.

Most important in this period between graduation and entrance into university was his relationship with Hazel Kramer, which had a profound effect on his whole personality, and perhaps on the ultimate course that his sexual development was to take.

Tom and Hazel were close emotionally; yet their physical relationship was almost unbelievably distant, even prim. He wrote that Hazel allowed him to kiss her on the lips only twice a year, on Christmas and her birthday.

He was never sure whether this was from frigidity on her part, or simply a coquettish ploy to bring out a more aggressive attitude on his part. In any case, it didn't work.

However, he does say that the episode of the fig leaf in his "Three Players of a Summer Game" really took place with Hazel at the St. Louis Art Museum. Hazel did indeed lift a fig leaf on a male statue (*The Dying Gaul*) and did ask him, "Is yours like that?" The New Yorker cut this line from the story, Williams later put it back and Dakin swears there are no hinged fig leaves in the St. Louis art gallery. Fig leaf or no, the implication was that Hazel wasn't as cold as all that, and maybe Tom was not getting the whole message.

The sad part was that the relationship did break up, and it was possibly Cornelius who caused it. Tom and Hazel graduated from high school the same year, 1929, Hazel from Mary Institute and Tom from University City Public High School (with a B average). He had transferred there from the St. Louis schools, Ben Bluett and Soldan, when the family moved from St. Louis to an apartment at 6254 Enright Avenue in the suburb of University City. (The Williams family moved nine times during their first dozen years in the St. Louis area.)

Cornelius knew that Tom and Hazel were very close, and was determined to avoid an early marriage. And he had a strong lever, Hazel's grandfather, who worked for International Shoe under Cornelius. C.C. persuaded Mr. Kramer to send Hazel to the University of Wisconsin. Tom, meanwhile, had decided to go to the University of Missouri, in Columbia, far from St. Louis, instead of nearby Washington.

Edwina accompanied him to Columbia to help him find a place to stay. That very first night, in the hotel, he wrote a letter to Hazel at the University of Wisconsin proposing marriage. A week later she replied that they were too young to think about anything like that.

Tom saw Hazel again, but the romance was over. Years later, Dakin remembers, Hazel's divorced mother, Miss Florence, dropped in on the Williams family. Flamboyant as ever, she sashayed in and went to the piano, as was her custom, and started to spank out a popular tune.

"Not so loudly!" said Edwina, fearful of the landlady.

Miss Florence stopped abruptly, and said she was leading up to the fact that Hazel would be singing on the radio that very night. That was true. Hazel had a good voice, and had found a number of professional singing jobs.

But Miss Florence was saving the big news for Tom. When he came into the living room she kissed him on the lips and said, "I've got news for you, sonny boy. Hazel has gone and got herself engaged to be married."

Tom was shattered, and couldn't believe it, but Miss Florence had a letter to prove it. She also said that Hazel was coming back to St. Louis, and invited them to come over on Sunday for tea to meet Hazel's fiancé, a young man named Terrence McCabe.

And so they did, and found that Terry McCabe was about as different as possible from Tom, a tall, thin, extroverted, back-slapping fellow who was the life of the party.

Tom, quiet, shy, introverted and heartbroken, listened as Terry told a joke that Dakin still remembers as the only thing he can recall clearly about McCabe.

"Did you hear this one about the stockbroker?" said Terry. "He was telling his new client, 'Hold your gas, let your water go, sit on your American Can! Scott tissues went down three points. Thousands were wiped clean!'" Great guffaws from Miss Florence.

Tom never asked another woman to marry him. Hazel's marriage ended in tragedy. She broke up with Terry years later, and this affected Miss Florence so much that she committed suicide. Hazel died mysteriously on a trip to Mexico, of alleged food poisoning.

No one can say that if Hazel and Tom had not been separated they might have married and Tom's whole sexual life would have been different. Dakin believes it could have been.

CHAPTER 3

Tom entered the University of Missouri almost at the moment the Great Depression began. Edwina remembered those hectic days. While they were getting his things ready to go, she and her mother had one other preoccupation. They needed to replace an old upright piano, and went shopping for it at Baldwin's. It seemed to them rather odd that few other people were shopping that day. However, they did buy the piano, on the installment plan.

At dinner they told Cornelius about the big purchase. He said, "I don't suppose you know the bottom dropped out of the stock market today."

Cornelius did not feel he was able to finance the whole cost of sending Tom to the university; it was possible only because grandma had contributed a thousand dollars. Since the Reverend Mr. Dakin's income was quite small, and since old Grand made very little money giving music lessons, this must have been a great sacrifice.

Cornelius had been a fraternity man at the University of Tennessee, Pi Kappa Alpha, and wanted Tom to join a fraternity, too. Edwina thought a proper boardinghouse would be better, and before she left Columbia she made sure Tom was installed in one, run by a lively widow who drove a bright red Buick convertible. The fact that it was segregated by sexes pleased Edwina.

Tom's roommate was a young blond farm boy who either accidentally or deliberately walked in his sleep, once as far as Tom's bed. Nothing happened. The boy sleepwalked back to his own bed.

But, as far as Tom has revealed, this was the first time a young man ever had walked to his bed, and he rather hoped it would happen again. And when it didn't, after a few nights, Tom says he loosened some of the bolts on the boy's cot. Sure enough, it collapsed. But instead of moving over with Tom, the boy fixed it, meanwhile glancing rather suspiciously at Tom.

Back in St. Louis, Cornelius was pulling strings. There were some cousins at the University of Tennessee who were influential in the Alpha

Tau Omega fraternity, and Cornelius persuaded them to make contact with the University of Missouri chapter of ATO. They were told that a scion of the Williams and Sevier families was actually slumming in a Columbia boarding house.

The ATO brothers sent a delegation immediately, and took him back to their temporary quarters; they were careful to pass by the new chapter house, which was just being completed. Tom was impressed by the imposing pseudo-Tudor mansion, and by the charm of the brothers. Decades later he wrote that one of them was surely homosexual, though he was far too innocent at the time to know.

They took him to supper, then up to their council chamber, where they asked him to join ATO. He told Edwina that their membership was not limited to a single type of young man. This later proved to be true in more senses than one.

They told him the history of the fraternity, and put a pledge pin on him, and everyone congratulated him. He wrote, "I never felt so important." It is clear the brothers gave him a big sales talk, because he told his mother that after a person left the university, being a fraternity man helped a great deal in business and social life. Actually, Tom never seemed to have reaped any of these benefits.

The fraternity was probably a good thing for him in some ways. Shy as he was, and in a university as big as Missouri, he needed friends.

An unexpected facet is revealed in a letter written to his father on October 14, 1929. It was not full of accusations about his broken love affair. It was a chatty letter thanking his father for the golf clubs, which he said he was using pretty often. His roommate, Harold, who played in the finals of the university golf tournament, was teaching him a lot about the game. He had also been on a geology field trip, and had become so excited about the rocks and fossils in a quarry that he lost his grip and fell about twelve feet, with no injury except to his trousers, which were ripped. The letter must have sounded very friendly to Cornelius. Of course he was also asking for money.

Another letter, handwritten to his grandfather in October 1929, is a further indication that the breakup of the relationship with Hazel seems to be considerably exaggerated in the *Memoirs*. There is a simple statement that Hazel, her mother and his sister Rose were planning to drive to Columbia for the first football game in the home stadium.

He entered the Missouri School of Journalism and, as he later told an interviewer from the university paper, he intended to be a journalist when he graduated. And Edwina quotes another interview in which he said that his favorite author was Louis Bromfield. He was already a minor celebrity, since he had already published something.

In those days fraternity pledges were kept on their toes by the rule of the paddle. This was a sturdy piece of wood at least half an inch thick, about three inches wide and about two feet long, with a handle. Until they became full members, around the middle of the freshman year, pledges could be paddled. The victim was ordered to "assume the angle." He would then hold his ankle with one hand and his genitals with the other, making sure they were well forward, to avoid castration. The administering brother would then swat him on the buttocks as hard as he could, often taking a run-up to hit harder. Afterward, sitting down was unpleasant.

At Tom's fraternity a "kangaroo court" was held once a week, at midnight. The sins of the pledges were solemnly read out and those who had, in the brothers' opinion, sinned the most, were paddled the hardest. Tom was often sentenced to ten swats, which he said was almost spine breaking. He could barely make his way upstairs to bed.

His crimes were various and, he wrote, practically innumerable—everything from borrowing his brothers' clean shirts without asking to writing rubber checks.

In his spare time, however, Tom was studying and, as always, writing. In his freshman year he wrote his first serious play and, according to a clipping from the university newspaper, he was "the first freshman to win honorable mention in the Dramatic Arts Contest." He was signing his work with his real name, Thomas Lanier Williams, and would do so for years. His play was titled *Beauty Is the Word* and was the sixth selection. The paper says it was "a missionary play with an original and constructive idea, but the handling is too didactic, and the dialogue often too moralistic." There is no record of any production.

Tom was conscientious about his studies and in the three years he was at Missouri he failed no courses except ROTC, the Reserve Officers Training Corps, which all male students at land-grant universities were required by law to join. Over the years his grades became steadily lower, probably because he was concentrating more on writing than studying.

His sexual activities, at least according to *Memoirs*, were considerable.

In any case, sex in universities in those days wasn't the permissive mixed-dormitories affair it is today. Sexes were rigorously segregated. No male was ever allowed in the women's dorms; no female was ever allowed, officially, to go upstairs in a fraternity house. Punishments for these crimes were swift and dreadful. Students could be expelled from the university. This didn't mean the crimes weren't committed; they were intricately plotted, like prison breaks. And the basic law of sexual segregation applied: the more rigorously the sexes were prevented from mixing, the more likely they were to do it anyway, without mixing.

In Tom's case, however, it may already have been too late to shut the stable door.

Edwina wrote: "Tom and I never discussed sex." But she said she did take him to the family doctor just before he went to the university, to be told the facts of life. At this point, according to the *Memoirs*, it is evident he had not yet fully consummated sex with either a female or male.

So nothing really naughty at all happened his first year, and Tom got safely back to St. Louis, where he found a job selling magazines door to door. His companion was a "pretty" blond young man from Tulsa, who was, "an outrageous young camp," he would say afterward, but at the time he just thought the fellow was acting silly.

Not until the autumn of his sophomore year was Tom tempted strongly to "cross the line," if only he had known there was a line, or where it was. During homecoming weekend, called Old Home Week, the alumni came back to the fraternity house, using up a lot of beds, and the members had to double up. So there was Tom in bed with his roommate, a well-built young man called Smitty (not his real name) whose eyes seemed to glow in the dark. There weren't enough blankets, so they had to lie close together to keep warm—"sleeping spoons," he called it. And then Smitty started to caress his arms and shoulders and to press against his buttocks. He didn't know what was *supposed* to happen.

At the time both he and Smitty were dating girls. On a double date Smitty "made it" with one girl, but Tom didn't with his. But he wanted to.

It was becoming obvious to the ATO brothers that Tom and Smitty's relationship was going beyond brotherly friendship; Smitty was considered the instigator, or aggressor. He was dropped from the fraternity but Tom was not. Toward the end of his sophomore year Tom did have his first complete homosexual experience. He and Smitty had gone to a kind of home-brew beer garden, where couples could drink and enjoy privacy in wooden arbors, each with a table and benches. He wrote in *Memoirs* that he and Smitty wrestled amorously and then took a taxi back to Smitty's room. And there they made love. It was, according to *Memoirs*, his first time with a person of either sex.

Meanwhile the greatest tragedy of his life was developing. The story of Tom's relationship with his sister Rose is so complicated psychologically, and so heartbreaking, that it could almost make a book in itself; it did form the nucleus of a number of his plays and stories in addition to *The Glass Menagerie*.

The Reverend Mr. Walter Dakin had once been asked to become the dean of an Episcopal school in Vicksburg, Mississippi, called All Saints College, so he was able to get Rose a scholarship there. Edwina said this pleased Cornelius because it was free. But when Rose was eighteen, in 1927, Cornelius decided to take her out of All Saints so that she could make her debut in Knoxville society. His family, as even Miss Edwina admitted, were members of the "400" in Knoxville. Rose was sent to Cornelius's sister, Isabelle Sevier Williams Brownlow—the name itself sounds social register. She was called Aunt Belle. Party dresses, paid for by grandma, were sent with her and expectations were high. She would meet and marry a young man who would be at the summit of Knoxville society.

The whole affair was a disaster. The tone and mood of the debut of a sad and socially inept young girl is captured in a heartbreaking short story written by Tom much later called "Completed." The girl is not Rose; Rose was much prettier than the Rosemary McCool of the story, but she was probably no less tragic.

A death in the Knoxville family caused the big party to be postponed, and a few small ones were held instead. Edwina, always seeking excuses, thought Rose was put off by the fact that the "boys all drank from hip flasks," but Tom's statement has a truer ring. When he asked her, on her return, what had happened, she said that Aunt Ella and Aunt Belle liked only charming people and she wasn't charming. Tom thought she had fallen in love with a young man who had been indifferent.

Rose was then sent to the Rubicam Business School in St. Louis to learn shorthand and typing. At that time living in the Williams apartment on Enright Avenue was an unsettling experience. Edwina and Cornelius were in a state of open warfare, and Rose was often in the line of fire. Edwina wrote that Cornelius would order her out of the house "once a month" and on other occasions tell her that if she *did* go he would "give away every cent I have rather than pay you alimony."

Once, when Edwina suggested he leave and go to a hotel, he packed his bags and walked out. Rose burst into tears, thinking he'd never return— but he did, the next day, and the war went on. One night, when he was drunk, Cornelius told Edwina he would kill her. Edwina fled, running first through Rose's bedroom, where, as Dakin remembers, Rose was crouching in a corner, terrified. "Mother let out a piercing scream, which frightened Rose so badly she ran in terror from her room, out the front door."

Dakin remembers: "Mother uttered an agonized gasp as C.C. reached the door to her bedroom, and attempted to slam it in C.C.'s face. Dad gave the door a sudden shove and it flew inward, striking mother on the bridge of her still-perfect aquiline nose. Mother give a bloodcurdling second scream, falling backward on her bed in what I believe was a genuine faint. Blood trickled from her nose in a volume sufficient to convince C.C. that he had done all the damage he could safely do. He snorted a couple of times and went out the kitchen door to the garage, where he furiously backed out the Studebaker, striking a fender in his rage.

"'This time he can't blame the dented fender on Tom,' I thought, as I witnessed the scene of his departure through the sun room curtains. I went to the icebox and got a towelful of ice to revive mother. She was in an angry mood when she came to and discovered the injury to her once beautiful nose.

"'Well,' she said, 'I will call Paul Jamison first thing in the morning. If your father thinks he can divorce me, he will have another think coming.' Dad did not come home that night and Rose spent the night with a friend. I remember falling asleep with my eyes full of tears.

"However, the next day mother received a phone call from the credit manager at Famous-Barr Company, the big St. Louis department store, advising that her charge privilege had been canceled, a call that galvanized her like a clarion call of a Civil War bugle boy to action. A call from Miss Edwina and C.C. was called on the carpet by his boss, Paul Jamison. C.C. was ordered to fire his amorous secretary (or be fired himself) and to immediately restore mother's charge account at Famous.

"Sheepishly, our father returned to the apartment that evening, and mother prepared her famous pork chops with bow-tie macaroni, all just as though nothing had happened."

On another occasion, according to Edwina, Rose was expecting a gentleman caller and Cornelius refused to leave the living room. When Rose complained, he slapped her. She ran out into the street in tears, crying that she was going to find a policeman to lock up her father. Grandma persuaded her to come back, but Rose would not speak to her father for days.

Even if they were not the whole cause of Rose's mental breakdown, such episodes must have hastened it. She began to have stomach pains, and claimed someone was trying to poison her. Doctors could find no organic cause for the pains and she was sent to a psychiatrist.

Edwina wrote that "the psychiatrist told Rose her trouble was sex," that she was frightened of it. Whereas Dakin wrote, "She began psychiatric treatment from a Dr. Beckman . . . he diagnosed Rose's condition as a result of sexual repression. 'Go find yourself a lover,' he counseled." Whereas Tom wrote in his *Memoirs* that the family doctor, named Alexander, believed that Rose was normal but highly sexed, and was suffering because of Edwina's puritanical restrictions. The family doctor, Tom wrote, believed that Rose should have an arranged "therapeutic marriage." This naturally seemed monstrous to Edwina.

"Arranging a marriage" or "getting a lover" were easier said than done. Dakin recalls an incident that happened some time later. Tom had gone out with Rose and a young shoe salesman named Colin. Rose had decided to take seriously Dr. Beckman's advice ("get a lover") and, thinking that Tom was not listening, suggested to Colin that she would welcome any attempt at lovemaking. Tom heard this and said to her later, "Rose, I heard you offer yourself to Colin, and I want you to know you disgusted me."

CHAPTER 4

There is little doubt that in Tom's third and last year at the University of Missouri he was concentrating more on playwriting than journalism. One play he wrote at this time, and the first one to be preserved, is *Hot Milk at Three in the Morning*, "a one-act play by Thomas Lanier Williams." It is marked "Honorable Mention. No. 13."

The play is really a first draft of one he later called *Moony's Kid Don't Cry*. A man with wanderlust wants to leave his wife and baby, who are tying him down, but the crying of the child persuades him to stay. It's a strong, simple and emotional play, but the *Moony's Kid* version (which won a prize) has sharper character development, and more sympathy for the people.

Tom must have been lonely that year. Smitty had left the university, and apparently he had no sexual partner. Smitty had been the prime mover, the aggressor, in their affair, and at this stage Tom was probably too shy to make overtures to anyone else.

The only emotional liaison he mentions is a friendship with a girl named Anna Jean, who lived at the Alpha Chi Omega sorority house across the street. She was witty and they had good times together, but nothing more. He wrote a sad little poem about her, how she waited beside her door expecting he would kiss her good-night. But he was too shy to do it.

Although he had failed ROTC that year, his other grades were acceptable and he could have gone on to his senior year. He had been especially good in English. Edwina quotes a letter Tom received after he left the university, from Robert L. Ramsay of the English Department:

> Your absence from the University this year has been a matter for
> real regret to all of us who knew the excellent work you did here the
> last few years, especially in the field of creative writing.

The letter went on to give advice about placing a "fine story" titled "Big Black" that Tom had written.

Tom wanted to stay on, but Cornelius would not hear of it, and took him out. One reason, in that depression year, was money. The other reason, Edwina thought, was rage because Tom had failed the officers' training course. Cornelius had gone to military school and had served as a lieutenant in the Spanish-American War. To Cornelius, failing ROTC proved that Tom was "not doing any good in college."

Cornelius put Tom to work at the International Shoe Company, in the warehouse at sixty-five dollars a month.

Tom had to work hard to earn his small salary. Edwina remembers riding on a bus in St. Louis and seeing a young man trying to cross heavy traffic carrying a box "almost as big as a sofa." She thought it frightful that anyone should have to work like that—and then noticed it was Tom. The box was full of shoe samples.

Every morning Tom had to dust hundreds of sample shoes, spend several hours typing factory orders, and every afternoon he had to carry huge packing cases of shoes to the J.C. Penney company, a major client. The cases were so heavy he could hardly lift them.

He made friends with a Polish fellow named Eddie, who showed him the ropes, and Eddie's girl friend Doretta, and a plump little spinster named Nora. They talked about the local movies and stage shows and radio programs like "Amos 'n' Andy."

But no matter how tired he was, every evening when he came home he would go to his room with black coffee and cigarettes. Edwina says she would hear the typewriter going until late at night, and sometimes found him in the morning still dressed, sprawled across his bed. He didn't want to be disturbed for any reason. Once, Edwina wrote, she tiptoed in with something for him to eat. "He looked up from the typewriter and glared at me. He said, 'I *did* have an idea.'" So she didn't do it again.

Dakin remembers: "His room was a tiny one and quickly filled with cigarette smoke... At six in the morning mother would open the door. A cloud of stale smoke would issue forth from his room. Mother would cough once or twice before waking Tom with her familiar, 'Rise and shine, Tom!' As in *Menagerie* he would reply, 'I'll rise, but I won't shine.'"

He was writing both poems and short stories. Weekdays he wrote verse, and weekends stories. After work on Saturday mornings, he would buy a thirty-five cent lunch and then go to the Mercantile Library, a good private library in downtown St. Louis, and "read voraciously." Saturday afternoon and all day Sunday would be devoted to finishing the short story. He tried to finish one every week, usually sending them to *Story* magazine. Nearly all of them came back, some with encouraging letters, others with the standard rejection slips. His only successes during these years were a few poems printed in the newspapers and a local prize for a short story, "Stella for Star." It won first prize for amateur authors in a contest sponsored by the St. Louis Writers Guild.

He came of age in 1932 and voted for Norman Thomas, the only time he ever voted in any election. He said he had become a Socialist. In 1933 he wrote his grandparents that he was going to night classes at a high school, and that he was thinking of taking a shorthand course so he could be a stenographer and make more money.

There was very little social life and apparently little or no sexual activity. If Tom was in love with anyone at this time it was probably with his sister, a pathetic, even tragic affair. During the shoe-company years he and Rose often spent their evenings together. They would walk over to Delmar Boulevard and look in the shop windows. Rose, who was never given enough money to buy pretty clothes, would tell Tom which dress she would like to have, if she could. Then they would stroll to an open-air root beer stand, where one could buy a stein for a nickel, with free pretzels. And after this sad little night out they would walk back and sometimes dance to a windup phonograph.

Tom admitted in his *Memoirs* that their feelings for each other were stronger than for anyone else, all their lives, even enough, perhaps, to prevent their wanting to marry any other person. It went beyond normal love of a brother and sister.

Tom was always haunted by the idea of incestuous love between brother and sister, and had a special obsession about one of his plays on the subject. *The Two-Character Play* was rewritten many times, and produced in three different versions in three different cities over a period of seven years (1966–73), and was finally called *Out Cry*.

There was nothing physical between Tom and Rose. He denies it categorically. There was not even (he wrote in his *Memoirs*) any "casual physical intimacy." They were shy with each other physically, and didn't even touch hands except when dancing. They would spend many hours in her bedroom, talking and dancing, but nothing more.

Dakin remembers one odd story from this period that shows how Rose could stumble unwittingly into psychological disasters. The whole family attended the St. Michael and St. George Episcopal Church, also attended by some of Shepherd Mead's family.

Edwina made a special effort to bring Rose into church work, thinking it would help. Both Rose and Tom sang in the choir and Dakin was an acolyte. All three children were sometimes startled by Edwina's fancy dress and uninhibited singing.

Dakin remembers: "Mother had become one of the well-known eccentrics of the congregation by virtue of her stentorian voice, especially in singing hymns such as 'The Church's One Foundation Is Jesus Christ Our Lord.' Both Rose and Tom, members of the choir, were embarrassed to hear comments from other choir members that could in no way be construed as flattering. To make matters worse, mother's choice of hats was truly unbelievable. I can still see her with a thirty-year-old velvet (you know how velvet shines when the newness vanishes!), with a green parrot feather perched on the brim. Tom soon dropped out of the choir, but Rose was persuaded to continue and even to take on teaching a Sunday school class."

The minister at St. Michael's was Dr. Karl Morgan Block, perhaps the most popular pastor in the St. Louis area. On Sundays the church was full; his sermons were famous, as much for his dramatic, even Shakespearean, manner as for his message. And also, as Dakin remembers, because "he never disturbed anyone's conscience by his sermons." He would quote— even intone—Shakespeare along with the scriptures.

So now the stage is set, except for one thing: anti-Semitism was beginning to seep into St. Louis. Along with the large German immigration to St. Louis in the mid-nineteenth century came a number of Jewish people. By this time both groups had become assimilated and Germanic accents had disappeared. Many of the Jews had become distinguished citizens, like Morton ("Buster") May, of the famous May Company family, the foremost philanthropist of the city.

A number of Jews had moved to University City, called by everyone "U. City" and by anti-Semites "Jew City." There was a rumor that the famous Dr. Block had Jewish blood. There was no reason why there should be anything evil about this, but in that atmosphere it sounded scandalous. Rose had heard the gossip, and without thinking had repeated it to a member of the congregation, an eccentric artist named Florence ver Steeg, who sometimes invited the Williams children to tea (often spiked with rum).

Word of what Rose had said reached Dr. Block and he is reported to have told her, "Being Jewish, or half Jewish, is not something I would be ashamed of, but I cannot tolerate your spreading rumors like this. You will have to turn in your materials, as I can no longer permit you to teach in my Sunday school."

Rose was so shattered by this that she had to be taken to Barnes Hospital for treatment. By this time Tom had stopped singing in the choir, but Dakin and Edwina continued at St. Michael's. When Dr. Block learned how seriously Rose had reacted to his scolding, he said he was sorry. Later he became dean of Grace Cathedral in San Francisco and Episcopal Bishop of Northern California.

The shoe-company years were bad for Tom, but he had some fun, too. His salary was tiny, but he could keep most of it. One of the first things he bought with his new wealth was a framed copy of the Mona Lisa for his mother. He also bought an antique lyre for five dollars. A lyre was supposed to be part of the equipment of a poet. He tried picking tunes on it, and finally gave up.

The best thing he bought was an old convertible, complete with rumble seat, for twenty-nine dollars. He called it "Scatterbolt" because that was how it sounded. Tom and Rose would put Dakin (then about boy scout size) in the rumble seat and drive out into the country. A favorite place in summer was the Tree Court swimming pool, where the spring water was cold with a smell of minerals.

St. Louis is like a furnace in summer, with temperatures over a hundred in the shade. The only air conditioning in those days was at the big movie houses on Grand Avenue. At the Fox and the St. Louis, twenty-five cents would buy an afternoon movie, a stage show, the Wurlitzer organ—and three hours of cool air. At home people would keep their windows open only at night. During the blazing hot days they would close them tightly, pull down dark shades and sit in the semidarkness with the electric fans going. The grass and the flowers would be burned down if they weren't watered.

Growing things in the Williams family was Dakin's department, even when he was pint-size. The garden behind their apartment on Enright Avenue was quite small, but Dakin filled it with hollyhocks, tall in the background, and bordered by four-o'clocks and tiny portulacas. Tom, however, remembered only the vegetables, squash and pumpkins.

One summer the family escaped during July and August to the trees and gardens of Webster Groves, a pretty suburb of St. Louis. Their wealthy cousins, Ned and Agnes Hartford, had a cottage up in Michigan where— like everybody else who could afford it—they went to escape the St. Louis heat. The Williamses borrowed their Webster Groves house for the summer. Cornelius joined the nearby Woodlawn Country Club, where Rose would play golf with Dakin and tennis with Tom. The only tragedy was that Tom jumped off the diving board and crashed into the side of the swimming pool, knocking out two teeth. Edwina noted that Cornelius was of little help, since he was "somewhere else at the time." And so, in her eyes, no doubt the cause of the whole thing.

While they were at the Webster Groves house a minor episode occurred that Tom might have made into a one-act play. All the actors were strictly in character. Dakin remembers it well. It was a Saturday midnight in August and still very hot. Tom telephoned. He was in his old Scatterbolt jalopy out on Sappington Road, and had run out of gas. (Very much in character. Tom never did and never would remember to put either oil or gas in cars.) "What *can* we do?" cried Rose frantically. (And in character.)

"Well," said Edwina, organizing things (in character), "your father has the car—and it's Saturday, so *he* won't be home until dawn." (Cornelius in character, and Edwina in character for putting it that way.)

Edwina decided that Rose and Dakin should get a taxi, stop for a can of gas and find Tom. They followed his directions, and there he was, standing with Scatterbolt beside a closed gas station.

"Oh, where have you been, Tom?" said Rose.

Tom answered, "To the movies."

"Mother won't believe that," said Rose, who didn't believe it either, knowing that Tom always said that as a cover story when he'd been with anybody his mother didn't approve of, which was practically everybody.

And that was what happened. When they reached home, Edwina was wearing her standard look of advanced suffering, like Amanda's in *The Glass Menagerie*.

"I was at the movies, mother," Tom said.

"I don't believe that lie!" Edwina said, in character.

"Well, you can go to hell then!" said Tom, going a bit beyond his character.

And then, Dakin remembers, "Mother's eyes shot up in their sockets toward the ceiling. She staggered backward as if struck by a physical blow. Cunningly she glanced behind her to be sure there was an overstuffed chair in the correct position, and proceeded to fall backward in a well-planned and frequently performed faint."

"Oh, my God!" gasped Rose (in character). "Tom, look what you've done! You've killed our mother!"

But Dakin wasn't worried. He had seen his mother "pull this on a monthly basis when arguing with dad over bills." He was, however, impressed by the performance, which he thought was better than usual.

If there'd only been a gentleman caller around, the whole scene might have come right out of one of Tom's plays.

Tom's salary of sixty-five dollars a month wasn't enough for good theater seats, but he often climbed up to the "peanut gallery" of the American Theater in downtown St. Louis. That third balcony was so steep it was like hanging on the side of a cliff, and only the tops of the actors' heads could be seen. But some of the great road company shows came to the American, and the gallery seats were only fifty cents.

As he told John Gruen, he remembered many of the plays. He saw Katharine Cornell in *The Barrets of Wimpole Street* and liked it. But the one that really excited him was Ibsen's *Ghosts* with Nazimova. He said it was "so fabulous, so terrifyingly exciting that I couldn't stay in my seat! I suddenly jumped up and began pacing the corridor of the peanut gallery, trying to hear what was being said on the stage, but at the same time I couldn't stand to watch it anymore. It was the scene in which Mrs. Alving realizes that her son, Oswald, you know, is afflicted with syphilis and that it has gone to his brain."

He said that he had also been reading O'Neill and Shakespeare. He said he was "particularly enchanted by all the very violent plays." However, he believed that his major influence at this time was Chekhov.

CHAPTER 5

In February 1935, Tom heard the news that Hazel Kramer had married Terry McCabe. It had been six years since Tom had proposed to her that day when he first entered the University of Missouri. Tom had seen her from time to time since then, and was still very fond of her, but the close relationship was finished.

Tom had always resented the separation forced on them by his father, and his own passive resistance to it. His mother reported that he had told her: "... under this hopeless nonresistance there must have been an unconscious rage, not just at dad but my own cowardice and impotent submission. This I realize because as I have grown older I have discovered a big underground rebellion was there all along, just waiting for a way out."

Tom's first reaction to the news about Hazel was to redouble his work, to move the short-story writing into the weekday evenings, too, drinking too much black coffee. He was in the midst of writing a story called "The Accent of a Coming Foot" when he noticed that his heart was palpitating. His reaction was to jump up, go outdoors and start walking downtown — that is, from University City due east toward downtown St. Louis. He got all the way to Union Boulevard, about two miles away, walking faster and faster, as though trying to keep ahead of the attack, expecting he might drop dead at any time.

Later he wrote a story, "Oriflamme," in 1944, when he was depressed after the death of his grandmother. The story is a stream of consciousness. A woman in a blazing red banner of a dress is running away from death — or from herself *to* death — along almost this identical route through St. Louis. While writing this crazed, almost psychotic (but beautiful) story of headlong flight to nowhere, he must have remembered that night, nine years before. It was not unusual for him to transfer his own feelings to those of a female character.

Finally the mania wore itself out. He began to notice buds on the trees. Spring was coming. He turned and walked back home. The palpitations subsided.

47

He told no one about this flight, but went to a doctor, who found that he had high blood pressure. He continued working at the warehouse for one more week.

On Saturday he took Rose downtown to see a film, *The Scarlet Pimpernel*, with Leslie Howard. They took a service car—a kind of bus service—along Delmar Boulevard toward University City. Tom began to feel ill. He whispered to Rose that he was losing all feeling in his arms and legs, and that his heart was pounding.

They were just passing St. Luke's Hospital and Rose asked the driver to pull into the emergency entrance. Tom was taken upstairs.

Dakin remembers when Rose came home and told their mother. Edwina said to him, "Your brother has had a heart attack and I fear he is dying."

Tom stayed at the hospital for about a week. In spite of Edwina's dire predictions, the doctor said it was not a heart attack. He was just exhausted. But the whole family was thoroughly shaken up, even Cornelius. Dakin says that for the first time his father did not complain about the expense.

Rose was affected most of all, and had what Tom thought was her first serious mental disturbance. When Tom returned to the apartment, Rose wandered into his room and suggested they all die together. It was a proposal that didn't tempt him at all.

Edwina recalled that Rose was almost out of her mind, wandering around the apartment in a panic. She woke up her father, screaming, "You're going to be murdered! We're all going to be murdered!"

Tom resigned the next week from the International Shoe Company. He received a letter from a Mr. Fletcher, head of the Continental Division, who said they all appreciated his "many sterling qualities," meaning, presumably, they liked the way he dusted the shoes and carried the boxes. They hadn't given him a chance to do anything else.

He wrote a play that is partly about his years at the shoe company called *Stairs to the Roof*, subtitled *A Prayer for the Wild of Heart that are Kept in Cages*. On the manuscript in the Texas archives there is an introductory note dated New Orleans, 1941. He said he had written it as a catharsis for a period he had spent as a clerk in a large company in the Midwest. The main character is plainly Tom, described as small and nervous, made frantic by "regimentation," but still unbowed. This young man, named Ben Murphy, has discovered a flight of stairs that leads from the offices up to the roof, where he can see the open sky. Later Ben and his girl break into a zoo, at night, and set free a vixen who is about to have cubs. The whole play is full of his claustrophobic feeling of being shut up in an office.

Tom wanted desperately to go somewhere, away from home, to write full time. Grand came to his rescue once again. The Reverend Mr. Dakin had retired and bought a small house in Memphis, Tennessee, and they invited Tom to come down there, to get well and to write.

His subconscious must have thought, "Precisely what I had in mind!" and evidently called off the hysterics. Everything was perfect. The Dakin house on Snowden Avenue was a few blocks from Southwestern University and even closer to the house of Knolle Rhodes and his wife. They were Virginians and he was head of the university's English department and would later become the president of the university. Through him Tom was able to use the university library, as well as the Memphis public library. It was then that he felt he had really come under the influence of Chekhov, the short stories rather than the plays. A certain literary "sensibility" in them suited his mood at the time.

He wrote a play and had his first production. Luckily, another of the Dakins' neighbors was a young woman named Dorothy Shapiro, a member of the local little theater, called the Rose Arbor Players—their "theater" was the sloping backyard of a lady named Mrs. Rosebrough.

The play is called *Cairo, Shanghai, Bombay!* and the title page of the manuscript lists the authors: "By Dorothy Shapiro and Tom Williams." No "Lanier" there. It is described as a "one act melodrama." The cast includes Millie, "a coarse affable girl of the Mae West type"; Chuck, "a sailor who has been around"; a noted author, "middle-aged cosmopolitan"; and an Unknown Author described as "a pretentious young intellectual." It is a sex comedy involving two "light ladies" and two sailors, and two observing authors. The dialogue is all colloquial, and there is very little of the Williams poetry.

On June 25, 1935, Tom wrote a long and happy letter to Dakin praising the penmanship and literary style of Dakin's last letter, and continuing on to tell about his coming production. It all sounded very pleasant, lunch under the peach trees and rehearsals in the garden. He wrote the main part of the play, and Miss Shapiro the prologue and epilogue. He intended to be an actor himself, playing the blind man, with a dog and a tin cup. He said he was beginning to feel much stronger.

The production went well. Edwina wrote that he "found it surprisingly amusing, even laughing out loud with the audience... and decided right then and there that writing was fun." Tom decided later that it was the theater that saved his life.

No homosexual incidents, nor sex of any kind, are recorded during the shoe-company years; in fact nothing since the Smitty affair. But the temptations returned in Memphis. There Tom wrote that he began to notice, even more, that he was attracted to young men.

He had gone to a lake near Memphis to swim with two university students whom he'd met through his grandfather. One blond young man attracted him very much. Apparently the feeling was mutual. The young man invited Tom to dinner at the Peabody Hotel restaurant. Tom was so excited that during the course of the meal he had heart palpitations so violent that a doctor was called. The doctor, a woman, gave him a sedative and told him to do everything slowly.

It wasn't recorded whether they did anything else, slowly or not.

When Tom came back to St. Louis that fall he was much more interested in writing plays. He enrolled in several courses at Washington University, a few blocks from home. He was trying to earn credits so that he could qualify as a senior at Washington the following year.

One of the courses he took was a popular one on the short story taught by "Sandy" Buchan, a bright little Scotsman with a strong brogue and a liking for classical, well-made short stories, like those of Wilbur Daniel Steele and other followers of O. Henry. Sandy prefered the "snapper" endings of O. Henry and de Maupassant, which could turn around the whole plot in the last line; he was probably a bad influence, since this style, like rhymed poetry, was already becoming obsolete. Both these two biographers, as well as Tom, took Sandy's course, and all survived.

Tom was being realistic. He must have known it would be a long time before he could support himself by writing. In a letter to his grandfather he wrote that he thought he would like to get a degree, and then perhaps teach high school English.

But meanwhile he was writing plays as well as short stories. He met Clark Mills McBurney (who later used only Clark Mills as his pen name) at the university. Clark was the leading undergraduate poet and the first editor of the new university literary magazine, called Eliot, because in its earlier years Washington University had been the Eliot Seminary. T.S. Eliot had studied there as an undergraduate.

Tom and Clark set up a "literary factory," as they called it, in the basement of Mrs. McBurney's house. There, and at home, Tom wrote two full-length plays, *Candles to the Sun* and *The Fugitive Kind*. (The later title was borrowed years later for the film version of *Orpheus Descending*, but has no other connection with it. The play takes place in a men's flophouse.)

There is no better way to understand the huge amount of work he was doing—and would always do—than to look at the manuscript of this one play, *Candles to the Sun*. There are at least four hundred pages, done on many different typewriters, in many different kinds and colors of paper— and in most cases not even numbered. Yet with all this mass of work, the writing itself is always "clean," almost error-free, with few if any typographical errors, and almost no misspellings. The title changed a number of times, from *The Lamp* to *Place in the Sun* to *Candles in the Sun*, with the *in* penciled out and *to* written in. He had written his full name, Thomas Lanier Williams, on the title page.

In the depression days all young writers thought they should be preaching social significance. (In fact, it was hard to get a grant from the WPA Writers' Project if you didn't.) This was Tom being socially significant about Alabama miners, about whom he knew nothing. The play took place in a miner's cabin (convertible into a different miner's cabin by changing the furnishings). The central character, Bram, is a forerunner of *Streetcar*'s Stanley Kowalski, a tough, sometimes uncouth but honest man. There are long, twenty-line speeches, almost orations, deadly serious, and not especially poetic. He was learning his trade.

Edwina reported that at this time he was reading Rimbaud, Lorca, Rilke, Melville, Hart Crane and D.H. Lawrence. Tom himself spoke mainly of Chekhov, Crane and Lawrence.

In the spring of 1936 the Webster Groves Theatre Guild announced a one-act-play contest. Tom heard about it shortly before the deadline and wrote one quickly. He called it *The Magic Tower*. In the archives there are several different versions of this, indicating that, like almost all his plays, it was later reworked a number of times. The original title had been *State of Enchantment*. The main characters are Linda, an ex-vaudeville actress, and Jim, a young artist. They live in a garret-studio, which becomes, to them, their magic tower. This begins to be closer to the Williams mature style and gives a foretaste of his later dramatic poetry. There is no indication that he ever expanded this into a longer work.

He sent the play to Webster Groves and soon received a letter saying that the judges had unanimously chosen it for production. It was performed in October, along with two other one-act plays. After the last curtain went down, the judges met to decide the winner. Sure enough, *The Magic Tower*, by "Howard Williams," had won. But where was Howard? A man named Howard Buermann (that's probably where they got the "Howard"), one of the other authors, was there, talking with Louise Francis Butler, the third author, but Williams could not be found—even though he was sitting in the audience with Rose and Edwina and Dakin. Tom was too shy to tell them where he was. But he was finally pushed forward, and walked up to get his prize, a sterling silver plate. It was the first material reward he had ever received for being a playwright and he was disappointed. He'd hoped they would give him money.

The St. Louis *Star-Times* of October 19, 1936, described it as a "poignant little tragedy with a touch of warm fantasy" and added that it was "exquisitely written by its poet author." The play had been signed "By Thomas Williams."

His leading actress was criticized, however, for being too nervous and hurried. After all, the critic said, she was better at hysterical parts. Perhaps she should have waited for a later Williams.

Meanwhile Tom saw what was probably his first Chekhov play, *The Cherry Orchard*, produced by the St. Louis Little Theater. Tom went with his mother, who may have been too excited at the time to pay full attention. She had just been chosen Regent (meaning head lady) of the Jefferson Chapter of the Daughters of the American Revolution because they were so pleased with (as she quotes) her "tact," "charm" and "graciousness," all qualities a lady had to have to be a regent of the D.A.R. His one-act play, *Something Unspoken*, often performed as a curtain raiser for *Suddenly Last Summer*, takes place during the election of a Regent for the Confederate Daughters. The main character, Cornelia, who might be described as a monster of graciousness (though she is not Edwina), is trying to manipulate the election by telephone.

Another St. Louis women's group, the Wednesday Club, held an "original verse contest," and Tom won the first prize, twenty-five dollars, in the senior division, with a sonnet sequence called *Sonnets for the Spring*. There are three of them, quite beautiful, and they adhere precisely to the formal rhyme scheme of the classical sonnet. At the time he changed his pen name to Tennessee, Tom said that Thomas Lanier Williams was a name better suited to writers of sonnets about spring, a literary form he had abandoned.

Even Aunt Belle, of the Knoxville Williamses, and generally conceded to be the most gracious (and richest) of them all, was impressed by Tom's literary victories. She wrote to him with much praise, but also cautioned him to "never let anyone discourage you by attempting to measure your success by the money you make." It was good advice, easier for a rich woman than a poor young man to follow.

At this time, Tom had forty-five dollars of his own money, including the twenty-five from the Wednesday Club, and hoped to scrape together enough to attend summer school at Washington University. He had only one good suit, and that was won for him by Edwina, after a pitched battle with Cornelius over the cost. He needed something to wear for his Memphis and Webster Groves first nights.

He was becoming increasingly aware of his young brother. He wrote that Dakin was learning an English accent to take part in a high school play. The rest of the time, he complained, Dakin was listening to baseball games on the radio. At the age of seventeen, Dakin was already becoming a problem to his brother.

CHAPTER 6

In the fall of 1936 Tom Williams entered Washington University as a full-time student, an event not mentioned in his *Memoirs*. That whole year was completely dropped out of his life and became "the secret year of Tennessee Williams."

Tom registered for courses in Greek, general literature and William G. B. Carson's English 16, the course in playwriting. His close friend, Clark Mills McBurney, had gone on to Paris, to the Sorbonne, but he and two other student writers, William Jay Smith and Louise Krause, formed the St. Louis Poets Workshop. They even had letterheads printed. They met at the Williams house on Arundel Place to discuss poetry, and tried to convince editors that there was a great poetic flowering in St. Louis. Poems would be sent out by the fictitious secretary of the society, with a letter on the official stationery. However, as Jay Smith wrote, "The editors were less impressed by our flowering than we were; the poems all came back."

Tom was also an actor—and in French. The French department produced Molière's *Les Fourberies de Scapin* and, as Smith wrote, "Tom was persuaded to take the part of the old father. He read the French lines with a kind of hound-dog ferocity and deliberation, as if he were chewing on a large section of the Mississippi Delta. When he moved woodenly across the stage with absolute seriousness, pounding the floor with his cane, small and square in his satin suit, an enormous blond wig flopping about on his shoulders, he gave a performance that a more sophisticated audience would have taken as deliberate high camp."

Further research indicated that a catastrophe may have occurred in W.G.B. Carson's playwriting course.

"Pop" Carson, who died in December 1976, at eighty-five, was one of the beloved characters of the university. His English 16 course was a club, a contest and a tradition. Pop, also nicknamed "Boops," delighted in giving the class his own dramatic readings of plays. The group would go off to attend performances, usually at the St. Louis Little Theater, and then take the plays apart in class.

But the main thing was the contest. All students had to write one or more one-act plays. Carson would read these, or bits of these, aloud in class, and give advice and criticism. At the end of the school year an independent jury selected the three winning plays, which were produced by Thyrsus, the dramatic club, the following year. Another jury watched the productions, all done together in one evening, and awarded the grand prize of fifty dollars to the author of the winning play.

Shepherd Mead had been one of Carson's students the previous school year, and his play, a science fiction called *Eternity Unlimited*, had been selected as one of the three for 1937 production—the year that Tom was in the class.

Among the students in the 1936–37 group was Aaron ("Hotch") Hotchner, who later became Hemingway's friend and biographer. Another was Wayne Arnold, now head of the drama department at John Burroughs School in St. Louis. Both Hotch, whom Mead knew at the university, and Wayne Arnold, whom he hadn't met, wrote to him about the controversial 1936–37 class. Pop Carson, too, had written Mead a letter some years before he died.

Here was Williams, at twenty-five older than the others, and probably the only one in the class who'd had anything produced anywhere. At this time he was almost pathologically shy and very sensitive. (Tom never mentioned any of this in his *Memoirs*, not the fact that he entered the class, nor even that he entered the university.)

Because of his shyness he was hardly noticed. Arnold wrote: "In English 16 he sat at the back of the class, mixing with no one and known to the rest of us as the SNCD." (Student Not Candidate for a Degree, as they thought. Actually he was a candidate, and did want a degree.) "I remember that his silent, dark (he stays in my memory there as always wearing dark clothing) figure seemed to me then someone considerably older."

Hotchner wrote: "He did come to class but not often. During the semester he wrote fragments of a play about his mother and sister, fragments which bore a strong resemblance to what was to be *The Glass Menagerie*, years later. Professor Carson read these fragments (as he read all our works in progress) with great spirit and afterward expressed his high approval of them. I took it for granted that when Williams got around to doing the one-act play . . . that these characters of his work scenes would be the principal ones in his one-acter."

But Tom evidently wasn't yet ready to write *The Glass Menagerie* and submitted, instead, as his contest one-acter, a melodrama called *Me, Vashya!* Wayne Arnold had access to the script files and read it a number of times.

He wrote: "*Vashya* concerned a peasant (Russian? Polish?) who became a munitions magnate selling arms to a world which seemed constantly at war. As a boy he had fallen in love with a child princess and—guess what?— he has now married her. End of exposition. As the curtain rises Mrs. Vashya is in a bad mental state. It seems that she had had a deep friendship with a young poet who had managed to arouse the jealousy of her husband, who saw to it that said poet was shipped off to the front lines in some war or other and got it in the head. The princess is distraught and has been having visions of her friend standing at the front of her bed urging her to kill her husband for what he has done to mankind. A psychiatrist is brought in, the princess has a tirade against her husband, and finally shoots him dead. Dying, he kisses the hem of her garment."

Me, Vashya! is intended as a kind of extravagant fantasy "suggested by the career of Sir Basil Zaharoff," the great munitions magnate, Tom wrote. It was never intended to be realistic, yet it doesn't really come off; it was an experiment that didn't work. He had already written much better plays.

When *Me, Vashya!* was read aloud in class, Hotchner wrote, "there was considerable half-suppressed laughter."

Meanwhile Hotchner was writing a play about a campus gossip columnist titled *Who's Aunt Tillie?* and Wayne Arnold was doing one about a best-selling book, called *First Edition*. And during all this, the three plays from the previous year were produced.

All the new scripts were now in, and, according to Hotchner: "On the final day in class, Professor Carson announced the winning three plays: Arnold's, mine and a third one called *Bangtail*, about a guy who was a compulsive horseplayer. Williams was present that day. He rose slowly from his seat, suffused with anger, and left the room. None of us ever saw him again. Certainly not at the performance." Actually Wayne Arnold did see Williams again once or twice, briefly.

Tom, however, was asked to appear with the three winners at Graham Chapel. Wayne Arnold says that Carson told him: "He [Williams] refused— in fact, stormed into Mr. C's office and delivered a tearing denunciation of the judges' intelligence, said that he approved the choice of my [Arnold's] play, but that to choose the other two over his was an insult he could not countenance. He slammed his way out of the office and so far as I know it was the last time he ever spoke to Carson."

In the following year the Arnold and Hotchner plays were produced, and Wayne Arnold's *First Edition* won.

The official records of Washington University show that in the academic year 1936–37 Thomas Lanier Williams was registered for William Carson's

English 16, both semesters, that he failed Greek during his second semester, and received a D for his second semester in general literature. He did not receive a degree.

For many years there were countless red faces at Washington University, including that of Professor Carson, though it must be added that he had had nothing to do with judging the plays. *Me, Vashya!* was well below Tom's standard at that time. *The Magic Tower*, for example, was probably better than any of the three produced.

But the whole episode was shattering to Tom, and it may be the reason why he dropped that year and Washington University from his *Memoirs*.

There is a happy postscript to this story. After Mead's article "The Secret Year of Tennessee Williams," these facts appeared in the university magazine, Dakin joined the university in sending an invitation to Tom to be a special guest on the campus. Tom accepted in 1977, and made a triumphal reentry. He read from his works in Graham Chapel, which was packed with cheering students, gave a press Conference and had his smiling face all over the St. Louis newspapers.

The year is no longer a secret.

Meanwhile, an extraordinary little theater group, the Mummers, and Tom discovered each other. This group was to have a profound influence on him during the crucial period between despair and the beginning of maturity.

In a preface to his volume of short plays, *27 Wagons Full of Cotton*, Tom gives a loving account of this brave, scruffy and impoverished little company, fighting to stay alive and solvent, like so many many amateur theatrical groups.

No one could make a living at it. They were waitresses, workmen, students, prostitutes, even a debutante or two from the Junior League. Their leader was a down-at-the-heels genius-director, with overgrown hair, a shiny blue suit, who wore a scarf instead of a shirt. His name was Willard Holland.

Holland called Tom, whom he had never met, and asked how he felt about compulsory military training. Tom said he'd flunked ROTC, and took a dim view of it. Holland was pleased, and asked if Tom could write a one-act curtain raiser against militarism. They were producing Irwin Shaw's *Bury the Dead* in the auditorium of the Wednesday Club—and they had a bit of time. Could he write something quickly?

Tom wrote *Headlines* quickly, and it was produced. He said that the Mummers did a marvelous job on the Shaw play, which simply "paralyzed" the St. Louis audience. As for his own—they even forgot to put his name in the program.

In spite of that, he was much impressed with them, and apparently they with him. They produced both of the full-length plays he had written the year before, *Candles to the Sun* and *The Fugitive Kind*. Tom said he thought both the plays were bad, but *Candles* had excellent audience reaction, with cheers for the author. He was pulled on stage with the greasepaint coal miners—the first of any kind he had ever seen.

Tom remembered that he got rave notices from all three of the St. Louis papers. Edwina quoted the *Post-Dispatch* critic as saying that it was a drama "of poverty, degeneracy, accidents on the fifth level below ground, a strike and a brutal murder, ending with beans for everybody, hope and the singing of 'Solidarity Forever.'"

Tom thought, in *Memoirs*, that *The Fugitive Kind* was a better play than *Candles*, but it was savaged by the critics. Afterward there was a drunken party in someone's hotel room in downtown St. Louis, where, Tom wrote, he made a dash for a window. Someone tackled him before he could, presumably, jump out, though he was never sure whether he really would have done it.

CHAPTER 7

Tom was still determined to write plays, and also to get a university degree. He had heard of the playwriting seminar run by Professor E.C. Mabie at the University of Iowa and began to plan some way to get there.

At the same time, the tragedy of Rose was reaching a dreadful climax. There was a whole series of catastrophes.

Rose had suspected that something was wrong. In *Memoirs* Tom told about a conversation during a drive in the country with friends. They were laughing about the odd behavior of an acquaintance who was losing his mind. Rose did not join the laughter and said people must never make fun of insanity, which was worse than death.

Being pretty, Rose attracted men, but the episodes of her gentlemen callers was sadder than the one in *The Glass Menagerie*. One of these was a bachelor named Roger Moore, who lived across the street from the Williamses after they had moved to their house on Pershing Avenue. Moore was running for mayor of University City, and both Tom and Dakin were helping him in the campaign, handing out literature. It was the first of Dakin's many electoral battles. Tom was interested more in Roger's sister, Virginia Moore, a published poet and author of *Virginia Is a State of Mind*. Tom showed her his poems and she gave them, as he said, tactful praise. Roger Moore admired Rose, and took her out on dates. The two were quite serious about each other.

The University City election was held and Moore lost. He was so upset by this that he had a nervous breakdown. His family had to take him to a private sanitarium. While there, he broke away from attendants, ran in front of a truck and was killed. Rose was shattered.

One gentleman caller must have struck Rose as the most serious and most desirable of all. He was a junior executive at the International Shoe Company, good looking, socially charming and extremely ambitious. Tom said they were dating several times a week, almost "going steady." Rose

61

would tremble every time the telephone rang, hoping it would be the young man, and often it was.

Cornelius was rising once again in the company. The earlier episode of the poker night and the infected young prostitute was beginning to be forgotten. Cornelius might still have become a power at International, and the ambitious young man knew it. Cornelius, who had been a salesman out there alone on the road for so long, could talk to his salesmen in their own language. He could be tough, and tell them, "If you don't get your sales up, you're going to be fired." He could also make speeches that made them all love him. They knew that he knew what it was like to live out of a suitcase, and have a cigarette for breakfast.

But then it happened again, the second big Cornelius scandal, the Episode of the Ear. Cornelius and the boys were having another wild Saturday night, this time in a private dining room of the Jefferson Hotel in St. Louis. The poker game was hotting up, and all the players were well lubricated with beer and bourbon. Cornelius saw, or thought he saw, one of the boys dealing off the bottom of the deck, and then win a big pot. Cornelius suggested that his companion keep his dirty paws off the chips.

"You filthy son of a bitch—" the fellow is reported to have said, and that was enough for C.C. He turned over the table, and the battle was on. It is said that Cornelius fought fair, throwing punches. But his opponent clinched, caught him in a headlock—and bit off his ear!

Both Dakin and Tom vouch for this incident, but Edwina could not bring herself to report it. It wasn't one of the things one brought up at a meeting of the Daughters of the American Revolution.

In time plastic surgeons were able to construct an ear of sorts out of skin taken from C.C.'s bottom, but it was too late. Poor Cornelius had finally gone too far. The top brass at International voted to give C.C. an "early retirement" and a pension. His salesmen still loved him. They gave him a big party, and they all chipped in to buy him a diamond ring. Dakin said he used to sit for hours on the sofa at home and look at the diamond. There wasn't much else for him to do.

The ambitious and unscrupulous young junior executive could see no reason to continue calling on Rose. It broke her heart.

After the disaster Cornelius told Rose she would have to get a job, and she tried very hard. Hours and hours of looking at the typewriter keyboard still hadn't imprinted it completely on her mind, but she managed to be hired as a kind of secretary and receptionist to some young dentists. Right away she had problems addressing envelopes. Tom wrote that she lasted only one day; Dakin and his mother believed it was a bit longer, but she was fired quickly. She ran into the lavatory, locked herself in and cried.

The dentists couldn't get her out; the family had to come downtown and persuade her to open the door. It was her first and last employment.

Even Tom, who loved her so much, gave her one last blow that he says he has regretted all his life. One weekend, while Edwina and Cornelius had gone off in the car, Tom brought some of his friends, mostly Washington University students, to the house. Among them were Clark Mills McBurney and William Jay Smith. They all drank a good deal, and one of them got very drunk and started making obscene phone calls.

Rose was there, heard all of it and when their parents returned told them about it. Edwina was furious and told Tom that none of these friends could ever come into the house again. Leaving his mother, he met Rose on the stairway and screamed that he hated the sight of her face. She was speechless and horror-struck as he ran out of the house. He felt it was the cruelest thing he had ever done in his life.

Dakin believed it was "the final straw that separated my sister from her sanity." But at least it was one of many straws; the process had been continuing for years. After this she began to suffer delusions, believing people were trying to poison her. Edwina wrote that a psychiatrist had told Cornelius: "Rose is liable to go down and get a butcher knife and cut your throat." Tom reported that she was actually about to leave for her psychiatrist's office with a kitchen knife in her purse, but that Edwina took it away from her.

She was sent to St. Vincent's Sanitarium. The diagnosis was, according to Tom, dementia praecox; according to Dakin, schizophrenia and acute paranoia. It is doubtful that anyone can have all those at once, but there was no question that she was seriously ill.

Dakin, who was home all during Rose's illness, was closer to it than Tom was, and saw all the really frightful part. To Tom it was heartbreaking and dreadful, yet with an aura of bittersweet tragedy.

At the worst phase of Rose's illness, Tom went off to Iowa University. Grand had come through with the money again, and Tom joined Professor Mabie's seminar in playwriting.

Dakin said he spent a large part of his senior year at the University City High School driving his mother, and sometimes his father, to the mental hospital. At times, he said, "Rose was like a wild animal. Often I would hear her screaming long before the Catholic sisters would usher us into her presence at St. Vincent's. Our visits were almost always depressing disasters. Between screams and the most vile cursing, she would be chain-smoking and pacing up and down the corridor or visiting room. Finally the mother superior advised us there was no future for Rose at St. Vincent's, which was primarily equipped for 'custodial care.'"

Tom, who was away during most of this period, never reported seeing Rose in these disturbed states. The only visit he recorded was one to the Missouri State Asylum at Farmington, sixty miles south of St. Louis, where he found her relatively calm.

Something had to be done; and the family has argued and searched their souls and their consciences ever since about what was done, and whether it should have been done. The doctors at St. Vincent's suggested that the family talk to Dr. Emmett Hoctor at the Farmington Asylum. Dr. Hoctor was one of the pioneers in the growing field of brain surgery.

At Farmington Rose's condition was studied and evaluated for several months. Dr. Hoctor had been experimenting with a new kind of operation called prefrontal lobotomy, in which a hole was drilled in the skull and an instrument inserted to sever a connecting nerve. At this point, according to Tom, no one in the United States had ever had this operation. The doctor thought Rose would be helped by it, but permission would have to be given.

Cornelius, extremely depressed, was becoming more and more an alcholic, so the decision was up to Edwina. She decided to let it be done, and it was.

Afterward Rose ceased completely to be violent and became, as Dakin puts it, "a mental vegetable." Edwina said in her memoirs that it was "a grave mistake" and was sorry she had allowed it.

Tom's opinion of lobotomy in general is stated clearly in his play *Suddenly Last Summer*. A monstrous mother (nothing like Edwina at all) threatens the heroine with lobotomy to wipe out the memory of her son's unspeakable murder. Tom considered it to be a kind of living death. He says he would never have permitted Rose's operation, and blames his mother for having it done.

As this is written, Rose is still alive and in good physical condition, drifting through life with a perpetual faraway smile. Ever since Tom became rich he has paid her bills at the best and most pleasant sanitariums. For many years she lived in her own cottage in a pretty wooded area at a sanitarium near Ossining, New York, and Tom would often drive her into New York to the Plaza Hotel, for dinner. As Dakin remembered, when her limousine drove up, Rose would proudly wave at passersby, for in the imaginary world she inhabited she was Queen Elizabeth, or perhaps Cleopatra, Queen of the Nile.

Later Tom bought a house for her, near his own, in Key West, a pleasant place with a swimming pool. One of their cousins lived there with her.

The person who probably suffered most from the tragedy was Miss Edwina. Dakin wrote this postscript: "It may appear from these pages that our mother was a comical character with many of the attributes of Amanda in *The Glass Menagerie* but in this ordeal of my sister's mental demise she showed an abundance of courage and determination to do all that could be done to salvage the wreck that life had inflicted upon Rose."

Edwina stated that Cornelius never visited Rose after the operation.

CHAPTER 8

Apart from the sadness about Rose, the year at Iowa University was much happier and more productive for Tom than the one at Washington. This was partly a matter of physical equipment. Washington University now has an elaborate theater complex in a big new building, but in 1937 there was nothing. The plays written in English 16 were performed in a kind of lecture room in the law school. There were no real theatrical facilities, no place to experiment, to tinker with sets and effects, or to try out bits of experimental plays.

Professor E.C. Mabie had persuaded the University of Iowa to build a large theater and theatrical workshops. Projects were going on all the time. Student playwrights did more than just write. They could take a course in stagecraft, learning how to design and build sets, and they were required to act in plays. They were learning all about the trade.

But it was difficult to enter the course; Tom was able to do it partly because Holland, the Mummers director, sent Professor Mabie a long telegram and a copy of one of Tom's plays. Colvin McPherson, the drama critic of the St. Louis *Post-Dispatch*, also sent an urgent letter.

Tom later wondered if all this was necessary, but he got in, and also took courses in Shakespeare, modern drama, stagecraft and experimental playwriting.

Tom threw himself into all this with great zest and made his acting debut as a black preacher in a "living newspaper" dramatization. With his accent, it was obviously typecasting.

At the same time he was working part-time in the cafeteria of the university hospital. He was invited to stay at the local ATO chapter house, but decided to go to a boardinghouse closer to the campus where there were many graduate students and English majors, including one Russian communist, who tried unsuccessfully to convert him.

He began writing immediately, and soon wrote his mother that two of his new short plays were being produced. One was a satire on Hollywood producers, about which he then knew nothing.

He received an A for the first term in experimental playwriting with Professor Mabie, whom he described as a splendid teacher. Unfortunately, Mabie had an inoperable brain tumor, which gave him periods of mental lapse, enough to have to be sent to the psychopathic ward of the university hospital. Once the professor became so upset at a rehearsal that he threw his eyeglasses at the actors, and kept them working all night long until noon the next day.

When Tom arrived at Iowa his suitcase already contained the partly completed manuscript of a full-length play titled *Not About Nightingales*, another of his early forays into social significance. In the Texas archives there is a stack of about four hundred pages of writing and rewriting on *Nightingales*. He obviously did more work on this while at Iowa. It is a "social problem tragedy" in three acts. Prisoners rebel because of bad food, spaghetti with rotten meatballs every day. The central characters, a woman prison administrator and a trusty convict (who fall in love) battle the corrupt warden. Convicts are punished in a hot-box cell, where some of them die. The play is grim and very serious.

At least one version must have been ready before he entered Iowa, because he submitted it to an agent, Olga Becker, who wrote him on September 22, 1937, saying that she might be able to find a producer if certain things were done. One producer, not named, suggested speeding up the first act, better curtain lines and making it "less like *Tobacco Road*." Olga Becker's comments were that there was no central character, the structure was "very bad" and that there was "no first act." But it wasn't beyond repair, she added.

Tom was doing well in all his studies. He wrote to his mother to say he had received two B's and two C's. Things, he told her, were going along smoothly except that his boardinghouse was serving potatoes three times a day, seven days a week, driving him occasionally to the campus restaurant. He added that he was having a series of short plays broadcast over the radio every Tuesday evening. A short story and some poems would appear in *American Prefaces*.

But he wasn't telling Miss Edwina everything.

The year at Iowa, he wrote in his *Memoirs*, was the time he had his "first and only consummated sexual affair with a woman," and it was of such violent passion and such giddy frequency that it would seem a flight of the imagination, except that Tom said it really happened, and he is an honorable man.

This is what he said took place. The girl's name, "Sally," is fictitious, but she was real, and a "genuine nympho" and an alcholic, too. This was about the time when *The Fugitive Kind* was being performed by the Mummers in St. Louis, and the panache of a produced playwright attracted Sally to him. Sally had an Etruscan profile, a sensual mouth and a pair of the finest breasts on campus. He even liked the fact that her breath smelled of beer and cigarettes.

A girl with all these attributes must have had every wolf on the campus wildly howling, but she overlooked all that and, he claimed, borrowed an apartment from a friend just to seduce him. She lured him there, tuned into the sexiest music on the radio—and in a trice they were in the buff on the sofa. But he couldn't perform, and instead went to the bathroom and threw up. End of round one.

This apparently excited her all the more. He had brought out her maternal instinct, he said. The next night he took her home to her boarding-house. She was wearing red ski pants and a white sweater, stretched tightly over her bosom. Instead of going to her room they stayed in the parlor. She switched off the light and pointed to the sofa. In no time she had him wildly passionate, unzipped her ski pants, and he did it, all the way, with his overcoat on.

Tom said that people kept coming in during these festivities, but it didn't bother them. She would zip up, and he would button his overcoat, and no one minded. The people would go on upstairs, and the two of them would go at it again, in a variety of positions. Tom said they repeated the "same scene" (presumably the zipper, the overcoat and casual observers) every night for about two and a half months, and it was getting better all the time because he was learning to hold back his orgasms. By this time the other roomers, or audience, (who were "raffish" people, he said) would have had time to set up bleachers. One time, on the sofa, she wanted to perform fellatio, but he wouldn't let her.

For their last date, just before Christmas, they checked into a hotel room and did it for the first time naked in bed. He wrote that after the holidays she told him she was pregnant, but that was not true. She had another boyfriend. He tried to get dates with other girls but couldn't. And he said that he then had no sexual interest in males. But he never again made love to a woman.

The whole "Sally" affair was told in his *Memoirs* with a perfectly straight face, but Tom is a master of black humor and he often made fun of heterosexual coupling. The most hilarious example is the first act of *Period of Adjustment*, probably the funniest act he ever wrote.

Tom's main preoccupation at Iowa must have been work, and huge amounts of it. He was rewriting *The Fugitive Kind*, he was doing vast reading for his literature course—"all literature from the Bible to *Babbitt*"—and he did more work on *Nightingales* and wrote another full-length play, *Spring*

Storm. He was overcoming his shyness, and read all of the play aloud in class. It was surely his sexiest play to date. It is called "a tragedy of sex relations" and also had another title, *April Is the Cruelest Month*. It tells of the lovemaking of two couples, and makes it seem rather unpleasant. There are two acts, each of three scenes.

Reading the play aloud must have been quite a performance. When he finished he said that Professor Mabie's eyes "had a glassy look as though he had drifted into a state of trance," and there was an embarrassed silence. Then Mabie said gently, "Well, we all have to paint our nudes."

He was also writing both poetry and short stories. In a letter to Edwina he said he had just done some new lyrics, which he would send to *Poetry*. One of the stories was perhaps the first of his strange "cat series," which he did both as short stories and one-act plays. They have many titles; one of the first was "The Beetle of the Sun," changed from "The Ghost of a Man and a Cat," and it finally appears in his *One Arm* volume of stories as "The Malediction" and as a play in the *27 Wagons Full of Cotton* collection, called "The Strangest Kind of Romance," that is, man and cat. These versions vary slightly, but all are about a little man, a factory worker, who finds a cat called Nitchevo that he loves (but not sexually), a landlady who sleeps with him but whom he does not love and a factory that eventually fires him.

People who see symbols in everything might say that the cat is a symbol of homosexual love. And the little man from the factory is another facet of the social significance that Tom was trying so hard to write about. It was the fashion, in the depression and postdepression years, for all writers, especially young ones, to be committed. Tom was breaking his head on it, writing thousands of pages—*Candles to the Sun*, *Not About Nightingales*, *The Fugitive Kind*—and for him it would never really work; it wasn't his way.

The story of the cat was written "in an individual style." It doesn't sound like Williams at all. It is written in a kind of poetry, but as though the poet were standing somewhere on higher ground, looking down.

But the other story, written about this time, is entirely different, lovely and truly poetic, and here the poet is right in the midst of it, lying down. In it he becomes Tennessee Williams for the first time, and perhaps not by coincidence; it is his first known work to be publicly signed "by Tennessee Williams." The story is "The Field of Blue Children," and was published in 1939 by Story magazine. It is about a poet at a big state university, a bit of an outsider, who falls in love with a girl, a sorority girl who is an insider, and makes love to her in a field of blue wild flowers. Then she goes back to her insiders and marries one of them. The boy seems very much like Tom—like Tennessee, we should say now—though the girl is about as far away as possible from "Sally."

Why Tennessee rather than Thomas or Thomas Lanier? For one thing, it is obvious he had to choose *something*. The old triple-barreled names for authors were going out of fashion. He once told his mother that Thomas Lanier Williams reminded him of bad poetry. Thomas Williams would not have been an identification, since there must be thousands with that name.

Edwina lists two reasons why he chose Tennessee. One was that his friends in Iowa could tell from his accent that he was from *some* southern state, and just picked out Tennessee. The other was that the Williamses had fought the Indians for control of Tennessee, and a young writer had to be like that, defending the stockade against savages.

Another theory is that Tennessee, with the accent on the first syllable, sounds good to the ear, whereas Mississippi Williams and Missouri Williams simply don't.

In addition to enormous amounts of writing, Tennessee was also acting. Once he was made up as a page boy for *Richard of Bordeaux*, with painted lips and cheeks and curly hair. He was startled to note that he looked like a young girl. But he had stage fright and could only squeak out his one line.

For a while he shared an apartment with a Middle Eastern student who tried to sodomize him, and whom he says he refused.

He admired passionately the university's best (and handsomest) actor, Walter Fleischman, who played Christ in a passion play. And he thought Lemuel Ayers, a postgraduate student, looked like a saint in an Italian Renaissance painting.

He also studied under Professor Conkle, who was becoming famous for his play *Prologue to Glory*, produced by the WPA Theater. Tennessee thought he was a first-rate teacher.

The result of all the writing was that he failed some courses and had to stay for summer school to make up his credits. In late summer of 1938 he received his B.A. from the University of Iowa.

In August he wrote to Professor Mabie saying that he had finished *Spring Storm* again and would mail it to him as soon as he could get it typed and bound. He also said that he was spending some time on the public beaches taking down "colorful idioms of speech" in a notebook, and that he planned to stop at a cheap hotel to get material for his "flophouse play," which he planned to rewrite (almost certainly *The Fugitive Kind*).

He went back to St. Louis to finish revisions on *Not About Nightingales*, which the Mummers had planned to produce. But this fine, small, but financially shaky semiprofessional group had run out of money and had to disband.

He then went to Chicago to try to join the WPA Writers' Project, but they would not take him because his family wasn't sufficiently destitute. So he returned to St. Louis. Clark Mills McBurney was back from Paris. Tennessee relaxed with him and other friends. C.C. let him use the Studebaker and they picnicked on the Meramec River. It is a pretty wooded stream southwest of St. Louis, and in those days was clean enough for swimming, with rapids for sporty canoeing.

This was a momentary recess. He knew he wanted to go away alone to write. But before he took off he read about a play contest sponsored by the Group Theatre. For many young playwrights that was a magic name. With the plays of Clifford Odets the Group Theatre was becoming a kind of new wave in the New York theater. Tennessee packed up all the scripts he had and sent them to New York. The package included the four long plays *Candles to the Sun*, *The Fugitive Kind*, *Spring Storm* and *Not About Nightingales*, and also three short plays, *Moony's Kid Don't Cry*, *The Dark Room* and *The Case of the Crushed Petunia*. The three short ones together were called *American Blues*.

After he put that bundle in the mail he was ready to cut loose, really cut loose, for the first time.

CHAPTER 9

With no job, no money, and no real prospect of making any, Tennessee took a bus to New Orleans. He wanted to get away from St. Louis and his family, to write and to live for as close to nothing as possible. And, no doubt, he also wanted privacy, because it was in New Orleans that he "came out," the gay way of saying that he had decided on his way of sex and no longer wanted to suppress it.

Miss Edwina, back in St. Louis, had no idea what was really going on in New Orleans, although Tennessee wrote her many letters, telling her the kinds of things a young man tells a mother who is a Regent in the D.A.R.

He said he was fascinated by the city, which was true. He did love New Orleans; he has always said it is his favorite city in America, perhaps in the world. He walked the city for miles, explored every stone of the Vieux Carré, the old French quarter where he lived, and he wandered through the campuses of Tulane and Loyola universities, listened to the Dixieland jazz in Jackson Square, explored the bayous and the Cajun country. And he loved the food, which was delicious and cheap.

He almost ignored this first New Orleans period in *Memoirs* because he had covered it well in an almost totally autobiographical story called "The Angel in the Alcove," which is in his *One Arm* volume. The "angel" part is about the only thing that didn't happen, since she (it was a female angel, theology to the contrary) was the imagined ghost of his grandmother, old "Grand," who had not yet passed on, though she would about a year later.

The story tells about a young writer who lived in a rooming house in the Vieux Carré. Tennessee did live in a replica of one, for $2.50 a week. It was run by an eccentric and highly suspicious southern gentlewoman turned harpy by poverty. (In real life there had been three women.) She would sleep in a cot, down by the front door, so that she could look suspiciously at her tenants as they came in at night.

The angel he imagined was not only "Grand," she was also his conscience. After he turned off the light in his room he imagined she would

73

come and sit quietly in the little alcove by the window and watch him.

One night, while the angel was, as usual, watching, the writer was in bed and was wakened by a visitor, who was leaning over his bed. He was startled, but the visitor, a tubercular artist who slept in an adjoining room, persuaded him in whispers to lie back and let him do what he wanted to do, which, we are led to believe, is what Sally wanted to do and he wouldn't let her. (The later play version seems to confirm this.)

The writer came to the conclusion that the angel, and his conscience, had allowed it to happen, without either blame or approval. So it was stamped "OK" by conscience and the ghost of Grand. The real Grand, alive and well and living in Memphis at the time, was not consulted.

In fact, he wrote a letter to Grand during that period and hoped she would come down, in the flesh. He said she could get a room for four dollars a week, which would include use of the kitchen.

In the story he had written about the plan he had worked out with the landlady to start a restaurant—"meals for a quarter in the Quarter" (i.e., the French quarter)—but in his letter he told Grand that the operation had lasted only a week, because the cook became exhausted and left. And he, as the waiter, got pretty tired, too.

He also told Grand that he had started a new play with a New Orleans background, and had finished rewriting *The Fugitive Kind*. He was going to send this revision to the Group Theater.

Tennessee later expanded *Alcove* into a full-length play, *Vieux Carré*, which was produced in New York at the St. James Theater in 1977, and had a successful run in London, at the Piccadilly Theater, for several months in 1978. The play dramatizes a fantastic but true incident: the landlady was so angered by a wild party on the ground floor that she poured boiling water through the floorboards. She had to go down to the police station, where she was charged with "malicious mischief" and fined fifteen dollars. Tennessee was a witness. Fearing he might be charged with perjury, he wouldn't say that she had not done it, only that it was "highly improbable that a lady would do such a thing."

An item not noted in the play was that one of the doused people was the wife of Roark Bradford, and the incident led to Tennessee's meeting Bradford, from whose stories *The Green Pastures* was made.

He was hoping to have the revised *Fugitive Kind* produced by the New Orleans WPA Writers' Project, and in the course of this he met the project director, Lyle Saxon, author of *Fabulous New Orleans*.

Tennessee was still living on handouts from Edwina and his grandmother, and trying desperately to get any kind of writing job. One of his radio plays was being produced by a local station, but without any payment.

But he was happy and claimed he already knew more people in New Orleans than he had ever known in St. Louis. He wrote that to his mother, but he didn't tell her about some of the far-out gay types, such as the one he calls "Antoine" in his *Memoirs*. This fellow carried around a cut-glass bottle of smelling salts, which he would sniff ostentatiously if any female came too close, whispering "poison." He liked Antoine and visited his beautifully decorated apartment, but generally he disliked any form of "swish" or "camp," which he considered then, as always, a form of self-mockery. In spite of his manner, Antoine could be serious; he and homosexual friends produced Gertrude Stein's play *Four Saints in Three Acts* in his apartment. It was performed seriously and well.

At the end of *Vieux Carré*, the young writer leaves the rooming house with another young man, who plays the clarinet. Their plan is to drive to California, which is what happened. The real musician was Jim Parrot (Tennessee pointed out that Jim was not a homosexual).

Apparently there were two different young writers named Williams in the car with the clarinet player. One was Tennessee, the romantic, suffering (even starving) young poet, as remembered in *Memoirs*, and the other was Tom Williams, who was writing letters to his mother, Miss Edwina, in St. Louis. Neither, of course, was telling fibs; they just saw things in a different light.

Tom carefully sent advance addresses, so that the checks from Edwina and Grand would arrive safely. He sent word from San Antonio that things were progressing nicely; they had no real worries because his musician friend had relatives who owned a squab ranch near Los Angeles. They beat an Indian squaw out of payment for a night's lodging by slipping out before dawn—and were followed by two barrels of buckshot that luckily went over their heads. Grand meanwhile was sewing ten-dollar bills into letters and sending them west.

Tom and the musician had a leisurely trip, staying at Phoenix for a few days and then stopping at Palm Springs to envy the movie millionaires in their desert oasis. They drove into Los Angeles, where they stayed at the YMCA, and Tom saw one of Cornelius's salesmen, Sam Webb, who thought he could get him a job selling shoes. Then they went to the pigeon ranch owned by the musician's uncle, where they treated Tom "like their own nephew" (Tom's words, in a letter to Edwina). And on one day they killed and plucked one hundred squabs.

Sam Webb came through with a job at Clark's Bootery in Culver City, half a block from the MGM studios, where Tom could fit high heels to the starlets for twelve dollars a week. Meanwhile, Tennessee, according to *Memoirs*, was able to endure semistarvation. There is a heartbreaking passage telling how he scratched for food, eating an occasional dried pea or a stolen avocado. He told how, after three days or so without food, the stomach contracts and the pangs of hunger subside. He thought that God helped starving people this way. Tennessee was unaware of Tom in the bootery.

Tom was leading a hard life, nevertheless. The shoe store was twelve miles from the squab ranch. He bought a secondhand bicycle for five dollars and rode the twenty-four miles every day. Without a car, and with no public transportation, there was no other way.

Both Tom and Tennessee report the bike.

Edwina worried that he would be hit by a car; the only accident was that he ran into a cow, which scared him more than the cow. All this cycling impressed Sam Webb, who wrote to Cornelius that "any boy who will ride a bicycle twenty-four miles a day to work is bound to succeed."

The big news came suddenly. There was a telegram from the Group Theatre, where Tom's bundle of plays had been sent. The date was March 20, 1939, six days before his twenty-eighth birthday:

THE JUDGES OF THE GROUP PLAY CONTEST ARE HAPPY TO MAKE A SPECIAL AWARD OF ONE HUNDRED DOLLARS TO YOU FOR YOUR THREE SKETCHES IN AMERICAN BLUES.

It was signed Harold Clurman, Irwin Shaw and Molly Day Thatcher.

They had created a new award to fit Tennessee. The main prize of $500 had been won by Roman Naya for a full-length play called *Mexican Mural*, but *American Blues*, Molly Thatcher wrote, was "so outstanding that it deserved recognition, and at our request the Group Theatre has made possible this extra award."

It was the first really professional recognition he had ever had for his plays. Of the three short dramas, *Moony's Kid Don't Cry* is the best known, and is included in the volume of the best one-act plays of 1940. As noted above, it is a revision of that early (probably 1932) one-act play called *Hot Milk at Three in the Morning*. The young man, in the new version, has been made into more of a free soul: the fugitive kind, the wild bird who doesn't want to be put in a cage. Here he is, a former lumberjack, trying to escape a factory life. This character, really Tennessee's own idealized image of himself, would appear in many of his later plays.

The Dark Room, one of the other short plays, is about a pregnant Italian girl who is kept in a darkened room by her mother. In *The Case of the Crushed Petunias* a homosexual young man steps on a woman's petunias and then goes off with her to a cemetery, possibly to make love.

Even Cornelius was impressed with his son for the first time. "We were all very proud you won the $100 prize," he wrote. He sent his son a pair of shoes and signed his name, "Affectionately, C.C. Williams."

Tennessee quit his shoe-store job. He and Jim left the squab ranch on their bicycles and rode south to Tijuana and Agua Caliente. They went down the Camino Real, whose name he later borrowed for a play. Then they cycled back to California and spent a lazy summer at Laguna Beach, swimming and cycling. He wrote that the summer was the happiest and healthiest and most radiant time of his life. In his journal he called that season *Nave Nave Mahana*, which is the Tahitian name of his favorite Gauguin painting. It means "the careless days."

The news of his Group Theatre award spread around Broadway and he received a number of letters from literary agents. One said she wasn't interested in serious plays but wanted a "good vehicle." He told her that the only vehicle he had to offer was a secondhand bicycle.

But one letter looked intelligent. It was from an agency called Liebling-Wood and was signed "Audrey Wood." She said she wanted him, sight unseen. He agreed to let her represent him and to give her the usual 10 percent of all the money she earned him.

Now his typewriter was rattling faster. On July 29 he wrote a three-page, single-spaced letter addressed to "Miss Wood," outlining the plot for a full-length play about a poor woman in a cheap apartment in a Los Angeles suburb who was dying of cancer.

He also told her he had been working at a bowling alley, and had a badly bruised kneecap because he hadn't jumped out of the way of a strike fast enough.

Nothing further was heard about the cancerous lady, but Audrey Wood went to work immediately and effectively. She sold "The Field of Blue Children" to *Story* magazine for twenty-five dollars. She also sent him an application form for a Rockefeller Fellowship grant.

But he was out of money again, and Grand sent him enough for bus fare back to St. Louis. He set up shop with his portable in the attic of the family house. In Laguna he had had an idea about a young, wandering adventurer in a snakeskin jacket who comes to a sleepy little Mississippi town and causes great commotion among the females. He finished it quickly in Edwina's attic that autumn. He called it *Battle of Angels*, and sent it to Audrey Wood.

He followed the play to New York soon afterward, hoping to find a job and live there. Audrey Wood had not yet been able to sell the play, and couldn't even find him a job at Macy's department store. Discouraged, he took the bus back to St. Louis and his attic workroom.

He wasn't there long before a telegram arrived from the Dramatists Guild, which he had joined. (All playwrights had to join the guild if they wanted to have a play produced on Broadway. A producer cannot sign a contract with a nonmember, and the guild protects dramatists with standard minimum-fee contracts.) Luise Sillcox, the executive secretary of the guild, reported that he had received a $1,000 Rockefeller grant, to be paid over a period of ten months. Audrey Wood telephoned, too, with the news and suggested that he come to New York.

Edwina was so happy she cried. Tennessee said it was the first time he had ever seen her in tears.

He was now a local celebrity. The St. Louis *Post-Dispatch*, the *Globe-Democrat* and the *Star-Times* all interviewed him. The family was becoming known for something else besides the wild Saturday nights of Cornelius.

CHAPTER 10

Tennessee arrived in New York at dawn on a Greyhound bus, tired, unshaven, dressed in a badly wrinkled suit. He waited until it was time for offices to open, then walked to Rockefeller Center to the RCA Building, where the main NBC radio studios were located as well as the offices of Liebling-Wood.

When he went in, the outer office was full of leggy chorus girls, and the Liebling half of Liebling-Wood was studying their legs and other attributes. William Liebling, usually called Bill, was a small, dark man, a casting agent who specialized in performers for vaudeville and musicals. At the moment he was selecting girls to audition for a show.

He told everybody to line up; they all did, except Tennessee. After Liebling had winnowed out the girls, nobody was left except the young man who looked like a vagrant, sitting on the bench. Liebling said there was nothing for him.

Tennessee said he only wanted to see Miss Wood. And on cue Miss Wood, who was really Mrs. Liebling, came out, as tiny as Liebling, with bright red hair and looking like a china doll, except for her eyes, which were very bright. She was energetic, witty and bouncy, and had one of the brightest minds in the business.

"Well," she said to Tennessee, "you've finally made it."

He thought it was a bit early to say that.

He moved into the West Side YMCA, where he could swim every day. Then he enrolled in the seminar in advanced playwriting conducted by Theresa Helburn and John Gassner at the New School for Social Research, on West Twelfth Street in Greenwich Village. The most important thing about the seminar was that Theresa Helburn was the codirector of the Theatre Guild, then the most respected and successful producing company on Broadway; John Gassner was its principal play reader. Gassner, a small, plump, gray-haired gentleman, with a precise way of talking, was the professor most frequently seen. Miss Helburn, whom Tennessee said had light lavender hair, appeared less often. Mead, who took the course about four years later, cannot remember having seen Helburn at all.

Gassner was always preoccupied with audience acceptance. He was not an ivory-tower man. He was forever seeking empathy, and the phrase he kept using over and over was: "Who are you *rooting* for?" The spectator had to be pulling for some character or he would lose interest. Gassner's influence in this direction must have acted as a kind of counterweight to Tennessee's poetic fancies.

Tennessee was enthusiastic, and stimulated, and was working feverishly. He wrote to Edwina that he was revising the last act of an old play, probably *Battle of Angels*, and finishing a new one, possibly *The Long Goodbye*, a one-acter.

And for the first time he was really living in the center of the professional theater. He spent many afternoons watching rehearsals of the new Clifford Odets play being produced by the Group Theatre. One day Harold Clurman, the head director (and one of those who had signed his award telegram) introduced himself and said that Tennessee's new play was on his desk. That was exciting—but nothing happened.

He went to many performances of Broadway plays. This was the day of Gray's Drugstore on Times Square. Downstairs there was a kind of flea market for theater tickets. Just before curtain time unsold tickets would be sent to Gray's, and with luck a $2.20 seat could be bought for fifty cents, and the buyer would have to run to get into his seat before the curtain rose.

Sometimes the Dramatists Guild would send him free passes. That way he saw Elmer Rice's *Two on an Island*. Another evening he went to a poetry reading by W.H. Auden and talked with many of the poets in the audience.

On the opening night of Sean O'Casey's *Juno and the Paycock* he didn't expect to get in. He had no ticket. He was standing outside looking at the celebrities when Audrey Wood and Bill Liebling came along and gave him a ticket to a box seat. There he was, looking down on Robert Benchley, Elissa Landi, John Beal and other notables. He loved the play, and said it was the only really good one he had seen in New York.

So though he had an income from the grant of only $100 a month, he was living like a king; but what made him different from most young hopeful playwrights in this position was—he didn't like it. Excited, yes; fascinated by the theater, yes—but he wanted to get away. He was and always would be his own man. He had no intention of imitating anyone. And he would never be able to work for long in the city; there were too many diversions. He would have preferred an attic in St. Louis or a cabin anywhere. And that would remain true. He did most of his writing far from Broadway.

He always liked to live where he could swim every day, if possible. At the Y he often started his day with a swim, then wrote for several hours, had a workout in the gym, went out for dinner and then to a play.

* * *

In January 1940 he met two young men from Atlanta who were living together in a furnished room on West Fifty-second Street, above a jazz club. They were Donald Windham, aged nineteen, who had been working in a barrel factory in Georgia and hoped to become a professional writer; and Fred Melton, age twenty-one, who had been lettering show cards in a department store and hoped to be an artist. All three would occasionally go swimming at the YMCA where Tennessee lived.

On February 14 all three went down to the New School's basement theater to see Tennessee's first New York production. The student actors were doing his one-act play *The Long Goodbye*. This play is short and sad, about a poor writer and his sister who live in a tenement apartment in "a large Midwestern American city;" all the references are to St. Louis. It is a step on the way to *The Glass Menagerie*, though not so close to the auto-biographical facts as that play. The only live people are the writer, a writer-friend and the moving men who are taking away the furniture. But there are flashbacks to his mother, dying of cancer, and his sister, who is not at all like Rose. She is being treated with sexual contempt by a young society dandy. At the end the writer is crying. The frustration and the portrayal of the underside of St. Louis reflect the sorrow of his own life in that city.

Edwina was excited to have the play mentioned in the drama column of the New York *Times*. Fleet Munson, a New York drama critic, saw it and wrote Audrey Wood that he had been "profoundly moved by the play-writing talent of one whose ability is...clearly recognizable...Gentle him, for Pete's sake. He's a honey. Don't let the drones get him."

A sharp observer of Tennessee at this period was Gilbert Maxwell, another of the Atlanta contingent. Maxwell had known Donald Windham and Fred Melton in Atlanta, and had rooms in the same building on Fifty-second Street. He was an actor and poet, as poor as the rest of them. Years later, Maxwell wrote a book about Tennessee *(Tennessee Williams and Friends: An Informal Biography)*. Their first meeting was at Windham and Melton's place in early 1940.

Maxwell found Tennessee sitting in the kitchen half of their one-room walkup. It seemed to Maxwell that Windham and Melton were somewhat in awe of him. Melton told him, "I've decided Tennessee is a visitor from another planet."

Maxwell was bowled over by Tennessee's energy and his obsession for work. He and his roommate, a Time researcher, invited Tennessee, Windham and Melton down for a party. It lasted until four in the morning, too late to go back uptown. That left five young men with two twin beds.

Tennessee agreed cheerfully to sleep on the floor and rolled up in a blanket. Before anyone else was up, he borrowed Maxwell's typewriter. While the other four were dressing, shaving, shouting and listening to the radio, Tennessee pounded away like a machine gun, totally unaware of anything else. When he rolled out the last page Maxwell asked him what he was writing.

He said it was the new scene for *Battle of Angels*.

This behavior simply boggled Maxwell's mind, but it was nothing un- usual for Tennessee, long used to sleeping anywhere and writing almost immediately on awakening.

That revision, and others, were all put together and the new version of *Battle of Angels* was handed to Gassner, with the hope that he would show it to Theresa Helburn and Lawrence Langner. Tennessee had planned to go to Mexico to write after the seminar was over, but, as he wrote his mother, sudden news changed everything. Audrey Wood telephoned to say that Gassner was "tremendously excited" over the play, and wanted Elmer Rice, the playwright, to look at it. Tennessee then talked to Gassner, who said it was the best play he had read in a year. Gassner wanted two other Guild play readers to see it, and if they liked it, too, there would be a production in the fall.

Tennessee felt like dancing in the streets. The Theatre Guild, he pointed out to his mother, had had five straight hits, including *The Philadelphia Story* with Katharine Hepburn, Hemingway's *The Fifth Column* and Saroyan's *The Time of Your Life*. Their record was the best of any producing company in New York.

Audrey also took him over to Harper's, the publishers, who had been reading, and admiring, his short stories. They said they would like to see a novel. If he would write the first fifty pages, and if they liked them, they would give him an advance. But he told his mother that he didn't feel this was the time to start a novel.

Theresa Helburn visited the class at the New School, where the play was discussed and changes suggested. She took Tennessee home in a taxi and said that the Theatre Guild would take out a $100 option on the play the next day. According to the Dramatists Guild contract, they would have to pay $100 every month. She wanted many revisions, some of which he thought were silly, but he wasn't going to tell her so.

On May 8 he telegraphed his mother:

THEATRE GUILD SIGNS REGULAR CONTRACT TODAY. MUST STAY NEAR NEW YORK. FALL PRODUCTION LIKELY.

The swimming and the writing weren't the only things going on at the West Side YMCA. Tennessee had finally come out of the closet. He had a good body from swimming and was handsome; his only defect was that the pupil of his left eye was turning gray from the cataract. He was still shy when sober, but with a few drinks inside him would "cruise" Times Square looking for sexual partners. He and another young writer would approach sailors and G.I.'s, who often thought they were pimps and asked them where the girls were. The writers made it clear that no girls were required, and sometimes took them back to the friend's place in Greenwich Village—or to the Y, where, of course, one couldn't bring a girl.

Tennessee admitted that no real love was involved, only the joy of pursuit and the companionship of his fellow pursuer. The act itself was repetitive and with only superficial satisfaction when love was not involved, as it would be later. It wasn't that important to him; work was his main concern.

In the spring of 1940 he wrote a letter, never published, to his mother that gives a marvelous and now-it-can-be-told insight into the revered Theatre Guild. He said that Gassner wanted him to push the play into a one-character story and, even worse, to make the lone character a female instead of a male (in a snakeskin jacket) because they had a chance to sign up Joan Crawford, who wanted to do a bit of legitimate theater. Tennessee said he had a low opinion of her acting, but Gassner insisted she would be a big box office attraction and make a lot of money. Tennessee was shocked, since he thought that the guild was interested only in artistic production. And, as he told his mother, having a good production was much more important to him than making money. This was at a time when he had almost nothing; in the summer the option money was reduced to fifty dollars a month.

Luckily, the Crawford threat eventually disappeared.

He had to stay close to New York, so he went up to Lake George, hoping to swim. The water was too cold and he spent his time climbing around the Adirondacks.

In June he moved into an apartment that he, Donald Windham and Fred Melton had subleased for sixty dollars a month. It had two rooms on the ground floor and a studio above, which he planned to use. The roof had porch furniture and a good view of skyscrapers and the East River. It even had a piano.

He had scarcely settled in when he packed up his portable typewriter again and was off to Provincetown, on the tip of Cape Cod, one of the gathering places of the gay world.

He rented a bike and a room, and wrote his first major letter to Windham, the first of a long series that would later be published by Windham as

Tennessee Williams' Letters to Donald Windham 1940–1965. He reported that he was shocked by the P-town way of life. It was his first real contact with the "swish" and "camp" side of homosexuality, the limp-wrist, whoops-my-dear, flowered-hat exhibitionism. He disliked it then, and he has disliked it all his life. He would never dress or act that way. What happened in bed did not shock him; what happened on the street did.

He soon settled down to a productive regime, even though it was one he could not have described to Miss Edwina. As usual he was working hard every morning, swimming and drinking every day and "fucking every night." He was experimenting with writing a play in verse for the first time in any serious way.

In Provincetown he first fell in love with a male, a dancer of striking proportions named Kip. Kip was making clam chowder on Captain Jack's Wharf when Tennessee first saw him. He was built like Nijinsky and had green almond-shaped eyes. Tennessee rented a room on the wharf and the two of them slept in it together. At night they could see the stars and hear the water lapping underneath.

He had no desk, but he put his portable on a box. He was trying hard to write *The Purification* in blank verse, a serious artistic challenge. The letters to Don Windham must have been a kind of relief, a relaxation from the hard, pure poetry. They were also erotic, and he cautioned Windham to be careful with them. They should be seen only by those who had gone "beyond shame."

What has happened is interesting. *The Purification* contains some beautiful lines. It is a one-act play in which Tennessee first touches on a brother-sister incestuous relationship. Perhaps the only way he could approach it, in those days, was in the form of a fantasy. It takes place in a poetic never-never land, on a mythical Spanish ranch in a place like New Mexico, and is done in the form of a family trial. A daughter, who has been having an affair with her brother, has been killed, though she reappears, materialized in two different forms, as Elena of the Springs (lovely) and Elena of the Desert (somewhat desiccated). This was experimental writing for Tennessee, and though he can never write very badly, there are bits in this that are about as purple as he ever gets. For instance, a kind of Latin cowboy makes a speech about a treble choir and the Angelus ringing—a far cry from cowboy talk. But it was a step toward the natural and beautiful poetry of *The Glass Menagerie*, which is not broken up, like *Purification*, into verselike lines.

But the strange thing is that possibly on the same day he wrote about the cowboy and the Angelus, he was writing to Don about Kip. It is an extraordinary piece of writing, honest and strong and understandable. There is not an iota of "swish" or "camp" in it, and is far better writing than anything in *Purification*.

It is about a night with Kip in their room on the wharf, with the sound of the wind and the gulls and the lapping of the sea under them. And the beautiful bronzed body of Kip. They made love three times, and he knew that he was in love with Kip. But Kip, who had two strings to his bow, decided he was becoming too homosexual and stopped. Kip later married and died very young.

When Kip left him, Tennessee was deeply hurt and fled to New York, and from there to Mexico. Edwina thought he was going by boat, but he said that he drove down with a young Mexican who came to the New York World's Fair and married a New York prostitute, whom he was taking back with him. Tennessee says the girl gave him the idea for Myrtle, the prostitute bride in *Kingdom of Earth* (later called *The Seven Descents of Myrtle*).

When they finally reached Mexico, after getting lost innumerable times, Tennessee checked in at the YMCA. He spent a week there, was lonesome, took a bus to Taxco and then got a ride with American students to Acapulco. He first stayed with them near a surfing beach, then went on to the Hotel Costa Verde, which was to suggest the locale of *The Night of the Iguana*, in the rain forest above a stillwater beach.

Long before he wrote *Iguana*, he wrote a short story using this location, and even the same title, but with an entirely different cast of characters, the main ones being a spinster and two homosexual writers. A real iguana, caught by Mexican boys, was actually tied up for fattening and eating, as it would be in the story and play.

At Acapulco he first met Jane and Paul Bowles, who were to become his close friends. Paul, then known as a composer, would become famous for his novel *The Sheltering Sky*. Tennessee thought Jane was one of the greatest living writers.

Paul Bowles, in his memoirs *Without Stopping*, tells what it was like to meet the young and unknown Tennessee Williams:

> One morning when we were getting ready to leave for the beach someone arrived at the door and asked to see me. It was a round-faced, sunburned young man in a big floppy sombrero and a striped sailor sweater, who said his name was Tennessee Williams, that he was a playwright, and that Lawrence Langner of the Theatre Guild had told him to look me up. I asked him to come in and installed him in a hammock, explaining that we had to hurry to the beach with friends. I brought him books and magazines and rum and coke, and told him to ask the servants for sandwiches if he got hungry. Then we left. Seven hours later we got back to the house and found our visitor lying

contentedly in the hammock, reading. We saw him again each day until he left.

Wandering around Mexico, Tennessee was cut off from the world and remittances. He was down to his last ten cents. He tried frantically to reach his mother and the Theatre Guild, and both eventually came through with eating money. But no one told him the latest on *Battle of Angels*; on his way back he read, in the theater column of the New York *Times*, that Miriam Hopkins might play Myra.

He returned to St. Louis to discover that Cornelius had actually bought a house, after renting apartments and houses for so many years. It had happened like this: Cornelius, still drinking heavily, was going regularly to the hospital for periodic "cures." He returned from the latest one, and there was a temporary truce between him and Miss Edwina. For a change she hadn't scolded him about drinking. So he told her he would buy her a house—and he did, a "Georgian Colonial," she called it, three stories high, at 53 Arundel Place in Clayton, a suburb of St. Louis, adjoining Washington University.

Edwina redecorated the third floor for Tennessee as a bedroom-studio. It had dormer windows and was far nicer and more spacious than anything he had ever had before. And there, while waiting for rehearsal dates for *Battle*, he finished *Stairs to the Roof*, based partly on the International Shoe Company years.

He also heard from Audrey Wood that CBS would like to hire him at $100 a script to do a radio series about Lincoln. Word arrived, too, that his one-act plays *This Property Is Condemned* and *At Liberty* would be included in a play anthology called *American Scenes*, to be published by John Day.

Theresa Helburn reported that Miriam Hopkins was definitely signed for *Battle* and that Margaret Webster would direct. She was English, probably best known for directing Shakespearean plays and was highly respected in both New York and London.

Tennessee arrived in New York in November, wearing jodhpurs (Windham reported) and just in time for rehearsals. Webster wanted to sample the atmospheric background of Mississippi, where *Battle* takes place, and they traveled there together. Once she asked him how he would feel if the play failed, and he told her he was trying to "insulate" his feelings, to reduce his suffering. Miss Webster told him that was a dangerous thing for a writer to do; a writer *should* suffer. At the time he seemed a bit skeptical, but some fifteen years later, in a letter written to the critic Kenneth Tynan, he acknowledged that it was a perceptive remark. He should not insulate himself, he had to live with suffering. So he recognized, long ago, that his plays were indeed a by-product of his own inner tensions.

Rehearsals began. The play would try out in Boston, with final rehearsals there. Tennessee was the man in the middle, surrounded by three strong-willed women—Webster, Helburn and Hopkins. The first time he saw Theresa Helburn's copy of the script it was covered with red marks, changes she wanted made.

Dakin remembers a letter from Tennessee that said Miriam Hopkins invited him to her suite at the Ritz-Carlton for champagne and a private supper. Was the motive seduction? Not at all. She wanted to suggest additional changes in the script, to build up her part, and to cut down the lines of the other principal actress, Doris Dudley. And although Miriam was supposed to be shot at the end, she wanted the hero to carry her body upstairs, so that she would be the center of attraction, even after her death. This one they couldn't quite manage.

The play was scheduled to run for two weeks in Boston, then continue the tryout in Washington before the big New York opening. Dakin, then at Washington University, was rushing to the library every day to check the drama news in the Boston *Globe*. And it came, soon enough.

CHAPTER 11

The first night of *Battle* was one that Boston will never forget. As darkness fell over Massachusetts, Tennessee's hopes were high. Theresa Helburn had sent him a precurtain telegram: SAINT MICHAEL AND ALL GOOD ANGELS BE WITH YOU. It was signed CONNECTICUT UPDYKE. The "Updyke" was her married name; and "Saint Michael and All Angels" was Edwina's church. She threw in one more state for luck.

It was the night before New Year's Eve and the Wilbur Theatre was crowded with a well-dressed audience full of well-bred cultural expectations. After all, this was the Theatre Guild, and unlike that rather leftish Group Theatre, the guild didn't usually ruffle any feathers. And there was Margaret Webster, so Shakespearean, and Miriam Hopkins, and a young playwright named after some southern state—and a play about angels.

Actually, no angels appeared. At a time of great stress in the third act, with a storm brewing, a character remarks that a battle of angels is going on up above. The only angels are meteorological and symbolic.

What did appear was a handsome young vagabond writer in a snakeskin jacket, fleeing from a charge of rape (he did it, but she let him), who goes off in the first scene to fornicate with the richest girl in town (she led him on) and who in later scenes becomes a sales clerk in the general store of a small southern town, and drives the whole female population into a sexual frenzy by his physical beauty and by the way he manipulates their knees when he fits them with shoes, and who finally sleeps with and impregnates the wife of the dying store owner, and is incinerated with a blowtorch.

At first the audience was lulled by the beauty of the words, but their eyebrows were rising, scene by scene. And when finally the town's lady artist, who is painting portraits of the twelve disciples, falls in love with the writer and makes her Christ look exactly like him—there were mutterings of "blasphemy." Before the audience could rise in proper Bostonian indignation the blowtorch scene started and the whole theater was filled with black smoke. That was an accident. In the dress rehearsals there hadn't

89

been enough smoke, so for the opening extra smoke pots were brought in and nearly asphyxiated the audience. Even before the curtain came down (the fire was the last bit) the audience was in full flight. When Miriam Hopkins (who was theatrically both pregnant and dead at the moment, shot by her cuckolded husband) rose up for her bows, all she could see through the smoke was the disappearing backs of coughing Bostonians, their eyes streaming, their sensibilities ravaged.

Tennessee would write better plays; his later revision of this one, re-named *Orpheus Descending*, is much more beautiful, yet *Battle of Angels* is an honest play, with a well-drawn portrait of a free-flying, idealistic young man, a dream image of Tennessee himself. If it had not opened in Boston, if Christ had not looked like Val Xavier and if the smoke had been less choking, it might have survived. Many lesser plays have.

Tennessee said in his *Memoirs* that the Boston critics and censors treated the play as they would an outbreak of the bubonic plague. Edwina quotes a critic who called it a play "about a half-wit living a defensive life against predatory women"; yet one critic said that it held occasional lines of beauty. The Boston censors demanded a number of cuts, and wanted the business about the resemblance to Jesus removed.

Tennessee gives a vivid account of the immediate aftermath in his preface to *Orpheus Descending*. Tennessee and Audrey Wood had gone back to their hotel after the disaster and the next morning had read the grim reviews in the Boston papers. They struck out across the wintry Boston Common for a meeting at the Ritz-Carlton. As they walked they heard several loud bangs, probably backfires, and one of them said, "They're shooting at us!" They laughed and entered the hotel.

Miriam Hopkins wasn't there; she was still licking her wounds. (But she did remain loyal to Tennessee and defended the play.) Waiting for them were Margaret Webster, Theresa Helburn and John Gassner, and the stage was set for one of the finest epithet-hurling matches of the period. The various contestants, who were among the best in the business, have re-membered and quoted or misquoted various hurled *bon mots*, and the en-counter, in slightly differing versions, has become a classic.

Tennessee, who had, of course, been rewriting most of the night, and was clutching a handful of pages for the final scene, said he would crawl through brimstone on his belly if these pages could be incorporated into the script.

But even more changes and cuts were demanded, and in any case the play would close at the end of the two-week Boston run and would not go on to Washington and New York.

Tennessee pleaded that he had put his heart into the play. Margaret Webster, flouncing her skirts, flung out, "You must never wear your heart on your sleeve for daws to peck at!"

Then Helburn made the killing remark: "At least you are not out of pocket!" Tennessee thought, sadly, that he had nothing in his pocket to be out of.

The guild gave him $100 to go off and rewrite the play and said they would consider doing it again the following season. A letter was sent to subscribers, refunding money to those who had reserved tickets beyond the closing date, with this explanation: "The play was more of a disappointment to us than to you. *Battle of Angels* turned out badly. But who knows whether the next play by the same author may not prove a success?

"In view of the unfortunate publicity caused by the Boston censor's protest about *Battle of Angels*, we feel it is only fair to give you the Guild's reasons for producing the play. We chose it because we felt the young author had genuine poetic gifts and an interesting insight into a particular American scene. The treatment of the religious obsession of one of the characters, which sprang from frustration, did not justify, in our opinion, the censor's action. It was, we felt, a sincere and honest attempt to present a true psychological picture."

Tennessee wrote his mother that the audiences were "non-poetic" and didn't understand the allegorical nature of the play. And in a letter to his father he complained that the people in Boston were "small-minded," they saw nothing but the sex in the play and thought it was dirty, and that this was frightening to the Theatre Guild people, who were, he thought, getting old and too conservative. He worried that the changes the guild wanted were mainly to satisfy the "narrow-minded" elements in the audience.

He was going blind, he feared, in his left eye from the cataract. In fact, he seemed almost as worried about his looks as about his sight. The cataract caused the pupil of his eye to look milky white, and he had always thought of his eyes as his most compelling feature. It had probably been caused by a childhood injury when he was hit in the eye with a stick during a wild Indian game. He felt he had to have an operation, which was performed under local anesthetic with a needle. He complicated the procedure by vomiting in the middle of it.

Altogether he would have four eye operations, vomit and all; each improved his vision—and his looks—only partially and temporarily.

After that he wanted to go someplace where he could swim and write a lot. He decided to go as far south as he could in the United States, which meant Key West. He met up with Jim Parrot, his squab-farm friend, and they drove down the incredible seagoing bridge to the island that it once was, inhabited by the native "Conchs," sailors, smugglers, artists and writers.

They found Mrs. Cora Black, the widow of an Episcopal minister, who had taken over an attractive mahogany house called Trade Winds and made it into what Tennessee called a "genteel boarding house." They spent one night in a fancy suite for five dollars; Tennessee told Mrs. Black he loved it, and wished he were rich enough to stay and write. She said he didn't have to be rich; she had some old slave quarters in the back, and he could have the whole building for eight dollars a week.

He took the slave quarters; Jim drove back after a few days, and Tennessee went straight to work on his revisions. He rented a bike, and every morning rode it to a Cuban restaurant that served strong coffee. He was afraid, as always, of what it would do to his heart, but he drank lots of it and wrote voluminously, poems, stories, as well as patching up the play.

Mrs. Black had a charming daughter, Marion, who was married to a rich alcoholic, Regis Vaccaro, an heir to the Standard Fruit Company fortune. Marion was a southern lady who had attended Smith College on a scholarship and wrote poetry. She and Tennessee became close friends and remained so until her death, many years later. She was to become his favorite traveling companion.

He fell in love, platonically, with Marion and with Key West itself. There were many interesting people around: Grant Wood, the painter; and Arnold Blanch and Doris Lee, Max Eastman, James Farrell; Kuniyoshi, the Japanese artist; Elizabeth Bishop, the poet; and the eighty-two-year-old philosopher John Dewey, still as spry as a monkey. Hemingway had left but his ex-wife, the former Pauline Pfeiffer, was still there, and so was his autographed bar stool at Sloppy Joe's.

The main problem was Marion's husband, who was alternately high on alcohol and ether. The alcohol Tennessee didn't mind, but the smell of ether drove him crazy. Regis had a glass eye and one evening, during dinner, to emphasize a point, he threw it at his mother-in-law. It landed in her soup. A lesser woman might have fainted, or screamed, but not Mrs. Black. She rose to the top of Tennessee's list of gentlewomen. As though nothing had happened, she removed it gracefully with her soup spoon and passed it to Marion, saying she believed it was something that Regis had lost.

He was still working hard on *Battle*. He wrote to his father on February 28 saying he was doing a whole new pattern of action in the first half of the play. He believed the guild might try it out in a summer theater. And he was swimming a great deal. The salt water was clearing up his sinus trouble, which had been giving him earaches and headaches.

But he had writing problems, too. Mrs. Black wrote to Edwina, whom she had known through the church, that the floor of Tennessee's "slave quarters" would sometimes be covered with crumpled papers. On one of them was written, over and over again, "My head is a block of stone."

But he did finish the *Battle* revisions, and in April headed north. He stopped at Edwina's house on Arundel Place to wait for a check from Audrey Wood. The Theatre Guild had agreed to pay him another $200, in spite of a disastrous season, notable mainly for flag-waving, drum-beating plays, and musical comedy.

From Clayton he wrote to Fred Melton, in New York, that he was becoming more and more a hedonist. With the world in such a state, he thought he should grasp all the pleasure he could. However, his main problem as a hedonist was that his greatest pleasure was work, and at the moment he was exhausted from too much of it.

He also noted that Dakin was directing, and playing a leading role, in *Hedda Gabler* at Washington University.

That spring he received another $500 from the Rockefeller committee on the recommendation of Audrey Wood, which was to be paid at the rate of $100 every month. So he went back to New York and brought the revised version of *Angels* to Laurence Langner at the Theatre Guild. There was no word at all for some weeks. Finally he telephoned Langner, who said, as Tennessee quotes: "About this rewrite, Tennessee. You have gone like the Leaping [sic] Frog of Calaveras County, you know, the Mark Twain story. I mean you wrote it too much like the frog jumped out of the county."

As far as the Theatre Guild was concerned, that was the end. Yet in spite of this cavalier treatment, Tennessee said that he continued to like Langner.

During this spring he moved in briefly with Paul Bigelow, the man he usually refers to as "the legendary Paul Bigelow." Bigelow has a vast affection and respect for Tennessee, and an encyclopedic knowledge of the past half century of the theater.

In the 1940s he was a deliberately mysterious uncle-figure (a young uncle, since he cannot have been much older than Tennessee) to the Atlanta group, though he was not, apparently, from Atlanta. He was a small, thin-faced man with bright, bird-like eyes and tightly curled black hair. No one was quite sure where he was from. Gilbert Maxwell, who had met him in Atlanta and knew him for many years, could never get him to reveal anything about his background. He had gone to school in England, he had lived in Greenwich Village in the twenties, he had been a reporter in Hollywood and

Mexico. He told Maxwell he was born in Maine, but only because it was summer. In other words, he had been born of summer visitors, not Maine Yankees.

Bigelow's New York apartment became headquarters for the Atlanta group and Tennessee moved in, shortly after the Key West visit. But his mind was so full of writing that, as Bigelow told Maxwell, "He's just not here, and I am so weary of telling him, all day long, 'Get up, go wash your hands for lunch, eat, Tennessee, pick up your shirt off the floor, Tennessee.' The last straw was when Bigelow asked him what had happened to two checks he had received from Audrey Wood. Tennessee finally remembered he had sent them out in the laundry. Bigelow ran down to the Chinaman's just in time. The checks hadn't yet been washed.

Bigelow was going crazy, just trying to communicate with Tennessee. They might be sitting on a bench in Central Park, and Bigelow might be trying to tell Tennessee a story, of which he had not heard a word. And then, Bigelow said, "You will then remark, simply to break the silence, 'I saw a most unusual bird this morning,' whereupon he will jump up shouting, 'Bird? What bird? Where?' Now what explanation can there be for that?"

Bigelow thought the only solution was to ship him off to Provincetown. Tennessee, still groggy from the Boston beating, and punch drunk from constant writing, said that people were always putting him on trains or buses.

Bigelow got Tennessee shaved and dressed and led him to Grand Central Terminal. Tennessee wanted to know where they were going, and Bigelow told him he was going to Provincetown. Tennessee said he didn't want to go.

Bigelow told him he was going to Provincetown anyway, and told the conductor not to let Tennessee off until he got there. When Bigelow left him in the carriage, his nose was pressed against the window and he was looking very sad.

Tennessee arrived safely, typewriter in hand, and was immediately writing poetry, short stories and plays. He was also, according to Bigelow, writing "imploring letters and strange postcards" to him. One of these letters, quoted by Maxwell, scolds Bigelow for sending him to live in a broken-down rooming house filled with "faggots and lesbians." The oddest inhabitant was a girl named Rachel who washed his feet every night and dried them with her hair.

The main thing he wrote that summer in Provincetown was a short play about the death of D. H. Lawrence, who had always fascinated him. Tennessee knew the true facts of Lawrence's death, in 1930, in a sanitarium. But in this play, *I Rise in Flame, Cried the Phoenix*, he chose to dramatize it poetically and symbolically. There are only two other characters, representing the two sides of Lawrence: his wife Frieda, large and handsome, and looking like a Valkyrie, his carnal side; and Bertha, the small, sprightly English aristocrat who represented his spiritual side.

Lawrence's favorite symbol, the Phoenix in a nest of flames, is shown on a red banner. Lawrence dies, bleeding and clutching the curtains beside the window, as the sun sets. He forbids the women to touch him before he is dead.

Tennessee, almost penniless, in Provincetown, wrote one play just for the sheer poetic beauty of it, not giving a second thought to the fact that a one-act play had almost no chance of being profitably produced.

It would later be produced many times, but largely by small art theaters. Frieda Lawrence herself admired it and wrote a preface for a special edition. "When I read this short play, I forgot it was supposed to be Lawrence and me; it happens in the other world where creation takes place. The theme of it is the eternal antagonism and attraction between men and women. This was between Lawrence and me too. But the greater reality was something else... it was life in its freedom, its limitless possibilities, that bound us together."

This is the only play of Tennessee's that Miss Edwina would never read, or even look at, because she knew that Lawrence had written *Lady Chatterley's Lover*, and that was a dirty book. Actually she needn't have worried. Nothing dirty happens in the play about the Phoenix.

He returned briefly to Bigelow in August. Maxwell reported that he looked very brown and muscular. He went off again to New Orleans to do some more work on *Stairs to the Roof*. Then he bought another bike and rode it along the Gulf coast. He came back to St. Louis because Edwina had told him that Grand was dying of cancer. But tough little Grand held on.

Cornelius was there, and they had scarcely said hello when he told his son to start shifting a pile of firewood from one side of the backyard to the other. Miss Edwina, who heard him making smacking noises when he ate— perhaps he was so glad to have some home cooking—told him brightly: "Turn left at the foot of the stairs, son Thomas. There's a trough for you in the kitchen."

He wandered sadly back to New York again, staying for a while at the apartment of an abstract painter he had met in Provincetown. He lived in the warehouse district of the West Village, a location Tennessee probably remembered years later when he wrote his novel *Moise and the World of Reason*. The artist was really "freaked out," he said, and that was before this was the "in" thing to do.

Tennessee must have made considerable progress against his shyness, because he worked for a time as a poetry-reading waiter at a bistro called the Beggar's Bar, run by a refugee from Nazi Germany named Valesca Gert. Tennessee created a minor sensation because he had just had another cataract operation and wore an eye patch, which had been painted by his artist friend with a glaring white eye. He was reciting his own light verse, and doing well on tips, until there was a big blowup. Madame Gert decided the three waiters would have to split their tips with each other and with her. This led to a noisy confrontation. Tennessee's friend, the painter, was present and started throwing soda bottles, one of which struck Madame G, who had to have several stitches on her scalp. The waiter with the eye patch was unemployed once again.

About this time Erwin Piscator, the wild genius director of the New School basement theater, almost produced *Battle of Angels*, until Tennessee discovered he had "rewritten" it with scissors and paste, switching around the speeches and making it into a protest play about the South. Tennessee said no.

Finally he was thrown out of the artist's place because some casual guests, for whom he was partly responsible, had absconded with some of the furnishings.

So he was on the street with not enough money to pick up his laundry. He appealed to the Dramatists Guild, which gave him ten dollars. Somehow he was able to get down to New Orleans again and worked as a cashier in a restaurant, meanwhile making further revisions on *Stairs to the Roof*.

He went back to Clayton long enough to have a case of the seven-year itch, so pronounced even by a doctor, and he spent three days greased, in long underwear.

Tennessee returned to New York, to the West Side Y, and became embroiled in the *You Touched Me* affair which is the main subject of the series of letters to Donald Windham.

This was a time of great crisis for Windham, and his situation might have seemed funny to an outside observer, but it certainly wasn't to him. He was in a really desperate fix. Here he was, only twenty, a young man who had come to New York without having gone to college, to make his fortune as a poet. The odds against such a proposition were simply incalculable. One considerable asset was his striking good looks. Maxwell describes him as he was at eighteen, in Atlanta. He was "a modest youngster with a fresh-skinned boyish face, curly dark hair, clear short-sighted eyes behind rimless glasses, and a laugh which usually doubled him up with glee at the sheer, exultant joy of being alive... He did not drink liquor, swear, or use four-letter words, and sometimes made up little poems that had something memorable about them."

Windham had not yet had any literary success, and then a dreadful thing happened—Fred Melton left him *for a woman*. He had married a pretty girl named Sara, from Macon, Georgia, and Don was thrown out of the apartment to be on his own, for the first time in his life. So he, too, went to the West Side YMCA, which he couldn't afford.

Don had just fallen in love with one of D.H. Lawrence's short stories, "You Touched Me." He thought it would make a good play and started to write it. He showed the first pages to Tennessee, who felt it had possibilities, and they agreed to collaborate, the first and only time Williams had ever, or would ever, collaborate with anyone. Whether there was ever any romantic or intimate relationship between the two is a matter that both of them, in all their writings about their times together, absolutely refuse to discuss.

They soon roughed out a draft, Tennessee almost certainly supplying most of the professional expertise, since Donnie (as Tennessee called him) had little experience in playwriting. Windham was by this time living a kind of grasshopper existence. He could no longer afford the Y, and he couldn't sleep at Fred's, since Fred's wife was there. So he slept at the studio of Paul Cadmus, whom he'd met the year before, until Paul had to go to work. Don then hopped over to Fred's to write, because Sara had a job and would be gone. The rest of the time he spent at a local diner, or just walking around.

Meanwhile, *This Property Is Condemned*, one of Tennessee's one-act plays, was produced at the New School. *Property* is one of Tennessee's "tell-about" plays, almost a speciality of his, which reached a high point in *Suddenly Last Summer*. Very little actually happens onstage, but the characters tell a strong story in dialogue. A boy meets a young girl on a railroad embankment. She is dressed in tattered finery, lives alone in a condemned house, scavenges in garbage cans and tells how her sister, a prostitute, and her family all came to bad ends—it seems virtually certain she will, too. It takes good writing to make this sort of thing work, and *Property* does.

But it is interesting how a good screenwriter, Francis Ford Coppola, and a good director, Sydney Pollack, could change the play massively, as they did in 1966, and make one of Tennessee's better films. All the "told-about" action is dramatized, and the main starring parts, Robert Redford's and Natalie Wood's, are two of the told-about characters.

He also finished "One Arm", which would become the title of a short story collection. It is written like a profile of a young navy boxing champion who loses an arm in an accident, becomes a male prostitute in New Orleans, commits a murder while drunk and is finally executed in the electric chair. In one extraordinary passage, Tennessee tells of the inner conflict of the Lutheran minister who visits the sailor in his death cell, and of the minister's struggle with his own latent homosexuality. It is a strange and poetic treatment of the subject.

At this point Tennessee was again totally without funds, and went to visit an older man he never names but who was, he said, a composer of popular music who lived in a Madison Avenue penthouse. Windham thought the arrangement was "nightmarish," and his friends alcoholic. Tennessee stayed there until spring.

Audrey Wood had been sending *Stairs to the Roof* to producers without success. Nobody wanted a fantasy about the International Shoe Company. Edwina quotes a letter from David Merrick as "fairly typical." Merrick found it "interesting and beautifully written. However, I think it is unlikely that you can get a Broadway production. I don't think a producer would be likely to risk a more than average amount of production money on a fantasy or semi-fantasy at this time...." But he added later on, "I don't think I should advise you to write about more commercial subjects because I feel you write so well and with so much genuine feeling in your present form. Let's just hope that soon they'll get around to wanting something better."

The play never had a Broadway production, although Margo Jones directed two different productions at the Pasadena Playhouse in 1945 and 1947.

He must have been really desperate, then, to agree to go to Macon, Georgia, one of the hottest places in the country in the summer.

The reason for Macon was that it was the home town of Jordan Massee, another of the Georgia writing contingent who had come to New York. Massee was a first cousin of Carson McCullers, later a great friend of Tennessee's, and he had been collaborating with Paul Bigelow on a novel.

Massee lived at home while Tennessee and Bigelow had to take a room in the attic of a boardinghouse. Bigelow said it was "an apartment on the top floor of a house in Macon, an old Victorian house which Tennessee and I shared." Tennessee said there were only two windows, "the size of transoms." There was only one electric fan, which Paul needed because he had a jaw infection and couldn't sleep without it.

Tennessee says he was soaked in sweat the whole summer. They were also visited by another sweat-soaked wretch, a "somewhat retarded" youth who worked at the A&P, who never had a bath or a change of socks and filled the attic with a mighty stench.

This black-hole remembrance, in *Memoirs*, is somewhat blacker than the situation as described to Windham in his letters. The retarded young man is upgraded to a redheaded sex object. Tennessee said he was swimming in the lake, had joined the Y and generally liked Macon.

He was visiting an unnamed but particularly flamboyant member of the gay world who had decorated his house with lamps made of yellow parasols and tables made of mirrors. He was also becoming a local celebrity. The Macon paper, tipped off by Bigelow, ran a feature story about the visiting playwright.

He wrote to "Mary" (probably Mary Hunter) that he was working nights as a busboy in a "light-drinking" establishment called the Pig 'n Whistle. He thought, for the moment at least, that he might stay in the South, which, he said, he hated and loved so intensely.

He was working "every day, without letup," he wrote Windham, apparently on *You Touched Me*, but there was no indication of any exchange of manuscript pages between Tennessee and Windham.

Audrey Wood had persuaded the Lawrence estate to let them use the story (Frieda, of course, was still alive). They would receive 40 percent of the royalties, and Tennessee and Windham 60 percent. Tennessee did a finished version, and had it ready for final typing, but no money to pay for it. Even poor playwrights felt they had to have plays professionally typed in those days. Special hard-punching typists would make seven or eight carbons of a play, with the top copy usually done in both red and black ink. Audrey finally paid five dollars to have it done, with five copies.

He also finished three long one-act plays about the Deep South to which he gave the composite title *Dragon Country*.

Once again he was so punch drunk from work that, as Bigelow reported to Maxwell, he was "absolutely withdrawn from present reality." They were out walking one evening when the police asked for their draft cards. Bigelow produced one but Tennessee couldn't find his. He thought it might be in the pocket of some pants he had left in St. Louis. Bigelow tried to explain that "Mr. Williams was a writer who simply lived in a world of his own," but the explanation didn't help. Tennessee was questioned for three hours at a police station. Someone had taken him for a German spy because of his crewcut, his cigarette holder and the fact that he had been singing a song in German.

Bigelow and Jordan Massee had to keep him indoors after that until Edwina could find his draft card. They amused themselves by having a group reading of Chekhov's *The Seagull* at the Massee house.

He also kept a journal during this time. It indicates he was swimming and working with weights. He exercised a great deal. The image projected by his father that he was a flabby little sissy is totally false. He also said he felt neurotic, but that was all right, he wrote better that way. He read O'Neill's *Desire Under the Elms* and was shocked, as most young playwrights are, at how incredibly bad the writing was. He wrote that he would like to live simply but have "epic fornications." He reread some of his old poetry and decided to stop writing poetry forever, a vow that he soon broke. And he came to the conclusion, as all writers do on bad days, that he was totally hopeless, and promised he would drink lots of coffee the next day and *write*. Other days he wrote that he had knots in his head, and really felt he was close to insanity, which was his greatest fear.

At the same time, he was writing whooping, Rabelaisian letters to Don Windham, sending him, in one totally uninhibited note, a recipe for a "meat dish," telling how to cook in a very warm climate. Actually it was a hedonistic set of instructions about making love in the afternoon on a bed covered with an oilcloth, the participants smeared with mineral oil, and with side orders of ice water, sherry, cigarettes and music. All the details can be found in Windham's book of letters.

Audrey Wood, who had received *You Touched Me*, wrote to him expressing mild approval. She was getting contracts signed with the Curtis Brown agency, which represented the Lawrence estate, and was discussing a fifty-fifty arrangement on the playwriting share with Donald Windham. This deal would mean that Tennessee would eventually receive 50 percent of the 60 percent left after the Lawrence share, or 30 percent of the royalties, as opposed to 100 percent royalties on one of his own plays not based on another work.

Audrey was beginning to get a few nibbles on *You Touched Me*, enough so that she wanted Tennessee to come up to New York, and phoned him in Georgia. It wasn't easy to find him because the Massees had taken a house on Sea Island, where Tennessee and Bigelow were visiting.

Finally the word reached them, and Bigelow felt responsible for getting Tennessee to New York by himself. At a time of artistic preoccupation this could be, Paul knew, easier said than done. He recalls:

"We took him over to the mainland and put him on the train, with some remarks from me like 'Don't get off the train, and remember you have your typewriter with you.' Well, the next day we had an agonized wire from Tennessee, and he wasn't in New York, he was in Washington, and money must be wired at once.

"We said, 'What in God's name!' We told him not to get off the train—and why did he get off in Washington, why did he need money? Audrey had sent him some money, and we knew he had money. Well, we sent money—but he didn't pick it up. But why not? We had to find out. The telegraph company said the money is there, but no Mr. Williams. It was sent in care of a hotel in Washington. Well, he never did pick it up. We became very worried about this."

Bigelow knew he couldn't telephone to his own apartment in New York because the phone was cut off; he phoned a friend, who went over there. No Tennessee.

Finally Tennessee did drift into New York, and Bigelow discovered what had happened. In Washington Tennessee got off the train under the impression that the train was going to be there for several hours. As Paul said, "He decided to go sightseeing, but he'd put his money, for safekeeping, in his suitcase, so logically enough he left the suitcase with the typewriter on the train, so he could come back and get on and go to New York. Well, of course no such thing was going to happen. The train went off. So then he walked up the street to the first hotel he saw which had, in those days, a telegraph office, and he went in and wired us. But then he forgot where the hotel was, so he never got back to the hotel, and so he never got the money."

How, then, did he ever get to New York?

Paul said, "Remember Blanche's last line in *Streetcar*? 'I have always depended on the kindness of strangers.' That was the only explanation he ever gave us." And he never recovered the typewriter.

No one in New York was about to pay Tennessee any option money on *You Touched Me*, so he headed south again and in mid-August found a job in St. Augustine, Florida, working for the War Department, in the U.S. Engineers office. Nobody would pay him to write, but he could type, and they had a teletype machine. Someone was needed to run it between 11:00 P.M. and 7:00 A.M., and he would be paid $120 a month. He liked that. It would leave the mornings free to write.

Thus, he said, he abandoned his ivory tower.

Meanwhile the Curtis Brown people thought *You Touched Me* was "damned good" and suggested certain changes.

Tennessee was living at the Y again and riding a bicycle to work. There were only two people on the teletype night shift, one of them a big fellow who had just been let out of an asylum, and a failed playwright who had not yet, he said, been committed to one. Yet they were receiving coded war messages. Tennessee said he had a lot of free time, which he spent writing short plays.

Back at the Y his adolescent roommate was either a hotel bellhop or a theater usher, depending upon whether one can believe *Memoirs* (bellhop) or the Windham letters (usher). A good rule of thumb is that letters written at the time are usually more accurate than *Memoirs*.

Since the Y was run by a "sanctimonious couple" he tried to establish a pious and righteous profile, whistling a church hymn as he walked through the lobby. Nothing specific is reported about any relationship with the usher-bellhop, except that his older brother tried unsuccessfully to get him out of there and into a defense plant.

Back in New York the play changers were busy. Audrey Wood had shown *You Touched Me* to John Gassner, who liked it and said the Theatre Guild might be interested in producing it with the Gish sisters, if they could change the time to the present, Britain in World War II. Tennessee was trying to convince Windham, by letter, that they might be able to do this without turning the play into another *Mrs. Miniver*. Audrey thought he should be in New York.

His success at the teletype didn't last, and things began to wobble. The boss wanted to fire him, but, as Maxwell reports (based on conversations with Tennessee later), nobody else was around to take his place. "Please, Williams, don't make me fire you in times like these when there just aren't any men." But he managed it anyway. A really important message came through and they blew it. Somebody had to be fired, either Tennessee or the other guy, a "certified loony." Tennessee was fired.

This somewhat melodramatic remembrance is modified considerably by the account written to Windham at the time, in which Tennessee said he had asked for a "release without prejudice." His main point was that working and writing all day and night was too much. Using his new RAF research (because they were moving the play to the Battle of Britain, more or less), he said he was getting "browned off," an English way of saying he had had all he could take.

Meanwhile, Windham had found a job at twenty-five dollars a week helping Lincoln Kirstein edit a publication called Dance Index. Fred Melton and his wife had left New York, and Don moved back into the apartment.

Tennessee returned to New York, rented a furnished room for a short time and on November 18 moved into Melton's room in Windham's apartment. In fact, Don moved him in, bringing his things from the furnished room, which Tennessee had managed to turn into a kind of dump, if Windham's description is accurate. All his clothes and manuscripts were piled up, mixed with cigarette butts, dirty paper, old magazines and underwear. He needed somebody to look after him.

CHAPTER 12

And so began his last five months as a virtually penniless drifter. The most unpleasant episode of this period was a night involving two sadistic sailors and the Claridge Hotel.

In *Memoirs*, Tennessee used the cover name "Dreamy Eyes" for his companion of that night, but Windham, in an introduction to some of Tennessee's letters, described how two sailors beat them up in the Claridge Hotel.

That night the two of them "cruised" together in Times Square, where Windham had reserved a room at the Claridge Hotel. They were approached by two sailors after midnight outside the Crossroads Inn. The sailors said they would go up to the room in the Claridge. Tennessee and Windham were to go first, with the sailors following.

Tennessee was suspicious but agreed. He and Windham went up and soon after the two sailors came in and subjected them to what Tennessee called "the brutal sex bit," which didn't please him much. Then the sailors pulled out the telephone cord and stood Tennessee up against the wall while they beat up Don, "knocking out a few teeth." Then they pulled a switch knife on Don and stood him up, bleeding, while they beat up Tennessee, hitting him in the face until his upper teeth cut through his lower lip.

Tennessee said he was almost driven out of his mind by the violence and terror. They went to the Y, where a sympathetic doctor sewed up his lip. That was the end of Times Square cruising for some time.

It was the kind of incident he never told Miss Edwina about, and in her book there is a bland disregard for anything sexual. But she published bits of his journal covering this period, and in it he mentions that he met William Saroyan, whom he found likable but disappointing. He felt there was "too much space" between them.

At about the same time he met Margo Jones, the "Texas Tornado," who would become such a close friend and theatrical dynamo. Margo had inherited a Texas oil well and had acquired an insatiable passion for the theater. She began her work in amateur theaters in Houston and Dallas and soon became an official in the national organization of little theaters.

She had never met Tennessee, but had read some of his plays and admired them deeply. Paul Bigelow has recounted the story of their meeting. Margo had written Audrey Wood that she wanted to meet Tennessee. Bigelow then had a flat in a brownstone house on Forty-ninth Street just off Fifth Avenue, close to Audrey Wood's office. He recalls:

"I knew from Audrey that Tennessee was to go to her offices and meet this great admirer, Margo Jones, and about ten o'clock in the morning Tennessee turned up with this very handsome Amazon from Texas, and that was Margo, the first meeting I had with her. After getting her into my apartment and coffee being produced, Tennessee said, Well, there was an errand he had to do, and he'd be back. I knew what was going to happen and it happened. (He didn't come back.) She scared the daylights out of him, he couldn't get out of there fast enough."

So Bigelow spent the day with her, drinking black velvets (champagne and stout). He said, "She amused the hell out of me, people like that always do. I loved her, she had a kind of wonderful wild quality...she was a rather big, rawboned woman."

Tennessee later overcame his fright and loved her, too, in his fashion.

His most pressing problem, as usual, was eating money. A friend who was ushering at the Strand Theater told him there was a job for another usher. The problem was that movie ushers in those days were dressed like Prussian generals, and they had to find somebody who could fit the only uniform left. Tennessee went to the theater and the uniform fit. He was hired and was delighted, not only because the ushers were paid seventeen dollars a week but because *Casablanca* was playing, and he could hear Dooley Wilson singing "As Time Goes By" five times a day.

During the war years picture palaces were mobbed, and the customers had to be restrained in the long roped-off lines. One time a lady broke out of the lines and Tennessee chased her, almost to the screen. She slugged him with her handbag, which "seemed to contain gold bricks." So he was put out in front, under a spotlight, proclaiming, "There will be a short wait for all seats." It was his first spoken line on Broadway, and somebody else had written it.

After a few weeks of this, the playwright Horton Foote suggested that he try running elevators and put him in touch with the union. Gilbert Maxwell helped, too. He was working at a hotel on East Sixtieth Street that would hire almost any warm body. Tennessee was hired immediately. There they were, two writers, both totally incompetent at running hotels, running one.

This was no ordinary hotel. Its residents were almost all permanent, nearly all aging ladies from ancient families, and they had had plenty of time to hate each other, each feeling she was too good to speak to the others. One exception was the actress Cora Witherspoon, whom they liked.

Life soon became exciting for the ladies. One evening Miss Witherspoon and her poodle landed in a heap beyond the front door because Gilbert and Tennessee had forgotten to turn on the portico lights. And on another occasion Tennessee had wandered away leaving the elevator door open— with no car there. Before any of the dowagers had time to fall down the shaft, word reached the management. Maxwell, who was held responsible, was fired, and Tennessee crept away before he could be fired, too.

Miss Witherspoon missed them both, but is reported to have said later to Donald Windham: "... somehow the hotel seems a so much safer place to be in, now that they're gone."

Tennessee had almost hit bottom. His revised *Battle of Angels* was rejected and nobody wanted *Stairs to the Roof*; the Lawrence play was being pushed around, and he couldn't even hold a job as an elevator man. He was thirty-two, broke and a failure.

He fled to St. Louis and found things were even worse there.

His mother and father were totally estranged, though living in the same house. They arranged to eat at different times. C.C. scolded Tennessee, ordered him to do all kinds of menial jobs, like shifting the woodpile, and Grand was dying of cancer, trying to hobble around to pretend that she wasn't. Rose was writing deranged letters, saying she was glad Tom was in the penitentiary because "hordes of hungry people were clamoring at the gates of the city." And Dakin was finishing his army basic training. He could have been commissioned as an officer, but C.C. refused to pay his board at Harvard.

Tennessee had to get away. He walked down by the Mississippi riverfront, in those days, before the arch, an old and beautiful sight. In a letter to Windham he said he had written to Guthrie McClintic again about *You Touched Me*. Nothing was happening on it, and he advised Don to be patient. In desperation, living in this tragic household in Clayton, he started doodling around with another play idea, writing several hours a day on it.

There is an early manuscript of a one-act play in the Texas archives titled *If You Breathe, It Breaks*. It is about a shy but pretty girl who has a "sissy" brother who plays the violin and another extrovert brother. The mother, Mrs. Wingfield, has tried to get a gentleman caller to visit her daughter, who would rather be a "front porch girl" than have callers pulled in for her. A glass unicorn has just arrived for her collection of glass animals.

It is so delicate that "if you breathe, it breaks." The play is marked as one of the "Mississippi Sketches," and the subtitle is *Portrait of a Girl in Glass.* Penciled in are the words "Landscape with Figures."

In a letter to Windham, Tennessee called the work in progress *The Gentleman Caller.* He wrote that he was working on it several hours every day. But he added, in a letter written a few days later, that he had stopped working on it. The strain was too much. He felt he was going to "blow up."

His father was due back in Clayton in a few days, so he returned to New York, broke, to the Strand movie palace, where he put the uniform back on, and was paid seventeen dollars a week.

Meanwhile, back at Liebling-Wood, Audrey was talking on the phone to MGM in Culver City, California. She then telephoned Tennessee and said she had found him a job as a screenwriter. Two hundred and fifty dollars!

Tennessee thought that was wonderful. Would he get two hundred and fifty every month? Audrey said no. Every *week.*

Audrey later swore that he replied, "That's dishonest."

The contract was for six months, no matter what he did. The "no matter what" part was to prove important. Actually he was part of a talent agency arrangement called "a package deal." The buyer had to take the whole package or nothing. Part of the package was Lemuel Ayers, the set designer, whom Tennessee had known at Iowa; another was the dancer Eugene Loring, who would later create the ballet role of Billy the Kid. No one was saying which part of the package MGM wanted, and which part they had to take.

CHAPTER 13

In the forties New York-to-Hollywood commuters usually went by train, three nights and two days, the *Twentieth Century Limited* overnight to Chicago, and the *Super Chief* to Los Angeles. Windham saw Tennessee off, *The Sun Is My Undoing*, a romantic novel, in his hands. His job was to write a screenplay of the novel.

He had a hard time finding any decent place to live in Los Angeles because of the huge numbers of war workers. He finally located a garishly decorated two-room apartment in a rather honky-tonk part of Santa Monica, with a plaster statue of Mae West on the dresser.

The episode is recounted in a story called "The Mattress by the Tomato Patch." It is written in the first person and he is even called "Tennie" and "Villyums" by his Marxist landlady, who does grow tomatoes and lolls about on a raggedy old mattress all afternoon. Evenings she is busy renting short-term accommodations to servicemen and girls, and mornings picking up (and counting, with some vicarious pleasure) the contraceptives from the floor. She gives Tennie bright red tomatoes and bright red propaganda from the *Daily Worker*. He is eating the tomatoes, but not buying the party line.

It is one of Tennessee's most relaxed and most amusing stories, and it sets the whole mood of his stay in California, where he seems to have been, in spite of the studio, happy and at ease.

One of the first things he did was look up Christopher Isherwood, whose *I Am a Camera* stories about Berlin developed into *Cabaret*, and who was also working as a screenwriter. Tennessee had been given a letter of introduction by Lincoln Kirstein, Windham's former boss on *Dance Index* (who had himself gone into the service, leaving Don in command). Isherwood was in his Vedanta period and was living in a monastery. When Tennessee arrived he was told in whispers that Isherwood was meditating, and was invited to do the same. He tried it, but it didn't do anything for him, perhaps because he lived inside his head all the time anyway, and it wasn't much of a change.

109

But later they had lunch at the Brown Derby and went off to buy Tennessee a motor scooter, so that he could get from Santa Monica to the studio. Los Angeles didn't have then, any more than it does now, any workable system of public transport. Everyone was terrified that he would kill himself. Bigelow heard about the motor scooter and wrote to Audrey to get somebody to do something about it. Tennessee parked it among the Rollses and Dusenbergs and Cadillacs in the studio lot.

Bigelow and the other worriers were entirely right. In the first month he blew a tire on Wilshire Boulevard, was thrown off and knocked unconscious. The people who picked him up thought he was dead, but when he came to, it appeared that only his glasses were broken.

That didn't stop him. Two days later he blew another tire. He abandoned the scooter and finally bought a bicycle. He and Isherwood became good friends.

Meanwhile there was considerable corresponding with Don Windham, much of it, from Tennessee's end, trying to dampen Don's enthusiasm for California. It was clear that he wanted to be brought out there. In the Texas archives is a letter to Audrey Wood saying that Windham had been "angling" for an invitation to join him, but he had "scotched" that in his last letter. He added that he felt sorry for Don.

In another letter to Audrey he said he had had dinner at the Brown Derby with Margo Jones, who wanted a script of *You Touched Me*, perhaps to do at the Pasadena Playhouse. He was working on *The Gentleman Caller* and told Audrey that she might be terrified at his using "so special a character as my sister is." That is probably the first direct statement that Laura is based on Rose. He felt a bit guilty about the time he was not spending on the Lana Turner script, but just looking at it brought on "amnesia."

Like almost every writer imported to "Hollywood" (actually MGM was miles from Hollywood, located in Culver City) Tennessee could not fathom the ways of the studio. He wrote to Bigelow that he was sent out there to write *The Sun Is My Undoing*, but so far they'd only wanted him to help build Lana Turner's "latest celluloid brassiere."

Lana Turner was pregnant, but the studio was getting ready to shoot *Marriage Is a Private Affair* immediately after she had the baby. Tennessee did work hard on the script, and he did try to keep it simple, and in words more or less of one syllable. It is written to be understood by a child, or Miss Turner's dimmest fans, and is notable largely for a pencil sketch, by the author, of Lana before and after, in the plot: "old Theo" and "the new Theo."

But at times something in him snapped, and he would lock his office

door. He wrote a wonderful letter to Isherwood, describing how Lana
Turner and Pandro S. Berman were galloping up and down in "Time's
Winged Chariot" in the corridor outside his locked door while he was
writing *Portrait of a Girl in Glass*, "about my sister."

Nevertheless, he and his producer, Jane Loring, spent hours trying to
think up new sexy situations that would slip through the Hays Office—
the censors hired by the movie industry to enforce an almost Victorian
production code. In those days, if a male and a female were alone together
in any room, the door had to remain open. Who knows what might happen?

Most of the details from this period are in letters to Windham, which
record the interminable agonies of trying to get *You Touched Me* produced.
The irresistible force in the whole affair was the unstoppable Texas tornado,
Margo Jones, who during that summer was to be the director of the Pasadena
Playhouse, then the main stronghold of the legitimate stage in southern
California. Many of the inmates of Hollywood's loony bins cheerfully made
the long drive to Pasadena to see real live actors doing intelligent plays.

Tennessee had heard through Lem Ayers that Margo was planning to
do *Battle of Angels* there. Then she managed to get a copy of *You Touched
Me*. "I've gone completely off my head about it," she wrote. Gilmore Brown,
who ran the Playhouse, thought they might be able to produce it.

Later Margo invited Tennessee and Gilmore Brown and Lem Ayers to
dinner. Lem agreed to do the sets, but then they couldn't get the main
Playhouse and would have to use the little Playbox theater. It held only
about one hundred people, with no admission charges and no royalties.
Ayers was not interested in doing sets for this.

Meanwhile, romances were continuing. Tennessee would cruise the Pal-
isades, looking for willing servicemen, the most memorable of whom was
a gay marine. He wrote in his journal (and might perhaps have sent it to
the *Guiness Book of World Records*) that he "screwed him" seven times in one
night.

His relations with the top brass at MGM were becoming more and more
strained. He was finally taken off the Lana Turner script; the reason he
gave to Windham was that he was "too fey" for Lana. He shed no tears
over this, but was shocked when the studio asked him to submit a story
idea for Margaret O'Brien, whom he described as a "smaller and more
loathsome" version of Shirley Temple. He told Don that any story he had
about Miss O'Brien would be "unprintable," and did nothing.

The only project that interested him was a "folk opera" version of the
Billy the Kid material. This was being planned by Arthur Freed, MGM's
musical film maestro, with Lem Ayers and Gene Loring. Tennessee wrote
lyrics for it.

He was finally told that MGM would not pick up his option. He would be paid for the six months, and then dropped. Where writing was concerned he was simply incapable of not being his own man, no matter what the alternative. And the only economic alternative at the moment seemed to be to go back to the Strand, put on the uniform and make seventeen dollars a week. He could easily have thrown MGM a fish, or a lollipop for Miss O'Brien, and kept his $250 a week for another six months or so, but he would not.

He was almost physically thrown out. He wrote Audrey Wood that a young man simply burst in without knocking and told him to move his stuff out. He could not keep the office during his layoff.

Audrey Wood had been putting away some of his salary every week, and he knew he would be able to write for a few months after the contract expired, which was enough. After the break with MGM, but still on salary, he did most of his writing beside the tomato patch in Santa Monica. As he remembered, a day's work went something like this: he started with strong black coffee, sometimes with the Marxist landlady, who called him "Tennie," then wrote for six to eight hours, had a fish dinner on the pier and a look at the lads on Muscle Beach and then rode his bike to Venice for a swim at a club he had joined.

The interminable conversations and finaglings about *You Touched Me* continued. Sometimes he would go out to Margo Jones's cottage in Pasadena, and sometimes "a personable young poetry publisher" would join them. Tennessee had the second bed, the publisher had the sofa. And even though he was invited to share Tennessee's bed, he politely declined.

Horton Foote arrived and stayed with him a while, bringing word that the Actors' Company in New York was also interested in doing *You Touched Me*, and that Mary Hunter might direct it. This pleased Tennessee, who thought that she was the most intelligent woman he had ever met, and felt she might do a better job than Margo. There was talk about its being done at the Cleveland Playhouse, too.

He was working on *The Gentleman Caller*, and he was not being dishonest toward MGM. He submitted it, in original screenplay form, to the studio with a note attached. He said that like *Gone with the Wind* (then a huge box office hit), it was about a southern belle and he thought it would run twice as long. So MGM had a chance to pick up *The Glass Menagerie*, at no extra charge, but they turned it down. They said they didn't want a second *Gone with the Wind*.

He was rewriting and polishing it as a stage play. The process of putting all his scattered bits and pieces together was always a nightmare to him. He describes it in a wonderful letter to Don Windham, and anyone who looks through his piles of manuscript can understand it. The hundreds of pages, even though well written and cleanly typed, are rarely numbered, and there are often different versions of the same page.

While in California he was chosen to receive a $1,000 award from the National Academy of Arts and Letters, with this citation:

> To Tennessee Williams, born in Mississippi, in recognition of his dramatic works, which reveal a poetic imagination and a gift for characterization that are rare in the contemporary theatre.

Even Tennessee, the indefatigable writing machine, was becoming infected with the Hollywood disease, which seems to attack all writers who go there. He was trying to write *The Gentleman Caller* but, as he wrote to Windham, the atmosphere was making him lazy. He was losing interest and wondered if it was because the play lacked violence, which "excites me."

With the growing excitement about *You Touched Me*, there was some tension between the two authors. Windham worried that his original idea might be dominated by Tennessee, who was reassuring Don that it wasn't so, and promising that profits would be equally divided between them. At the same time, however, he continued to persuade Don to stay in New York.

The unsinkable Margo Jones was pushing ever onward. Tennessee was amazed by her unlimited energy, and said that she wore him out completely that summer. He also thought then, or at least told Don, that she was a good director. He had seen some of her student productions and thought her work was better than anything in New York.

Margo Jones wasn't able to do the Pasadena production soon enough, so she traveled to Cleveland and directed *You Touched Me* at the Cleveland Playhouse in October. Windham was there. Tennessee had planned to join them, but at the last moment had heard some "vague but terrifying comments" from Margo, and decided to stay in California.

The Cleveland reviews were good.

Margo rushed back to Pasadena to get that production started. While she was, as usual, moving mountains, Tennessee had word that Dakin, a brand new second lieutenant in the air force (in spite of C.C.) was training in New Jersey.

Tennessee had his first contact, in a long time, with his father, who was staying at a Los Angeles hotel, being entertained by some of his salesmen. Tennessee brought Margo along. She was so bored that she got drunk and did a wild solo dance. C.C. was shocked, and terrified that Tennessee might marry her. Dakin remembers that C.C. said that the Williams men always drank—but their women did not. To have a drinking Williams man marry a drinking Williams wife would be a disaster. Needless to say, no such marriage was ever planned by Tennessee.

Father and son had a conversation for the first time that Tennessee could remember. But as C.C. drank more and more he became a "maudlin old buzzard." Yet Tennessee began to feel sorry for him in his loneliness and hunger for affection.

You Touched Me was produced in the Pasadena Playbox and both of the first two important audiences were obviously "delighted" with it. Saturday night they had "the Hollywood crowd" and on Sunday the "elegant old ladies" because it was Founder's Night. Windham was not there but Tennessee, who was, said there was great warmth and charm in the play and thought Don would have liked it more than "the mess" he saw in Cleveland. No reviewers were allowed in the intimate Playbox.

The studio wanted copies of the script. Mary Hunter talked to Tennessee from New York and said she would try to get money for a New York production. And in the midst of all this pie-in-the-sky, Tennessee was hurrying to skip town because the scooter company was suing him for nonpayment. He hadn't received a dime from the Pasadena production, and virtually nothing from Cleveland.

James Laughlin of New Directions, who would henceforth publish most of Tennessee's works, visited him during the last days in California. Laughlin saw and liked the Pasadena production, and had lunch with Tennessee and Isherwood. Both Laughlin and Isherwood had seen his apartment in Santa Monica, and exchanged views of it. Isherwood said he had seen nothing like it since he had visited a cheap abortionist in the slums of Berlin. Far from denying this statement, Tennessee's own description of his apartment documents it accurately. Dishes, unwashed for weeks and partly covered by fungus, were mixed with pages of old manuscripts, "joy rags" and other "conveniences of pleasure."

He decided to go back to St. Louis for Christmas and stopped on the way in Taos, New Mexico, to see Frieda Lawrence, who was happy with her Italian lover. He said she "adored" the play. She was running a pottery shop. Just after Christmas, Tennessee wrote a letter to Mary Hunter from Arundel Place, in Clayton, describing Frieda, who obviously fascinated him. She was "huge" and wore a cap made of bobcat fur on her straw-colored hair. Here eyes were "lit with lightning." Frieda had a few suggestions about the play.

A dreadful thing happened in St. Louis. According to Edwina, Tennessee was called back suddenly from California because Grand was so ill, and at the moment he arrived in Clayton, Grand "literally died in his arms." Grand did die while he was there, but it was not like that at all. It didn't happen until after Christmas, and it was much more frightful.

At first all was serene. He said good-bye to Dakin before his brother left for the Pacific war. The only real clue about his destination was some mosquito netting in his pack. Tennessee said his brother was "sweet" but that they disagreed about everything. Dakin believed that the country would remain Christian, democratic and capitalist, and Tennessee called that "reactionary."

Tennessee wrote in a letter to Windham, on January 3, 1944, that his grandmother was still well and beautiful, "all silvery and warm."

She died a few days later. He wrote a tragic little book about it years afterward and had it privately and beautifully printed, mainly for the family. It was probably written with more pain than anything else he ever did.

Tennessee was at home in the early part of the evening, and remembered that Grand had washed the dishes and, as he left the house, was at the piano playing Chopin.

When he returned, a few hours later, the terrible hemorrhage had taken place. At the top of the stairs he could see quantities of fresh blood, leading to the bathroom. The toilet bowl was full of blood and bits of lung tissue. Old Grand was still alive in her room, with the doctor and Edwina. His grandfather was kneeling by a chair, praying. The old lady seemed to be trying to tell something to Edwina, and kept pointing toward the bureau. She died before anyone could discover what she meant.

Afterward they discovered a corset in the bureau with several hundred dollars, carefully stitched in by the old lady. She and Gramps had always been poor and all her life she had made great sacrifices to save money, buying her eyeglasses at Woolworth's, losing teeth to save dentists' bills, making over old clothes and giving music lessons. She had sewed the money into a corset for safekeeping, as she had in letters to her grandson.

That month, after the death of Grand, Tennessee wrote his beautiful but terrifying story "Oriflamme," remembered his own night of palpitations, and his midnight flight into St. Louis. The heroine in the flame-colored dress died with blood pouring from her mouth.

On the day that Grand died, on Epiphany, January 11, Dakin's troop ship sailed to India via South Africa.

Tennessee had another eye operation, his most successful, and wrote to Audrey Wood that it gave him 20/30 vision in his bad eye, with a thick lens. This contradicts the statement made in Edwina's book that he never had *any* sight in his left eye. Cornelius gave him $100 toward the medical expenses.

A few weeks later he wrote that C.C. had returned to work but was "feeble and irritable." The household was once again driving Tennessee crazy. He was having feelings of panic, palpitations, nausea and chills, followed by drowsiness and a heavy appetite.

He was all set to leave immediately. But the only cure his perennial hypochondria ever needed was a good idea, and he had it. The symptoms stopped and the typewriter started to rattle. On March 4 he wrote to Windham that in five days he had written sixty pages of a new play. It was probably the first draft of *Summer and Smoke*.

So, with another play spilling out of his bursting suitcase, he arrived in New York again. In May he rented a cottage on Fire Island, the sandbar off the south shore of Long Island, sections of it gathering places for the gay world. He came back to New York briefly to accept his National Institute of Arts and Letters award of $1,000. Windham was with him and the two of them were amused by the old-fashioned academicians, but were happy to meet another award winner, Eudora Welty.

Then in June he was back on Captain Jack's Wharf in Provincetown. He settled down to finish *The Gentleman Caller*. He had a new title for it: *The Glass Menagerie*. He rented a one-room studio apartment and of course, a bike. He saw a good deal of Fritz Bultman, who was recovering from measles, and his wife Jeanne. And he had word from Dakin, in Burma: a python was killed just outside his tent.

The usual indoor sports were going on in Provincetown, during one of which, a sort of sexual battle royal, Tennessee won the prize, a sexy blond sailor, a regular Billy Budd, as well as the deadly venom of his hosts, who thought both of them were theirs. All the details are in the Windham letters.

But these shenanigans did not interrupt the work at all. He did finish the play he still referred to as "the Caller" and began retyping it.

He was practically driven off the cape, however, by amorous summer visitors, one of whom caused him to ride around all night on a bike, just to get away. He continued to be nauseated by the twittering queens in their prettily flowered creations. The natives were beating them up, and he wasn't sure whose side he was on. He never liked this part of it, and when it interrupted work, that was the end. He fled to Cambridge, to the dormitory room of a student friend at Harvard.

He seems to have dropped out of the frying pan into the fire. The student, whom he calls Bill, was, according to his *Memoirs*, very appealing physically and part of a wild group. One of his friends had slashed his wrists in a theatrical semiattempt at suicide. Bill himself seemed to be willing to play games, but he was above all a peeping Tom. He had a map of Cambridge with all the best windows marked with X's. He would go on regular tours from midnight until 2:00 A.M. A few years later, while drunk and leaning out of a rapidly accelerating New York subway train, Bill literally lost his head. It was cut off by a steel column.

But Tennessee's work went on, regardless. He finished *Menagerie*, which of course he had already finished before. There is no contradiction here; a play is finished again and again; a play is never finished.

James Laughlin reported having trouble with the printed version of *Battle of Angels*. Two sets of printers had rejected it because the text was "sinful." They were trying a third. And Margo Jones was producing his verse play, *The Purification*, at the Pasadena Laboratory Theater.

He was back at Provincetown again, a boat ride from Boston. He entertained the poet Blanchard Kennedy for a week. He thought Kennedy was the most appealing person he had seen since Kip, and lectured him on the "charming fallacy." Beauty and charm gave those possessing it a license to exploit others. He made it clear that the beauty and charm were Kennedy's, not his own.

In Provincetown in late August he finished "the Caller" again. Resigned, he wrote that it would have to go into his reservoir of noble efforts, and would be the last play he would try to write for the "now existing theatre." He really seemed to be at the end of his tether.

On the beach at Wellfleet, a few miles from Provincetown, Mary Hunter teased him by taking a copy of *You Touched Me*, which he didn't know she had, out of her beach bag. She had ideas about producing it. He was being pulled between her and Margo Jones, both of whom had the desire, but neither one the money, to produce it.

CHAPTER 14

Suddenly, after all the years of grubbing and finagling and endless writing, it happened, so quickly that Tennessee and everyone else was amazed.

He went back to New York, had *The Glass Menagerie* typed and gave it to Audrey Wood. She read it, liked it very much and thought carefully about a producer. Eddie Dowling, once a singer and dancer and actor, had been doing some producing and directing. She thought he might be right for it.

She gave him a script. Dowling took it home and read it. The story usually told is that he went whooping right away to Audrey Wood. However, a letter in the Texas archives from Tennessee to Margo, dated October 18, 1944, says that Dowling first sent the script to George Jean Nathan, then the foremost theater critic in New York—and a close friend of Julie Haydon, whom he would later marry. Nathan not only liked the script, he also saw in it a role for Julie, to play Laura, the crippled sister (and a dream image of Rose Williams).

Nathan had great admiration for Dowling. As he wrote in *Theatre Book of the Year*, "He has been a poor man in worldly goods, this Dowling, and at times having less than two hundred dollars in the bank to support his wife and child has been compelled to undertake pitiable jobs for others... but let him find a play that no other producer would touch and which his critical sense tells him has some qualities of worth and loveliness... he will go out and beg, borrow or steal... the money needed to get it a hearing."

Dowling decided to option the play, and to direct it and play the part of Tom, who was almost Tennessee himself. He didn't really believe it would be a hit, and he did not have the money to produce it himself. He went to Louis J. Singer, a Wall Street broker, and told him he had a play he loved. "I don't think it will make a dime, but it will make me very happy to do it." Singer said, "You've got a partner."

Laurette Taylor's daughter wrote that Nathan had told Dowling there was only one actress who could play Amanda Wingfield, the mother. So, early in November, Dowling stopped by Laurette's apartment with "a script by an unknown author." She sat up most of the night reading it. The next morning she was in Dowling's office. She told him it was the play she had been waiting for.

Everybody who had read the script liked it. Tennessee was really surprised. Nothing like this, he wrote to Margo, had ever happened before. The material was so close to him that he wondered if it would mean anything to anyone else. Writing it, he said, was hell.

Laurette wanted the part, but everyone knew it was a big gamble. True, Laurette had been a great actress, but at this time she was close to being an alcoholic. After the death of her husband, the playwright Hartley Manners, she had gone on what she herself called "the longest wake in history." She had been on Broadway only once in the previous thirteen years.

Dowling and Tennessee heard her read the role at the Hotel Fourteen. She didn't have quite the proper Mississippi drawl, not yet. But they decided to take the chance.

Margo Jones was signed on as assistant producer and director and Anthony Ross as the gentleman caller. Dowling had the full $75,000 he needed, all from Singer, and he reserved the Chicago Civic Theatre for the tryout.

Since everyone fancies himself a play doctor, the play changers were at it again. George Jean Nathan is reported by Windham to have said that he and Dowling might make something good out of the play if they could take it over. Nathan thought Tennessee was just a short story writer who knew nothing about the theater.

Both Windham, writing at the time (in a letter to Sandy Cambell) and Tennessee, remembering, reported that Nathan and Dowling had concocted a drunk scene, which they thought was essential. It included, Tennessee recalled, things like having Eddie Dowling sing "My Melancholy Baby."

Tennessee was shattered by this, as was Margo Jones, who produced an instant Texas tornado. She said that if there was going to be a drunk scene, Tennessee would write it. He did.

They had no theater in New York for rehearsing. Some of the rehearsals were held in Dowling's office, some in Laurette's hotel and some in Donald Windham's apartment.

Everything depended on Laurette Taylor, who certainly didn't look promising, not even to her daughter, who wrote this account of Laurette in rehearsals:

Laurette gave little indication of what she was going to do with the part of Amanda. She was up to her old trick of watching the others, seemingly much more interested in them than her own part, neither learning her lines nor her business. Tony Ross tried to pump heart into the others by recalling how magnificent she was, but as time went on he began to worry along with the rest. As Laurette sat hunched over her script, peering nearsightedly at the lines through a large magnifying glass, murmuring through her speeches, or walking about like one achieving a hesitant, tactile familiarity with a world and people not yet clearly seen, Dowling was heard to murmur more than once, "That woman is crucifying me!" Intermittently he talked of procuring another actress for the role.

By the time they left for Chicago, on December 16, the other three actors were well up on their parts. Nobody was sure about Laurette.

The company arrived at Chicago's Union Station on a bitterly cold morning. The actors stepped down on the platform but Tennessee, as usual, had forgotten something and ran back to the train. When he reached the platform again, the rest of them were gone, except for a little old lady in a sort of pirate hat and a mangy muskrat fur coat. But in spite of everything Laurette looked to him like a star, and together they walked out of the station to find a taxi.

During the first rehearsal in Chicago, Laurette seemed to be incredibly bad. She was ad-libbing outrageously, and Tennessee thought the play sounded like the "Aunt Jemima Pancake Hour." He started screaming at her, and she screamed back. Finally they broke for lunch, and after that she began to act so beautifully that both he and Julie Haydon cried.

Laurette was drinking, but wasn't drunk. In fact, everybody except Julie and Eddie was drinking. Otherwise, Tennessee wrote to Windham that he was living luxuriously on his daily allowance of ten dollars and was going for swims.

Rehearsals continued to be alarming. Louis Singer, the backer, walked into one of them and was flabbergasted. He shouted to Dowling, "What are you doing to me, Eddie?"

Miss Edwina had come up from St. Louis for the rehearsals, too. She thought that Laurette sounded like a colored mammy trying to imitate a southern lady. Tennessee tried to tone down the accent.

"But I'm trying to imitate yours, Tennessee," Laurette said.

"Mah accent?" Tennessee said, "Ah don't hayev any ayaccent." (At least that's the way a northern newspaperman put it.)

In the end Laurette got it right, and a considerable rapport grew up between her and Tennessee. They began to respect each other. For instance, Laurette questioned a speech in scene 6, where Amanda was talking about a long-lost spring. The word *jonquil* cropped up a dozen or more times. "It's just too many *jonquils*, Tennessee," Laurette said. "Can't you cut a few?" "Laurette," he answered solemnly, "it's got rhythm. Ah need all those jonquils."

Laurette took the lines home and sort of sang them to herself. Tennessee was right. Not a jonquil came out.

The dress rehearsal was on Christmas night and the audience was the soldier cast, four hundred strong, of *Winged Victory*, which was playing in Chicago. The soldiers seemed to like it.

On opening night, December 26, Chicago was covered with ice, a gale was blowing out of Lake Michigan and the taxicabs were staying home. Just before curtain time, Laurette was dyeing an old bathrobe she was supposed to wear in the second act. It was still wet. Miss Edwina had a hard time getting to the theater. She wrote that her son was very nervous, unable to sit still. He went backstage. Edwina had not read the script, and had seen only one of "Tom's" plays before, *The Magic Tower*.

The curtain rose and she settled back to enjoy the play. She thought it was going very well—she had no idea that the mother, Amanda, had anything whatever to do with her.

It is the quietest, the most tragic and probably the loveliest and most poetic of all his plays. It is the one he must have felt the most deeply because it grew out of his heartbreaking love for his sister Rose. But Laura is not exactly Rose. The Laura of his short story "Portrait of a Girl in Glass" is closer. He didn't believe the *Portrait* Laura was insane, only that fear had closed "the petals of her mind." Neither the Laura of the short story, nor the real Rose Williams, was physically crippled, like the Laura of *Menagerie*.

The device of the narrator-actor Tom, the brother, enabled him to enclose the play in a frame of memory and allowed him to use poetry that might have sounded incongruous in dialogue.

The ending is very quiet. The gentleman caller has left, and we are sure there won't be any more. As Tom leaves, he says, "Blow out your candles, Laura—and so good-bye..." She blows them out, and the curtain falls.

At that moment, in the Chicago Civic Theater, Edwina said there was no sound at all, and she was afraid that the audience did not like the play. And then the applause broke like a wave, and continued on and on. At the age of thirty-three Tennessee Williams had finally ended his apprenticeship.

Laurette Taylor had been marvelous. The old pro had never bothered to impress anyone at rehearsals, and had been more interested in watching the others. She needed an audience. Tennessee has said that her performance in *Menagerie* was the greatest of all, in any of his plays.

Edwina went backstage to congratulate Laurette on her performance. The actress was sitting with her feet up on the radiator, keeping warm. To quote Edwina: "Before I had a chance to get out a word, she greeted me: 'How did you like you'seff, Miz Williams?' I was so shocked I didn't know what to say."

But Edwina finally told Laurette that she was magnificent. And even afterward, Edwina said, "I am *not* Amanda. The only resemblance I have to Amanda is that we both like jonquils." But everyone else, including Dakin and Tennessee, knew that she was, and with love, too, as well as a smile. Tennessee's description of Amanda in the opening pages of the play says as much, and is gentle and affectionate. He knew she was trying to cling to another time and place.

Edwina later asked Laurette why she wore bangs as a hairstyle for Amanda. Laurette replied, "I have an awfully high forehead. I wanted to cover it up so I could look like a silly little thing."

Edwina took off her hat and said, "My forehead is just as high as yours." Some people thought that was a confession that she was really Amanda.

The reviews were ecstatic. Chicago's most famous critic, Claudia Cassidy of the *Tribune*, said it "holds in its shadowed fragility the stamina of success... If it is your play, as it is mine, it reaches out tentacles, first tentative, then gripping, and you are caught in its spell."

Ashton Stevens of the *Herald-American* said it was "a lovely thing and an original thing. It has the courage of true poetry couched in colloquial prose. It is eerie and earthy in the same breath." He said of Laurette that he "had not been so moved since Eleanora Duse gave her last performance on this planet."

Did that mean it was an instant hit? Quite the contrary. People stayed away. George Jean Nathan reported that in its opening week in Chicago, "the play took in a mere $3,300 at the box office, which represented so heavy a loss that Singer, Dowling's co-producer... was all for closing it then and there. Supporting him in his decision was not only Alex Yokel, the company manager, but even Harry Davies, the press agent."

The only thing that saved it was the loyal Chicago critics. Claudia Cassidy attended three times in three days and Ashton Stevens "practically lived at the Civic Center for a week." They mounted a crusade, scolding the Chicagoans for not supporting such a great play. Slowly it began to work. Box office receipts rose and climbed to capacity at $17,500 for the last six weeks. At the end they were turning people away.

Paradoxically, the odd man out among the critics was George Jean Nathan himself, the man who had almost "discovered" the play, or at least had given it the first critical recommendation. Though he admitted grudgingly that the production was good, he thought that the play was "rather less a play than a palette of sub-Chekhovian pastels brushed up into a charming semblance of one." Perhaps he was bitter about not having his way as a play doctor.

By the time Cornelius came up to Chicago to see what his son had done, the theater was completely sold out. They had to put a chair in the aisle for him. He was not especially impressed by the play. Laurette Taylor was nothing like Edwina, he thought, and it couldn't have been *his* family. It said right in the play that the father had left home years before, and he knew he was still there, more or less.

After the show, Cornelius, Tennessee, Eddie Dowling and Laurette went to the College Inn. Old C.C. was shocked by the prices and pulled a bottle out of his pocket and plunked it on the table.

Tennessee had to leave early for a date at the University of Chicago. He left Laurette to entertain his father. She telephoned Tennessee the next morning and scolded him for leaving her with "that dull old man."

Tennessee was now really in the money for the first time. His royalties were more than $1,000 every week. The play, and Laurette's performance, were already becoming a legend in New York, and people were coming from there to Chicago to see it.

One of the New York visitors was Theresa Helburn of the Theatre Guild, the one who had told Tennessee he wasn't "out of pocket" in Boston. Dowling had hoped, Nathan said, that the guild might "lend the play its subscription audiences" when it came to New York. Miss Helburn said no. She felt it was "much too dangerously fragile to be sure of making money in New York."

Tennessee wrote to Windham that success was a bore. He was trying to avoid the people who wanted to lionize him—but that didn't include the gay young students.

He was trying as usual to write another play. Katharine Cornell had told him she hoped he would write a play for her. In the Texas archives there is a rather rough-draft version of a one-act play called *Interior Panic*. The central character is called Gladys, but that is crossed out and "Blanche" written in. There are two sisters, poor survivors of a great southern plantation called Belle Reve. One sister has married a lower-class character called Jack, who does a lot of bowling. It is only a nineteen-page vignette. In March, while still in Chicago, he wrote Audrey Wood saying he had about sixty pages of a play for Cornell. Among the titles were *The Moth*, *The Poker Night*, *The Primary Colors* and *Blanche's Chair on the Moon*. He outlined the story, and of course it is *A Streetcar Named Desire*. He was having trouble with it.

The Chicago success of *Menagerie* was creating more interest in *You Touched Me*. Mary Hunter phoned him from New York to say that she thought the money for it was now "in sight." Word of this reached Dowling, who was determined to bring *Menagerie* to New York before the other play could open. Dowling decided to end the Chicago run in mid-March, even though they were still playing to full houses.

Meanwhile Guthrie McClintic wanted to do *You Touched Me* and Audrey Wood was preparing contracts, this time giving Tennessee 40 percent of the royalties, the Lawrence estate 40 percent and Don Windham 20 percent, an arrangement that Don did not like. McClintic really had the money to produce.

The *Menagerie* company moved to New York to prepare for the opening date, March 31, Tennessee's first Broadway opening night. Several theaters magically became available and they took the best one, the Playhouse.

Once more all were worried about their great but fragile star, Laurette. On the day of the opening, Eddie Dowling did his best to keep her in the theater all day. He was really afraid that if he let her out she might get drunk. He kept her there from 10:30 in the morning until he dismissed the company at 5:30. During this time she was retching or vomiting into a bucket set in the wings. She ate no supper and was so weak that Julie Haydon and Anthony Ross had to help her take her place on stage at the dining table.

Dowling said that when the curtain rose she actually started to deliver her opening line in the second act, and caught herself just in time. After that, Dowling said, he was sure she would be all right. "And Christ Almighty, what a performance she gave that night!"

Tennessee had two tickets and brought Don Windham with him.

This time the audience not only liked it; they had been told they *should* like it by everybody who had been to Chicago. The combination was explosive. There were more than twenty curtain calls, and screams of "Author! Author!" One press report said that "for fully five minutes, evening gowned dowagers joined the gallery—clapping, shouting, whistling, shrieking approval."

Finally Eddie Dowling helped Tennessee up to the stage. Five days before he had celebrated his thirty-fourth birthday. He was wearing "a gray flannel suit with a missing coat button, a conservative pale tie and a water-green shirt... with his hair cut short, Mr. Williams appeared more like a farmboy in his Sunday best than the author of a Broadway success."

When Edwina, who wasn't there, read about the missing button, she almost cried, but Tennessee wouldn't have been aware if all his buttons were missing. (In fact, not long afterward, he couldn't go out with Audrey to meet an important producer because he couldn't find his other sock, and didn't have another pair. Bill Liebling had to go out and buy him a pair.)

The reviews were full of superlatives. Burton Roscoe wrote, "Here is make-believe so real it tears your heart out." Brooks Atkinson of the New York *Times* loved it. In a later retrospective account he summed up his feelings: "*The Glass Menagerie* speaks the truth as delicately as a piece of violin music. The theatregoer shares Mr. Williams' compassion and perception." *Newsweek* called it "a simple, sentimental story that offers Saroyan's fresh approach to people without Saroyan's facile dismissal of the people's problems."

Tennessee's telegram to Edwina read:

REVIEWS ALL RAVE. INDICATE SMASH HIT.
LINE BLOCK LONG AT BOX OFFICE.   LOVE.
                                                        TOM

A few days later she received an envelope full of legal papers. Tennessee had signed over half the royalties of the play to her. It would give her a comfortable income for the rest of her life.

The New York Drama Critics' Circle met a few weeks after *Menagerie* opened and gave it their award as the best play of the 1944–45 season. The vote took only fifteen minutes and, for the first time in their ten-year history, the critics chose the winner on the first ballot, with only one dissenting vote, that of Louis Kronenberger of *PM*. He preferred George Kelly's *The Deep Mrs. Sykes*.

Tennessee agreed. He thought *Mrs. Sykes* was better than his own play. Laurette Taylor won the acting award for the best performance of the season.

Once again, the only important dissenting voice was George Jean Nathan's. He said the play hardly mattered except for the performance of Laurette, to whom he had sent a bottle of liquor on opening night, an odd present for an alcoholic. Laurette wrote him: "Thanks for the vote of confidence."

The play later won just about all the other awards, with the exception of the Pulitzer Prize: Billboard's Donaldson Award, the result of a poll of 2,000 Broadway workers, from stagehands to stars; the National Catholic magazine's "Sign" Award, and the $1,500 Sidney Howard Memorial Award, given to "a new American playwright, having had one or more plays produced in New York during the current season." The citation stated that Tennessee had "brought a vigorous new talent into the theatre. He has the sense of poetry and of character of which great drama is made."

Tennessee was often his own worst enemy in his public relations. He had already enraged Dowling and his angel, Louis Singer, by his statements in a guest column he wrote for Ashton Stevens in the Chicago *Herald-American*. It was a bitter complaint about the fact that the theater had fallen into what he called the "receivership" of businessmen and gamblers. Singer, of course, was a businessman and putting money on a play was then, and still is, one of the most dangerous forms of gambling.

But Tennessee had been rubbed the wrong way by Singer, and wrote angrily. The result was that Dowling and Singer told their publicity agent to leave his name out of publicity for the show.

Shortly after the New York opening he did it again. In an interview with the New York *Times* he said, "No one means a great deal to me, anyway. I'm gregarious and like to be around people, but almost anybody will do. I'm rather selfish in picking my friends, anyway; that is, I prefer people who can help me in some way or another, and most of my friendships are accidental."

Windham tried to explain to "outraged acquaintances" that Tennessee hadn't meant it quite that way; that "no one meant a great deal to him compared to his work," and so on, but to the general public, the new Broadway sensation, Tennessee Williams, whom hardly anyone had heard of a few months before, was an unpleasant character, much more so than he really was. He was showing his worst side only. It was to become a habit.

Actually the next move of the apparent public monster was to bring his mother and grandfather to New York. He threw a lavish cocktail party at Sherry's "to meet Miss Edwina Williams and Miss Laurette Taylor." And yet, with both Edwina-Amandas on hand, who was the star of the Sherry show? Grandpa! Reverend Mr. Dakin, with his snow white hair and his clerical collar, was the life of the party. Edwina was not surprised. She wrote: "He entertained everyone, which he loved to do."

Yet Tennessee was depressed, and people could not understand why. But crushing, overwhelming success *can* be depressing, partly because the immediate aftermath is a letdown from great excitement and partly because heavy success gives an artist, certainly a writer, that most terrible of all rivals, his yesterday's self. He cannot let yesterday's self be better than tomorrow's; it is always stepping on his heels. Yesterday's self is invulnerable and mocking, its pages all written; today's self has nothing but hope and plain white paper. A blank piece of paper can be a terrifying sight.

One evening, in his room in the Algonquin Hotel with the Lieblings and his mother, he was so exhausted he was lying on the sofa. He suddenly felt so sick he went to the bathroom and vomited.

His mother thought he needed a rest. He went to the hospital and had another eye operation. While he was under the bandages, Don Windham read Plato to him. As soon as he could see again, he left town. From this time he could afford to go anywhere. And for decades that is what he would do. But, as Kazan once told him, he always had to bring Tennessee with him.

He was on his way to Mexico, which he had liked so much in 1940, when he was poor. He stopped in Dallas to see Margo Jones, who was putting on an early draft of *Summer and Smoke* in her Arena Theatre. This play, which contains his favorite character, Alma Winemiller, would haunt him all his life. It is close to being his most underrated play. (The most underrated is *Kingdom of Earth*.) It would be produced in various versions for more than thirty years, and would later be given a new (and probably worse) title, *The Eccentricities of a Nightingale*.

One reason why he was so obsessed with the play was that it went beyond individual characterization and attempted to compare two major facets of life: the spiritual side, personified by the preacher and his daughter Alma; and the material, scientific side by the young doctor. The two facets are symbolized by the two houses on either side of the stage. He often ran into trouble when he became more extroverted, when he went beyond his tendency to write from the inside out. In any case, he had a frightful time trying to make this one work and Margo, too, was bogged down by it. He said that her production was "awful," but pretended to like it because of his affection for her.

According to his *Memoirs* he took a train from Dallas to Mexico City, though he actually flew (he wrote a letter about it the next day) and stayed at the Lincoln Hotel, an annex of the distinguished Reforma. He liked it because there was a relaxed attitude about the guests he brought to his room. But he was still lonesome until he met a rich man who gave all-male parties, where he learned how to "follow" while dancing. He located an appealing part-Indian student as a regular companion.

Invigorated by the high altitude he wrote "One Arm," the title short story of that collection. Or perhaps, since he said that he wrote it earlier, he merely rewrote it. And he did a bit more on *Blanche*, by which he meant *Streetcar*.

He met Leonard Bernstein there, said he was very kind, but was also embarrassed by the way Bernstein insulted some "very effete American queens" who had asked them to lunch. Bernstein said that when the revolution came they would be stood up against the wall and shot. This of course was long before he was accused of "radical chic." Ruminating about this luncheon later, Tennessee tried to locate himself on the left-right spectrum. Was he left or right of Bernstein? He was certainly not interested in shooting anyone, and he was surely not a communist. Perhaps we needed an "enlightened" form of socialism. That is the way he felt, looking back, in the 1970s, when he wrote his *Memoirs*. His politics were usually a bit left of center, rather generalized and vague and they rarely surface in his plays.

Tennessee saw Bernstein several more times, and later wrote some of the most quoted lines in *Memoirs*, complaining about L.B.'s extreme egotism. If the conversation wasn't about him, L.B., he pretended to go to sleep. This was natural, because egotists are always troubled by other egotists. But for the most part Tennessee liked him.

He was being lionized. He met Dolores Del Rio, and Norman Foster, and Balanchine, and had a telegram from Katharine Cornell, signed "Kit," asking him again to write her a play like *Menagerie*. Guthrie McClintic was wiring him, too, about casting problems for *You Touched Me*, which was scheduled to open in the fall in Boston.

Then, about the end of July, he left Mexico City and had a traumatic time at the Mexican customs across the river from Laredo, Texas. All his manuscr:pts were confiscated, and when he got them back he thought his story "One Arm" was missing, but it had been with his dirty shirts the whole time. The episode was conducted with great emotion and almost caused an international incident.

He headed for New York, where McClintic and Lee Shubert were going into rehearsals with *You Touched Me*. They had some very good actors. The young RAF pilot was to be played by Montgomery Clift and the father of the girl would be Edmund Gwenn.

By this time the play had been pushed (mostly by others) so far away from the original story that Lawrence himself might not have recognized it. The story, only twelve pages long, is about two unmarried sisters who live near a British coal field and whose adopted brother returns from Canada, after the 1914 war, and is accidentally touched, while in bed, by one of the girls. (She mistakes him for her father.) This makes the brother think she may want to marry him. There are no more than a dozen or so lines of dialogue.

So two young southern American writers leaped in where few Englishmen would have dared to tread. Windham had never set foot in Britain, and Tennessee had been there once, for a few days, with grandpa and the Episcopalian ladies. To embark on this project was like two Londoners, one of whom had visited Niagara Falls for a week, attempting a dramatization of *Huckleberry Finn*, in which Huck has been transformed into a captain of the U.S. Air Force. It is a tribute to Tennessee's genius that such a moon shot was ever taken seriously, as it was indeed by a number of knowledgeable theater people.

The best and funniest scene in the play was the telling, by the father, of his love affiar with a female porpoise. There are no porpoises, male or female, in Lawrence's *You Touched Me*.

Both Tennessee and Don Windham were in Boston for the tryout. There was no disaster, as with *Battle*, but no triumph either, and they decided to bring it to New York, where *Menagerie* was still running. And that, Windham thought, was one of the problems. Perhaps by itself *You Touched Me* might have made it, but the comparison was deadly.

By this time, December 1945, Dakin was back from the Far East and went with Edwina to the New York opening. Edwina liked it, but remembered hearing a remark by a gentleman sitting behind her: "It won't last a week." Unfortunately, he was one of the critics.

The audience had not been enthusiastic, and they all left the theater sadly. Audrey Wood predicted mixed notices, and she proved to be right.

But for a few weeks, Tennessee had two plays on Broadway. *You Touched Me* closed January 5, 1946. Audrey Wood and Tennessee had finally agreed to give Don Windham equal royalties; he reported that his 30 percent of the total take, including his advance on amateur rights from Samuel French, was $4,239.72; Tennessee must have made the same. But on top of his *Menagerie* money, most of it went to taxes.

You Touched Me would never again have another major production, Tennessee would never again collaborate with Windham nor with anyone else, nor would he ever write another play based on a work written by anyone else. For better or worse, everything would be his own work, based on his own ideas.

Dakin was delighted to see *Menagerie*, which had opened while he was gone. When he visited the cast backstage, Julie Haydon did her famous "humility act" for him, falling on her knees before him, saying, "Oh, Dakin, I never thought that *you*, Tennessee's brother, would come to see little me!" Laurette told him they had had humility problems with her. At first she had fallen on her knees during curtain calls, kissing the hem of Laurette's dress. Laurette told her to quit it.

Dakin took Laurette for a drink at Duffy's Tavern. She was exhausted from her performance, and Dakin thought she was overweight and puffy looking. She knew she would have to do two shows the next day and told him, "I have to be on my good behavior." So she limited herself to a triple scotch on the rocks.

The play had been running—counting Chicago—for a full year, and there was open war between actor-producer Dowling and the rest of the cast. The only time Laurette, Julie and Tony Ross spoke to him was onstage.

CHAPTER 15

Around Christmas, a few weeks before *You Touched Me* closed, Tennessee left New York for his favorite American city, New Orleans, to be alone and quiet. He stayed at the Pontchartrain, in the affluent Garden District, and wrote a short play called *The Unsatisfactory Supper*, which is funny and rarely produced.

He advised Don Windham to leave New York, too, and to go south. Or, Windham thought, anyplace except where Tennessee was. After the debacle, there was a noticeable coolness between the collaborators.

But it was lonesome in that big hotel, so he went back to the old French Quarter, the Vieux Carré, and this time he rented a "lovely furnished apartment on Orleans Street, half a block from the rear of St. Louis cathedral." He had four rooms and a pretty gallery, with a view of the cathedral garden and the statue of Christ.

The main object was to be quiet, and to write. By mid-March he had finished a draft of *Camino Real*, so totally different from anything he had written before, and was also "working slowly on a longer play," which was to be *A Streetcar Named Desire*.

He makes a mysterious reference in his *Memoirs* to a deliberately unnamed "friend" who lived with him at this time, and relieved him of his "greatest affliction," loneliness. No other identification is given in the *Memoirs*, but it is now known that this is the same young man later called "Santo" in the *Memoirs*. He would become a strong, passionate, explosive, even dangerous influence in Tennessee's life.

Tennessee was now beginning to be a celebrity, and had his first fling in New Orleans society. He was invited to several debutante balls in the Garden District. Apparently the mamas hadn't discovered he was not husband fodder. He and Santo entertained a group of bluebloods at the apartment, but made the tactical error of keeping a couple of likely looking lads after the party for a late date. They kissed and told, and after that their Garden District apartment was off limits to the posh crowd. This did not seem to worry either Tennessee or Santo very much.

133

That is probably what really happened, because he wrote it at the time. But he made it into a funny one-page play in his *Memoirs*, which is much better. He brought the debutantes and their boyfriends into his lovely bedroom, and they asked him where his apartment mate slept. The mate, Santo, was struck dumb, but Tennessee said simply that they shared the room. This created a thunderous silence, since the only visible bed was somewhat smaller than double size. Everyone left, deeply shocked. But one of the young men returned, alone, naked under his raincoat. It was not stated how many young men slept in the bed that was slightly smaller than double.

He sent his early draft of *Ten Blocks on the Camino Real* to Audrey Wood in New York. She telephoned him with the crushing verdict: "Put it away and don't let anybody see it."

Depressed again, he decided to drive to Taos, New Mexico, to see Frieda Lawrence and her friends. He bought a slicked-up ruin of a 1937 Packard convertible, and decided to drive it to St. Louis on the way to New Mexico. Not wanting the family to see Santo, Tennessee left him behind. Already set in motion was a kind of catastrophic black comedy.

The car, as expected, broke down before he got it to St. Louis, and he had to wait until the radiator was repaired. Meanwhile Santo, knowing that Tennessee was heading for New Mexico, quit his job and took off for Taos; he sent a telegram to Tennessee at Edwina's house, where of course it was opened before he arrived.

His mother, who up to this time had no inkling of his sex life, cross-examined him closely about the telegram. Then, when Santo telephoned— many times, collect—she ran downstairs to listen on the other phone. Tennessee assumed that some of the truth must be reaching her.

Meanwhile Cornelius, retired, was drinking all the time, and old Gramps was hiding from him in his room. Dakin was home again, too, and was suffering under a continual attack of Edwina's mother-love, with the full force of *Menagerie*'s Amanda. She was after him to chew every bite of food. Unfortunately he had expanded her mother-love by bringing many gifts, including a bracelet of opals, a sapphire and a ruby ring set with diamonds.

It was clear to Dakin that there was something odd about the frantic calls from Santo, though as he remembers he did not then realize that his brother was homosexual. However, Tennessee wrote to Don Windham at the time that he suspected Dakin knew what was happening.

Finally the Williams madhouse was more than Dakin could stand. "Things were so bad," he said, "that I went down to the air force office at Scott Field, Illinois, and reenlisted. It was a lot rougher at home than slugging it out in the service during World War II." He was sent to Lowrey Field in Denver, Colorado, that summer.

Edwina maintained total silence about this whole period in her memoirs. At this point she retreated abruptly to thirty pages about her early childhood.

And suddenly, within a couple of weeks, Tennessee was dying. He wrote his will, gave up the ghost—and that was that. He said so himself.

The disaster had been carefully unplanned, in Tennessee's best form, and the whole saga was so terrible that he didn't speak about it until years later, except in a private letter to Windham. But in a letter to Kenneth Tynan, the British drama critic, written in 1955, he first made public his "death" in the spring of 1946.

It began, he wrote Tynan, during this time in St. Louis. He had been wandering around town with his friend, Bill Inge. Bill had been a reporter in St. Louis and was at the time in the English department at Washington University. Bill had seen *Menagerie* and it changed his life; it made him realize that this kind of play, the kind he wanted to write, could be produced, and he began writing his own.

After leaving Bill, Tennessee returned home to Clayton, where he had an attack of cramps, which later developed into a sharp pain in his abdomen. Most people, at this point, might have suspected appendicitis and called a doctor. Tennessee simply climbed into his patched-up Packard and headed west toward Frieda Lawrence, and Santo in New Mexico.

When he reached Alva, Oklahoma, the Packard collapsed with burned-out bearings, and he abandoned it, taking a train to Wichita, Kansas. He was suffering sharp pains in the abdomen, and went to a hospital and stayed for three days. Apparently the doctors said he had appendicitis, but since it was not yet acute he went on to Taos.

He had a high fever but no pain. The doctors in Taos thought the appendix had already burst. His blood count was enormous and he was convinced he was at death's door. Santo came to his bedside. While the doctors were shaving his groin for surgery, which he believed would be his last, he wrote out his will. He left the playscript of *Battle of Angels* to Santo—who thereupon tore up the will.

As he was put under the ether he shouted, "I'm dying, I'm dying!"

The length of the operation varies in the telling. In his letter to Windham, written at the time, it took two hours. In the letter to Tynan, written in 1955, it was four hours. In his *Memoirs* it had grown to seven hours. In any case, the doctors found that his leaking appendix had infected his diverticulum and took them both out. In a few days he was out of the hospital, feeling fine, and the dying was momentarily over.

He refused to give up the idea, however, and for the next three years was sure he was dying. Later, when Bill Liebling said he really ought to get a new suit, he refused to buy one. It would be a waste of money, he said, for a dying man.

Frieda Lawrence picked him up in her car and they went driving off through the mountains toward the Lawrence ranch. He was feeling marvelous. They bought a jug of wine and drank some of it—and then, suddenly, he shouted for her to stop, he couldn't breathe. They were then up to about eight thousand feet. Frieda turned around and brought him straight back to the hospital, where the doctor told him he certainly shouldn't go up that high after a seven-hour operation.

The main thing he was dying of, one suspects, was Audrey Wood's telephone call reporting that she didn't like *Camino Real*.

During this trip he must have met Lady Brett, whom he had imagined as a rather fancy character when he wrote his *Phoenix* play. He was startled to discover (as he wrote to his mother) that she wore a cowboy hat and blue jeans (which he then called blue denim trousers) and was amazed that the daughter of a viscount and sister of the Ranee of Sarawak could act so simply and naturally.

He seemed to crave these psychological storms the way a thirsty man craves water. He wasn't faking, at least not consciously. The Taos incident was the beginning of his "desperate time," which was, as he wrote to Tynan in 1955, to produce his best work, *Streetcar* and later *Cat* and perhaps all the ones written between 1946 and 1955. He believed that this fruitful period was to a considerable extent caused by his feelings of desperation; the more emotional tension, the better the writing. And this meant that he was playing a losing game, he said, because his emotional reservoir was continually being depleted.

There may be truth in this, but perhaps not the whole truth. He was finding himself at last; after the long and dreadful apprenticeship he was discovering his own style, learning how to use his great strengths. His finest decade had begun. The colored lights were on.

But still, the best stuff of his work was built out of inner turmoil, and where could he buy the raw materials for that?

CHAPTER 16

Tennessee brought Santo to New York with him. In his *Memoirs* he claims it was at this time that he *met* Santo in New York. They were staying at the luxurious apartment of Miss Elizabeth Curtis, just off Park Avenue. Miss Curtis was old and very rich and liked to think of herself as a patron of the arts and a friend of young creative people.

Tennessee had rented a cottage on Nantucket for the summer, and was marking time until he and Santo could go there. One evening he was in bed reading a new novel, *The Member of the Wedding*, by Carson McCullers. It was his kind of writing, an emotional story about a young girl set in the Deep South. He thought it was beautifully, poetically written, and a work of genius. He wrote Mrs. McCullers a letter saying he thought he would soon die and wanted to see her before he did.

Although he had never met Carson McCullers, he had known about her. She had been born in Georgia, and though six years younger than Tennessee had been well known as a writer for a long time. Her novel *The Heart Is a Lonely Hunter*, published in 1940, had been a critical success and a best-seller. Her next one, *Reflections in a Golden Eye*, had also done well. And she was, as Gilbert Maxwell wrote, a cousin of Jordan Massee, whose home Tennessee had visited so often in Macon.

Tennessee suggested that she visit him in Nantucket and she agreed. She had not seen *The Glass Menagerie* but had read and admired it. She left her home, then in Nyack, New York, and arrived by ferryboat on the island. She was a tall woman who wore trousers, a baseball cap and what Tennessee called her delightful crooked-tooth grin.

They seemed to have fallen virtually in love with each other almost immediately and Santo sensed that right away. Tennessee and Carson cycled to the beach, and Santo went into a tantrum. He shouted an obscenity at a row of old ladies in rocking chairs.

This created quite a sensation. Santo needn't have worried, though. The two writers weren't in love *that* way. Tennessee and Santo shared the same bedroom and Carson, who had been married for years to an ex-marine, had a separate bedroom of her own in the Nantucket cottage.

They got along so well that Tennessee asked her to stay the whole summer. She wrote later that it was Tennessee who suggested, "Why don't you make a play out of *Member?*"

That was a challenge to her, "because The New Yorker in reviewing the novel said I had many of the components of great writing, but the chief thing I lacked was a sense of drama."

For Carson it was a built-in bonanza: here was a newly celebrated dramatist, offering her encouragement, room and board. She accepted happily, and they seem to have had a marvelous summer. She cooked and played the piano, and the two of them worked every morning, sitting in the same room with their portable typewriters at opposite ends of the table. (Tennessee said later that he had never been able to work that way with anyone else.)

The old gray frame house on Pine Street had a windup Victrola and wonderful old records, which they played. Once a storm blew in the downstairs windows and a pregnant cat jumped in and had kittens on Carson's bed. Carson cooked for him, things like canned pea soup with frankfurters and mashed potatoes with olives and onion. As Tennessee ad-libbed to Rex Reed, in the September, 1971 Esquire:

> "She was in love that summer and mooning over somebody. Her husband Reeves had not yet committed suicide, but it was not him she was mooning over. She would go out and buy Johnny Walker and sit in a straightback chair at the foot of the stairs and...sit up all night mooning over this romance in her head. I'd come down in the morning and the bottle would be empty. It was a crazy but creative summer. We read Hart Crane poems aloud to each other."

Strangely, almost eerily, he remembered, or *thought* he remembered, that he and Carson had made a kind of shrine to Laurette Taylor, "who had just died," a portrait of her with a funeral wreath around it. The strange thing is that Laurette did not die until the following December.

They wrote all morning, swam all afternoon and in the evening read to each other what they had written during the day. It seemed like a wonderful regime for good, productive work. He was still working on *Summer and Smoke*, and she was trying to write her first real play.

Actually, Carson had only seen six live plays in her life, four of them in high school. So the nightly readings and discussions must have amounted to a highly advanced course in playwriting. She encouraged him, too, to keep on with *Summer and Smoke*. And she talked him out of his dying mood and helped him to face up to life again.

With his help she finished the play in a few weeks. Her husband Reeves arrived later. Tennessee didn't particularly like him. He said Reeves was morose and introverted, but then so was he.

Soon after Reeves arrived, the McCullerses left on the *Île de France* for Paris, where they would stay for more than a year. During all that time no one wanted the *Member* play, until finally Tennessee took it to Audrey Wood, who optioned it to Robert Whitehead in 1949. It was produced triumphantly the following year and won the New York Drama Critics' Circle Award for 1950. In second place that year was *Come Back, Little Sheba*, written by Bill Inge, Williams's other drama protégé.

Tennessee never publicly claimed any share in the writing (nor of the royalties) of *Member*, though he did write to his mother at the time, saying he was helping Carson dramatize her latest novel. He had really made the play possible in two ways: first in his advice during the writing of it, and secondly in establishing a climate for such a play. As Brooks Atkinson wrote in the New York *Times:* "If it were not for *The Glass Menagerie, A Streetcar Named Desire* and *Summer and Smoke*, Mrs. McCullers might have had difficulty in finding the proper audience for her play, and audiences might have difficulty in surrendering to it so completely. Tennessee Williams is the pioneer in this particular genre, which has rescued one aspect of the theatre from mathematics and geometry."

Tennessee and Carson remained close friends until her death in 1967.

Late in the summer he and Santo left Nantucket and stopped off in Martha's Vineyard to see Katharine Cornell and show her a rough draft of *Streetcar*, which he was writing for her.

Meanwhile, Dakin was returning from his air base in Colorado. He stopped in Oklahoma on the way back to pick up the Packard convertible that Tennessee had left there. It was in such dreadful shape that he said it was touch and go whether it could creep over the dusty Oklahoma roads to St. Louis.

By this time Cornelius was drinking constantly and Dakin finally had to draw up legal separation papers. C.C. gave Edwina a couple of hundred shares of shoe company stock and his half interest in the Arundel Place house, then went off to Knoxville to live with his sister Ella.

After his return from New England, Tennessee went back into the hospital, this time St. Luke's in New York. He feared once again that he was dying. He was sure it was "pancreatic cancer," but he didn't get much encouragement from the doctors on this, and finally picked up his grandfather and took him down to New Orleans. The old gentleman had cataracts in both eyes and was almost totally deaf, but remained serene and cheerful. Tennessee said he was a wonderful traveling companion.

Margo Jones visited with her friend Joanna Albus. Tennessee had finished another draft of *Streetcar* and read it to them. He believed they were shocked. Margo preferred *Summer and Smoke* and decided to schedule it for the following summer in Dallas.

Menagerie had closed because Laurette could play it no longer. She stayed long after she should have stopped, and finally had to be carried out of the Playhouse on a stretcher. She told Eddie Dowling she was dying, and she didn't want him to come to her funeral.

"Why not?" Eddie asked.

"Because I know you'd bring the understudy!"

In December, while Tennessee was in New Orleans, he heard that Laurette had died of a heart attack in her room at the Hotel Fourteen in New York. He was bereaved because their relationship had been so close, in fact the closest he would ever have with any player. He immediately wrote an appreciation of her to the New York *Times*, including these words:

> There was a radiance about her art which I can compare only to
> the greatest lines of poetry, and which gave me the same shock of
> revelation as if the air about us had been momentarily broken through
> by light from some clear space beyond us.

Tennessee had bought a white Pontiac and he drove his grandfather along the Gulf Coast, all the way down to Key West. They took a two-room suite at the top of the Hotel La Concha, where he settled down to put *Streetcar* into final shape. He and old Gramps were happy together. He was working well every morning and swimming every afternoon, while Gramps sat by the water's edge and let the waves lap over him. Everything in Key West seemed better. The wartime feeling was gone. Pauline Hemingway was there, and so was Miriam Hopkins, and both of them entertained him and grandpa, and presumably Santo, too. Miriam Hopkins gave a big cocktail party in their honor.

Santo was being difficult again, threatening to leave. Tennessee bought him railroad tickets several times, but he just cashed them and stayed.

Far and away the biggest event was that he "finished" *Streetcar* again and sent it to Audrey Wood. She liked it a great deal.

Grandpa wanted to be in New Orleans for the Mardi Gras, a festival that never impressed Tennessee very much. He sent grandpa on ahead to his New Orleans place, and started off in the white Pontiac to join him. As usual, the moment he stepped into a car alone disaster struck.

He was stopped by police near Jacksonville; he had no taillights, something he hadn't thought to check. They asked him for his driver's license, and he didn't have that either. The police were convinced he must be either criminal or crazy, and handcuffed his wrist to his ankle. He was thrown into jail, spent a night with a crowd of whores, dope addicts and drunks, put up $300 bail and finally had to study for and pass a driving test before he was allowed to move on. He reached New Orleans and grandpa safely.

Grandpa had a fine time at the Mardi Gras. Both his eyes and his ears were weak, but it was gaudy enough and noisy enough to get through to him.

Tennessee was pacing up and down, waiting for news from Audrey about a possible producer for *Streetcar*. Finally word arrived. Audrey wanted him to come, secretly, to Charleston, South Carolina, for a conspiratorial meeting with Irene Selznick. Mrs. David Selznick, the daughter of Louis B. Mayer, the head of MGM, was very rich. Tennessee had heard she was worth sixteen million and, on top of that, actually had good taste. He was skeptical.

Audrey had arranged everything like a cloak-and-dagger operation. She wanted him to come—alone. And by that she meant, presumably, not to bring Santo. Santo was "inconsolable," as Tennessee wrote, referring to him as "the Princess." Relations between them were already becoming strained. However, Santo did know more about Mrs. Selznick than Tennessee, since he read movie magazines. Tennessee didn't even know her first name was Irene, but Santo did.

It was at this time, while Tennessee was away seeing Irene, that Dakin had his first clear view of his brother's sex life. He was amazed and distressed. Dakin took the Panama Limited down to New Orleans and was met at the station by Santo, who waited for him while he attended mass at St. Louis Cathedral.

Dakin remembers: "Santo took me immediately to the Old Absinthe House. Some of Tom's friends, a young married couple, had invited Santo and me to lunch at their home, which was a very massive ante-bellum southern home with columns and a beautiful decor, but now serving as a mortuary. I could hardly stagger inside as a result of downing four absinthe cocktails on an empty stomach."

They had lunch, visited the artist's studio in the attic, where Dakin was puzzled by a blank piece of white canvas titled "the White Cliffs of Dover at Dawn," then drove around the French Quarter in the rain, stopping at bars, and finally to Galatoire's, where Dakin bought them all dinner. While they were driving around, Dakin couldn't help noticing that Santo was holding his hand warmly, in fact *very* warmly.

"Don't you enjoy holding hands?" Santo whispered to him.

"Doesn't everyone?" said Dakin, who was already keeping company with a pretty young lady named Joyce Croft at a Texas air force base.

He and Santo were finally deposited at Tennessee's place, the upstairs flat on St. Peter Street. He recalls: "I started to undress for bed and had peeled down to my jockey shorts, when Santo barged into my bedroom. Seating himself on my bed, immediately next to me, he draped his arm over my shoulder, giving me a friendly pinch on the nipple.

"'Dakin, I want you to sleep with me tonight.'

"'Oh, no, Santo, not tonight. After all we have scarcely met one another,' I protested.

"Santo persisted. 'Dakin, you are beautiful, you are a younger version of your brother. Surely you will not say no to Santo. Please, Dakin, I shall probably die if you do not say yes. I will guarantee that you will not regret it.'

"Santo was dark and with large brown eyes, certainly a most attractive and persuasive individual. Nevertheless I persisted in my rejection and Santo finally withdrew into his own sleeping quarters."

Since Tennessee was off with Audrey Wood and Irene Selznick, Dakin returned promptly to St. Louis. "Very tactlessly I wrote Tom exactly what had happened. I told him how much all the family had suffered from the stigma attached to 'having insanity in the family.' What had happened to Rose was indeed tragic, but what would follow from public knowledge of Tom's indiscretions would make bad matters far worse! 'How can you do this to me and to our family?' I asked.

"I was very young and immature at the time I wrote this letter, which had the predictable effect of terminating the warm brotherly relationship that had once existed between us. Tom was very angry upon receipt of my letter, and wrote me a blistering note telling me to mind my own damn business, adding that he was shocked at my callous insensitivity toward my sister's pitiful condition."

This episode created a block in the relations between the two brothers for many years.

Meanwhile Tennessee met Irene Selznick at the finest hotel in Charleston. She and Audrey Wood greeted him warmly. They talked a long time and he discovered that Mrs. Selznick did indeed have taste, that she loved and understood his *Streetcar* and was prepared to give it the very best possible production.

He and Irene and Audrey Wood made a firm agreement, and wired a code message to her New York office:

BLANCHE IS COMING TO STAY WITH US

And Blanche, as everyone was to learn, was the woman who took the streetcar named Desire on the way to Elysian Fields, and had a ravishing encounter with her Polish-American brother-in-law named Stanley Kowalski.

Tennessee said good-bye hopefully to Irene and Audrey and took the train back to New Orleans. Later he drove his white Pontiac (with taillights and driver's license) to New York, where he and Santo stayed briefly at the Royalton Hotel.

One thing he wanted to do was to see Arthur Miller's *All My Sons*. He greatly admired the direction by Elia Kazan and decided that he would like Kazan, above all, to direct *Streetcar*.

While they were in New York, Santo was beginning to make big trouble. He discovered that Tennessee had many friends in New York, and since some of them were male, Santo assumed they were all his lovers—something that was, of course, far from being true.

One day Tennessee stepped across Forty-fourth Street from the Royalton to the Algonquin Hotel. The lobby of the Algonquin has long been a popular cocktail lounge, and because of the Round Table publicity, almost a tourist attraction. It was then, as usual, filled with many plump suburban ladies straight out of Helen Hokinson cartoons.

Tennessee was having cocktails with Don Windham and one of Don's friends, when Santo came bursting in, shouting that Don and his friend were "the biggest whores on Broadway." Santo continued this tirade until all the matinee ladies had fled in terror.

Then Santo told Tennessee to go across the street to their hotel to see what he had done. Tennessee went, and found that the room had been wrecked, his clothes, including a new suit, and his books torn up, and a typewriter, borrowed from Audrey, smashed. Only his manuscripts were spared.

At first it didn't look as though Tennessee could get Kazan as his director. Kazan was then on the way to being probably the best director on Broadway. Only two years older than Tennessee, Elia Simanoglou, born in Istanbul, had come as a boy to America, had gone to Williams College and then took a master's degree at Yale, after which he married Molly Day Thatcher. She was one of the three people who had signed that first telegram to Tennessee, in 1939, giving him the Group Theatre's special $100 award. She was their main play reader.

Kazan read *Streetcar* but wasn't sure he wanted to direct it, but Molly, who had become a good friend of Tennessee's, persuaded him. Later, after working with the play, he needed no further persuasion. Years later he said, "I think it's the best play I've ever done. It ranks with O'Neill's best plays as the best America has ever done."

It was a summer of much movement and steady work. In June Tennessee and Santo were on Cape Cod in a shingled bungalow that he had rented, between Provincetown and Truro. He called it the Rancho Santo (it rhymes rather better with Santo's real name). Margo Jones and Joanna Albus visited them to talk about the August opening of *Summer and Smoke* in Dallas. Tennessee was also doing more polishing on *Streetcar*. Both Margo and Santo were consuming much alcohol, but Tennessee wrote that in those days he was not drinking heavily himself. At the Rancho he thought of Blanche's famous exit line about depending on the kindness of strangers. He felt this was true of himself, too. Strangers were usually kinder to him than friends. He thought it was because people who knew him well did not like him. As always, he was seeing the worst in himself.

Irene Selznick invited him and Santo to come out to Los Angeles to talk about the production, especially casting. Santo, the fanzine buff, was delighted. He would be able to see his gods, the movie stars. And for Tennessee this was far from the mattress by the tomato patch in Santa Monica. He was being treated like a Hollywood star, and he loved it. He later toned this down considerably, since it is thought rather bad form among intellectuals to be giddy about Hollywood, but in a letter to his grandfather, on July 28, 1947, he was simply raving. He wrote that the red carpet was out for him. He stayed the first week as the guest of George Cukor, had a swimming pool outside his door and his meals brought on silver. Santo is not mentioned.

After that, Irene Selznick provided him with a beach house at Malibu, next door to Fanny Brice. And, as he wrote to Don Windham, she had also provided a secret work place, secret from Santo. Irene also loaned him a car.

He went everywhere, including a champagne party at John Huston's, where he danced with many film stars. He told Gramps that they all lived like Roman emperors. He had lunch with Ethel Barrymore, Dame May Whitty, Rex Harrison and many others.

But the star who impressed him the most, and was the most difficult of all to meet, was a woman who went by the name of Harriet Brown, also known as Greta Garbo. His letter to Don Windham about her has been extensively quoted. She was beautiful, she drank straight vodka, she would have preferred above all to play a part that was neither male nor female and she wished she could have played Dorian Gray. She seemed cold toward him, yet asked to visit him later. She scared him, he said.

All that was a lark. The serious business was casting an actress to play Blanche. They heard that a little-known actress was playing locally in one of his short plays, *Portrait of a Madonna*. Her name was Jessica Tandy, and she was already playing Blanche Dubois of *Streetcar*, or very close to it, because the leading lady of *Madonna*, called Miss Lucretia Collins, was an aging and faded southern belle, about to be taken from her apartment to a mental home. Miss Lucretia was Blanche as she might have been a few years after *Streetcar*. Tandy played her magnificently. She had been directed by her husband, Hume Cronyn, and the play was a big success. Cronyn thought that the character of Miss Lucretia was closer to that of Alma Winemiller in *Summer and Smoke*, as he said to Mike Steen, in his *A Look at Tennessee Williams*. And Jessica confessed to Mike Steen that it wasn't entirely an accident. She and Hume knew Tennessee was coming out there. "We actually did that revival of *Portrait of a Madonna* for him, really."

Jessica feared that the performance she had given the night Tennessee and Kazan and Irene were there was not very good. She had been shooting a film all day and was exhausted. Nobody said anything to her after the show, and she thought they didn't like it. But next day Kazan told her she had the part.

They also thought they had John Garfield to play Stanley Kowalski. He probably would have done a good job, but his commitments and conditions made it impossible.

Tennessee went directly to Dallas to meet Margo Jones in her fancy air-conditioned suite in the best hotel. (Margo's oil well, left by her father, was still pumping.) He saw her production of *Summer and Smoke*, which pleased everyone enough for Margo to start making plans to bring it to New York the following year.

Then he went back to the Rancho Santo on Cape Cod, where, in the next few weeks, he would meet two men who, in very different ways, would have a considerable effect on his life.

The Rancho was full of people, including Santo, Margo Jones, her assistant Joanna Albus and several of Irene Selznick's employees. The electricity had gone off and the plumbing wasn't working very well. Guests were using the bushes instead of the bathroom.

But all this ended. Kazan wired that he was sending out a young actor to read for the part of Stanley Kowalski. After a few days he arrived with a girl. Nobody had ever heard of him. He was very handy. He got the electricity working again and also fixed the plumbing.

Then he started reading the lines written for Stanley. He hadn't read very many when Margo jumped up and shouted that it was the greatest reading she had ever heard.

Tennessee wrote that the actor, whose name was Brando, was not especially excited. He just smiled. He got the part. And when Kim Hunter was signed to play Stella, the main roles were filled.

Tennessee needed one other role filled—for himself. Santo was becoming more and more of a problem. John LaTouche, the lyricist who wrote *Cabin in the Sky*, had come to Provincetown accompanied by a former sailor, a young man of Sicilian extraction named Frank Merlo. He had served for six years in the navy as a pharmacist's mate, was slightly shorter than Tennessee, but had a body like a Greek statue. LaTouche had to leave the cape suddenly, but Frank stayed.

One evening Tennessee and Santo went to a Provincetown nightclub called Atlantic House to hear Stella Brooks, a jazz singer whom Tennessee liked. Santo began shouting obscenities at her and rushed out, leaving Tennessee alone. Frank Merlo was there, also alone, and he and Tennessee went off in the white Pontiac and proved, on the dunes, that they were highly compatible sexually. He drove Merlo back to Provincetown and for a while wandered about blissfully.

Santo later found the empty Pontiac and assumed that Tennessee was with Stella Brooks. He was not, of course, but Santo went to her place, gave her a black eye, made a mess of her room and then took off in the Pontiac. Meanwhile Tennessee, finding his car gone, started walking home, a long way. Santo, in the car, overtook him and, Tennessee believed, tried to run him down. Tennessee ran across the marsh grass and Santo followed in the car until it bogged down. Then Santo ran after him on foot, cursing in English and Spanish. Tennessee finally escaped by hiding under a pier. Then he walked back to Provincetown, rented a room in Atlantic House and barricaded himself in it. Santo drove back to the Rancho and terrified Margo Jones and Joanna Albus.

The next morning Tennessee came back to the Rancho and they put Santo on a bus—but he hitchhiked back. Finally they all made peace, and went out for a lobster dinner.

But after this episode, Santo's days with Tennessee were numbered.

CHAPTER 17

B ack in New York rehearsals were beginning. Irene Selznick managed somehow to persuade Santo to leave and Tennessee rented a one-room apartment in a brownstone in the Chelsea district, just north of Greenwich Village.

The extraordinary Williams-Kazan partnership began. Their talents were beautifully complementary; together they were unequaled. Tennessee sensed this on the first day of rehearsals. Kazan worked close to the actors, tilting back on a wooden chair, and speaking to them softly. He never shouted at them, never scolded.

Kazan understood Brando's "method" acting, and let him try various pieces of business again and again, letting him feel his way forward.

At the end of one of these exercises he came over to Tennessee and asked him quietly what he was doing wrong. Tennessee said, "Nothing, Mr. Kazan, it's completely right." Soon after that he would call Kazan "Gadge" like everyone else. They were in almost complete agreement during the entire rehearsal period.

Kazan respected Tennessee completely, but he once made a shrewd comment on their inner differences:

> I realized there was a difference between the way he and I approached life. I think he is closer to the feeling of death moving in on him. Somebody once said that you couldn't do good work in dramatic form until you had included the possibility of your own death. He lived with this, he lived with death all the time, he was brought up to it.
>
> Let me make a parallel. Blanche Dubois, the woman, *is* Williams. Blanche Dubois comes into a house where someone is going to murder her. The interesting part of it is that Blanche Dubois–Williams is *attracted* to the person who's going to murder her. That's what makes the play deep.

Kazan, usually called "Gadge," liked Tennessee to attend rehearsals as much as possible, and even asked him to come up onstage, from time to time, to demonstrate action. Tennessee tells of showing them how the Mexican woman would walk along the street selling tin flowers for funerals. He did it realistically enough to make Jessica Tandy scream. "That's it," said Gadge, "do it just like that."

Tandy said Tennessee came to every rehearsal but didn't communicate directly with the actors. "He communicated with Kazan . . . but didn't really talk to any of us, at least not to me, about it all. I think he is a very, very, very shy man. I think he is not able to be outgoing."

She said, as Laurette had said, that it was impossible to cut anything, "because he writes so poetically, so musically, that you can't chop it."

So things were going very well in rehearsals. His main worry was Santo. Once, when he was alone in his Chelsea apartment, Santo discovered where he was and tried to break down the door. Failing that, he hammered on the window until it broke. A policeman came and ordered him to go away. By this time both Santo and Tennessee were crying.

Since Santo knew where his apartment was, Tennessee had to hide in a hotel room.

They had decided to give *Streetcar* a long tryout tour, with the first stop New Haven. After the opening night, they were invited to Thornton Wilder's home. Wilder, of course knew Kazan well, because Gadge had directed *The Skin of Our Teeth*, Wilder's whooping fantasy.

Tennessee took a dim view of Wilder and his pontifical and academic pronouncements. Wilder had no respect for the play, which he thought was based on a false premise. No woman born an aristocrat, like Blanche's sister Stella, could possibly marry a vulgarian like Kowalski. Tennessee's earthy reaction: Wilder had never been properly laid.

They moved on to Boston, making little adjustments all the way. Since the progress of the cavalcade was well publicized in the papers, Santo knew where they were. He burst into Tennessee's room at the Ritz-Carlton, full of contrition, and since Tennessee wasn't buying it, Santo smashed some of the bric-a-brac. Irene Selznick heard all this from her room across the hall and came in. Santo scolded her, too, and finally went away.

By this time everyone had had enough of Santo. Paul Bigelow has this to say, on tape, about Santo:

BIGELOW: I knew him; he was rather frightening and psychotic . . . all of us became very afraid for Tennessee, and we had every reason to believe that Santo had made attempts on Tennessee's life.

SM: Stabbing or what?

B: No, the thing they were all afraid of was poisoning. We were all afraid of that, and Bill Liebling managed through police connections in the theater district to get Santo the hell out.

SM: Santo mainly did these things when he was drunk, didn't he?

B: No, he was quite sober.

Santo bothered Tennessee no more, and was not seen by him for years after this. Apparently Santo joined Alcoholics Anonymous, settled down and became a good citizen. Tennessee wrote that their later meetings were "serene and pleasant."

Boston liked the play and business was good. The last stop before New York was Philadelphia. Crowds were swarming around the theater. Kazan thought it smelled like a hit.

It certainly was in Philadelphia. The audience loved it, and the reviews were excellent.

They were ready to go into New York. Carrying this big production around had cost a fortune, about $100,000. (Today it would be closer to half a million dollars.) Irene Selznick had put $25,000 of her own money into it and the "angels" were practically archangels, some of the country's biggest social and show business names, including Mrs. John Hay Whitney, Howard Cullman, Robert Lehman, Cary Grant, Yip Harburg and many others. Audrey Wood herself invested $5,000.

On opening night both Edwina and Dakin were sitting in the Barrymore Theater. Dakin had already given his opinion on the title, when his brother asked him which one he preferred—his working title, *The Poker Night*, or *A Streetcar Named Desire*. Dakin chose *The Poker Night*, but admitted to himself, as the evening went on, that he liked the whole package, title and all. (Kazan joked later that it should have been called *A Streetcar Named Daisy Rae*, because in partially francophone New Orleans that's what it was called, Désiré. Eventually, in the film, which Kazan also directed, it was pronounced that way. In the opening scene, Vivien Leigh, playing Blanche, asks about the streetcar to "daisy rae.")

Unlike *The Glass Menagerie*, there are no Williams family members included among the characters (unless Kazan's Blanche-Tennessee is included) though it is full of Tennessee's special brand of magnolia-scented nostalgia, mixed with his sad mockery of the airs and graces of the now threadbare southern aristocracy. He had heard this, almost in counterfeit, all his life from Edwina, who always pretended to be a southern blueblood but never really was, unlike Cornelius, who was close to the real article and never put it on at all. If there is any false note, that is it: the real ones don't usually put it on, only the pretenders. The two sisters of *Streetcar* are supposed to be the real thing, the last members of a great family, owners of the once splendid and now bankrupt plantation, Belle Reve (pronounced Belle Reeve). Stella, the sister who found happiness with a Polish-American ex-master sergeant, does sound like a real aristocrat; she doesn't lay it on at all. Blanche, the sister with the airs and the fancy but faded clothes, who has fallen all the way down to prostitution, is the one with Miss Edwina's brand of partly imagined silver spoons. Perhaps it is these echoes of Edwina that make her, along with Amanda, the best theatrical female of the decade.

Otherwise, Blanche is almost the opposite of Edwina-Amanda. Edwina was always prissy and apparently cold about sex, whereas Blanche is all passion. She even tries to seduce a paperboy. After putting up a broken-bottle token resistance to Stanley's rape, it is pretty clear that she is going to enjoy it, and then hate herself afterward. Note the stage directions, just before the blackout and the rape. Blanche is directed to drop the bottle and sink to her knees, and Kowalski to carry her "inert" body to the bed. The key word is *inert*.

Menagerie happened in a St. Louis near-slum that Tennessee hated; *Streetcar* in the Old Quarter of New Orleans, which he loved.

There is all the difference in the world between the two plays, yet they are both stamped indelibly with his trademark, the passions, the deep insight into tormented characters and the poetry, the beautiful writing. No one else could have written either one, and no one else had ever written anything like them before.

Technically, *Streetcar* is more expert. *Menagerie* might not have worked without the narrator. *Streetcar* has none, it stands on its own feet, and that is the harder way to do it. But emotionally *Menagerie* seems the stronger. We are very sorry about Blanche, but Laura breaks our hearts.

Blanche's speech in the first scene puts a whole dying family into one page. She tells how Stella came home for the funerals; but she had been there for the deaths. No one moves in the theater during that speech.

After the curtain came down, the actors took a dozen curtain calls. Then, as *Life* magazine reported, "the audience began to shout, 'Author!' Finally, the stubby little man who wrote the play, Tennessee Williams, came out from the wings and, in a daze of happy embarrassment, gave a few choppy bows. He wasn't sure whether he should bow to the actors or the audience."

Dakin remembers; "Tom joined Mother and me in the taxi outside the Barrymore Theater to ride with us to Club 21," where Irene Selznick was giving a party for the cast. Dakin said he knew they had a big hit, but Tennessee was still cautious. He knew the New York critics were unpredictable.

Dakin and Edwina were sitting with Audrey Wood and Bill Liebling, and although the waiters were bringing in champagne and caviar and a trolley of prime ribs of beef, Bill Liebling would not touch a morsel.

There was a standing ovation when Marlon Brando and Jessica Tandy entered. And then, finally, Kazan came in with the papers—and the reviews.

Everyone was quiet as he read them aloud. Brooks Atkinson of the New York *Times*, the most influential of all, loved it. So did John Chapman of the *Daily News*, and finally Walter Kerr of the *Herald-Tribune*—all raves. Each one seemed to be trying to outdo the others in superlatives.

"All at once," Dakin recalls, "a warm smile appeared on William Liebling's hitherto ashen face. He grasped his knife and fork in both hands and said, 'Now we eat!'"

Lincoln Barnett, writing later in Life, said, "Williams wandered easily among the guests, accepting their congratulations with felicity and pleasure. But there came a moment when later he found himself temporarily alone and as always his thoughts turned inward and his eyes gazed far away. Then someone appeared at his elbow and said, 'Tenn, are you really happy?' It was Audrey Wood.

"'Of course I am,' Williams replied in surprise.

"'Are you a completely fulfilled young man?' she asked sternly.

"'Completely,' said Williams. 'Why do you ask me?'

"Miss Wood looked at him searchingly, 'I just wanted to hear you say it,' she said."

The afternoon papers raved, too. Just about everyone liked *Streetcar*—except, of course, George Jean Nathan, who wrote that in the play "Tennessee Williams had made of the sewer a broad sea in which to sail little poesy boats..."

Atkinson's later retrospective view was that *Streetcar* "is a harsher play than *The Glass Menagerie*...but it is a masterpiece."

But in spite of what Tennessee had said to Audrey, he was not fulfilled. He would never be. He wrote in the New York *Times* perhaps the saddest and strangest lament about triumphant success ever written, about the dreadful storm of checks beside a swimming pool in Beverly Hills, and being dragged away from the very conditions that had made him a playwright. Oblivion and furnished rooms were better for the artist than fame and riches.

He was trying to arm himself against the dangers of success. He did need conflict, and perhaps even some privation and he was not, like Shaw, being paradoxical, or witty. He almost meant it, though not, of course, to the extent of giving everything away like Tolstoy.

These dangers would be with him all his life. He wrote his lament-for-glory long before the massive, crushing success of *Streetcar* was apparent to him. For a man apprehensive of success, *Streetcar* could scarcely have been more threatening. It was as successful as any play could be. It won almost every major prize, including his first Pulitzer, his second New York Drama Critics' Circle Award and the prestigious Donaldson Award. He gave the Pulitzer money to the University of Missouri for a graduate scholarship in journalism. *Streetcar* would be, and still is, produced in almost every city in the world. For the rest of his life there would probably be no single evening in which it was not playing somewhere, in some language.

He stayed a few weeks longer in the apartment in Chelsea, putting up a Christmas tree, and throwing a big party, his little place jammed with people, including Helen Hayes and Garbo.

He saw Garbo again that month in her apartment in the Ritz Tower. He had been working on a screenplay called *The Pink Bedroom*, and George Cukor thought she might be interested. Tennessee told her the story while they had a few drinks. She kept saying, "Wonderful!" but finally suggested that he show it to Joan Crawford. There is no evidence that he showed it to anybody else. Probably at this stage it was not a complete screenplay, more of a treatment. There is an eleven-page vignette called *The Pink Bedroom* in the Texas manuscripts, a two-character dramatization. The bedroom is the boudoir of a mistress. Her protector enters and there is an argument about the fact that he doesn't see her enough, and doesn't even telephone her before he arrives.

And then the great blizzard of 1947 hit, right after Christmas, the biggest New York snow since the blizzard of 1888, twenty-six inches. All of New York was paralyzed, Tennessee's building ran out of fuel and he huddled in front of a log fire for several days. He kept warm in bed, he wrote, with a young circus roustabout whom he had found curled up in a doorway.

His main problem, after the snow was cleared, was publicity. He now owned one of the hottest names in town, and much as he liked attention he couldn't stand too much of it. So he boarded a ship and sailed to Cherbourg for his first major stay in Europe. The North Atlantic in winter is dark and rough and unpleasant, but he was not seasick, just queasy enough so that he couldn't write.

CHAPTER 18

From Cherbourg he went to Paris, at first to the swank George V, recommended by Garbo, which he hated, and then to the old Lutetia, on the Left Bank, which he liked much better, though it was then almost unheated.

The press was still after him, and since he didn't want to be actually ignored, he held what was probably the first bathtub press conference. The room was freezing, but there was plenty of hot water. He sat in the hot suds, soaking and answering questions.

At night he went to the gay spots. He wrote to Don Windham that there were at least three places where the boys danced together. He brought one of the boys home a couple of times, finding him "unimaginative" in bed, and a crook. He stole 30,000 francs from his wallet—thirty dollars.

He found the French theater appalling—"Dallas, Texas, is better," which isn't entirely fair, since he couldn't have understood more than 10 percent of the words.

He soon convinced himself that he was dying again and went to the American hospital at Neuilly, where someone mentioned that he might have either hepatitis or mononucleosis. Fascinated by these new words, he wrote "The jig is up!" in his journal.

But he was cured by Mme Lazareff, the editor of Elle, the fashion magazine, whose daughter he had met on the boat. She gave him a good dinner and sent him to Vence, in the south of France. That appealed to him because it was where D.H. Lawrence had died.

Vence was such a big improvement over Paris that he decided to go still farther south and try Italy. As soon as he crossed the border he was miraculously healed. So much for hepatitis and all that. He was immediately in love with Italy, and the feeling would last. He died only when he had nothing better to do. An interesting idea, a new place or a new young man could bounce him back like Lazarus.

He traveled around a bit, to Sicily and Naples, and finally settled in Rome. That was the city of his dreams. He had seen the Coliseum, and

153

all the sights, with Gramps and the Episcopalian ladies. What appealed to him this time was the sex, meaning beautiful boys, who were everywhere; all you needed to say was *Dove vai?* or "Where are you going?" and *Quanto costa?* The answer to that was a thousand lire, or two dollars. In fact, he didn't even have to ask. As he wrote to Don Windham, the most extraordinary specimens offered themselves on nearly every block. By May, Windham, too, was there, with Sandy.

And so began the Roman spring of Mr. Williams. Actually this title came first, before his novel about that spring called *The Roman Spring of Mrs. Stone.* In 1948, a Roman newspaper, noting his capers, ran a story with the headline *La primavera Romana di Tennessee Williams. Mrs. Stone* was published in 1950.

Don Windham wrote later that the novel was really a self-portrait of Tennessee, and a knowledgeable one. A reader's first reaction is that Windham must have been mistaken, since there are no important American males, no successful playwrights, no obvious Tennessee Williams at all in *Roman Spring.* The central character is Karen Stone, an American woman of the theater, an actress who is beginning to lose her youthful beauty, and who is very rich following the death of her multimillionaire husband. So where is Tennessee Williams, the newly rich American man of the theater?

Karen Stone has just retired from the theater, and her tough, rational friend, the writer Meg Biship, asks why. Karen answers that she had had enough of it. At that moment Mrs. Stone is interested only in beautiful young men, buying them and putting them into her bed.

Meg describes the young men as elegant and pretty, the kind who make love nicely, and asks Karen if that is enough to ask of human society. Karen says she thinks it is.

The young men, the reader begins to realize, are really "pretty" young men, gay young men, not the kind of young men who appeal to women. And they are beautifully, erotically described, in the most sensual way.

There are two descriptions of a pretty young tramp who wears a tattered old overcoat without a shirt, or much of anything else, underneath it, and broken shoes tied on his feet with string. One description appears in *Mrs. Stone,* written in the late 1940s, and the other in his *Memoirs,* written in the early 1970s. One is fiction, about the young Italian who waits on the Spanish Steps beneath Karen Stone's window, and the other is a description of Rafaello, the Italian youth whom Tennessee met while he was walking near his hotel, in Rome, and who would become a most important companion. The two descriptions are almost identical.

The Roman Spring of Mrs. Stone may not be precisely the Roman spring of Mr. Williams, but essentially Windham has a point. The book is his first novel, and it is obvious to any playwright that it is a converted play, or play idea. The relevant question is, why was it *not* a play? It is much shorter than a full-length novel, about the same length as a playscript, about a hundred pages, and is broken into three "acts" (called Part One, Part Two and Part Three). All of the important action can be played in Mrs. Stone's living room and on her balcony.

And it does work very well dramatically, as Gavin Lambert proved later in his first-class screenplay for the film made in 1961, beautifully directed by Tennessee's friend José Quintero, with Vivien Leigh as Karen Stone and Lotte Lenya, who really stole the show with her superb characterization of the contessa, the woman who procures young men for Mrs. Stone. The men look definitely heterosexual.

Perhaps, at the time, Tennessee thought that the material was too subjective, since a great deal of the story, as written in the novel, takes place in Karen's head. Or perhaps, in the late 1940s the material was simply too blue for Broadway.

Rafaello, the real-life young Italian in his scrawny overcoat, was sitting at a cafe when Williams was returning to his hotel. He and Tennessee exchanged smiles and he brought Rafaello, broken shoes and all, into the lobby of the posh Ambassador Hotel, to the consternation of the employees. He might as well have brought in a team of mangy mules.

Rafaello became his every-other-night lover. Tennessee quickly rented a beautiful apartment on the Via Aurora, near the Via Veneto, close to the Borghese Gardens. He had a living room with huge windows looking out over the old wall of Rome, and a bedroom with a huge bed, a *letto matrimoniale*, though very little matrimony entered into it.

He bought Rafaello beautiful new clothes, and they would spend every other night together in the big bed. In the morning breakfast would arrive, eggs and bacon and toast for Rafaello, *caffè latte* for Tennessee, who would be working hard all morning. The landlady, Mariella, thought he was crazy because he paced up and down, speaking the dialogue.

His friends would ask if this was Rafaello's night, and if not he would "cruise" with them, and drink Frascati, the wine of Rome. He wrote to Carson McCullers that he was creatively in the dumps, he couldn't write. He was just poking over old scripts, unable to start new work, even though he was drinking so much coffee he had violent palpitations and spots in front of his eyes.

In the same letter he said he had recently met Frederic Prokosch, the novelist, and Gore Vidal. Vidal would remain a good friend for a long time. He was then twenty-three and a "real beauty," as Tennessee wrote to Carson. Vidal was already known for his novel *Willaway*, published three years after he left his upper-crust prep school, Philips Exeter, and his new novel, *The City and the Pillar*, had just appeared. It was one of the first important novels about homosexuality. Tennessee had read it and told Carson he thought it was absorbing, but not a good book.

Tennessee gave a housewarming party at his Via Aurora apartment, and Gore was there. It must have made a huge impression on him, because he wrote a hilarious account of it twenty-eight years later for the *New York Review of Books*. He called it *Some Memories of the Glorious Bird and an Earlier Self*. The "glorious bird" was Tennessee; Vidal couldn't remember how the nickname started, though it may have had something to do with the later *Sweet Bird of Youth*.

The historian Sir Harold Acton was there, too, "floating like some large pale fish through the crowded room," as Gore Vidal put it, having come down to Rome from his stately home in Florence to inspect the new crop of American writers and artists who were invading the city. Gore naturally quoted Acton's highly flattering description of him: "aggressively handsome in clean-limbed sophomore style, [with] success written all over him." And he couldn't resist quoting Acton's put-down of Tennessee, "a pudgy, taciturn, moustached little man without any obvious distinction." Acton felt sorry for Tennessee's "protégé" Rafaello, whom he called "Pierino," because the boy spoke nothing but Italian and no one else (except himself) did.

Acton's rather cruel comments on Tennessee are essentially endorsed by Vidal: Tennessee was indifferent to place, art and history. "The Bird seldom reads a book and the only history he knows is his own; he depends, finally, on a romantic genius to get him through life."

And Tennessee, writing at the time to Don Windham, was almost as critical of Gore, whom he found to be extremely conceited, and he rather resented the fact that Gore, a ballet student, was always prancing about.

Yet in spite of all that, and the difference in their ages, Gore and Tennessee had a great deal of fun together. As Vidal wrote, "We became friends largely because the same things made us laugh. Driving from Rome to Naples in a jeep, we invented several imaginary characters whose exploits we gravely recounted to each other. Particularly memorable was the hazardous and vicious journey of one Lesbia Ghoul to Outre-Mar, where— But my lips are sealed."

Together they visited the aging philosopher Santayana at the Convent of the Blue Nuns. Gore quipped that neither Tennessee nor Santayana had ever heard of the other, but Tennessee was much impressed by the deep understanding and humor of the octogenerian semi-invalid. His gentleness and kindness reminded him of his old grandfather.

Tennessee also met the director Luchino Visconti, who had already directed the Italian stage version of *Menagerie, Zoo de Vetro*, and was about to do *Streetcar*. He also met Visconti's brilliant young assistant, the blond Florentine Franco Zeffirelli.

And he landed in jail again because of a wild escapade in the woods of the Borghese with Italian black-market cigarette boys. But he was able to spring himself quickly because, as he said, in 1948 Americans could get away with anything in Rome.

He and his friends drove all over the countryside in his old American jeep. On wild nights they would counteract the effects of too much Frascati by driving through the spray of the Roman fountains. He thought these were the best days of his life.

During most of May Don Windham and his friend Sandy visited him, and in June he drove the jeep down to Naples with Rafaello to pick up Margo Jones. They made excursions to Capri and Ischia and Sorrento. He said that Margo seemed to be completely indifferent to the beauty of these places. She was thinking only of the theater and their project, her coming production of *Summer and Smoke*, scheduled for the fall in New York.

One night Margo was afraid to sleep in a room alone, so all three of them shared a bedroom. Rafaello didn't quite know what to make of it, and wondered if Tennessee was going to sleep with her. He was most puzzled that this did not happen. As Tennessee wrote to Windham, Rafaello said that the lady liked to *parlare* and *mangiare*, and even to drink, but she didn't like *amore* or *poesia*. (But surely he must have been wrong about the *poesia*.)

However, Margo as usual handled all the arrangements, and managed to transfer both Tennessee and herself to London, where massive preparations were underway for the *Glass Menagerie* production in the West End.

No one has ever put together all the pieces that made up the great *Glass Menagerie* disaster in London. The anticipations were boundless. Absolutely everything was being done to make it a glittering event, a kind of bright summer prelude to the opening of the London theatrical season.

Helen Hayes, generally considered in 1948 to be the "first lady of the American theater," was signed to play Amanda. John Gielgud, with one of the most illustrious names in the London theatrical world, was to direct. "Binkie" Beaumont, the Flo Ziegfeld, more or less, of the West End, was producing, and a huge opening-night party was to be given, with royalty coming no less, by Lady Sybil Colfax, London's most famous hostess. It would be a gala celebration of the inevitable triumph, London's extravagant welcome to America's young lion, Tennessee Williams, who had just won two New York Drama Critics' Circle Awards and the Pulitzer Prize.

After his long stay in Rome, Tennessee didn't like London at all. It was dull, the people were stuffy and it was full of middle-aged "fags." He missed Rafaello. He did admit that everyone was being nice to him and was glad that Isherwood and Gore Vidal were there. The only play in town worth seeing, he thought, was a translation of Jean-Paul Sartre's *Crime Passionel*.

They would try out in Brighton, the seaside town south of London, where many big London shows did their trial runs. Soon the company, and Tennessee, were down beside the sea.

Meanwhile Dakin and Edwina were on the way. Dakin was finally back in civvies and was teaching at the St. Louis University Law School. The students had already given him a nickname. He had contracted a bad case of poison oak on his feet, and had to appear in class wearing tennis shoes, so he was now dubbed Tennis Shoe Williams. Everyone knew about his famous brother.

Edwina, now rich from her *Menagerie* royalties, had asked Dakin to escort her to London on his summer vacation. They boarded a Cunarder in New York and sailed to Liverpool. Helen Hayes's mother, Mrs. Brown, was also on board.

There were mix-ups when they arrived in London. No rooms were available because of the Olympic Games. Tennessee wasn't in London, nor anywhere else that they could discover, and though he had reserved them a suite at the Savoy, he hadn't told them about it, nor had anyone else. It was hours before the clerk of another hotel discovered by cross-checking reservations that the Savoy was ready and waiting for "Mrs. Dakin Williams and her young son Cornelius."

Audrey Wood had left a message for them at the Savoy. Everyone was in Brighton. So they took a train down there, to the Royal Crescent, the hotel where the *Menagerie* company was staying. The play had already opened in Brighton, but Tennessee wasn't there either. No one knew where he was.

Both Helen Hayes and her mother were charming to them. Helen, knowing that in those days no British hotel supplied soap, brought them some. And her mother invited them to her room for tea. Mrs. Brown was sure that Helen would be far better than Laurette Taylor as Amanda, and thought that John Gielgud was marvelous. They all loved Frances Heflin (Van's sister) as Laura. Helen was with them for a while, but had to leave to get ready for the performance.

Her mother then told them, confidentially, about Tennessee. He had been to Brighton, but had left. Her story was that Tennessee had had a falling-out with John Gielgud. Gielgud was discussing curtain calls with the cast and it seems he requested that Tennessee not take a bow. Mrs.

Brown claimed that Gielgud said, "I don't want the beautiful effect of the play diminished by a perspiring little author with a wrinkled shirt and a messy dinner jacket coming up on stage." Mrs. Brown said she had this directly from Helen, and that Tennessee promptly disappeared and hadn't been heard from since.

John Gielgud had been very reluctant to direct the play in the first place. He feared that it was too American for him. However, as Ronald Mayman, Gielgud's biographer wrote: "...a recent visit to New Orleans had given him a feeling for the atmosphere, and Helen Hayes, his leading lady, persuaded him that the types were universal, and encouraged him to trust the American cast to provide all the national color that was needed. John had not seen the New York production but was given the use of Eddie Dowling's original prompt copy and Tennessee Williams, who came to the London rehearsals, seemed to approve of his direction."

Dakin and Edwina saw the Hayes-Gielgud version of the play that evening in Brighton. Dakin's reaction was that it was a perfectly competent but totally uninspired performance. Helen Hayes's Amanda was a studied portrait, with every surface detail carefully sketched. Lacking was the inner fire, the emotion, the quiet desperation that Laurette Taylor had brought to the part on the Broadway stage.

Even in Brighton the British reaction was cool. Dakin heard this typical comment in the lobby. Two English women were talking:

"How did you like it, dear?"

"I didn't. Didn't like it a'tall."

"Why ever not?"

"It was just too *beastly* real."

Dakin felt that the British, after their long war, were looking for lighter, more escapist entertainment. And perhaps they were a bit resentful of American wealth and power. This was not only American, but regional American, in a strong regional dialect.

Edwina and Dakin went back to their comfortable suite at the Savoy to wait for the London opening the following week. They saw the changing of the guard, Madame Tussaud's waxworks, the Tower of London, the British Museum and all the rest. Audrey Wood and Bill Liebling, back at the Savoy, kept asking them if they had heard from Tennessee. No one had. They also wanted to know if the Williamses had been invited to Lady Sybil's party after the opening. Edwina and Dakin had been, but had been instructed not to tell. Audrey and Bill had not been invited.

On the day of the opening, July 28, a telegram arrived from Paris:

DEAR MOTHER AND DAKIN STOP　AM IN PARIS
STOP　WILL BE AT THE HAYMARKET THEATRE IN
TIME FOR THE OPENING NIGHT CURTAIN STOP　TOM

Then another one arrived:

DEAR MOTHER AND DAKIN STOP　DEPARTURE
DELAYED BECAUSE OF LAUNDRY FOULUP STOP　MAY
NOT MAKE IT IN TIME FOR CURTAIN STOP · PLAN
ARRIVAL ON LATER PLANE STOP　LOVE TOM

And a few hours later still another:

DEAR MOTHER AND DAKIN STOP　MISSED PLANE
STOP　GO TO LADY SYBIL'S PARTY WITHOUT ME
STOP　I WILL BE THERE BEFORE IT IS OVER STOP
LOVE TOM

So Dakin and Edwina went to the gala opening night at the Theatre Royal in the Haymarket. Dakin remembers the audience, glittering with lords and ladies, even Princess Margaret. All the important people of London were there, as well as the financial backers of the play, including "Binkie" Beaumont. "Binkie" was personally taking care of Edwina and Dakin. The invitations were brought to them by hand, and they were told to go right to the carriage after the performance to be taken directly to Lady Colfax's party.

Dakin noted that Helen Hayes was especially charming as Amanda, but also that her performance was an exact carbon copy of what he had seen in Brighton, every gesture, every inflection, every foot movement carefully thought out and executed with precision. He found this to be true of all her other performances as well, unlike the freewheeling style of Laurette. Somehow, he felt, the play didn't quite get off the ground.

But the first-night audience was ecstatic. But still no Tennessee. The horse-drawn carriage was waiting for him and his family outside the theater. Edwina and Dakin had just stepped into it when two people came rushing through the crowd. It was Bill Liebling and Audrey Wood, who had not been invited by Lady Sybil but who were determined to crash the party. They climbed into the carriage.

Not to invite Audrey Wood to a party for Tennessee was certainly unusual. But not unusual for this party. No member of the cast except

In a euphoric moment, Helen Hayes and Tennessee Williams clasp hands at
Sardi's restaurant in 1978. Inscribed on the back of the photo: "To Dakin.
You'll make it. Love, Tom." —*Photo by Alpha Blair*

First anniversary party of *A Streetcar Named Desire*. Left to right: Elia Kazan, Jessica Tandy, Williams, Irene Selznick, Karl Malden and Kim Hunter. Missing: Marlon Brando. —*Photo courtesy of Humanities Research Center, University of Texas at Austin,* © *Friedman-Engeler*

A debonair Tennessee Williams at his ease in Hollywood, 1965. The glass he holds contains Coca-Cola.

An uncertain Anna Magnani gets a fine coaching point from Williams for her role in *The Rose Tattoo*. —*Photo courtesy of Humanities Research Center, University of Texas at Austin*

Tennessee Williams' great friend, Frank Merlo (left) with director Elia Kazan, the playwright and unidentified actor, at a high point of the relationship. —*Photo courtesy of Humanities Research Center, University of Texas at Austin*

The University of Missouri, Tennessee
Williams' alma mater, bestows the honorary degree of Doctor of Arts, 1968.

Tennessee Williams and Carson
McCullers in an animated mood
during the time they shared a house
in Nantucket. —*Photo courtesy of*
Humanities Research Center, University
of Texas at Austin

Tennessee Williams is initiated into an oriental ritual, en route to Japan in 1969. Later he wrote *In a Bar of a Tokyo Hotel*.

In younger and golden days: the "Glorious Bird" and a preppy-looking Gore Vidal chat it up at Key West, Florida.
—*Photo courtesy of Humanities Research Center, University of Texas at Austin*

Williams scratches a personal signature—
"10 WMS"—on photo taken with pop
guru Andy Warhol.

A handsome gift from the playwright established a cultural center at the
Key West Library.

A bemused playwright in a rare moment
of relaxation at his Key West home.
Photo taken in 1975.

The brothers: Tennessee and Dakin in a friendly mood outside Gatesworth Manor, St. Louis, the "old folks' home" where their mother spent her last days.

The brothers: Dakin and Tennessee in St. Louis, around the time the playwright was received into the Catholic Church. —*Photo by Herb Weitman*

Edwina Williams flanked by her two sons in the garden of the Beverly Hills Hotel, 1961, at the height of Tennessee's fame. —*Photo by Wilson Millar*

Helen Hayes had been asked, and no one else from the production except John Gielgud. Such a thing would have been scandalous on Broadway. After all, there were only three other people in the cast.

All four went to the party, which was triumphant, with champagne and caviar and fresh strawberries. It is said that Noel Coward and John Gielgud looked down their noses at the gate crashers, Bill and Audrey Liebling. Helen Hayes was there with her husband Charles MacArthur and their daughter (who was soon to die of polio). Princess Margaret made it, but Tennessee did not, and Lady Sybil was distressed that her guest of honor never arrived.

Why wasn't he there? Tennessee later told Dakin that it wasn't only the matter of the curtain calls. He didn't like curtain calls anyway. In his *Memoirs* he gave complicated reasons based on his opinions of the production, which he thought was doomed, and of Helen Hayes as an actress, and of John Gielgud as a director (not much of one, he thought). But in a letter written by hand to Gramps on August 13, 1948, he said it was simply because Lady Colfax had not invited the other members of the cast.

As remembered twenty years later, he thought of Hayes as a disaster, and in the Atlantic interview with Tom Buckley, published in 1970, he said baldly that she couldn't act, and "became a monkey" in front of an audience, with simian gestures. In spite of all that, he told Gramps that Hayes was not as good as Laurette Taylor but was "as good as any living actress."

Part of the reason he left was probably that he was fed up with what he told Gramps was the "snobbism" of England and wanted to be in Paris. He joined Gore Vidal at the Hôtel de l'Université on the Left Bank, which, as he wrote to Don Windham, seemed to prefer young bachelors of a certain kind.

He took a suite with large rooms and windows ceiling to floor, and gave a big cocktail party. Jean Cocteau couldn't come but invited him to his place the next day. Gore Vidal, who was there, reported the presence of a lot of French actors and actresses hoping for parts in Cocteau's stage version of *Streetcar*. Gore also said that Jean-Paul Sartre had been invited, "but instead sat all alone down the street in the bar of the Pont Royal and when one of the guests who knows him went to fetch him, refused to come. Very French. Williams was highly pissed off."

Jean Cocteau invited both Tennessee and Gore to lunch at the Grand Véfour, to talk about the part of Kowalski for his current lover, Jean Marais. Gore, who was acting as translator, wrote that Marais "looked beautiful but sleepy. Cocteau was characteristically brilliant... Between Tennessee's solemn analysis of the play and Cocteau's rhetoric about theatre (the long arms flailed like semaphores denoting some dangerous last junction), no one made any sense at all except Marais, who broke his long silence to ask apropos the character Stanley Kowalski, 'Will I have to use a Polish accent?'" But it was all for nought. Cocteau broke up with Marais, and finally produced *Streetcar* in perhaps the wildest version ever done, with naked blacks acting out the rape of Blanche in pantomime.

Tennessee also visited the Boeuf sur le Toit and the Bains Déligny, both *très gai* gathering places, and was having a marvelous time. He wrote Windham that he had not yet "collided with" Edwina and Dakin, but he had heard that his mother was furious. He couldn't understand why.

He said he had sent a number of wires to London on the day of the opening, including one that said he had been taken ill, though actually he had been quite well.

He received the London reviews through a young lady, Maria Britneva, who would become one of his closest friends, and remains so at this writing. Maria is part White Russian and part English and was then an actress. Her mother did translations from the Russian. Maria would later marry Lord Peter St. Just. Tennessee found her "honest and beautiful."

The reviews, however, were not beautiful. The critics liked Helen Hayes but not the play. One was headlined, "Bad Play Well Acted."

Dakin and Edwina finally located Tennessee at his strange hotel in Paris. He told them that Lars Schmidt, the Swedish multimillionaire (later to become Ingrid Bergman's third husband) had offered to take the entire Williams family to the Tour d'Argent, one of the finest and most expensive restaurants in the world.

Afterward Schmidt took them all to the Club Mayol. He should have known better than to take Miss Edwina to a place where the females often didn't wear *any* clothes at all. Sometimes they paraded around *naked*! Dakin said, "Mother, averting her eyes from the entire proceedings, stared fixedly at the ceiling above the rear balcony, deliberately missing the entire performance."

Miss Edwina recovered sufficiently to look at the sights of Paris, and then of Switzerland, with Dakin. Then they returned to London to find that the Haymarket Theatre was only about half full.

"Binkie" Beaumont wrote to Tennessee on August 3 from his offices in the Globe Theatre, saying that in spite of the notices the "tone is one of respect and admiration." On Monday, he wrote, they took in three hundred and eleven pounds, and he felt that this amount, small as it was, meant that they "will succeed financially." It did close soon afterward, however.

Tennessee had a most international laundry bag. Dakin had brought it from Paris to London, where it was picked up by Maria Britneva at the Savoy Hotel. This led to a swim with Maria and a boyfriend of John Gielgud's, and finally tea with Gielgud himself at his flat on West Eaton Place, where Maria was staying at the time. In spite of all that had happened, Gielgud was charming to them.

Dakin and Edwina returned to St. Louis, but Tennessee's laundry stayed behind with Maria, in London, and presumably got washed somehow. Tennessee returned with Gore Vidal, picked up the clean shirts and had a melancholy look at *Menagerie*, which he thought was as bad as he had expected, "tricked" rather than honestly performed.

Then, with Gore left behind, he and Truman Capote boarded the *Queen Mary* for New York. Capote, who was twelve years younger, had recently become famous for his novel *Other Voices, Other Rooms*, published that year, and almost infamous for the dust-jacket photo of the author, lying on a sofa, looking like a kind of male Lolita. This caper had pretty well caught him up with his rival, Gore.

Tennessee and Truman had a whooping good time on board. He wrote about it in fond memory more than twenty years later, at which time he seems to have thought that Truman had turned "bitchy." But then, in his youth, in 1948, he was not bitchy—not yet.

They played such pranks as switching around the shoes left overnight in the corridors for shining. Truman was followed around the ship, Tennessee wrote, by an alcoholic Episcopalian bishop, who was seeking heaven knows *what*, but Truman put him down with the now famous bishop's-ring ploy. Truman told the bishop, who had cornered him again, that he had always wanted a bishop's ring. The bishop said you had to be a bishop to get one. Truman looked the ecclesiarch in the eyes and said he would find his at a pawnshop, "hocked by a defrocked bishop." The bishop, still frocked, fled in confusion, never to return.

Margo Jones was on the dock when the *Mary* pulled in. She still had no *amore*, and maybe no *poesia*, but she kept on arranging things beautifully. She had found Tennessee a dream apartment on East Fifty-eighth Street, designed and decorated by the sculptor Tony Smith, with a two-story workroom, a patio with a fountain and a bedroom with an aquarium, fishing nets and, of course, an enormous bed.

Margo threw her tornado of energy into *Summer and Smoke*, the first Broadway production of which she was in full command. She was both producer and director. She had confidence because Brooks Atkinson of the *Times* had seen her Dallas production in August 1947, found it enchanting and said so in print. This in spite of the fact, as Tennessee pointed out, that the main character (and his favorite character of all, in any of his plays) Alma Winemiller, had been played by a tall, toothy girl with a Bronx accent. This time Alma would be Margaret Phillips, a lovely young woman of Welsh ancestry. Todd Andrews would play the doctor.

There is no question that Tennessee wished Kazan, his favorite director, could have directed, instead of Margo. Gadge would probably have done a better job. Margo was a permissive director. If actors asked her how to play a scene she might simply tell them to "feel" it. And Tennessee thought they were often confused.

Bigelow told a story of Margo in rehearsal. Before the opening "Margo called the company together, and mind you, Tennessee was there, and she said, 'Well, I want all of you to understand that it may not be the best Williams but it's a Tennessee Williams play—' and Tennessee was right there!"

Tennessee added that she had said, while he was *not* there, in a reverential tone, "This play is the final work of a dying playwright." It was *not* true, Tennessee had not been dying for months, and would not die again for several more.

A first-class production was in the making, and the deadline was October 6, when it was scheduled to open at the Music Box Theater, one of Broadway's best. Jo Mielziner was working on the rather complex two-house setting, one of the most beautiful of any for Tennessee's plays. It would be true to his specification that there should be a great deal of open sky as a backdrop for the action. Mielziner decided to use a kind of black-wire sculpture to sketch in the two American Gothic houses—the parson's and the doctor's. The sky would be able to shine through them. And he was designing a beautiful angel fountain for the center of the stage.

Tennessee and Margo wanted Paul Bowles to do the music. Paul and his wife Jane were in Fez, North Africa, when Paul received Tennessee's wire to come to New York. Paul was then known mainly for his music, but had just finished his book, *The Sheltering Sky*, which would make him even more famous as an author. He had just sent it off to Doubleday. He left Jane in Tangier and came to New York to write the score. During this time Gore Vidal would drop in occasionally.

In his memoirs, *Without Stopping*, Bowles tells a good Vidal-Capote-Williams story:

> Gore had just played a practical joke on Tennessee and Truman Capote which he recounted to me in dialect as it were. He had called Tennessee on the telephone, and being a stupendous mimic, had made himself

into Truman for the occasion. Then, complete with snigger, he induced Tennessee to make uncomplimentary remarks about Gore's writing. They gossiped a while and hung up. A few days later Gore saw Tennessee and during their conversation made oblique but unmistakable allusions to some of Tennessee's remarks made over the wire. To Tennessee it seemed quite obvious that Truman had run to Gore and maliciously repeated the telephone conversation. As a result he was angry with Truman, which had been the object of the ploy.

Bowles said he went with the company on tour to Buffalo, Cleveland and Detroit, and "for no apparent reason Gypsy Rose Lee came along with us." During this time on the road, Marlon Brando kept telephoning Tennessee from New York, trying to persuade him to put his name on a list of sponsors for a liberal organization. Audrey had advised Tennessee not to join anything even remotely political—so Paul Bowles would tell Marlon that Tennessee was in his bath, or give a similar excuse.

Dakin and Edwina arrived in New York, in time for the Broadway opening, staying at the same hotel as the Lieblings, the Royalton. Dakin was there not only for the *Summer and Smoke* opening, but to try to straighten out some of the tangled financial and legal affairs of his brother.

Through Audrey Wood's office, Dakin received word that a "Maria" would meet him at a New York bar at eleven o'clock that evening. He was not sure who "Maria" was, but the message said that Marlon would be there, too. That did it. Dakin wanted to talk to Brando.

Dakin went first to the final preview of *Summer and Smoke*, which he liked, and then headed for the Two Deuces bar. Sure enough, Brando's motorcycle pulled up, with a young woman hanging on behind. Dakin recognized her as Maria Britneva, of the laundry-bag episode. Brando had just finished his evening's work, playing Stanley in *Streetcar*, then in its second year and running strongly. He was still wearing Stanley's torn T-shirt. Maria looked a bit bedraggled and blown about.

Maria said brightly to Marlon: "Doesn't Dakin look like his brother? Tennessee and Dakin! Don't they look like Greek gods?"

"They look like goddamn Greeks," mumbled Marlon, in his best Kowalski mumble. And he didn't say much else all evening.

Maria was troubled because at the moment she was an illegal immigrant, having overstayed her visa. Marlon finally emerged long enough from his black silence to make her feel a bit better. He read their palms, telling Dakin a lot of nonsense, but predicting that Maria would marry "royalty." That didn't (or at least hasn't yet) come true, but she later did marry her lord.

Dakin believed that Marlon, so recently an Illinois farm boy, was putting on the Kowalski manner as a defensive mask.

Dakin had serious business the next day at the office of Audrey Wood and Bill Liebling. Tennessee had appointed him as a sort of watchdog over his financial affairs, and he decided to lay the cards on the table. There was no question that Audrey and her husband had acted basically to Tennessee's benefit, and had been good for him. But their lawyer, Eddie Colton, had been drawing up contracts between the Lieblings and Tennessee, and there lay a possible conflict of interest.

The Lieblings had made a great deal of money out of *Streetcar*, in addition to their 10 percent share of Tennessee's royalties, since they had a share in the production. It is, of course, not illegal for an agent to invest money in a client's production. And none of the money earned by this would come out of Tennessee's share, since an author's royalties come "off the top," from gross receipts, and are not affected by the producer's (or his angels') profits or losses.

Dakin was trying to find out whether the Lieblings' choice of producer had been influenced in any way by an inducement, such as a percentage of the profits; that is, a free "piece of the production." This would be unethical.

Dakin asked the straight question: "It has come to my attention that Irene Selznick has given 10 percent of the production rights to Bill and Audrey in exchange for letting her produce *Streetcar*. Is that correct?"

"An absolute lie!" said Bill, and told him that he had a canceled check to prove that he and Audrey had invested their own money in the play, and that their interest was 100 percent legitimate. Eddie Colton, who had written the contracts, confirmed that everything was legal.

Colton's statement cannot be disproved. But one factor made Dakin suspicious. Margo Jones had told him that the Lieblings had indicated to her that they expected a "gift" of a percentage of the production of *Summer and Smoke*—free, that is, without investing any money, in return for their influence in persuading Tennessee to allow her to produce the play, instead of another producer. If true, that would have been unethical.

Dakin confronted Bill Liebling with this information. Bill said it was not true, that he and Audrey had asked Margo to let them invest in *Summer and Smoke*, and she had said it was too late. Bill was very angry. By this time he and Dakin had walked out to the elevators. He said to Dakin, "That woman! They call her the Texas Tornado, but I tell you if she was standing right here beside us, I would pick her right up off the ground like a real twister and I would throw her down this elevator shaft."

This, of course, was only rhetorical, since Margo was about twice his size. But why was he so angry? And why was the meeting between Audrey and Tennessee and Irene Selznick held in such a secretive, cloak-and-dagger manner?

Tennessee took his old Nantucket friend, Carson McCullers, to the opening-night party of *Summer and Smoke*. She was the person closest of all to the writing of it, since she had been working at the other end of the same table. Carson had been having a hard time since that summer on Nantucket. Nothing yet had happened to her play version of *The Member of the Wedding*; she had suffered a frightful stroke and was physically disabled. Tennessee had kept in touch with her and had been quietly and privately sending her money.

He had helped her, not easily, to the table and they waited for the reviews. Atkinson's was good, as they expected, since he'd liked it in Dallas, and so was Coleman's, but Barnes and Chapman panned it horribly. Tennessee told Carson he wanted to leave immediately. Because she was unsteady, it was a long, embarrassing exit, and everyone was watching.

Carson was so sorry for him that she arrived at his apartment before he wakened, and put some Mozart on the phonograph. She thought the music would make him feel better. But all he wanted was to get to work, by himself, as soon as he could.

Two weeks after the opening they were still playing to full houses, and Tennessee gave a "bad notice party," inviting the critics who had given him the worst reviews. He invited all the cast, too, and gave them presents. They had hot turkey and ham and champagne and whiskey. Marlon Brando came after *Streetcar* and took people riding on the back of his motorcycle. Some of the cast from *Where's Charlie?* came in after their opening night. They were happy. They had a hit.

It was a pleasant wake for that production of *Summer and Smoke*. The business did drop off and finally Margo had to close it. Thus, if Audrey Wood and Bill Liebling had invested their money in the play, they would have lost it, as the Texans did who had put up theirs.

But it was not the end of *Summer and Smoke*.

CHAPTER 19

The biggest thing that happened to Tennessee that autumn was Frank Merlo. He had not seen Frank at all since that wild night on the beach near Provincetown. He was buying some food in a delicatessen on Lexington Avenue and there was Frank, with a wartime buddy. He asked why Frankie hadn't looked him up.

Frank knew about the success of *Streetcar*, which he had seen and liked, but he was against climbing on bandwagons, and had no intention of capitalizing on their night on Cape Cod. That was typical of Merlo.

All three went back to Tennessee's apartment and ate sandwiches and pickles. The friend, who was "straight," read the situation and suggested that Frank stay with Tennessee. He went back home to New Jersey.

Frankie stayed, and stayed, for many years. In addition to the sex part, which was mutually good, and the genuine affection they had for each other, they were probably more complementary than most male-female partners. Merlo was, unlike Santo and Rafaello, a steadying influence; he was competent at all the everyday chores of life, at which Tennessee was hopeless. He did the driving, the cooking, the packing, the picking-up, everything, leaving Tennessee free to do nothing but write. He was what a man wanted in a wife, before women's lib. Frank kept things running smoothly. It was an excellent arrangement.

Frank was beautifully built, muscular and physically tough, with absolutely no swish, no camp. Though he was handsome, his face was a bit long, giving him a horsey look—Tennessee often called him "the little horse." There's a charming bit of light verse in his book of poetry, *In the Winter of Cities*. The poem is titled "Little Horse" and is dedicated to "F.M."

Tennessee prefers a more serious treatment, in *A Separate Poem*. He thought at first they would have an "every other night" arrangement, as he had with Rafaello. Tennessee had to return briefly to St. Louis, leaving Frank in New York. He wasn't at all sure Frank would be there when he returned. But Frank was there, on the big bed in the aquarium bedroom, and they decided to stay together all the time, every night.

One evening he and Frank came back to the apartment to find Gore

169

Vidal and/or Truman Capote, who had entered more or less illegally, depending on whose story we believe. Tennessee has it that both of them had climbed in over the transom and were then in the clutches of "a female policeman." Vidal says he came in with Tennessee and Frank and found Capote telling both a male and female detective a story about the private lives of Mr. and Mrs. Charlie Chaplin. No arrests in either tale. (Tennessee's in *Memoirs*, Gore's in *The Matter of Fact*, and there is always the possibility they were *both* made up.) Tennessee's postscript was that the cop(s) searched the apartment for drugs, found only a few Seconal sleeping tablets and was (were) persuaded to drop the charges.

In early December, Tennessee, Frank and Paul Bowles took a ship for Gilbraltar. Both Tennessee and Paul wrote accounts of this, both highly original. Tennessee had them on the *Vulcania*, Paul on the *Saturnia*, which first reached either Gibraltar (Tennessee) or Tangier (Paul), but these are details. Tennessee and Frank had a first-class cabin with a veranda, and he was out there working every morning, probably writing about his (or "Mrs. Stone's") Roman spring.

At two different places they met Paul's wife, Jane, "for the first time" (he had met her eight years before in Acapulco). But the important thing was that he was with her again, and she totally fascinated him. Jane, then thirty-one, was beautiful, brilliant, slightly lame and hard drinking. In a short but extraordinary writing period she wrote a novel, *Two Serious Ladies*, seven short stories, and her one produced play, *In the Summer House*. She became a cult figure, extravagantly praised. Tennessee called her "the greatest writer of our century in the English language," and said Harold Pinter agreed with that statement.

The Bowleses, both so talented, seemed to have a workable though highly unconventional married life. She had no qualms about his male friends, and he none about her female ones.

The four of them had a fine time driving around in Tennessee's convertible, which he had brought with him, in southern Spain and Morocco. At one frontier post leading to Spanish Morocco, Tennessee's typewriter and several suitcases were almost confiscated by crooked officials. They were jealous. As Bowles wrote: "All those clothes for one man?" one of them said. "And three razors?" This referred to Paul, who always traveled, Tennessee said, with at least a dozen pieces of luggage. Tennessee's Buick Roadmaster started to roll down toward a ravine, and was rescued bravely by Frank, who reached it just before it dropped off. Finally they had to go back; they couldn't cross the frontier until the next day, when word was sent ahead that they were VIPs.

However, Tennessee was depressed. A cable had come saying that *Summer and Smoke* was closing. And it was raining all the time. He and Frank drove to Casablanca and put the car on a horrible old ship to Marseilles. They drove straight to Italy, and there they both began to feel a great deal better. Finally they arrived at the apartment on the Via Aurora in Rome, the one with the big windows and the matrimonial bed.

And so began the period of Italian writing, his first major step away from the surroundings and the people he knew best. It is the perennial situation of the expatriate writer, and it can be dangerous.

In early 1949, in his delightful apartment with Frankie, and in his favorite city, he was in heaven, and heaven is a difficult place in which to create. Few good plays or novels will ever be written there.

He was beginning to suffer from the expatriate's dilemma. He was moving away from his own native material. How could he use the new backgrounds and the new people? Like most wandering writers, he had to compromise. He shied away from writing about Italians in Italy, and chose to write about the reactions of his own kind of person to the alien environment. That was *The Roman Spring of Mrs. Stone*, or Tennessee, once removed, in Italy.

Then he decided to reverse the process, and bring the Italians back to his own home ground, the American Gulf Coast—and that became *The Rose Tattoo*. Actually it was Sicily he moved, because Frank was of Sicilian extraction, and he moved it over near New Orleans.

These were the things he was working on during this second Roman spring and summer.

It is more difficult to see deeply into alien souls, and a writer always wonders whether he can see clearly enough. It is always harder when the language is different. This can be deceptive at first. The writer is charmed by the new sounds, and once he begins to make sense out of what they are saying he is delighted, and forgets he has hardly gone beneath the surface. As someone said about riding a motorcycle: once you begin to think you're really good, that's when it kills you.

He must have wondered if he could ever write a play about Italy or Italians that would be as good as *Menagerie* or *Streetcar*. But he was trying hard. He wrote to Don Windham that he had mapped out two and maybe three plays, but he was having trouble getting down to work in Italy. He thought it might be the climate. Perhaps it was too sunny, too nice, too lazy, like Hollywood.

He and Frank were having wonderful times, some of the best ones with Tennessee's closest Roman friend, Anna Magnani. She was then at the height of her fame, living like an empress in a gorgeous Roman penthouse, summoning her young male lovers like Catherine the Great.

Tennessee and Frank would have drinks on her terrace overlooking Rome and then she would drive them, along with her current male plaything, to some fabulous place for dinner, which would last for hours. Then, with a bag of leftover food from the restaurant, they would drive around feeding the stray cats of Rome. After that, they would take her big black alsatian for a run in the Borghese, stop for a nightcap on the Via Veneto, and finally Tennessee and Frank would watch her go up in the elevator with her young man.

Tennessee thought she was the most unconventional person he had ever known. What seemed to buoy him up when he was with her was that she was assured about her life and did not have his ever-present sense of guilt. He wrote *The Rose Tattoo* with Magnani in mind, even though she was a Roman and not a Sicilian.

He was also beginning to discover that big money meant big taxes. He had just paid $110,000 to the government and had only $65,000 left, in government bonds. He was complaining that Dakin had agreed to pay Colton, the Lieblings' lawyer, twice as much as before, and had paid himself $1,000.

He was still giving large amounts of money to many of his less commercially successful writer friends. He did this all his life. Paul Bigelow knows this himself. When he needed money desperately for an operation on his jaw, Tennessee gave it generously. Bigelow speaks of "an endless number" whom the playwright helped, "and I must tell you that he never talks about it."

Tennessee later discovered that he could give money through the Authors League Fund, which was set up for needy writers. But, as Bigelow said, "He wouldn't have done it that way if Audrey hadn't suggested it." That made it tax deductible. Many of the gifts were to theater people other than writers, such as Bigelow. Among those he helped were Carson McCullers, Oliver Evans (who later wrote her biography), Donald Windham and Paul Bowles.

He was trying to get Rose taken out of the sanitarium and brought to a private home. Later he made an effective compromise, finding her a luxurious sanitarium that provided her with her own cottage in the woods.

But he was still having trouble with the writing. He wandered around Italy, to Florence and Naples, and the island of Ischia. He had a spat with Truman Capote because Truman repeated that story about Margo Jones, who said he was a dying writer, and he could not make up his mind whether

Truman was bitchy or not. Sometimes he seemed to be acting like a vicious old lady.

Tennessee was buying yards of blue and beige shantung silk for matching suits for himself and Frankie.

By April he had finished a short story that would be the basis for *Mrs. Stone* and was making a start on *The Rose Tattoo*.

In May he and Frank made an extraordinary visit to the reigning king and queen of the English theater, Sir Laurence and Lady Olivier—Sir Larry and Vivien Leigh—who were interested in doing *Streetcar* in London. Like so many of Tennessee's expeditions, it became a kind of wild tragicomedy.

Before going to the Oliviers' country place, he met Irene Selznick in her hotel room for a strategy conference. Irene talked for an hour and a half, which made it almost too late to leave for the Oliviers, who lived in a thirteenth-century abbey more than an hour from London. By the time they arrived, Sir Larry was already in bed. Irene was livid. What an insult! Even her diamonds, Tennessee said, seemed to be flashing angrily.

But they stayed overnight, and the next day was really splendid. Vivien, at that time possibly the most beautiful woman in the world, was totally charming and very sweet to Frankie, and that made them both happy. Tennessee had seen her in repertory at the Old Vic and was not too impressed by her *Antigone*, but liked her *School for Scandal*. It was her offstage personality that convinced him she would make a good Blanche. And everyone knew that the southern accent would be no problem for Scarlett O'Hara.

He wrote to grandpa in Clarksdale, telling him that Irene was so upset she had three doctors, and was eating charcoal biscuits all day. He wasn't sure whether it was something she'd eaten or just the general excitement.

There was plenty of that. Sir Larry really let his hair down and did almost a cabaret performance for them, even acting out the horses in his *Henry V*. Danny Kaye was there, too, and even he was subdued by Sir Larry's histrionics.

Between biscuits, Irene began smiling, and all was soon set for the Oliviers and *Streetcar*, Vivien to star and Sir Larry to direct. They would try for an opening in London in the autumn.

Tennessee and Frank went back to London, met Maria Britneva and tried to find a restaurant that was still open. They tried three places, all closed, and when they did find one, Tennessee was so upset by everything, including the excitement of the day, that they had a fight with the waiter and were thrown out. Tennessee ran off, leaving Frankie and Maria in

Piccadilly Circus, hoping they would bring him a piece of bread.

Back in his room he took a sleeping pill and felt a great deal better. Somehow, wherever he went became wonderland, full of mad hatters and crazy queens; they were always after him, they would never leave him alone.

He always seemed to be suspicious of the English. He wrote to Irene Selznick that he even had it put into the *Streetcar* contract that no mention should be made of him as "short and squatty."

He and Frank returned to Rome, where he kept on trying to write, but without great success. Rome was hot and crowded with tourists and American sailors. The whores had raised their prices a thousand percent. He saw Rafaello a few times, and even slept with him while Frank was visiting in Sicily, but Rafaello soon went into the Italian army and out of his life.

Rome was doing *Streetcar*, too, and doing it with the usual Italian genius for chaotic enthusiasm and anarchy. Somehow there got to be two warring factions of translators, and Tennessee finally had to pay both of them out of his royalties. The Blanche, he said, was all wrong, and they had an organ playing most of the time, so loud he couldn't hear her. But it was a smash hit and moved to a larger theater.

His writing was interrupted by Hollywood, which was beginning to produce his first motion picture. Charles Feldman, formerly the biggest talent agent in town, had bought *Menagerie* and declared himself to be a film producer, working for Warner Brothers. They had chosen Irving Rapper, a director famous for many fine films, including *The Corn Is Green*, and were willing to spend almost any amount to make it the world's greatest movie.

The process by which it became what Tennessee describes as an outrageously bad film is interesting to examine.

First Rapper was sent from Hollywood to Rome to talk to Tennessee. He had been in the New York theater, was well regarded by Audrey Wood and respected by Tennessee for *The Corn is Green*. Tennessee was gracious to him and showed him all over Rome. (Rapper was so taken with it that he later came there to live for two and a half years.) They had long talks about *Menagerie*, and Rapper suggested that Tennessee come to Hollywood to supervise the writing of the screenplay. He already had Peter Berneis working on it, "under the supervision of Jerry Wald," as Rapper told Mike Steen. In Hollywood a writer never sits down at a typewriter and writes a screenplay; he prepares a screenplay under the supervision of somebody. Tennessee was being given the opportunity to join the group. He was not especially enthusiastic, but finally agreed to come out there anyway.

Irving Rapper went back to the coast to grapple with the casting problem.

Feldman, the ex-talent agent, was determined to have each of the four characters played by a major star.

When Mike Steen asked Rapper if Laurette Taylor would have got the part if she had been alive, Irving reluctantly said no. "She would have been the last person to be asked . . . it was [then] always a question of distribution. Of name value. Of box office value." Rapper of course was against this reasoning, but he had to go along with it.

He had one marvelous idea, to have Tallulah Bankhead do Amanda. And Tallulah, an Alabama girl, "loved the idea." She agreed to do a screen test as Amanda. Tallulah's test was fantastic, Rapper called it "the greatest test I have ever seen or made."

Did Tallulah get the part? Not so. Jack Warner went over the heads of Feldman and Rapper and threw it out. He was afraid of her drinking. As Rapper put it, "He said Errol Flynn was enough."

In September, Tennessee and Frank flew from Rome to Los Angeles. The entire studio was atingle with anticipation. The head people, Jack Warner, Charlie Feldman and Jerry Wald, had a late lunch so that the small fry would be out of the commissary. Finally, as Rapper said, the trumpet blew heralding Tennessee's arrival. Jack Warner "fixed his tie and as the two arrived he got up from his chair. 'Well, well! At last, here you are! Welcome to Warner Brothers!' And he shook the hand of Frank, thinking he was Tennessee, but Tennessee was very timidly walking behind Frank, with that familiar cigarette holder hanging from his lips. The mistaken identity amused rather than annoyed Tennessee."

Later Jack Warner did discover which one was Tennessee, but he was puzzled about Frank. "And what do you do, young man?" he asked Merlo.

Frank looked him right in the eye and said, firmly, that he slept with Mr. Williams.

Casting went on. Kirk Douglas and Jane Wyman were cast, or miscast, as the gentleman caller and Laura. Bette Davis was almost cast as Amanda, but there were problems, and they finally settled on a really monstrous piece of miscasting—Gertrude Lawrence. She had already played another Amanda, the brittle, sophisticated starring role in Noel Coward's *Private Lives*, and no one else on earth could have done it better. As a witty, charming comedienne she was unequaled. Her husband, the producer Richard Aldrich, said, "Gertrude asked for my opinion. I was opposed to her accepting the offer and I made no bones about it." He knew the role was wrong for her, and said she should accept it only if they made flashbacks to the youthful Amanda, of *Menagerie*, showing her young and pretty. This was done. For the rest of the part she had to wear padding and gray hair and makeup wrinkles.

Gertrude Lawrence wrote her husband, "It's difficult to dress Amanda like an out-of-date belle, without making her look either like Whistler's Mother or Nurse Cavell after a night on the town."

But it was just as bad for Jane Wyman. Gertrude said they cut off all her hair so she could wear a blond stringy wig.

Tennessee had feelings of justifiable foreboding, but he went dutifully to Chicago and St. Louis to look at possible locations for exterior scenes. In St. Louis he noted that grandpa was at loose ends and promised to take him down to Florida later.

He finished up his version of the screenplay, saying that the film people seemed to be pleased with it, but adding the ominous note that they felt the ending should be a bit more "upbeat," that Hollywood weasel word meaning a happy ending. For *Menagerie* it would be like having Romeo and Juliet come bouncing out of the tomb on tippy-toes.

They gave him a big party with all the stars, and a solid-gold cigarette case with an amethyst clasp, which was so valuable he planned to put it in a safe deposit box.

After this experience, Tennessee and Audrey Wood were determined that the inevitable film of *Streetcar* would have to be arranged more skillfully. Audrey was also determined to get even more money. She prepared an ambush for Hollywood. She planted rumors that Twentieth Century-Fox had offered half a million dollars for it, but had been refused because Tennessee wanted a "quality" production. She managed to get that into Walter Winchell's column.

Naturally the phone began to ring. Charles Feldman was calling from Hollywood. He had read in Winchell that Tennessee was demanding quality more than money and he, Charlie, had lots of quality.

Audrey said she knew that. Look at the quality stuff going into the *Menagerie* filming. But she, Audrey, wanted something more than quality. Charlie wanted to know what that was.

"Money," said Audrey.

Charlie said he had money also. *Real* money. He would be glad to do a quality production of *Streetcar* and also pay $500,000 for the privilege.

Perhaps the key word was *real*, a half million in real, and not newsleak money. To the casual observer it must have seemed insane, after the dreadful mess that was being made of *Menagerie*. Was Audrey, a very shrewd operator, simply selling out for a huge price? And was Tennessee crazy to go along with it?

But Tennessee and Audrey had an idea that could change everything and the name of it was Kazan. They had a feeling that Gadge would make all the difference.

Kazan had never made a film from a stage play, and had "very great resistance to doing it." He did it only because, as he said:

> ...I feel closer to Williams personally than to any other playwright I've worked with. Possibly it's the nature of his talent—it's so vulnerable, so naked—it's more naked than anyone else's. I wanted to protect him, to look after him. Not that he's a weak man—he's an extremely strong man, very strong-minded. But when he asked me repeatedly to make the film of *Streetcar*, I finally said I'd do it.

Kazan first tried to do the obvious thing that almost anyone thinks of doing, in adapting a play to a film—to "open it up," as he said, with exterior shots, to bring it out of the stage set. Usually this is an intelligent approach. He and a screenwriter worked for several months, doing scenes in Blanche's past, scenes in New Orleans and so on. At first he thought it was good, and then he threw it all out. He decided that the strength of *Streetcar* was its compression, and he decided to shoot the play almost exactly as it was written. He even wanted to use the whole Broadway cast, but Feldman insisted on at least one star. Brando was not yet a movie name at all. So Vivien Leigh was brought in from London.

All that would take many months. Tennessee returned, exhausted, from the *Menagerie* operations, to New York, to the old Chelsea Hotel, and while there in October 1949 arranged to rent a house in Key West, which had three bedrooms. He hoped to have room for his grandfather. Soon afterward he would buy the house on Duncan Street, which would become his main home. A simple frame house, it was over the years to become the nucleus of a kind of compound, with covered patio, swimming pool, guesthouse and a virtual jungle of tropical plants.

He saw many of his old friends in New York. Don Windham was there, but the relationship was beginning to be strained. Tennessee was rich and went to expensive nightclubs. Windham wrote about one evening when he was going with Tennessee to meet Gore Vidal at the Blue Angel. He was without a tie and Tennessee suggested he go back home and get one. Windham's feelings were hurt, and he didn't join them.

Bill Inge was there, too. His play, *Come Back, Little Sheba*, had been well received in a summer theater tryout, and he was working very hard to prepare it for Broadway—so hard that he was driving himself to heavy drinking. (But he made it. *Sheba* was produced with great success, and chosen by Burns Mantle as one of the ten best of the year.)

Tennessee's main worry at the time was that Margo Jones was doing what he regarded as a poor production of *Summer and Smoke* in Cleveland, so poor that he was even thinking about taking legal action.

He and Frank went down to the house in Key West and spent most of the winter there. Gramps joined them, and Frank was very good with him. They liked each other. Tennessee settled down to his best work in many months. He was always in bed by midnight, up by eight, working hard all morning, and spending the afternoons on the beach.

Meanwhile the Oliviers' stage version of *Streetcar* opened in London— and the London jinx seemed to be as strong as ever. Kenneth Tynan wrote that Vivien Leigh "worked with Trojan intensity, and failed. After the initial shock at hearing Williams's play described by the critics as 'a shallow shocker' we shut our eyes tightly and forgave Miss Leigh." Tynan also said that "the English and French productions [of *Streetcar*] were both so blatantly sensationalized that Williams' underlying lyric fibre passed unnoticed."

This seemed to have little effect on the hard work Tennessee was doing at his new house. By early December he finished his first draft of *The Rose Tattoo*, the first major play he had completed in three years.

He wrote to Don Windham, partly in apology for his delay in sending a publicity blurb for his new novel, *The Dog Star*, which had just been published.

But the letter also seemed to be a kind of rationalization for the decline in their friendship, or at least the greater space that had opened up between them. He listed his priorities, normally, as 50 percent work, 35 percent for his struggle against what he called "lunacy" and 15 percent for love and friendship. But at this time he was so concerned about work—89 percent— and "lunacy"—10 percent—that he had only 1 percent left for love and friendship.

He did seem genuinely to regret the growing distance between them, but perhaps if he had been writing to Frank, the percentages would have been different.

He wanted to go up north to see the Philadelphia tryout of Carson McCullers's *The Member of the Wedding*, and also attend the rehearsals of *Come Back, Little Sheba*. So in early January he and Frank started the drive to New York. They got as far as Miami, and then thought better of driving all that distance in midwinter. They turned around and drove back to Key West.

He and Frank kept pretty much to themselves, and he was working steadily. He finished *The Roman Spring of Mrs. Stone* and sent it to Audrey Wood in New York. She submitted it to Jay Laughlin of New Directions, who bought it for fall publication.

He then did several more drafts of *The Rose Tattoo*, and was considering a different title, *Right or Wrong, It Is Done*.

In May he and Frank came up to New York and sailed from there to Europe. They spent three weeks in Paris, where he collected about five thousand dollars worth of French royalties, then drove to the Hotel Inghilterra in Rome, where they started looking for an apartment.

He wanted to go to Sicily as soon as possible with Frank, to hear some of the Sicilian talk at first hand, for the play, and to observe the people. Anna Magnani agreed to come with them. Frank took them to visit some of his relatives and Tennessee wrote down a great deal of real talk. Much of the incidental dialogue and background chatter would be done in Italian.

He put the new material into his script and gave it to Audrey, who sent it straight to Irene Selznick—who turned it down. She said it was material for an opera, not a play. However, Cheryl Crawford liked it very much and decided to produce it, with a tryout scheduled for Chicago toward the end of the year.

Mrs. Stone was published in New York in September, and received only moderate attention. He had some favorable reactions from Isherwood, Edith Sitwell, Carson McCullers and Rosamund Lehmann, but was disappointed that the book was not reviewed everywhere.

As novels go, it was a modest success. He told Gilbert Maxwell that it had sold about ten thousand copies, which is much more than the average sale of a novel. It would be published in London by John Lehmann in 1950, and again by Secker and Warburg in 1957, and in numerous paperback editions. The film made from it would become one of his favorites. However, he said he had never been happy artistically with the book.

He and Frank returned to the States with a reasonably complete version of *Tattoo*. They paid a brief visit to the West Coast, where Kazan was completing the film of *Streetcar*.

At first Kazan had been having trouble with Vivien Leigh. She kept on telling him how she had done Blanche "with Larry" in London. Kazan told her, "You aren't doing it with Larry now, you're doing it with me." Finally she agreed, and became enthusiastic.

There is an eight-page letter written in longhand at this time by Frank Merlo to the old Reverend Mr. Dakin. It is as interesting for its picture of Frank as it is for a chronology of the period. In the printed literature there are very few quotes from Frank, who wrote quite well, and was always polite and respectful.

About the *Streetcar* filming he wrote: "The picture is almost completed and Tom was delighted and excited over what he has seen of it. Mr. Kazan, as you know, is the director and is doing a magnificent job. We are quite fortunate to have Miss Leigh playing Blanche. She is better than any of the actresses who have played the part yet. You would love Miss Leigh. She is quite a charmer and a delightful hostess... She gave a lunch for Tom... We went to the studio almost every day to watch 'shooting.'"

While on the coast they visited what Frank called "Hearst House," which "is so well guarded we had to pass through two gates and many more armed guards. Even the manservant who served us coffee had a pistol attached to his belt. We were quite taken aback at the sight of this sinister manservant."

They returned to New York, where Frank's letter was written, and sublet Buffie Johnson's town house. Buffie was married to Gerald Sykes, whose novel, *The Nice American*, was about to be published. Frank and Tennessee had just been guests at a weekend house party. Another guest was Gore Vidal, who was, Frank wrote, "his usual unpleasant self. (You must forgive my lack of tolerance concerning Mr. Vidal's character, but I know you will appreciate my feeling about him, although you [Rev. Dakin] are inclined to be more Christian about people like him.")

The main job in New York was to cast *Tattoo*. Tennessee had written it especially for Anna Magnani. He must have pictured her, in his mind, as Serafina, all the time he was working on it. Tynan wrote that it was "the most thoroughgoing star vehicle of the last ten years." So naturally Tennessee wanted her to play it on Broadway. Anna wanted to do it, too; but she was afraid to try it live, on a stage, in English, even the Sicilian English of Serafina. She could learn the lines, but she knew that onstage there would always be emergencies and she would have to ad-lib. This was a frightful disappointment to Tennessee. He and the director, Daniel Mann, wondered if anyone else could possibly play the part.

Tennessee thought he had found an actress who might be able to do it. She was a young woman named Maureen Stapleton, and when he showed her to the others, they were skeptical. After all, Serafina was no child. Every night for twelve years she had made love, with huge passion, in fact 4,380 times (she kept score) with her late husband Rosario, the banana truck driver, until he died. It was always with Rosario, never with anyone else, even once. Could a girl play a woman like that?

Stapleton read the words beautifully, but she obviously did not look the part. They tried messing her up. They even dirtied her face and found her some funny clothes. And sure enough, Maureen made them believe it. She was indeed Serafina Della Rose.

Who could play Alvaro Mangiacavallo, Mr. Eat-a-Horse, the driver of another banana truck? He had to convince Serafina to chalk up number 4,381, after spending so long in her private, self-imposed nunnery. He had to have the body of Rosario and the face of a clown. Eli Wallach was perfect to play the funniest character that Tennessee ever created. It took a lot of living in Italy to make Alvaro Mangiacavallo come to life.

Tennessee described *Tattoo* as his "love play to the world," full of the love he felt for Frank. And Frank helped him to reach into the hearts of the Sicilians. The printed version of the play is dedicated "To Frankie in Return for Sicily." The play is a hymn to ecstatic, Rabelaisian sex—really monogamous sex, faithful but violent sex from Serafina's standpoint—and, comparatively speaking, from Tennessee's as well. In his own fashion, and at this time, he preferred a kind of monogamy, and was happiest living a (more or less) faithful sex life.

Who else could have written that love scene between Serafina and Mangiacavallo, with the dressmaker dummies, the ashes of truck driver number 1, the Virgin Mary and the condom dropping on the floor? It is one of the funniest love scenes ever written. Yet, according to its own lights, it is quite moral. These are not wanton or promiscuous people. For them, sex is for keeps.

Dakin remembers some of the rehearsals in Chicago. Incidental music had been called for in the script, and it was specially written by David Diamond (who was a close friend of Carson McCullers). Musicians were hired, and if you hire any musicians, you have to hire a lot of them, by the rules of the union. And when they all played, nobody could hear what the actors were saying.

Tennessee said, "Does David Diamond think I've written an opera with gestures?"

All but four of the musicians were removed—though the others would have to be paid anyway.

On the night of December 29, *Tattoo* opened at the Erlanger Theater. The Chicagoans, who knew *Menagerie* and *Streetcar*, were somewhat baffled by Sicily in Mississippi. Even Claudia Cassidy, the faithful Williams admirer, was puzzled. She wrote that it failed as a tragedy, but "could make a very good comedy."

Tattoo ran for more than a month in Chicago; Tennessee worked steadily on it, giving it a happy ending and emphasizing the comic elements.

Then, on February 3, *Tattoo* opened in a city that had almost as many

Italians as Rome—New York at the Martin Beck Theater.

Dakin and Edwina were there again. In her memoirs, Miss Edwina hops over this one rather lightly. Joyous hymns to sexual pleasure weren't for her.

The reviews were not wildly enthusiastic, and Tennessee stayed in New York to try to hold up the play with publicity. By this time he was a full-fledged celebrity, sought for newspaper interviews and talk shows, some on radio, some on the new medium, television. And he was getting better at it. After a while a shy writer gets used to a TV camera rolling at him like a tank, with its red lights flashing. The publicity was helpful but the play was still shaky.

Dakin and Edwina, meanwhile, went down to Key West to help take care of grandpa. A few days later, Tennessee arrived, still worried about *Tattoo*'s box office. Then Gore Vidal rode up to the Key West house on a bicycle. He noticed that Tennessee looked worried and asked Dakin the reason.

"Because of the reviews," Dakin said.

"The *Times* was good," said Gore.

"The Hearst papers were very unkind," said Dakin.

"That's easily remedied," said Gore, who happened to be a friend of Marion Davies, the movie star who was a close companion of William Randolph Hearst, the newspaper tycoon whose resemblance to *Citizen Kane* was not accidental.

Gore advised Tennessee to pack up a box of suitably inscribed and autographed copies of his books and plays, and send them along to Marion; Gore would tell her they were coming.

Soon after that, Dakin saw his brother rushing to the post office with a large box of books. And within two weeks a very flattering feature appeared in the New York *American*, a Hearst paper, with color photos of the cast, urging everyone to see *The Rose Tattoo*. A second review from another critic, also flattering, also appeared. The Los Angeles *Examiner*, and many other Hearst papers, began praising the play.

Whether or not there was any direct connection, business at the box office improved greatly and the play was a success.

Later, of course, Anna Magnani played Serafina in the film of *Tattoo* and won an Oscar for it.

The play is full of roses. Serafina's husband was named Rosario, her daughter Rosa, and their last name was Della Rose. Her husband wore the tattoo of a rose on his chest and so, beginning that day, did Mangiacavallo. Rosario's hair had always been perfumed with oil of roses, and so was Mangiacavallo's. There is a rose on a fan, a rose-colored silk shirt and roses are growing by the house. It is a celebration of Tennessee's almost mystic attraction to the rose image, growing partly from the names of the two women he loved most, old Grand and his sister. He wrote an article on the mystique of the rose, the *rosa mistica*.

He came back again to New York for the screening of the film of *The Glass Menagerie* and was as shocked by it as he expected to be. He had managed, by threatening a lawsuit, to keep them from having it end in a wedding, but Hollywood had to sneak in the upbeat. And there was another gentleman caller in the offing. Everything was going to be okay with Laura. He called it the most unfortunate film ever made of his work.

CHAPTER 20

Old Williams plays never die, they keep on being recycled, and usually improve in the process. He had not forgotten *Camino Real* even though, back in 1946, Audrey Wood had disliked it so much she refused to show it to anyone.

However, some typescripts had managed to find their way to the Actors Studio. As Kazan said, "One of the experimental works I did there was a scene from *Camino Real*. That's the way Williams got introduced to the Studio; he saw that experiment and liked it very much."

Tennessee said that Eli Wallach, Barbara Baxley and some student actors were performing scenes from it. It was the first time he had seen any of it acted, and was so pleased with the way it played that he suggested to Kazan that they might try it on Broadway, possibly with another play.

Kazan agreed. He was fascinated by it, not frightened as some others might have been, because he had directed Wilder's *The Skin of Our Teeth*, a fantasy just as wild as *Camino*. But he became involved in something else, and the project was postponed. Tennessee went to work again on the script.

He was moving around restlessly. A letter written in early June by Frank to the Reverend Mr. Dakin, from Paris, said that they had just spent twelve days in London, and "we *were hungry* most of the time. The English diet is mostly starchy foods and fish. Rationing still is with them although some bacon, ham and eggs is available. I gained weight from eating so much bread."

They went to the theater almost every night, had dinner with Sir Larry and Lady Olivier, and bought a black Jaguar convertible with tan leather seats.

They brought Maria Britneva with them to Paris, and sent her back to London "loaded with all kinds of things unobtainable in London, mostly clothes."

They drove the car down to Rome; the mistake was to let Tennessee drive it. As he wrote to his mother on August 24, 1951, he was driving at about seventy miles an hour when a truck came out of a side road without stopping. The Jaguar was smashed, and his typewriter flew through the

185

air and hit him in the head. His only injury was a small cut above the hairline on his forehead.

Then he was back in London, where there was some talk of producing *Summer and Smoke*, had lunch with T.S. Eliot, and was given an autographed copy of his play, *The Cocktail Party*, then a hit in New York.

Carson McCullers was in London, too, in dreadful health and depressed, in spite of the fact that her play version of *The Member of the Wedding* had won the 1950 New York Critics' Award. She was rich, and much more famous, but was drinking heavily. He found her in a lodging house in Chelsea, sitting on a sofa, very sad, and with a nearly empty bottle of sherry.

He had also been to a polo match with Maria, Hermione Baddeley, a young friend of hers, and a real maharajah. Hermione's friend had a terrible argument with Maria, spat in her face and called her frightful names.

He planned to go back to Paris and then to St. Tropez.

All that was just the frolicking of the afternoons. The serious business was going on every morning, the work on *Camino Real*. He wanted it pronounced in the Californian way, *Cam*-ino Reel, not Cah-*mee*-no Ree-*al*. The full title originally was *Ten Blocks on the Camino Real*, and each "block" was a scene. It was then short enough to require a curtain raiser. Rewriting expanded it. The printed version now has sixteen scenes. On the surface, *Camino* looks like a circus, with people in fantastic costumes strutting about, sometimes even running out into the audience: Don Quixote, Lord Byron, Camille, Casanova and Kilroy. There is a fancy hotel and a flophouse and an archway leading to the desert. It is a fantasy of decadence, full of people in declining years; Casanova is almost too old to love, and Camille is an aging courtesan who has to pay for her pleasures. Don Quixote of the drooping lance is older than old; Byron is an old gentleman sitting behind potted palms. The young hero, Kilroy, a boxer, enters this diseased world, and is treated and dressed like a clown. His only solution for this festering old place is to leave it. He goes out into the desert with Don Quixote. It is Tennessee's solution for a world like that: don't fix it, leave it.

There's some lovely poetry, some of his very best, like the muted love scene between Casanova and Camille, performed, as the author tells us, in the style of an antiphonal poem.

The play is full of symbols; in a preface to it he wrote his best essay on symbolism itself, which he called the natural speech of drama. Sometimes a gesture, or an object on the stage, demonstrates an idea better than pages of exposition. To illustrate his point, he tells of the old portmanteau of Casanova, which represents all his faded and fragile memories. It is thrown from a balcony and comes crashing to the ground.

He continued to write and rewrite *Camino*, and tried desperately to have it produced. But few people would invest in a fantasy, even one written by Tennessee Williams. He had to try hard to raise angel money. In early 1952 he was in New York and went to parties with rich people who had, he told Gilbert Maxwell, "been asked in the hope they'd put some loot into *Camino Real*." Many of them had more money than sense. One plump dowager congratulated him, instead of Saroyan, on writing *The Time of Your Life*, and then dragged him over to meet Edna Ferber. When told, in a voice like a fanfare of trumpets, that this was none other than the real life Tennessee Williams, Miss Ferber looked over her shoulder and drawled, "Well, the best I can manage is a mild yippee." Tennessee replied, "I can't even manage that."

The net result of all this was that *Camino*'s production was put off for lack of funds.

He took grandpa on a nice trip, down to New Orleans, where they discovered that Tennessee had become such a hero that the Hotel Monteleone would not let him pay for his room, and presented them with a huge basket of fruit.

They moved on to Miami, where they were entertained by Gilbert Maxwell. Old Gramps, even more blind and deaf than before, was still serene. Asked by Maxwell if he felt certain of an afterlife, "he answered in his musical, methodically measured voice, 'Oh, yes, indeed yes. I am quite sure that when I go, I shall cross over to the other side and my dear wife will be waiting there to take my hand.'"

Tennessee and Gramps went back to Key West, where the new writing studio was taking shape. Any sensible writer knows that a work place should be simple and functional, with a minimum of distractions, or outside stimuli of any kind, quiet, well lighted and well ventilated, with no frills. This one was about the size of a one-car garage, with room for one man to sit down at the typewriter. The windows were all fitted with jalousies so that air could circulate, and sunlight be controlled, but privacy maintained. There was a long worktable, big enough for spreading out a whole act at a time, and a ceiling fan. It became his favorite place to work.

He settled down once again to revisions of *Camino* and also experimented with a screenplay of his *27 Wagons Full of Cotton*.

While he worked, a revolution was just beginning in the New York theater; *Summer and Smoke* was more responsible for it than any other event. "Off-Broadway," which now has perhaps more artistic prestige than "Broadway," was born.

"Broadway" itself was never actually on Broadway. Broadway, the Times Square section, was full of movie houses, souvenir shops, delicatessens, pinball parlors and Howard Johnsons; all the "Broadway" theaters were then, and are now, on the side streets to the east and west (mostly west) of it, between Forty-third and Fiftieth streets, and contracts were specially written for this district with featherbedding clauses for all the theatrical unions. Production in the contractual "theater district" was becoming so fiercely expensive that serious, artistic theater was being priced out of business.

Then a wild, occasionally alcoholic and always brilliant young director name José Quintero took *Summer and Smoke* down to Greenwich Village to the Circle in the Square, an odd theater indeed. It had no proper stage at all, only a playing area with the audience sitting on both sides of it; actors entered through the bar on the landing.

Quintero, whom Tennessee didn't even know at the time, cast a virtually unknown actress named Geraldine Page as Alma Winemiller.

She told Mike Steen: "I was waiting by the bar to make my entrance for the second act, right after intermission. Most of the audience was back in, but there were two people going up the staircase ahead of me in the dark, and I was so annoyed that they weren't in their seats. I just got around them in time to make my entrance. And afterwards I said to the stage manager, 'Who were those two nuts in the way when I was trying to make my entrance?' And he said, 'That was Mr. Williams.' He came backstage afterwards and that's when I met him."

It was the beginning of a long friendship and much work together.

Quintero had done an earlier and longer version of the play. The actress said, "We did it at its own pace and didn't worry about getting people home on the commuter trains."

Brooks Atkinson of the *Times* went down to the Village and wrote that the play was magnificent. It was the first really big Off-Broadway hit, ran for almost two years and was a commercial as well as an artistic success. The Off-Broadway ice had been broken. The Phoenix, the Théâtre de Lys, the York and many others were soon producing plays that were better than Broadway's. (Ironically, the Circle in the Square itself later moved uptown.)

The London production of *Summer and Smoke* also succeeded, and *The Rose Tattoo* was running in Denmark and Norway.

That summer he and Frank went to Europe again. They had a pleasant crossing on the French liner *Liberté*, and stayed in France long enough to spend some of his French royalties, mainly from Cocteau's unbelievable production of *Streetcar*. They continued on to Rome, to the apartment with the tall windows and the big bed. He saw Anna Magnani again, many times. She said she wanted very much to do the English-language film of *Tattoo*.

By late summer they were in New York, and this time the *Camino* production was underway. Cheryl Crawford, who had produced *Tattoo*, had finally assembled a sufficient choir of angels, and Kazan had agreed to direct. He was casting it largely from the Method players of the Actors Studio. Tennessee agreed that their technique was well suited to the play.

Kazan said, "I tried to produce *Camino Real* in the style of the Mexican-Indian figures of death, the candy skulls and the little, wooden dancing skeletons; I took a lot from a Mexican artist named Posada who is a sort of primitive and influenced Diego Rivera a lot; and I used some of his works, like his dance of death. Williams approved of all this. I put a lot more music in the play than he had, and he liked that, too."

So with everything set for rehearsals after the new year, Tennessee went back to Florida, stopping for a Christmas party in Miami with Gilbert Maxwell and one of his favorite girl friends, Marion Vaccaro. Then he went down to Key West to write until it was time for rehearsals.

While rehearsals were going on, Kazan said that Tennessee would come in, after his morning's work, and lunch ". . . around three-thirty, and watch a while. If he saw something funny, he'd laugh very loud. If he didn't like something, he'd say 'No!' out loud, and I'd say, 'Shut up!'"

By this time, of course, they were old friends. Tennessee went with the company to Philadelphia for the tryout. He and Frank had a hotel room directly over that of the pop singer Johnny Ray, then famous for "The Little White Cloud that Cried," and they made friends with him, visiting him backstage. Tennessee's taste in music is wide, ranging from pop to classical, and he is reasonably well informed, but not elitist, or intellectual about it.

The opening-night audience at the Shubert Theater was somewhat baffled by this odd play and by the actors running around between the seats. Many were amazed and delighted, but no reaction was as dramatic as that of the producer Saint Subber, a few nights later. He threw himself on his knees before Tennessee, shouting, "Maestro!" Tennessee felt this rather unconvincing, since he never heard from the man again.

Camino opened in New York in March 1953, at the National Theater. Edwina came in from St. Louis, and Dakin flew in from Mather Air Force Base in California.

The day of the opening he was crossing the street near the National Theater with Kazan when Gadge said, "Dakin, what do you think of your brother?"

It seemed to Dakin that he was saying, "What do you think of his way of life?" All he replied was, "Why, Gadge, I'm enormously proud of him, of course."

Kazan merely said, "Well, you should be." He was "straight" and married and tolerant.

But Dakin was worried. He was still concerned about his brother's sexual life-style. He knew there was nothing he could do about it, except hope that he would not flaunt it in the media. At this time Tennessee's homosexuality was known to his friends but had not been publicized generally, as it would later be.

Dakin and Miss Edwina visited Tennessee's apartment, where Frank had accumulated quite a menagerie, including a huge shepherd dog named Satan, a monkey called Creature and a parrot named Laurita, whom Frankie had been teaching how to talk. The first thing Laurita said to Edwina was, "Fuck you, fuck you!" Frank quickly threw a cover over the cage, and Dakin swears the parrot said, "My God, what a short day," a routine Frank had borrowed from *Streetcar*. Miss Edwina was not amused.

The first-night audience was pleased, displeased and confused. As John Gassner might have asked, "Who are you rooting for?" And Tennessee could have replied, "It doesn't matter." He was not trying to write a simple story line.

Tennessee went to the opening-night party and stayed until the reviews began to arrive. Some were very bad. He and Frank ran off to his aquarium apartment on East Fifty-eighth Street. He tried to sleep but couldn't. Frank was sympathetic, but nothing helped.

Then Kazan arrived with his wife Molly, bringing along John Steinbeck and his wife. Gadge wanted to cheer him up, but it didn't work. Tennessee was angry, stalked into his bedroom and bolted the door.

Frank took over, served them drinks and tried to explain about Tennessee. Probably, if Kazan had just come alone, or only with Molly, it might have been all right.

In any case, one of the two men had lunch with him the next day. Tennessee, in his *Memoirs*, says it was Kazan, and they ate at a fish place. Maxwell wrote that Tennessee told him, soon after, in Miami, that it was Steinbeck who asked him to lunch, and he was "so completely understanding, so tactful, and kind I could hardly believe it." At least everyone was reconciled, but nothing could help the production of *Camino*. Cheryl Crawford soon closed it. Tennessee says she even cut out the confetti in the big carnival scene toward the end. After all, confetti costs money. But they were playing to capacity, even after the closing announcement.

Crawford's reluctant angels must have lost a lot. In a letter to Kazan, Tennessee wrote that she had budgeted it at $140,000. Fantasy can be expensive.

Brooks Atkinson's considered opinion, years later, was that *Camino* was "superbly written" but marked the beginning of "an increasing preoccupation with degeneracy, corruption and horror."

Tennessee was despondent about the failure of *Camino* because it represented a new step for him, breaking away, he thought, from his old manner and his old material. He felt that all this had been rejected. When Tennessee fled back to Florida, Maxwell tried to point out to him that the reviews had not been half as savage as he had thought.

Tenneseee's friendship for Don Windham led him into what was possibly another backwater, though at the time it may have served as a kind of occupational therapy after the traumatic experience of *Camino*. Windham had written a play, *The Starless Air*, and had submitted it to the Theatre Guild, where Paul Bigelow was then the play reader. Bigelow, who had little respect for Windham's talent, put him off for a long time.

Finally, Joanna Albus, Margo Jones's friend, thought she would try doing it at her theater in Houston. Then the Theatre Guild tentatively decided that they might try it out at the summer theater in Westport, Connecticut.

Tennessee had been thinking more and more about directing, and was wondering whether he might try directing one of his own plays. So when Windham suggested that he might start by directing *The Starless Air*, Tennessee agreed to try it.

Down in Key West, Tennessee studied the play and wrote Windham long letters of criticism and play doctoring. At this point Lawrence Langner of the guild thought they might produce it later on Broadway, if all went well. Windham naturally was quite excited about this.

Windham and Tennessee made many changes in the script, and Tennessee went to Houston and did direct it, his first real attempt at directing. Windham wrote that he was "an inspired director." But there were many differences of opinion, and many arguments. Windham wrote that Tennessee was putting in speeches that didn't belong in the play (and which turned up later in *Cat on a Hot Tin Roof*) and for a while Windham was barred from rehearsals. This is strong action to take against a playwright, and is in fact forbidden on Broadway by the Dramatists Guild contract. A playwright cannot be barred from rehearsals. They finally compromised. The script could be changed, but must be kept under the playwright's control.

Audrey Wood wanted assurances that Tennessee would be allowed to direct the play if it reached Broadway. However, Tennessee did finally leave the production. He wrote Windham many more letters about possible changes in the play, but he never again directed it.

Without Tennessee, others lost interest in *The Starless Air*. Langner felt that without Tennessee's name it would be hard to find backing.

The reverberations from all this, extending over many months and many letters, seem to have been the largest factor in separating Tennessee from Windham, and ending the mainstream of the Williams-to-Windham correspondence.

It was a time when artistic integrity had reached a point of obsession, and for good reason. Works of art, especially written ones, were being bought for huge sums by mass magazines, films, radio and television. They were processed, digested, bowdlerized and otherwise corrupted. The object always was greater public acceptance and this was, for the first time, being scientifically measured by polls and ratings. If the broadcast rating or the Gallup Poll or the audience cards given out at sneak previews showed that *they* wanted a snappier pace or a happier ending, give it to them. Sometimes plot outlines, titles, even alternate endings were pretested before the work was even written, if *written* is the right word.

Agents were accused of being pimps and writers called each other prostitutes. Ayn Rand and her far-out *Fountainhead* had people arguing seriously whether an architect had the artistic right to dynamite his own building because somebody had changed the front porch.

The descent of American radio and television into a bland, meaningless porridge showed what could happen when a potential art form pandered only to the lowest common demoninator.

The integrity obsession resulting from all this broke up many friendships. The Williams-Windham breakup was more complicated than this, but the integrity mania was surely one factor. Both had strong convictions about integrity; Williams had the writing strength to make his stick.

An interesting postscript to the Williams-Windham relationship is this "coded" comment in Tennessee's *Memoirs*, where "Dreamy Eyes" was a code name for Windham, a code broken by Windham himself.

It happened three years after this time, when Tennessee was in Florida working with Tallulah Bankhead on a production of *Streetcar*, in which Tallulah was playing Blanche. They were playing a "truth game" at Tallulah's mansion in Coconut Grove.

He was asked why he had stopped caring for Dreamy Eyes; he said simply that they had both found lovers. He of course had found Frank. That was why they had neglected their friendship.

In June he and Frank took a ship to Le Havre and went briefly to Spain. They met Paul Bowles in Barcelona. He had driven up with two Moroccans, one his chauffeur and one, Ahmed, his lover. They decided to drive to Rome, but Ahmed couldn't get a French visa, so he flew directly to Rome with Tennessee and Frank. All this Bowles told to Mike Steen.

Tennessee had a different apartment in Rome, this time on the Via Firenze, and was able to find another one on the same floor for Paul and his Moroccans. Tennessee had also arranged for Paul to work on a film being made by Luchino Visconti, called *Senso*, with Alida Valli and Farley Granger. Tennessee wrote that Paul was doing the script, and Paul, who should know, said it was music.

Mike Steen was curious; Tennessee had spent so much time in Italy— how good was his Italian? Did he speak it? Bowles replied: "Some. He is not a linguist. Oh, no. Not at all. He always used the present-indicative verbs instead of the proper form. And I think people abetted him in that when he was speaking with Italians. They would use it, too, because I suppose that they thought it was easier." Bowles added that Tennessee was always popular in Italy.

Tennessee's main worry that summer was the excessive stench of his bulldog, Mr. Moon. Frank tried hosing him down and stuffing him with chlorophyll tablets. Nothing helped.

But the important thing was that Tennessee, though in Rome, was returning to Williams country, after his excursions into Sicilian Mississippi and never-never land. The previous year The New Yorker had published one of his short stories, almost a novelette, called "Three Players of a Summer Game." In this story he was back in the sleepy, WASP South.

"Summer Game" is a beautifully written mood piece, and if it were a play would probably take place on a croquet lawn, with a newly painted house on one side and an electric car parked on the other. The central character, Brick, an ineffectual former athlete and now an alcoholic, comes here on summer evenings to drink, to play croquet and to sleep with Isabel, the pretty young widow whose doctor husband died not long before. Brick's capable wife, Margaret, who now runs their plantation, because somebody has to, would not appear very often. Isabel's plump little daughter, Mary Louise, would go about with a piece of ice in a handkerchief. She uses this to rub on mosquito bites. The electric car is where she sits while Brick and Isabel are making love. (The narrator is a young boy, and there is just the slightest misty memory of a boy named Tom and a little girl named Hazel.) Brick drinks more and more. Isabel has to sell the house and the electric car, and Margaret is seen driving Brick around in her car, almost like a mascot, or a prisoner.

That sounds very little like *Cat on a Hot Tin Roof*, but that is where it started, and the metamorphosis of this story into *Cat*, probably his most technically expert play, is what he was thinking about and working on for the next year.

When he was finished there was very little left of "Summer Game" except the names Brick and Margaret (usually called Maggie in the play). Even the sultry, lazy mood of the story had to give way, largely because of the demands of time unity. The play is precisely constructed to happen in continuous action. Technically that is the hardest way to write a play. All the events have to be fitted together into about two hours of crisis, in this case a gathering of the clan for the birthday and the dying of Big Daddy, a character who does not appear in the "Summer Game" story at all. Isabel and her house, her daughter and her electric car have gone, and the scene has moved to the bedroom of Maggie the Cat at the plantation. Maggie has been totally changed to an explosively sex-starved woman. Her tin roof is a husband who has no interest in making love to her, nor to any other woman.

Yet "Summer Game" works well as prose fiction, and *Cat* is simply dynamite in a theater.

But for Tennessee it was a brain-crushing struggle. He made little progress on *Cat* in Rome and came back to the States, this time to New Orleans, where he became ill and had to go into a hospital. When he came out he returned to his Key West house, where he felt he was good for nothing but the beach and the movies.

He soon pulled himself together and began hard work in his little studio. He finished a draft of *Cat* and sent it to New York, hoping above all to persuade Kazan to direct it. Kazan read it, had grave criticisms of the third act, but finally agreed to take it on.

Hollywood was after him again—and finally came, literally, to his front yard. Hal Wallis, the producer, had seen *The Rose Tattoo* in its first days, in Chicago, and had told Tennessee that he would like to make a film of it. He later bought it and Tennessee agreed to write the screenplay. He and Wallis met several times in New York to talk about the script, and Wallis said "his suggestions and revisions were brilliant."

Both Wallis and Tennessee wanted Anna Magnani for Serafina, and they flew to Rome to talk to her. They were able to calm her fears about doing a film in English by writing a bilingual script, with the Italian translation on the facing page.

Tennessee and Frank sailed with her to New York, and all day, every day of the voyage, worked with her, Frank speaking both Italian and English to her. By the time they reached New York, Anna knew the English lines perfectly.

Though the play took place "somewhere along the Gulf Coast between New Orleans and Mobile," according to the stage directions, everyone thought that the island of Key West would be perfect as a location. As Hal Wallis remembered:

"We drove all over town looking for a wood frame house that would best fit the requirements of Serafina's home. Finally, I saw one on a corner in an outlying neighborhood. It looked perfect but there was a fence too close to it which enclosed a goat yard belonging to the house next door. I asked my guide from the chamber of commerce if he thought the owner of the neighboring house would let us move the fence and provide our own needed goat yard. He said, 'Well, I don't think he will mind at all. You see, that's where Tennessee Williams lives.'"

The owner did not object, and even allowed them to use his house as the dressing rooms for the stars, Anna Magnani and Burt Lancaster.

But nothing stopped Tennessee's writing, not even having his house used as a film set. He worked every day until about 1:00 P.M., then came down to join the group.

There must have been times when he could hear the commotion above the rattle of his portable. Both Lancaster and Magnani were strong personalities with powerful egos. Naturally, they fought. Daniel Mann, who had directed the stage version, was directing the film, but sometimes Anna Magnani would decide she wanted to direct, and Burt would walk off the set. Magnani was screaming, Mann was going crazy and Lancaster was sulking.

But they all thought it would be a great picture. And it is certainly the only one in which not only Tennessee's house appears, but in which he is on screen himself. He and Hal Wallis agreed to appear as extras in one bar scene, which was shot in a real bar in downtown Key West. It is the scene where Anna rushes in looking for the girl friend of her late husband. Wallis said they stood there all day long in a hundred-and-ten-degree heat while the scene was shot and reshot.

Even the church scene was shot in a real church in Key West.

Hal Wallis said that everyone had fun, cast and crew alike. Tennessee enjoyed himself immensely. Harper's ran a picture showing him seated happily in the midst of film machinery, wearing blue jeans and sneakers. He wished he could stay for more of the excitement and, as he wrote to his grandfather, to act as referee, but Kazan wanted him in New York. He was casting *Cat*.

Kazan thought Barbara Bel Geddes would make a good Maggie the Cat and wanted Tennessee to hear her read the lines. Barbara, the attractive daughter of designer Norman Bel Geddes, had already appeared in several Broadway hits, and is now known everywhere as J.R.'s mother in "Dallas."

Tennessee saw her with Kazan. She was a cool-looking blond, on the surface not at all like the sizzling Maggie. But she could act, and proved to them that she could make her Maggie sizzle. And Ben Gazzara was very good as Brick. The big surprise was the choice of Burl Ives, known mainly as a folk singer, to play Big Daddy, the farm hand who had made himself into a millionaire planter. Ives was simply tremendous.

Tennessee and Kazan always worked beautifully together, but *Cat* was the biggest strain on their partnership, their most serious difference of opinion. Tennessee wrote about this in a true literary curiosity, probably the only known preface-to-an-alternative-third-act ever written. It was not an angry criticism of Kazan, and in fact was full of praise for him, as highly perceptive, and as a director from whom he had learned a great deal about his own work.

Kazan's criticisms were that Big Daddy, a pivotal character, did not appear at all in the third act, except as an offstage cry; that Brick's character should show some change, or development, as a result of the strong scene with his father in act two; and the character of Maggie should be more sympathetic to the audience.

Tennessee agreed with the third criticism. Maggie was becoming more sympathetic to him, too. But he was strongly opposed to the other two points. He did not want Big Daddy to appear in the third act, and he was against a turnaround in Brick's character. It was not believable that a conversation could bring about such a marked change in a man who had disintegrated to that extent.

But Tennessee did write the act as proposed by Kazan, and that was the one used on Broadway. Years later, Tennessee wrote a long essay for Playbill explaining the relationship of a playwright with intelligent professionals, especially directors, in the theater. He underwent three stages of development: the first, when the writer was young, and too frightened not to agree with any change; the second, when he was new to success and agreed to no changes; and the third, when he listened carefully to intelligent suggestions.

In the argument about the third act, they were probably both right, Tennessee psychologically and Kazan theatrically; Tennessee's version is more honest to the characters and is probably what they would have done, but Kazan's probably made for a more dramatic play.

Tennessee still prefers his original third act and considers that the play, with this act, is the favorite of all his plays, partly because he was proud of its unities of time, place and characters. But the main reason, as he pointed out in his *Memoirs*, was that in the second act and in the character of Big Daddy he had arrived at what he called an "eloquence of expression" that he had never equaled in any of his other characters.

He did accept the version preferred by Kazan without pressure. There was no ogre of a producer forcing either him or Kazan to do anything. The play was produced by the Playwrights' Company, organized years earlier by a consortium of Broadway's leading playwrights to produce their own plays and those of other playwrights. Their royalty percentages were more generous and their guarantees of self-expression more liberal.

During rehearsals, Grandpa Dakin died on February 14 in Barnes Hospital, St. Louis, two months short of being ninety-eight years old. Tennessee flew immediately to St. Louis.

Edwina wrote, "He appeared at the front door bearing a huge pasteboard box. There were tears in his eyes.

"I asked what the box held. 'It's a blanket for grandfather,' he said. He had carried with him thousands of Father's favorite flowers, sweet-scented spring violets, with white carnations outlining a St. Andrew's cross, to be placed on Father's coffin."

Paul Bigelow, who had been especially fond of the old gentleman, had flown from New York with Tennessee, and had already telephoned the church to have a special musical arrangement made of "Crossing the Bar," for the service. Bigelow had heard the old man say he wanted this played at his funeral.

Edwina accompanied the body to Waynesville, Ohio, the town where he had grown up, and he was buried next to old Grand. They were an extraordinary couple and their influence on Tennessee was incalculable.

Tennessee gave $1,000 to set up a memorial room in his honor at his alma mater, the theological school of Sewanee, the University of the South.

Tennessee returned to New York to the *Cat* rehearsals and followed the production to Philadelphia for the tryout. There he met William Faulkner for the first time. Faulkner was in love with Jean Stein, who was working with the play company. It wasn't surprising that the two authors had never met, even though they were born only a few miles apart. Faulkner was fourteen years older and Tennessee had left Mississippi when he was a boy. Faulkner had won his Nobel Prize years before, in 1949. At this time he was drinking heavily. Tennessee said of the Philadelphia meeting that Faulkner never talked to him, and even thought that the older man disapproved of him.

The company returned to New York for the March 24 opening at the Morosco Theater.

Dakin, then an air force captain stationed at Big Springs, Texas, was dating General Fred Dean's secretary, Joyce Croft. (He later married her.) Dakin put this proposition to the general: he might just be able to get four tickets to his brother's opening night if the general could manage to find an airplane to get them there. The general did find one, and since he was a pilot flew them to New York, where they met the general's girl friend.

The next day, only hours before the opening, Dakin had lunch with Tennessee, who "seemed more confident of success than I have ever seen him, beaming with praise for Kazan." So the battle of the third act had not changed the Tennessee-Kazan relationship. Anthony Quinn, who had played Stanley Kowalski in one of the *Streetcar* companies, joined them. Tennessee told Dakin that he and his friends were invited to the big cast party being held afterward at Gracie Mansion, the official residence of the mayor of New York.

Dakin remembers, "If I was not impressed by this bit of information, I was certainly overwhelmed by the sight of the immense crowd gathered in front of the theater. The entrance was roped off and mounted policemen were keeping the people under control as limousines pulled up to the entrance to discharge a glittering assemblage of first-nighters."

Everybody was there, including the honeymooning Debbie Reynolds and Eddie Fisher, Walter Winchell and Marilyn Monroe, who was in New York studying with the Actors Studio. She was in skin-tight gold mesh, her hair a shining platinum.

But this was to be one of Tennessee's weirdest opening nights, and it nearly destroyed his relationship with Audrey Wood. The story is complicated. When interviewed about it later by Gilbert Maxwell, Audrey said, "I'll tell you some time about this evening, my love, but the act takes a full twenty minutes." David Newman finally put the whole saga together in an article in Esquire.

In spite of his apparent confidence at lunchtime, Tennessee was unusually tense that evening. *Camino* had failed. It was more than four years since *Tattoo*. He wondered if he was finished.

That evening all the omens looked unfavorable. For one thing, as Maxwell wrote, Tennessee met Don Windham and Fred Melton in the bar at the first intermission. And, as Tennessee told Maxwell, "they didn't say one word. They just looked at me with scorn and contempt." He wondered if this was a real indication of disaster.

During the next two acts he became more and more anxious. He was sure he heard an unusual number of coughs from the audience, a sure sign they were bored and unhappy.

By the time the curtain fell he had retreated to the alley, and was pacing desperately up and down. Then it was over, and he saw the side doors of the theater—the emergency fire doors—burst open. Audrey Wood and Bill Liebling came out. Tennessee charged at them, head down, shouting,

"Rats! Rats! Leaving a sinking ship!" Audrey tried to tell him they had just come out the side doors to avoid the crowd. But he wouldn't listen and ran off.

Audrey and Bill were invited to the party at Gracie Mansion, and they thought surely they would find Tennessee there. They arrived—there was no Tennessee.

Dakin and General Dean and the two girls went there, too. Dakin remembers, "The party almost defied description. It was on an even more lavish scale than Lady Sybil's after the London opening of *Menagerie*." It had been given by Helen Hayes in honor of the costume designer Lucinda Ballard. All the celebrities were there. Dakin remembers having a long talk with Averell Harriman. Champagne and chateaubriand were being served.

But where was Tennessee? And where was Kazan?

Kazan, in fact, was having a little preparty gathering at his place for a few people, and of course Tennessee was invited. He went straight to Kazan's and looked for Audrey. She wasn't there. That convinced him the ship had really sunk, and Audrey was the rat who had left it. He was too upset to ask Kazan if she had been invited. She had not been, for no special reason. Kazan knew she would be at the other party.

Some of the people from Kazan's went to Gracie Mansion and reported that Tennessee was outraged. Audrey Wood had left him! All was over between them! Audrey heard all this and was almost in tears.

Then Tennessee did arrive, and would not speak to Audrey. He went to the far side of the room and sulked. Audrey, at her wit's end, left with Bill. And, as always happens in such cases, arrived at the checkroom at the same time as Tennessee. Bill tried to patch things up. He put them into a taxi and took them to Toffenetti's, a Times Square restaurant, the only place that was still open. Still, Tennessee sat in stony silence and finally left. Audrey couldn't sleep. She was afraid she had lost a good friend and a major client, and couldn't understand why.

The following morning she telephoned and invited him to lunch. And, she said, he arrived "as charming as always," and as though nothing had happened at all.

And that is how Tennessee celebrated the night of his greatest triumph—it was, at least, the biggest commercial or popular success, and close to *Menagerie* and *Streetcar* artistically.

Gilbert Maxwell says that Audrey told him later, "You know, it's funny sometimes about Williams. He really didn't know what he had in *Cat* until I told him, but I knew as soon as I read it."

And what about the terrible omen involving Don Windham and Fred Melton in the bar after the first act? Why did they observe the apparently contemptuous silence? Windham told Maxwell later: "The truth is he made Fred and me promise before he gave us our tickets that we wouldn't open our mouths to him at the theater about the play." There was no feeling of contempt, though Windham did say that he hadn't liked *Cat* as well as some of the others. Windham understood Tennessee's hang-ups as well as anyone. He wrote a novel called *The Hero Continues* and admitted that the central character was based on Tennessee. In his journal, dated April 23, 1952, he was already analyzing the leading character, as an exercise in the development of the projected novel:

> But it is the story of an individual with an extraordinarily complex resource of human and warm emotions. No single reaction of his is simple or cold. None abstract. He can be cruel, but he is cruel like a vengeful child. Or like a selfish lover. Never like a person of insufficient feeling. He suffers from a persecution complex—but never from self-pity, an important distinction. He resorts to hysterical surface movement for inner calm—never merely to excite himself emotionally, but to bring his emotional excitement to a climax from which calm will follow.

That is a shrewd assessment, and it throws some light on the peculiar (but in the end harmless) happenings of the night of March 24.

Dakin and Joyce and their general had to fly back to Texas quickly. Dakin was ecstatic about the reception of *Cat*. He knew that the audience loved it, and he had read the reviews, which were marvelous.

Cat ran longer on Broadway than any other of Tennessee's plays, and Audrey was able to persuade MGM to pay him $750,000 "off the top" for the film rights. This means that he received the entire amount, and that from the company that had once thrown out his screenplay about a gentleman caller and sent him off to the tomato patch in Santa Monica. The Lieblings' lawyer, Eddie Colton, also made MGM sign a 100-page contract even guaranteeing payments to Tennessee for every showing of the film on television. Clauses like this are standard now, but they were not then.

All this meant that *Cat* was his most successful play, to date, on a financial basis, but it was a critical success as well. It gave him his third New York Critics' Circle Award and his second Pulitzer Prize.

This total success was, as usual, totally crushing to Tennessee. It was even worse than *Streetcar*, and that had almost finished him. He said that once again he could not write.

He went down to Key West and shut himself up in his studio. Nothing happened. He drank coffee, and more coffee. For the first time, coffee alone was not enough. So he became what he called "a drugged writer." After several weeks he could stand it no longer, and started washing down a Seconal with a martini. He said he became "hooked" on it.

The terrible danger to a writer from this sort of thing is not that it doesn't work—but that it does, for a while. It often does help, or makes him believe that it helps, which is almost the same thing. He does write better. And then it becomes a crutch. And then he has to increase the dose to have the same effect. It must be remembered that he was not doing this for kicks, or for some kind of mind-blowing sensation. The sole purpose was to try to make the writing flow. At that point he would have done *anything* to make the ideas and the words come again. Momentarily gin and tablets worked, and this proves that it was not stimulation he needed but the reverse. Alcohol and Seconal are depressants, not stimulants, like caffeine and amphetamine.

Maxwell, who was teaching in Miami (and trying to write poetry) came down to Key West to see him, bringing along one of his writing students. Maxwell had no way of knowing that Tennessee was in this psychological cul-de-sac. Tennessee was glum and silent, and obviously in no mood to have guests. When Maxwell complimented him on the Pulitzer and the Critics' Award, he said, "The hell with the critics. I wrote *Cat* for money." That was not true, but that was how he felt.

However, part of this was certainly caused by his chronic impatience with Maxwell, who was then drinking too much. He was quite civil with Françoise Sagan when she and some friends visited him, and with Budd Schulberg and his wife at one of Schulberg's Key West parties.

CHAPTER 21

He and Frank left for a summer in Europe. In Paris he saw Faulkner again and had dinner with him and Jean Stein. Once again conversation seemed almost impossible. Once, when Tennessee asked Faulkner a question, he raised his eyes, and the look was so sad and terrible that Tennessee cried.

Of course he was crying for Faulkner, or mainly for Faulkner, but they were tears for a writer who had won everything, the Nobel and all, who had become almost a god, and it was plain that Faulkner was miserable and close to being a total ruin as a writer. It was a terrifying look into a possible future for a younger writer who had just begun to think he could write only with alcohol and Seconal.

He and Frank went on to Rome and there, driving himself along with his gin and tablet whip, he worked on a screenplay that would eventually be called *Baby Doll*. The project had started years before with Kazan. Kazan had been reading his volume of short plays, *27 Wagons Full of Cotton and Other Plays* and the two of them were thinking about combining the title play with three others to make a full-length work, for either stage or screen. Kazan said, "I told him there was a good movie in *27 Wagons Full of Cotton*, and he jumped at the idea and said, 'It would be great.' Then I thought to add something from the other three stories [*The Unsatisfactory Supper*, *This Property is Condemned* and *The Last of My Solid Gold Watches*] each one making a progress. It would go from one story, then the focus would change to another story, and I was not thinking of it as a unified story at the time. Then I changed my mind. There was a girl at the [Actors] Studio who was just a beginner, named Carroll Baker; she wasn't a member, even, she was just like an apprentice there. Williams' heroine in *27 Wagons Full of Cotton* is a big, fat girl, so I said to him one day, 'There's this girl who has so many of the inner qualities of your heroine, but she's not fat—would you like to see her?' So I did an improvisation with Carroll Baker and Karl Malden. The minute Williams saw Carroll Baker he wanted to put her in the film."

203

Kazan and Williams finally settled on a single, unified story, using only *27 Wagons* and *The Unsatisfactory Supper*. Kazan was doing considerable work on the construction, and Tennessee would send him additional scenes.

The original one-act play must already have been performed countless times, since its printed version is already in its eighth printing. It is one of his most effective short plays. It has three scenes and only three characters: Jake, the owner of an old, outdated cotton gin; his wife Flora, a fat masochistic lump; and Silva, the energetic Italian-American whose successful competing cotton gin Jake has just burned down. Silva brings his twenty-seven wagons full of cotton to Jake, to gin for him, worms the truth out of Flora about the arson and seduces her.

The principal change, as Kazan pointed out, was in the character of the woman. Flora became Baby Doll, a retarded, infantile twenty-year-old, shaped like a woman and treated like a baby by her husband. She sleeps in a baby's crib and sucks her thumb. Presumably she's a virgin—until tomorrow, if Silva doesn't get there today. She becomes a satirical symbol of a type of immature American girl-woman.

Tennessee, who was almost certainly writing first drafts of *Sweet Bird of Youth*, was also sending bits of screenplay to Kazan. As Kazan said: "He would suddenly write a few and send them to me with a note 'insert somewhere.' Some I used and some I didn't; he didn't seem to care." Kazan's main worry was that he didn't feel they had a proper ending.

Tennessee was moving around Europe, too, with his portable. Ken Tynan saw him in Spain about this time, and wrote a fine, affectionate profile, with this description:

> In Spain, where I saw him last, he looked profoundly Spanish. He might have passed for one of those confidential street dealers who earn their living selling spurious Parker pens in the cafes of Malaga or Valencia. Like them he wore a faded chalk-striped shirt, a coat slung over his shoulders, a trim dark moustache, and a sleazy fat-cat smile. His walk, like theirs, was a raffish saunter, and everything about him seemed slept in, especially his hair, a nest of small, wet serpents. . . . In Italy he looks Italian; in Greece, Greek; wherever he travels on the Mediterranean coast, Tennessee Williams takes on a protective coloring which melts him into his background, like a lizard on a rock. In New York or London he seems out of place, and is best explained as a retired bandit . . .

Meanwhile Kazan had sold the *Baby Doll* idea to Warner Brothers, and was ready to film it. He told Tennessee they still had no ending, and finally persuaded him to come down to the location in Greenville, Mississippi.

Tennessee did not want to come. Kazan quoted him: "I left the South because of their attitude towards me. They don't approve of homosexuals, and I don't want to be insulted. I don't want my feelings hurt." After a few days in the hotel in Greenville he told Kazan he was leaving because he couldn't find a swimming pool. Kazan found him a pool, but it had no water in it. They started to fix the pool, and put in some water—but Tennessee left town. And then, Kazan said, "The next thing that happened was typical of him—after he's done something bad like that, he does something brilliant. In a couple of days he sent me an ending, which I thought was wonderful."

But he must have stayed longer than Kazan implies. Karl Malden, who was down there on location (he played the husband) remembered that Tennessee was there for several weeks. As he told Mike Steen, "Every day he'd come in with something new and Kazan would read it and say, 'You can do better than that, Tenn,' and Tenn would kind of giggle and say, 'Well, you know, Gadge, I think that's good.'" He said they finally wound up with about six different endings.

But Tennessee had a date with Tallulah Bankhead. He had always been fascinated by her. He had even thought of her as Blanche in the first production of *Streetcar*, but Irene Selznick had vetoed it. At this time a revival of *Streetcar* was scheduled for the New York City Center, and Tallulah was to play Blanche. Tennessee brought Herbert Machiz, who was chosen to direct, to meet her in New York, at Tallulah's elegant town house on East Sixty-second Street. Young Machiz must have been impressed by Tallulah's beautiful living room, with her portrait by Augustus John over the fireplace.

Tennessee left, but Machiz stayed to dinner, and afterward read her the whole play. Tallulah said, "I can just tell you're going to be a great director."

The play was to rehearse in Florida and open at the Coconut Grove Theatre in Miami. Most of the rehearsing was done in the enormous house of the theater's director. He had turned over the whole place, swimming pool and all, to Tallulah.

Tennessee and Tallulah were thrown together professionally for the first time at Coconut Grove, and some kind of explosion was inevitable. Tallulah, the way-out princess of one of the Deep South's most powerful and aristocratic families, was far closer to the background of Blanche than either Jessica Tandy or Vivien Leigh, and she had done some tremendous things on Broadway, including her magnificent Regina in Lillian Hellman's *The Little Foxes*, and her equally stunning performance in the totally different leading role of Thornton Wilder's *The Skin of Our Teeth*.

The relationship between her and Tennessee was one of exasperation, leading to a combination of love and exasperation. He thought at first she was being too grand, as Blanche, or too flossy, and said, "This isn't Mayfair, y'know." One time he gave her a beautiful black Mark Cross handbag. She threw it back at him, saying, "A lady *always* travels in brown. But I suppose it's impossible for you to understand what a lady is!" They were often at each other's throats and rehearsals went better when he was away.

Tallulah settled down to the part and at the final rehearsal Tennessee said afterward that it was truly Blanche, fragile and lovely. She played it so well that it would be a beautiful performance.

And then a curious and almost cruel thing happened. On opening night, with the Coconut Grove Theatre packed, Tallulah came onstage with her little suitcase. Blanche is now close to being an alcoholic, and she finds a bottle of whiskey, pours herself a half a tumblerful and belts it down. Then, a few moments later, when her sister Stella comes in, she pretends to find the whiskey bottle for the first time, and says, "Oh, I spy, I spy!" This set off gales of laughter, and the audience continued to laugh throughout the play, which of course is no laughing matter. Tallulah, never trying for laughs at all, had to carry on as best she could.

Tennessee was furious, Tallulah was shattered and bewildered. Machiz thought it might have been her mannerisms, her voice, the way she shook her head. Maxwell even suggested it was because the audience was drunk. And mostly, no doubt, it was simply because she was Tallulah.

Afterward there were reporters. Time had sent a photographer and writer. And in the course of all this, Tennessee said something dreadful. No one seems to know the exact words, but we do know what he said to Tallulah the next morning, when he and Herbert Machiz visited her, because he wrote a letter to the drama editor of the New York *Times*. They found her curled up quietly in bed, looking more like a mouse than Tallulah. When she asked Tennessee whether she had been his best Blanche, he told her she had been the worst, and she agreed.

Both he and Machiz talked frankly to her and gave her notes for the next performance. He said she followed them brilliantly that evening.

Then Tennessee left town.

Tallulah's biographer, Lee Israel, also noted that Jean Dalrymple of the City Center (who had probably started the whole enterprise) had talked with Tallulah, too. "They tried to exorcize from Tallulah's performance every one of the mannerisms that had hardened sclerotically over the years."

Tennessee did go to New York a few weeks later to see her do *Streetcar* at the City Center. Tallulah was still having trouble with her wild claque of gays—even when her performance was highly disciplined. As Lee Israel wrote:

During the crucial scene with Mitch, her last-chance beau, she looked out into the audience and said, as Blanche, "I'm looking for the Pleiades, the Seven Sisters, but these girls are not out tonight. Oh, yes they are. There they are. God bless them! All in a bunch, going home from their little bridge party." There were more than seven sisters in her audience that night. And when Tallulah uttered those lines of Tennessee Williams, pandemonium ensued.

Tallulah wanted to stop right then, but she didn't, and her performance was great. Tennessee wrote that he had tears in his eyes throughout the performance, and afterward rushed up onstage to kneel at her feet.

He and Tallulah remained close friends. He loved her for the same reasons he loved Anna Magnani. They were both gallant, unconventional and without shame. If, in the midst of a good story, Tallulah had to go to the bathroom, he would be invited to join her, sitting on the bathtub while she did what she had to do, completely without embarrassment.

He didn't think that sex was of major importance to her. He thought she was a Narcissan. She was, he wrote, one of the wittiest people he had ever known.

Tennessee went back to Florida to begin one of his most interesting experiments in stagecraft. There is no better way for a playwright to work than with an unhurried resident acting company, always available to try out scenes and compare revisions.

There was a small theater on Bird Road in Miami called Studio M, owned and directed by a young man named George Keathley, who, like Gilbert Maxwell, taught at the Lindsey Hopkins Vocational School.

Keathley had asked Tennessee to write a play for him, and Tennessee thought he would try using Studio M as a laboratory theater, for working on his new idea, which would become *Sweet Bird of Youth*. At this point *Sweet Bird* was a long one-act play about an aging gigolo, Chance, who returns to his old home town on the Gulf Coast, with his employer, the "Princess Kosmonopolis," the cover name of a rich old movie star. Chance sees his former mistress, Heavenly, who has since married the son of a political boss, whose main vote-getting platform seems to be to castrate all black men who mess around with white women.

The most difficult part to play is that of the Princess, and Keathley found Margrit Wyler, once a well-known actress in Austria and Germany. He and Tennessee both liked the way she read the part, and they decided to begin rehearsals.

Many of the actors were amateurs, and what happened must have been both exciting and bewildering. As they were learning their parts, the one-act play was day by day becoming transformed into a full-length three-act play. New scenes were coming in and old ones dropping out.

Paul Bigelow, who was there part of the time, said that the actors, in spite of their confusion, were exhilarated, believing they were taking part in what might be theatrical history.

These days Tennessee was seeing a great deal of one of his favorite women friends, Marion Vaccaro, whose husband, Regis, the alcoholic heir to a fruit fortune, had died. (He was the one who threw his glass eye into the soup.) Marion was rich, drove a lavender Cadillac and lived with her mother, Mrs. Black, in a beautiful shorefront house.

There were many lavish parties, with numerous famous guests, Hermione Gingold and Billie Burke among them. Billie Burke was there to play in *The Solid Gold Cadillac* at the Coconut Grove. Her husband, Flo Ziegfeld, had been gone for a long time. She told them, "Flo Ziegfeld and I were lovers, you know. I suppose I should have married again, but I never could because Flo spoiled me for any other man."

Tennessee kept on adding scenes to *Sweet Bird* until it was indeed a full-length play. It could even have been longer than most long plays, but he cut out a number of new scenes.

He was enjoying himself. He and Frank were living at the Towers hotel, and Frank kept everything running smoothly. Maria Britneva was there some of the time, and also another actress, Cloris Leachman. Tennessee was driving his Thunderbird around Miami, between rehearsals. His only worry was Miss Edwina, who came down for the opening. He thought she would be shocked by the sick, degenerate people in the play. But Edwina declared she was not, she was a sophisticated woman!

Edwina came down to Miami to see the opening of *Sweet Bird*, and Tennessee was worried. As he told Maxwell, "Can you imagine how I feel, knowing she's in there seeing this *awful* play with all these sick, degenerate people in it?"

If Miss Edwina was shocked, she didn't let on. She told Maxwell, "What's wrong with Tom, getting upset about my seeing this play? Doesn't he know I'm a sophisticated woman?"

Sweet Bird, with a fine performance from Margrit Wyler, seemed to go well at the tiny Studio M. He wrote his mother that it played for two weeks in Coral Gables, the final week of which was mobbed, with so many folding chairs in the aisles that the actors had trouble reaching the stage. Yet it would be three years more before it would open in New York.

After that he went back to his workroom in Key West and pulled out the old manuscript of *Battle of Angels*, which he had been thinking about, off and on, for sixteen years, ever since that disastrous evening in Boston. He had a new title for it, *Orpheus Descending*.

The writing went on steadily, both at Key West and at his Miami suite in the Towers, where his mother joined him for Christmas. A dentist friend from Memphis, named Hugh Wyatt, was visiting down there, too.

Christmas Day itself was often a detail to Tennessee when he was working violently. Maxwell reported that the typewriter was rattling away furiously when Dr. Wyatt came in and told him his mother, Miss Edwina, was packing to go back to St. Louis. Tennessee asked why she should do such a thing.

The doctor said, "Well, it's two P.M. on Christmas Day, and she hasn't heard from you since yesterday."

Tennessee was quite shocked. "Oh, Lord," he said, "I'd forgotten it was Christmas!"

So he stopped writing and took Edwina out to lunch.

Meanwhile, Kazan's film of his screenplay of *Baby Doll* was released, by Warner Brothers, and the old double standard of morality came into effect. Almost anything could be said in a play (and sometimes in a film made from a play), but in an original film (which this seemed to be, to casual observers) beware.

Baby Doll, which is practically *Alice in Wonderland* compared with some of Tennessee's other works, was condemned by the Roman Catholic Legion of Decency, and denounced by New York's Cardinal Spellman.

Dakin pointed out, in an article for *Pilot*, a Catholic publication, that the most "morally offensive" bit in the film was a scene without dialogue for which Tennessee was not responsible. Today this scene would not raise the most timid eyebrow.

Kazan was really troubled by the denunciation. He thought *Baby Doll* was a serious film. He said: "I like the film *Baby Doll* better than the film *Streetcar* and the reason is, it's more ambivalent. It combines comedy and social significance, passion and farce."

The censorship battle of *Baby Doll* actually paved the way for greater freedom of expression on the screen. Kazan said that even the scene they were complaining about was to an extent caused by his fear of censorship and the production code. He said: "It was hurt a little by censorship. Because I meant to keep a certain mystery in the film, it was never made clear what happened. When Silva (Eli Wallach) lies in the crib and she's tucking him in, there's a fadeout. Then he's fast asleep and she's sitting at the foot of the crib. It's utterly unimportant what happened—the exaggerated importance attached to any physical act!—but because so much was made of her thumb in her mouth, there was an assumption by some people that she went down on him during the fadeout; or that some sort of overt physical sexual act had been performed. But it really doesn't matter at all, because that's not what the picture is about, and *I* never thought anything did. I just thought of him as first teasing her then falling asleep in the crib...because of the film codes I think I left it more ambivalent than I would have otherwise."

The picture was given a C (for Condemned) rating. Warners fought it by putting up a block-long sign on Broadway of Carroll Baker, sucking her thumb.

The war was on. The New York *Post* carried a big story saying that Cardinal Spellman hadn't even seen the picture. Priests were sent into motion picture lobbies to take down the names of parishioners who came in to see the film, and many theater owners were frightened to show it. Business was not very good.

And yet, as Kazan said, "Now, when you see the picture it's so mild you wonder what in hell all the fuss was about."

Yet Dakin, a converted Catholic, was still concerned and continued to defend his brother in Catholic publications. Later, a Roman Catholic spokesman publicly defended the morality of Tennessee's writing. It was never the church's purpose, he said, "to forbid genuine and sincere artists from raising questions that relate to man's relationship to the world and to God. Perhaps more than any other writer in the theater today, Tennessee Williams is dealing with these fundamental issues."

Tennessee was working furiously on *Orpheus Descending*. He told about it in the preface to his *Five Plays* volume. He said that *Battle of Angels* had never gone into his trunk but had remained on his workbench. He believed that this time he had finally finished it. Three-quarters of the writing was new. The *Orpheus* version, at last, said what he had wanted to say. The preface, titled "The Past, the Present and the Perhaps," bridges the seventeen-year gap between the two versions of the play.

Audrey Wood wasted no time in having contracts signed with the Producers Company. Harold Clurman would direct.

Rehearsals were beginning in New York. There was no problem about the leading female part, the character renamed Lady; that was Maureen Stapleton. Tennessee knew they could always rely on "Mo." But the real starring role in *Orpheus*, as in *Battle*, was Val Xavier, the young vagabond in the snakeskin jacket.

The first actor they chose was wrong for it. In the Philadelphia tryout Tennessee said he seemed like a lieutenant in the Mafia. He told Clurman the young man would have to be fired, and Clurman did it. The actor came to Tennessee's suite at the Warwick Hotel in tears because he said he loved the play. But it was no use.

Then they found Cliff Robertson. His first performance in Philadelphia was, for Tennessee, the best he ever did. Everyone, including Robert Whitehead of the production company, thought they might have a hit.

Orpheus opened in New York on the first day of spring, 1957, at the big Martin Beck Theater. Those few people who had seen Battle of Angels would have noticed many changes. The characterizations are sharper. Lady, formerly Myra, is most tragic; in the new version she has been virtually bought by her husband, old Jabe. The bit about the portrait of Jesus, considered blasphemous in Boston, is missing. The writing is even more beautiful. Val's lovely story about the high-flying bird, with the most poetic lines in the play, is all new. Val thinks of himself as a bird like that, with no legs at all. It lives on the wing and sleeps on the wind.

Tennessee seems to have more empathy for this play than for any other, perhaps because Val is a partly idealized, partly mythical portrait of himself, or his psyche, unlike his other major plays up to this time, in which his leading characters are women: Amanda, Blanche, Alma, Serafina and Maggie. Yet there is another difference; Val is, as he says himself, all wings and no feet, yet all the women have their feet firmly on the ground. There is poetry running through Xavier's veins; in theirs is warm, red blood.

The reviews were not good, but not as bad as he said: "They put it down with a vengeance." With hindsight he thought it was overwritten but "under-directed" by Harold Clurman, whom he still liked and respected as a fine critic.

Orpheus closed after a few weeks. And because it had been so close to him, this hurt him deeply. On the same day that The New Yorker came out with a "devastating" attack on him, he also heard of the death of his father.

The news about C.C. arrived just before a scheduled broadcast with Mike Wallace, too late to cancel, and he fortified himself with a few drinks. By the time Wallace arrived, he was in no condition to be interviewed.

He had not seen his father for more than ten years and had not realized how great a shock it would be.

Dakin had recently returned from Formosa, where he had served during the Korean War, and was settling down with his wife Joyce at Scott Air Force Base in Illinois, across the Mississippi from St. Louis. He had heard that Cornelius was ill and planned to visit him. Dakin experienced a strange, mystical happening on the night of C.C.'s death. He and Joyce were spending the weekend at Edwina's house in Clayton. Shortly before dawn he had a dream. A Catholic priest whom he knew, Father Jerome Wilkerson, stood over him and said, "Dakin, your father is dead." A few hours later the phone rang and a telegram was read from C.C.'s sister Ella, in Knoxville, reporting that Cornelius was dead.

Edwina, who had not seen him for years, remained bitter. Her memoirs state: "Cornelius died alone in a hotel room in 1957. He died after a bad attack of asthma, and that, combined with a spree, I'm sure, caused his end."

Tennessee and Dakin met in Knoxville for the funeral. Edwina told Lucy Freeman, who had collaborated with Edwina on *Remember Me to Tom*, that Dakin had told her, "Neither Tom nor I shed a tear." Tennessee made a point of telling Maxwell this was not true. He said, "I cried." And Dakin confirms that they did.

C.C. had been living at Whittle Springs, a large, rambling frame hotel on the outskirts of Knoxville. Both Tennessee and Dakin were happy to learn that he had not been, as Edwina had implied, left alone to die. He had struck up a happy relationship with a grass widow from Dayton, a pleasant, plump, brown-haired woman who visited him regularly. Knowing their father, the brothers assumed (and hoped) that it had been a warm relationship. She had been discreet enough not to attend the funeral, but they noticed she had placed a potted plant on his grave. Cornelius had been in character right to the end.

Tennessee, in his mature years, had much more pity than hatred for C.C. In Edwina's book there is almost a tribute to him. Tennessee felt that his father needed the release of drinking and poker and his wild weekends. And he did control the drinking. He was never arrested for drunken driving or public disorder. He was always truthful and honest and hardworking. He always got up at six and arrived home for dinner every evening at six, and usually listened to the radio in the evening. Tennessee never saw him strike Edwina, except verbally, and she could hold her own in an argument. It was simply a "wrong marriage," Tennessee thought, and it shouldn't have happened.

The most heartbreaking Cornelius story is one that Tennessee told Gilbert Maxwell. Father and son had gone to see Rose at the state asylum. Cornelius held up pretty well until they left her. Then, when they reached the hall, he put his face in his hands and tried not to cry. It was no use. He put his arm against the wall, leaned his face against it and cried like a helpless child.

Cornelius certainly had a large influence on Tennessee, if only through his son's reaction to him; or, as the psychologists put it, through compensation or sublimation. When the new breed of psychoanalytical biographers gets its collective teeth into Tennessee they will prove that if Tennessee had had a nice, understanding, cuddly daddy with a lopsided smile, he would have led a well-adjusted, heterosexual life as an assistant professor of English at some college, with a cute wife and three beautiful children. The plays? Simply catharsis. He would have had no psychological need to write them at all.

While Tennessee and Dakin were in Knoxville, Aunt Ella took them for a drive up Kingston Pike to visit the large brick residence of their great-great-grandfather, John Williams, United States senator. In the early nineteenth century it had been a showplace. It is now an orphanage. President James Polk, Sam Houston and Davy Crockett had all visited there.

CHAPTER 22

Tennessee returned to New York to begin an odd summer, the summer of the psychiatrist and the Chinese apartment, the summer in which he was "forbidden" to write—which was like forbidding him to breathe. And it was the summer in which he wrote the weird but haunting play *Suddenly Last Summer*.

Tennessee said in a long interview with Robert Jennings, published in Playboy in 1973, that his main conflict was between his creative and his personal life. Since he put a greater value on his creative life, the personal one was often at risk.

This summer he was seeing the psychoanalyst Dr. Lawrence Kubie, whom he liked very much, but with whom he had strong differences of opinion. Kubie told him that he had written nothing but "violent melodrama" because of the violence of the times. Who was wrong, Kubie or Tennessee's memory? What violent melodrama? In his four major Critics' Award plays there is no violent melodrama at all, except for the "rape" of Blanche, which was really by consent. Kubie, he said, used rather violent-sounding methods, imitating his father and screaming at him. He told Tennessee he should break with Frank Merlo and become heterosexual. Since he could not do that, he broke with Kubie instead.

In fact, he was not at all sure he wanted to be well adjusted. He said that if he got rid of his demons, he would lose his angels.

But Kubie's worst sin, by Tennessee's reckoning, was to tell him to rest, to stop working. He even seemed to trick him, he thought, into not working by making appointments in the morning—knowing that he always worked in the morning. If there was a 9:30 A.M. appointment, he would get up at 4:00 A.M., and do the writing beforehand.

At the time of the Playboy interview, he said he would not "get within a mile of a shrink now."

Gilbert Maxwell had come up to New York from Florida with him and

215

reported on the extracurricular activities. One of the first things Tennessee did was to rent a second or playpen type of apartment on the other side of town. He was visiting a friend, a Brazilian consul, who lived in a hotel apartment on the West Side. He liked the building, heard that there was a vacant apartment next door and immediately wrote out a check to rent it.

He then went down to Chinatown and bought paper lanterns, wind chimes and bead portieres. He announced, "This apartment is supposed to be tacky." He called it his West Side pad and it performed a serious function. His young friends, usually southern and often hungry, could meet there, eat delicatessen food and drink and read poetry, and leave the East Side apartment for Tennessee and Frank—and work. Frank Krause, a male nurse, was one who moved right away into the West Side pad. It was like a private club to which Tennessee could go when he was lonesome, and it gave shelter and nourishment to a number of artistic but often insolvent young men.

During that summer he also visited the Virgin Islands and Havana. And a while after that he finally gave up the West Side pad. That was about a week after a woman columnist had written: "What famous playwright is going regularly to an analyst and, at the same time, throwing Nero-like orgies in his West Side apartment?"

Maxwell said that the orgies consisted of "poetry readings and parlor games, topped off with a lavish banquet of cold cuts, potato salad and cole slaw from the corner delicatessen."

In between "orgies" and headshrinking he finished *Suddenly Last Summer* rather quickly, before the summer was over. He had a script with him one day when he was out at the Long Island resort of Southampton. He met Herbert Machiz and showed it to him. Machiz was delighted and showed it to John C. Wilson, the producer, and there was a quick production. Tennessee was impressed by the way Machiz could get things rolling.

They all decided that *Suddenly* was not quite long enough for a whole evening and found another of Tennessee's short plays, *Something Unspoken*, which also had a New Orleans background. The two, collectively, were called *Garden District*, after that fashionable section of the city.

They were able to use one of the best of the uptown Off-Broadway theaters, the York, on First Avenue, and made the wise choice of Anne Meacham for the difficult role of Catharine. (Tennessee dedicated the printed version of the play to her.) It opened on January 6, 1958.

Both the plays are dominated by monster-women, rich and imperious. Cornelia, in *Something Unspoken*, is derived partly from one facet of Edwina's life; she was the regent (or head lady) of the St. Louis chapter of the Daughters of the American Revolution. During the action of the play, Cornelia is deliberately staying away from a meeting of the Confederate Daughters, at which the regent is being elected. But the play is really about her domination, almost the enslavement, of her paid companion, Grace, a widow some twenty years younger, who is on this day celebrating (or mourning) her fifteenth year of servitude. There are overtones of lesbianism—unspoken. The finagling for the regency (here not successful) may well have come from Tennessee's observations of Edwina, but not Cornelia's cruelty and domination. Edwina was not like that. And Freudians will surely quiver over the Cornelia-Cornelius similarity.

The second female monster, in *Suddenly Last Summer*, Mrs. Venable, is not Edwina at all, but the horror of the play is the threat of lobotomy, the brain operation that destroys memory, as it did the memory of Rose Williams. Mrs. Venable wants to force Catharine, the girl, to be lobotomized so that she will forget the unspeakable thing that happened to her son while he and Catharine were in Spain the previous summer.

This play, more than any other of Tennessee's, is a triumph of sheer writing over conventional playmaking. By the copybook it has no right to succeed. It is scarcely a play at all, only a series of monologues. The two principal ones are probably the most overpowering in modern theatrical literature: the one about the massacre of the baby turtles by the sea gulls and the one about the actual devouring of Mrs. Venable's son by Spanish urchins. The main character, the son, never appears in the play. He can't; he is dead.

It is not an evening for the prudish, the squeamish or the fainthearted, since it is concerned with lesbianism, pederasty, cannibalism, brain-breaking and a soupçon of incest, perhaps the richest devil's brew ever stewed in a bouillon of beautiful poetry. No wonder there was extreme caution about its reception.

The opening-night audience seemed to be both stunned and delighted. Tennessee wrote that Anne Meacham tore into her part like a tigress. Hortense Alden (formerly married to James T. Farrell) was excellent as both Grace, the enslaved widow, and Mrs. Venable.

Tennessee said he was well fortified with both barbiturates and alcohol for the opening. He saw Kazan and his wife down front and asked them what they thought. Kazan would not commit himself, but the two of them joined Tennessee and Frank at their place to wait for the reviews.

The TV notices were poor and Tennessee became hysterical, shouting, "If the theater doesn't need me, I don't need it!" But then the *Times* and the *Herald-Tribune* reviews arrived and they were raves. Atkinson said it was "startling proof of what a man can do with words...an exercise in the necromancy of writing...no one else can use ordinary words with so much grace, allusiveness and power." Atkinson was simply bowled over by its beauty, and the beauty was surely there. Later, after long reflection, he wrote, "Mr. Williams' preoccupation with infamy culminates in *Suddenly Last Summer*—a perfectly written drama that is thoroughly repellent."

Suddenly Last Summer is a good illustration of the different arts of the stage and the screen. Tennessee said he sold it in one telephone conversation. He was sitting beside a swimming pool in Miami when the film producer Sam Spiegel called long distance. Spiegel asked how much he wanted for the film rights to *Suddenly*. Tennessee suggested $50,000, plus 20 percent of the profits.

Normally that is a dangerous kind of deal, because it is very difficult to discover what the real profits of a picture are, since the bookkeeping is largely controlled by the film company itself.

Sam agreed, and made the film, a big production, with Elizabeth Taylor as Catharine, Montgomery Clift as the doctor and Katharine Hepburn as Mrs. Venable.

The story that the play had told about was shown. The cameras looked at a mental institution and went to the Spanish beach where the homosexual poet had his confrontation with the Spanish boys. Tennessee called it "a bad film," but his judgment about the profits had been good, or lucky. It made a great deal of money, and his share was large.

But strangely enough the words, and the telling of the story on stage, were more dramatic than showing on the screen what really happened.

Tennessee spent a great deal of time the rest of the year moving back and forth between Florida and New York, partly because he was now becoming a producer as well as a playwright.

Ken Tynan, remembering the playwright's youthful *cri de coeur* at the time of *Menagerie*, about businessmen and gamblers in the theater, chided him about becoming, in his affluent middle age, one of them himself. He and Kazan were planning to produce *Sweet Bird of Youth* mainly by themselves, with their own money, though Cheryl Crawford would be the nominal and acting "producer." Tynan estimated that Tennessee and Kazan between them would own 75 percent of the production.

And that, of course, was gambling on a high-rolling scale. The budget on *Sweet Bird* was to be around $150,000, very expensive then for a straight play. It meant that if the play failed commercially, he and Kazan would lose a great deal of money. But if it became a hit, he would receive not only his royalties but a share of the profits as well, and a much bigger share in any possible film sale.

For better or worse, the Broadway theater was not only art, it was big-stakes gambling of the most dangerous kind; out of every five plans actually produced and opening, only one succeeded. The other four failed. A producer had one chance in five to win.

So he had a gambler's as well as an artist's reasons for working very hard that year on the revisions of *Sweet Bird*.

Another high-rolling Williams production was already underway; the gamblers were MGM, making a big-budget film of *Cat*. It would be Elizabeth Taylor's first Williams role (*Suddenly Last Summer* came later) and Paul Newman's as well. Richard Brooks was directing and working on the screenplay.

For a while it looked as though the production would be postponed or canceled. Just before shooting began, Liz Taylor's husband, Mike Todd, was killed in a plane crash. She later told Dakin that she was crushed. He was, she said, "the moon, the stars—everything—to me!" She said she cried for days. She thought she would give up doing *Cat*. But what, she said she asked herself, would Mike have wanted her to do? He would have wanted her to carry on, and she did so much want to do a Williams role. So she did and, she told Dakin, the film saved her life. She put her "whole heart—what there was left—and soul into acting," and found that she could face the cameras again. She certainly made a delectable Cat, almost hotter than the roof.

The film was highly successful and made a great deal of money. And Tennessee's name, in the celebrity sweepstakes, was boosted up to the same level as that of the President of the United States, and almost as high as that of Liz Taylor herself.

Dakin added that he was careful, during the above conversation, not to mention the name of Eddie Fisher, who became Liz's moon and stars a discreet interval later.

Paul Newman had scarcely finished his last retakes for *Cat* when he had to hurry on to New York to play Chance Wayne in the Broadway version of *Sweet Bird*.

By this time Tennessee thought *Sweet Bird* was in shape for rehearsals, and started writing another play, *Period of Adjustment*. More than ever before he was writing for laughs. It was the closest he had yet come to a drawing-room comedy, if Ralph's tacky living room, about to sink into an underground cavern, could be called a drawing room. This is the story of two couples, the men air force buddies back from the Korean War. One of the wives was from Big Spring, Texas, the hometown of Joyce, the wife of that air force character, Dakin, back from the Korean War. But there are almost no other similarities. The two are quite different from Dakin and Joyce.

The two men are seriously considering a business venture: raising Texas longhorn cattle for use in TV westerns. Ralph's wife has just left him, at the time when George's new bride, on her honeymoon, arrives alone, not sure whether her flight-shocked new groom is following her or has already abandoned her.

The first act is the funniest act that Tennessee has ever written—and at the same time one of the saddest. It is not black comedy, it is tragicomedy, the hardest kind to write, the most difficult to make viable. Chaplin did it. Few others have succeeded. If Tennessee had been able to sustain this delicate balance, *Period of Adjustment* would have been a masterpiece. The next two acts seem to be mourning the fact that a perfect one-act play has no place in the commercial theater.

Tennessee directed the play himself at the Coconut Grove Playhouse in Miami. It was just the thing for that slightly tipsy Miami audience at Christmastime, and the theatergoers seemed surprised and pleased at the happy ending. Not a single person was raped, castrated, lynched, committed or even eaten.

Tennessee considered it a tryout, to guide him in rewriting the play later for Broadway.

He came up to New York for rehearsals of *Sweet Bird of Youth*. Opposite Paul Newman, as Chance the gigolo, was Geraldine Page, who had, since the Off-Broadway *Summer and Smoke*, become a Broadway star. Madeleine Sherwood, Rip Torn and Sidney Blackmer, all very well known, were also in the cast.

About halfway through the first reading, Tennessee suddenly had violent misgivings, jumped up and told them to stop. He rushed out into Times Square, went home and took a drink and a pill.

That evening Kazan and Molly visited him, and talked to him quietly and gently. And gradually, he said, he became calm, decided he loved them and trusted them.

So they continued rehearsals. But Kazan was worried. As he said later: "*Sweet Bird of Youth* was a script with a fault, a serious fault: its interest was split between two characters. The central character in act one, the old actress, disappears in act two, and I thought that play needed some sort of directorial 'holding up.' So I had an enormous television screen and I projected things on it. I did some stunts with that play, because I thought it needed it."

Any first-class director, like Kazan, has to be, to an extent, a play doctor. Kazan must have recognized that *Sweet Bird* has another diagnostic problem. It is almost two plays, the romantic (in this case closer to antiromantic) relationship between Chance, and his employer, the Princess. This play, set in the bedroom, is in acts one and two. The other play is the political play, against the racism of Boss Finley. Kazan was concerned with helping Tennessee stitch these two together, as firmly as possible.

Walter Kerr stated that Kazan had even cleaned up the play: "an incest motif that had appeared in the original text was no longer stressed."

Geraldine Page was having trouble with the difficult part of the old actress, and at one point she said that "Kazan had given up. He didn't know what to tell me." The problem was the third act. Kazan and Tennessee called her aside. She said: "The atmosphere was so kind of strained. Finally Tennessee started talking to me. He used such wonderful direction. He really ought to direct sometime. He has fantastic directorial gifts, but he's so polite that maybe he has trouble forcing his opinions on people.... He was telling me that that big speech in the third act has to top in dramatic intensity the second-act curtain, which is a logical thing to say. But the second-act curtain was so powerful! I told him nothing short of an atomic bomb would top his second-act curtain. And with his southern charm, he said, 'Oh, yes, honey, you can do it. You can do it.'... And he was saying that the language, particularly in that speech, was heightened language, and that unless it had a vast emotional current underneath to carry it, it would sound pretentious."

It was during the *Sweet Bird* rehearsals that the strange and tragic Diana Barrymore affair began. Diana was trying out for the part of Catharine in Herbert Machiz's touring company of *Suddenly Last Summer*.

Diana, the daughter of John Barrymore and the poet Michael Strange, was at this time a troubled actress. One line spoken by her father, the "Great Profile," tells her story; on meeting her one day he said, "You are my little girl three wives back, are you not?" He didn't seem entirely sure; he'd hardly ever seen her.

John had been divorced from Michael Strange not long after Diana was born, and Miss Strange, née Blanche Oelrichs, was mainly preoccupied with her career as a poet and actress. Diana spent most of her life with governesses in Paris and New York and other places. By the time she was twenty she was drinking heavily. She tried too hard to become a great movie star. She certainly had the looks, and at twenty was gorgeous. One film critic described her in an early film: "Diana played the role to the hilt and right on past the hilt and up to the elbow."

Diana became an alcoholic and almost a derelict, even shoplifting, stealing vegetables from a supermarket. Her doctor told her, "You're on a dreadful merry-go-round: alcohol, barbiturates, stimulants. If you don't get off it quickly, you will die."

During the course of all this, she had three unsuccessful marriages. At the time of the *Sweet Bird* rehearsals she was thirty-seven, had given up drinking entirely about three years before and had "written" (told to Gerold Frank) her autobiography, called *Too Much, Too Soon*. It had been a bestseller, bringing her quite a lot of money. She was making a desperately determined attempt at a comeback, and decided that the key to it was Tennessee Williams, whom she knew, at first, only through his plays.

The gambit was clear to her: she had to have a great play, containing enormous depths of understanding, to lift her to the kind of stardom she imagined—and only Tennessee could write it. She laid her plans, deliberately, to get to know him, and to get him to write such a play for her.

The gambit would play itself out in less than a year, and would be almost as dramatic, and as tragic, as one of Tennessee's plays.

In the past two years she had served her Williams apprenticeship by playing both Blanche in *Streetcar* and Maggie in *Cat* in touring companies. She made a calculated point of getting to know both Gilbert Maxwell and Dakin well, and wrote innumerable letters and made many long telephone calls to them both. The whole affair is richly documented because of this.

Apparently she did come to like both a great deal, but she admitted later to Maxwell, "Did you actually realize I was using you for weeks after we met [at a *Sweet Bird* rehearsal] merely to get closer to Williams?" Maxwell said he did realize it, and didn't mind. He, in fact, fell in love with her, and creates an extraordinary portrait of her in his book and a fine, detailed account of the whole affair. Diana's first objective was to persuade Tennessee to give her the part of the Princess in *Sweet Bird* in the London production. So she came to the theater to watch Geraldine Page rehearse the part with Paul Newman. She sat alone nervously, chain-smoking cigarettes.

Diana already had strong feelings about Kazan, who, she felt, had kept her from this job. She later wrote to Dakin: "My hatred for Kazan burns black—if he had not wanted to play Svengali with Miss Page I would have done it [the Broadway production]. The woman is *me*—as I was finished at 36—I was! If I had been given a reading it would have been mine."

Diana did win the part in the touring company of *Suddenly Last Summer* and was rehearsing it.

Tennessee and the *Sweet Bird* company moved to Boston for a tryout. He flew back to New York only long enough to see the ANTA production of his one-act play about D. H. Lawrence, *I Rise in Flame, Cried the Phoenix*. When he arrived, there was Diana, escorted by Maxwell. She was in her new blue mink. The play was well produced, with Alfred Ryder as Lawrence, Viveca Lindfors as Frieda and Rosemary Harris as Brett. Audrey Wood was there, too, and both she and Tennessee were pleased with the production. There were no plans to make it into a big, commercial Broadway venture.

The Boston tryout of *Sweet Bird* went well, and the company returned to New York for the March 10 opening at the Martin Beck Theater. Dakin, who was still concerned about his brother's spiritual side, had come to New York for the opening, bringing several friends, including a young Catholic priest, Father Jerry Wilkerson.

On the day of the opening, Dakin invited Tennessee to lunch at the Algonquin Hotel. Without telling Tennessee, he brought Father Wilkerson along. Tennessee was upset and nervous, of course, because of the opening; he was reluctant to talk to a stranger, and his mind was far from theology.

But to his credit, he stayed with it, discussed Dakin's new book, *Nails of Protest* (which he had read twice, and had found well written and persuasive) and the doctrines of life after death and original sin, both of which gave him trouble. At the moment he was more concerned about life after the critics, in about twelve hours, and he could not understand why we should all be blamed because Eve had eaten that apple.

Father Wilkerson was kind and reassuring. He did not feel that Tennessee needed to worry about punishment after death, and said, essentially, there was nothing we could do about what Eve did.

After lunch they went over to the Martin Beck, where Kazan was giving his players their last instructions before the ordeal. Paul Newman, more used to cameras than starring in a Broadway first-night, was the most nervous of all, and the director was patiently going over lines with him.

A few hours later it opened, with a flourish. Geraldine Page was tremendous, displaying, as Tynan said, "knock-down flamboyance and drag-out authority." At one point she brought the whole house to its feet, screaming and clapping. They needn't have worried about Newman. He was excellent as Chance. There were countless curtain calls. It was almost a riot.

They all went to the home of the Renfields to wait for the reviews — Dakin, Joyce, Father Wilkerson, Paul Newman and Joanne Woodward (eight months pregnant), Lee Strasberg of the Actors Studio and his daughter Susan, and many others. Good news began to come in by telephone and finally galley proofs of the reviews. They were good. Tennessee and Kazan, as both artists and entrepreneurs, were delighted.

The play was a popular and commercial hit, though it won no major prizes. It would have a long run and was sold to MGM. Both Page and Newman played the same parts in the film.

Tennessee, greatly relieved but never satisfied, took off quickly for Key West to work on revisions of *Period of Adjustment* and a new play with a Mexican setting. He was continuing to use alcohol moderately in connection with his work, but was by no means an alcoholic. Diana had noticed a pint bottle in his jacket pocket at rehearsal, and said it reminded her of her past.

She was busy in New Haven, rehearsing with the touring company of *Suddenly Last Summer*. Maxwell, who was there for the New Haven opening night, wrote that Diana did a powerful performance as Catharine. "The Barrymore talent was there in this thing she projected, as well as the powerful, husky voice..."

Diana, remaining a sober, hardworking actress, continued on tour with *Suddenly*. Tennessee saw her during her successful run in Chicago, and it was there that Dakin and his wife Joyce saw her perform for the first and only time. They thought she had been very good. (The critics had been favorable, too. Sidney Harris, for example, wrote that it was "the restoration of a great name to the American theatre.")

Dakin and Joyce went backstage to talk with her, and made a date for Sunday brunch the next day at the Henrici. Dakin thought she seemed reasonably happy, though lonely—as most people are on tour.

But she was still pushing her thing about Tennessee. She wrote Dakin a letter immediately afterward.

> Sunday was a joyous, glorious day—you were a complete surprise (as was Tom). You emanate warmth, goodness, and love of your fellow man.... I hope you liked me as much as I did you. One thing, the most important thing, that we share is our love of Tom. I don't mean this in a sacrilegious way, but he is my saviour on earth. Through him I went on the wagon—I had to relearn Blanche after having played it with my dead husband for three years before—I told myself I had to stop drinking if I wanted to really be a good Blanche...

There is something pathetic about an effusive letter like that, written to a man she had just met. There is a kind of silent scream in it. She went on to say she had met Tennessee and had "fallen instantly in love with him." She had found through him the motivation to change her life. She

also added that she wanted to do the London version of *Sweet Bird*.
Dakin sent her a copy of his book, *Nails of Protest*, and they corresponded
about it. And when Diana came to St. Louis in May she visited Miss Edwina
at her home. Dakin arranged for her to talk with Father Wilkerson, and
they did, for several hours. He made it possible for her to be accepted back
into the church, and she went to confession for the first time in years.

Diana continued to telephone both Dakin and Gilbert Maxwell from all
over the country, as she continued on tour, sometimes talking for more
than half an hour. She kept telling Dakin of her plans to marry Tennessee.
Yet she must have known he had a different way of life, because she told
Dakin what had happened one evening at Tennessee's apartment. Frankie
was out and she was "alone" with him—alone, that is, with Anna Magnani
and Marion Vaccaro. Finally Frank came back and ran them all out. So
surely she knew about Frank.

In June Ethel Barrymore died, which left Diana the last of the Barrymore
acting clan. Maxwell invited her to a party to cheer her up. Tennessee,
who was in New York on a visit, joined them. They had a good time,
Diana didn't drink a drop and left alone, sober.

But she had taken two sleeping pills, and while cooking eggs for a late-
night snack in her apartment had "fainted," fallen on the floor and awakened
with her right thigh badly burned from hot grease. A doctor said she might
even los. her leg, but they were able to save it. When Maxwell asked her
if she had been drinking, she flew into a rage.

With her leg still bandaged, Diana rehearsed for a week's engagement
of *Streetcar* in Pennsylvania. She was desperate to have Tennessee come
and see her in it, and though he was working hard he did come for the
opening night. She looked thin and tired, but was determined to do a good
job for Tennessee.

Maxwell said she was very good. She had many curtain calls. Afterward,
Tennessee and Maxwell went back to see her. She was exhausted, "drenched
in sweat, shaking, crying." Tennessee put his arms around her and said,
"My darling, you were tremendous. You have a great voice and you are a
Barrymore."

That evening, Maxwell said, she ate a proper meal for the first time in
days. Tennessee's approval seemed to have meant everything to her.

One Sunday, Tennessee hired a limousine and drove her and Maxwell
north of Manhattan, along the Hudson, to visit two of his favorite women,
his sister Rose and Carson McCullers.

He had taken good care of Rose. She lived in a pleasant cottage at Stony
Lodge, near Ossining, in a pretty wooded area with a swimming pool and
tennis courts. Tennessee went in and brought her out to the limousine.

She was still pretty and seemed cheerful. They all drove off to have lunch at a restaurant.

Maxwell asked if she had seen any of her brother's plays. She replied, "Yes, one. *The Rose Tattoo.* Very poor."

Maxwell wrote, "Tennessee choked on his drink as he set it down, remarking, 'Very astute critic.'"

Then they drove up to Nyack, across the Hudson, to see Carson McCullers in her white Victorian house. Carson had been very ill but now was improved, sitting by the fireplace, smiling. She and Tennessee talked about the dramatization of her short novel, *Ballad of the Sad Cafe,* written after *The Member of the Wedding.* She was hoping to have Anna Magnani play in it. Tennessee suggested she give him an autographed copy of the book and he would take it to Anna. (These things often take a long time. The play version, as dramatized by Edward Albee, did not open for another four years.)

It was a strange group, Rose smoking cigarettes and smiling rather secretly to herself; Diana, who hadn't read any of Carson's work, sitting quietly and a bit tense; and Maxwell, quite subdued.

They drove Rose back to her cottage. As Tennessee left Diana and Maxwell to take her inside, Diana broke down and cried. She had seen Rose, and Tennessee's tragic love for her, and it was more than she could stand.

They didn't speak of Rose all the way back. It was not until they were back at Tennessee's apartment and had had a couple of drinks (coffee for Diana) that Tennessee finally broke down, and in a kind of violent catharsis let it all out, his love for Rose and his terrible sorrow about her. Maxwell said it affected him more deeply than anything Tennessee had ever put on paper. There were no tape recorders and no notes, and none of the three could have reconstructed it accurately. But, with apologies, Maxwell tried to put down an approximation of it:

> She was the best of us all, do you understand? More beautiful, more intelligent, sweeter and warmer than anyone. Not one of us was fit to stoop and tie her shoes... the torments this girl has endured are not to be mentioned, yet she stands there before you, triumphant, with her head up and her shoulders back and looks you in the face and silently tells you, this brave little creature, "Look at me. Somehow I came through. I am here."

Diana was crying again and Maxwell was almost numb with emotion. If Tennessee had put such a scene in a play, no one would have believed it or accepted it: a poet is in love with a beautiful and talented but sadly flawed actress who is (or says she is) in love with a famous playwright, who in turn is in love, spiritually, with his sister, who has become a kind of lovely china doll, and he is living in sin with a former pharmacist's mate of the navy. A critic, examining this, would say, "In his previous plays, Mr. Williams has given us some unlikely fantasies, but this one is simply incredible. Why can't he give us a slice of real life?"

After this almost unbearable trauma, they needed something even better than a psychiatrist. Tennessee suggested they go visit Anna Magnani, and that proved to be the right thing.

Anna cheered them up, told Maxwell he was beautiful, told Diana she was too skinny to be sexy and should eat more and told Tennessee he had better come out to the movie set the following day, where she and Marlon Brando were having a minor war over the filming of *Orpheus Descending*. (Hollywood, of course, would not hold still for a highbrow title like that, so they borrowed a different title from another of Tennessee's plays, which had nothing to do with *Orpheus* at all, called *The Fugitive Kind*. This was the play that almost made him jump out of a St. Louis hotel window, in 1936.)

He promised Anna he would go out to the set on Long Island the next day. Then they all went out and had a big Italian dinner.

He did go out to the Long Island set. The problem was complicated. Magnani was in love with Brando, and at the same time the language problem was driving both of them crazy. As Tennessee explained years later to Dennis Brown, Magnani didn't know English very well and had to learn her lines like a parrot. But Brando was never able, Tennessee said, to read a line the way it was written, or the same way twice. He was always ad-libbing. Magnani expected some definite word as a cue, and Brando would say "ummm," or "ahhhh," or perhaps just grunt, and Anna couldn't tell where she was and it drove her crazy. But that didn't stop her from being in love with Brando.

So she asked Tennessee to write a love letter to Brando for her. He did. It took about ten different drafts to say it the way Anna wanted it, and then she sent it to Brando. Brando didn't bother to answer it. So the love affair, which never got started, was over, and that made the language problem, and the grunts, even worse. It was a wonder they ever finished shooting *The Fugitive Kind*. In spite of everything, the film was a better-than-average translation of the play, and it followed the action of the play closely, perhaps even too closely. There are few exterior scenes, most of which are shots of Brando and Joanne Woodward riding around in a derelict Jaguar roadster. Sidney Lumet, the director, must have had a dreadful time with the diction. With Magnani's heavy accent and Brando's grunting, some of the dialogue really needs subtitles in English.

Tennessee kept on writing his Mexican play, which he called *The Night of the Iguana*, and that summer an early version of it was given in a tryout at the Spoleto Festival in Italy. He also visited the set where Elizabeth Taylor, Montgomery Clift and Katharine Hepburn were filming *Suddenly Last Summer*. He was being treated like a pasha. Sam Spiegel put his Mediterranean yacht at Tennessee's disposal. He also dashed down to Mississippi, where location work was being done on *The Fugitive Kind*.

Diana accompanied him on one of the junkets to Europe. And in case anyone should get romantic ideas, Marion Vaccaro went along, too. Diana had a good time, in spite of the third party, and wrote to Dakin: "It was an idyll!...I have never been so happy! Just to sit at your brother's feet, and to light his cigarettes!" The subtleties and complexities of these relationships were lost on the tabloid reporters, who were sure there was a romance. Maxwell quotes one headline:

TENNESSEE'S BACK, AND DIANA'S GOT HIM!

Not quite.

Diana later went on to the Virgin Islands without Tennessee, to visit friends. Meanwhile, another actress was doing fine things with Williams material and frightening Diana.

Claire Luce had done a highly professional job in *Portrait of a Madonna* and *Suddenly Last Summer* in New Jersey. Diana saw these performances, knew Claire Luce was good and knew she also wanted to play the Princess in the London production of *Sweet Bird*.

Then Tennessee came back to New York and Diana gave him, Cheryl Crawford and Audrey Wood a reading as the Princess. Part of it she did lying on her back, since the scene was played in bed. She had been visibly nervous. All three agreed that Diana was not right for the part. None could have realized how seriously Diana would take that decision. Tennessee said he was writing a part for her, so that she needn't be too disappointed.

Shortly before Christmas there was a double preview of Tennessee's films, perhaps the first time in history that a playwright has seen, for the first time, the finished films of two of his plays on the same night. He first went with Diana, Cheryl Crawford and Maxwell to Procter's RKO to see *The Fugitive Kind* with, as he wrote, the "two huge talents that clashed," those of Magnani and Brando. For some reason a rough crowd of people hissed and booed them as they left the theater.

Tennessee then took Diana in a cab to Sam Spiegel's apartment for a private preview of *Suddenly Last Summer*.

This must have been unsettling for both of them, for him to watch a film that had been changed so completely from his play, and for her to watch Liz Taylor playing the part that she had played so many times on stage, all over the country.

By this time Diana had only one more month to live. She was found on January 25 by her manager, Violla Rubber, lying naked and dead in her apartment. Various things were found broken. Some reports suggested suicide. Some even speculated there might have been foul play. And no one knows to this day exactly what happened.

But many events leading up to her death were known to many people, including Tennessee. Dakin, too, heard from her in the few weeks just before her death.

Diana persuaded Maxwell to bring Tennessee to her apartment for a pre-Christmas drink, and he did come, late, bringing a magnum of champagne, and was then embarrassed because he had forgotten she was on the wagon. (She later gave it, wrappings and all, to Violla Rubber.)

That evening Diana really pinned him down about *Sweet Bird*. She told him, "I was made to play this part and I'm going to have it."

Tennessee told her he still did not think the role was for her but said, "Suppose you did play it in London, would you be satisfied?"

She shouted, "No!" and then told him more calmly that it still would not be enough.

Diana was depressed over Christmas. She wrote to Dakin:

> Christmas has become a commercial monstrosity and, when you are alone as I am, it simply becomes too much. I may brave the crowds for a trip to St. Ignatius' Church where I was baptised, but that's all.

She was invited to spend Christmas Day with her half brother, Leonard Thomas, and his family, but didn't go. She had their daughters come to see her.

Sometime during the holidays Diana began to drink again. On New Year's Eve she went to a big party in the Village at Danny Blum's with Tennessee and Paul Bigelow. They reported that she had been pretty high.

She was going out occasionally with Glenn Stencel, who had a bit part in *Sweet Bird*. She was drinking then, too, but Stencel said only moderately.

Maxwell was worried. At one time he reminded her that she had written in her book that she had tried suicide, but would not try it again. Did she mean that?

She said she did mean it. "I've thought of it, yes—but I never would, because I've already brought enough disgrace on my family."

Dakin reported the same thing. He had talked with her on the telephone so many times. Once, shortly before Christmas, she had seen the film, *On the Beach*, in which the last survivors of the nuclear fallout were taking suicide pills. She told Dakin she thought this was "appalling" even though the people were sure to die very soon anyway. She did not approve of suicide under any conditions.

Later she told Maxwell that her doctor had prescribed "two glasses of sherry and at least one shot of bourbon daily" for her heart. Maxwell didn't believe it.

A few days later, while attending a performance of *Sweet Bird* on the night when Rip Torn took over the role of Chance from Paul Newman, she began to cry during the second act, and Maxwell had to take her home. There she poured herself a straight drink, but she "merely sipped it," he said.

There was a report that four policemen had removed her from the audience of a Broadway play, *The Andersonville Trial*, when she arrived intoxicated. Maxwell said she had told him later it was another girl in her party who caused the disturbance.

Tennessee had left New York by then. *The Night of the Iguana* was ready for an American tryout, and he was arranging to do it in Miami, at the Coconut Grove Playhouse. Violla Rubber was going to produce it.

On Saturday night, January 23, Diana telephoned Maxwell. Her voice sounded strained. He asked if she wanted him to come over, and she said it was not necessary. She had other guests; he spoke to one of them, who said he probably should come.

There was deep snow in New York that night, but he came right away. When he arrived she was on the telephone, talking to Violla in Florida. She had a drink beside her but was not drunk. Maxwell thought she was a bit high from Seconal, "but that was not unusual." She remained high-spirited throughout the evening.

The next night, Sunday, she had another party. Among the guests were Essee Kupcinet, wife of Irv Kupcinet of the Chicago "Kup's Show," Edward Thomajam, Kazan's assistant on *Sweet Bird*, Glenn Stencel and a pilot friend of his named Cook.

They were running low on liquor, and Diana telephoned Gene Cavallero, Jr. of the Colony restaurant to get two bottles of whiskey. He said it was illegal for him to sell her liquor in bottles.

At about two A.M. the last guest, Glenn Stencel, left. He was probably the last person to see her alive. He had scarcely arrived at his West Side apartment when Diana telephone him. She was terribly depressed and wanted him to come back. He refused. He had a cold and would be working Monday night. Afterward, of course, he felt awful about it.

Maxwell, who had not been at the party, phoned her the next morning. He said her voice was "no more than a husky whisper." She sounded exhausted. As far as anyone knows, that was the last time Diana spoke to anyone.

Violla Rubber telephoned Diana's apartment at 3:00 P.M., Monday, to tell her some good news. A Canadian producer wanted her to play Blanche in a production of *Streetcar*. Diana did not answer. Later her maid came into her apartment and found her nude body in bed. The maid telephoned Violla Rubber, who came immediately.

When Maxwell called Diana's apartment Violla answered, and said she would call him later. Moments afterward someone phoned him. It was on the radio. Diana was dead.

Maxwell telephoned Tennessee in Florida, who said he had just heard it himself on the radio, and would be in New York as soon as he could get there. The papers were full of stories, many of them suggesting suicide.

Tennessee arrived the next day. He flew up in cotton slacks and a khaki jacket, without an overcoat and carrying only an airline bag. He had even forgotten the keys to his New York apartment. His maid had to bring them down from Harlem by taxi. He sent a blanket of violets for Diana's coffin.

Dakin says she had never told Tennessee about her return to Catholicism, and was given a Protestant burial service. It was read by the Reverend Sidney Lanier of St. Thomas's Episcopal Church, Tennessee and Dakin's cousin.

Could Diana have been murdered? At the funeral Violla Rubber whispered to Tennessee that Diana's bedroom was a wreck, and certainly looked as though there had been violence. Diana had been lying naked, face down, with blood streaming out of her mouth. A heavy marble ashtray had been shattered against the wall, and there were other signs of a struggle. None of these facts, she said, had been reported to the papers.

The police report said there was no "evident cause" of her death, and no indication that she had committed suicide, no evidence of large suicidal doses of pills, and "no signs of violence."

There was nothing sinister about the fact that the body was unclothed. Diana usually slept in the nude.

Her doctor said she had died of a heart attack. It seems almost certain that she did not deliberately kill herself.

Tennessee was deeply disturbed by her death. He considered her a great person and a great lady. He once told Dakin that she was an actress of great talent, but no control. He thought that her heart just gave out. She was a terribly troubled girl who had been ill and was making a valiant battle.

Almost hidden beneath the many flowers surrounding Diana's coffin was a bright red apple, the traditional gift sent by one Barrymore to another on the occasion of openings—and closings.

CHAPTER 23

Deeply saddened by Diana's death, Tennessee went back to work in Key West, still polishing *Period of Adjustment* and *The Night of the Iguana*.

In March he received an advance copy of Don Windham's novel *The Hero Continues*, admitted by the author to be a *roman à clef* about Tennessee, and dedicated to him.

Windham's description of the main character, Denis, is a portrait of an initially impoverished and dedicated writer, similar in many ways to Tennessee. And Morgan, the younger character, who had also come up from the South, may be based upon himself. The young man, he wrote, was similar to Denis in "idealism and ambition."

By this time there had been a long hiatus in the Williams-Windham association. The main correspondence had ended almost five years before, after their failure to find a producer for Don's play, *The Starless Air*.

Tennessee read *The Hero Continues* and wrote Windham detailed letters about it. He felt that the author had been merciful to him, that he "loved" the book, though he thought the hero was a "zombie" and a "shadow."

Sweet Bird had by this time left Broadway but was still touring the country—amazingly, Tennessee had begun to rewrite it. He was, as he wrote Windham, trying to make *his* hero less shadowy, too.

In April Tennessee went to Hollywood, where arrangements were being made to film *Sweet Bird*. A whole crowd was out there with him at the Bevery Hills Hotel: Edwina, Dakin, Joyce and Maxwell. Also there, but not on his bill, were Marilyn Monroe and Yves Montand, who were shooting *Let's Make Love*. They remained close to each other, even off the set, in spite of distant spouses, Arthur Miller and Simone Signoret.

The Williamses had met Marilyn before, and she invited them to the set, which was closed to most visitors. Edwina was thrilled. Marilyn was doing her dancing number, supposedly in a little Off-Broadway theater, and was having a hard time. She admitted she was no dancer. Her dress, which was too thin, and too tight to put on, had been built on her. Afterward there was a birthday cake for her with candles and the next day she had lunch with the Williamses. Dakin noted she had become a bit plump, but also more mature and aware. The years with the Actors Studio and with Arthur Miller had changed her a great deal.

There were many other fanzine adventures for the family. Edwina actually had her picture taken with Elvis Presley on the set of *G.I. Blues*. Laurence Harvey met Dakin at the hotel bar and made a determined attempt to have Dakin persuade his brother that he, Harvey, should star in the *Sweet Bird* film. (Harvey had already been in the screen version of *Summer and Smoke*.) Dakin said he'd see what he could do—and the result is there for us all to see: Paul Newman played Chance again.

Edwina and her two sons were guests of honor at a Beverly Hills dinner party with one starlet, Mia Farrow, just divorced from Frank Sinatra, and two more-mature ladies, Rita Hayworth and Jennifer Jones. Edwina was not quite sure how to take Jennifer, because Edwina had got to know Irene Selznick well during the goings-on with *Streetcar*, and here was this movie star, sitting right at the same table with them—who now had Irene's former husband David! Edwina looked at the gold streetcar on her charm bracelet, given to her by Irene, and shuddered. Things like that simply didn't happen in Clayton, not to members of the D.A.R.

Tennessee was especially interested in Rita Hayworth, who was talking about Ali Khan; and Mia Farrow, at the time fascinated by Stanley Kubrick, was telling Dakin to sit in the fifth row when he went to see his new film, *2001*. She told him it was groovy. In fact, she said almost everything was groovy.

Another day they all went to a party given for Mary Pickford and her husband Buddy Rogers. This was a rare honor because by this time Mary had almost become a recluse.

There was much talk about Hollywood's favorite topic—money. About nine-tenths of the time, on this addled coast, it is pie-in-the-sky money, which can't be cashed at any bank. But these days, with Tennessee, it was legal tender. Tennessee went to see Hal Wallis, the producer, and others. There was a huge two-picture "package deal" that he considered, but finally decided that the money, though real, would almost all go in taxes.

They were beginning to shoot the film. Geraldine Page, who was doing her Princess role again with Paul Newman, knew that the screenplay had changed the characters a bit from Tennessee's play. The Princess now "was a totally different lady and it didn't have any of that grand passion in it. It was more of a light comedy performance in the film."

But she did feel that Richard Brooks was an understanding director. She told Mike Steen she was having trouble with the big telephone scene.

TENNESSEE WILLIAMS 235

It wasn't right and it wasn't right, and I was sort of lying across the bed with the phone, hanging on to it in a complete state of demoralization. And Brooks came over to me and very quietly said, "Now, there's no rush. Take it easy. There's plenty of time." And he started walking away to kind of calm me down so I wouldn't get too discouraged. And as he was talking to me, it was the weirdest thing. I could feel the scene coming on. I could feel it gathering, and he's talking away to me, and I said, "Will you get out of here and let me act?" And he caught what I meant right away and just backed up and said very quietly to the cameraman to roll and that's the time I did it that's used in the film.

At the screening of the film at MGM, with such film-lady dragons as Hedda Hopper and Louella Parsons, the scene was wildly applauded.

Tennessee wrote that Page and Newman "co-starred brilliantly" in the film.

Tennessee went back to Key West to work, and was joined later by Dakin. His main concern was *The Night of the Iguana*, and he was desperately anxious to make this play a success. He was still planning the Coconut Grove tryout. There would be no limit to the number of tryouts or the amount of rewriting.

Dakin feared there was no limit, either, to the strain to which he was willing to subject his body, or his health, to do this. Dakin could see, in the bedroom and bathroom that Tennessee and Frank shared, pills of every kind, on every dresser and shelf. Tennessee was still obsessed, Dakin thought, by fear that he would have some fatal illness before he could finish putting down all the writing that he felt was still inside him. He had pills to wake up by, pills to tranquilize and, more deadly, Doriden (a morphine derivative) for effective sleep.

In the fall, Tennessee returned to New York for rehearsals of *Period of Adjustment*. He had hoped that Kazan would direct but he was already committed to directing a film, so Tennessee settled for George Roy Hill. In the cast were Barbara Baxley, Robert Webber, James Daly and Rosemary Murphy as the two air force couples.

The tone of the play was changing slightly. Shelley Winters, who kept hoping Tennessee would become more politically committed, read an earlier draft and bemoaned the fact that the version in rehearsal was less political. As she told Mike Steen, "If you really read the first draft of the play, there are two couples discussing potency, but meanwhile the house is sinking and the walls are cracking. And the actors pay no attention to the house sinking." Winters felt, correctly, that the sinking house was symbolic of society as a whole. (In fact, Tennessee got the idea from one of Edwina's houses in Clayton, which was built over an underground cavern. The play was originally called *High Point Is Built on a Cavern*.) Whether Shelley liked it or not, the play was light and funny, and had little political propaganda.

Before the opening, Tennessee gave a big party at Nicholson's Cafe for his cast and the casts of *A Taste of Honey* and Brendan Behan's *The Hostage*. Maxwell was there, and said that the life of the party was Tallulah, who had come up from Florida with the writer James Herlihy. He had practically forced her into a health routine, with lots of swimming, and she looked much more fit than usual.

Miss Edwina came to the opening at the Helen Hayes Theater. Between acts, Tennessee held court at a nearby bar, with Brendan Behan and his wife, Frank Krause, Maxwell and others. As usual, on opening nights at this time, Tennessee was well fortified with pills and a few drinks.

The production was not up to Kazan's standards. Winters said, "I was very sorry to see that the production was so bad, when I believed the play was so good." But the audience was relaxed and seemed to enjoy it.

Tennessee took Edwina to a big party given at the Plaza. The reviews came in, and they sounded a bit surprised. Williams had written a light comedy! The critics thought it touching and romantic. On the other hand, it was not considered one of his major plays. In summing up Tennessee's work later, Atkinson said it "is so far below Mr. Williams' standard that it proves nothing one way or the other. His heart is not in that mediocre jest."

Tennessee knew, himself, that *The Night of the Iguana* was the more important work. He felt that with this play his reputation was at stake.

He went back to his work studio in Key West for more revisions of *Iguana*, then took a suite in the Towers hotel in Miami. He would be directing rehearsals at the Coconut Grove Playhouse.

Maxwell visited him there one morning, and found him exhausted from writing and also worried because one of his friends (not named) was in trouble with the police and needed a thousand dollars. He sent it. This was not unusual. Audrey Wood, through whom the money flowed, said, "It's not just one or two people by any means. It is a whole group he's helping, and it goes on all the time."

Tryout number one in Miami gave him ideas for more revisions and in the spring he and Frank went to Italy for tryout two in Spoleto. They spent time first with Marion Vaccaro in Rome, then went to Sicily to visit some of Frank's distant cousins and then, for business, they went to Spoleto.

Every year Gian-Carlo Menotti, who first became famous for his short operas *The Medium* and *The Telephone*, returned to this pretty little town in the middle of the Italian boot to be the maestro and the impresario of the Spoleto Festival of Two Worlds, an uninhibited circus of music and drama and even fireworks, always culminating in the birthday party that Menotti threw for himself. Tennessee referred to it as an "ego-trip" for Menotti and his friend Thomas Schippers. It was fun for everybody.

Frank Corsaro, a young director, put on *Iguana* and did such a good job that Tennessee recommended him for the American production. It was hard to judge audience reaction at Spoleto. Some of them could hardly understand the English words. Tennessee made more notes and more revisions.

Then he and Frank Merlo went back to New York to prepare for the Broadway opening. This time they were going to do it the hard way, with a long tour first. Charles ("Chuck") Bowden and Violla Rubber were the producers, and the cast was extraordinary, with Bette Davis as Maxine, the proprietess of the old Mexican hotel; Margaret Leighton as Hannah, the poor artist who is touring the world with her grandfather, Nonno, the world's oldest poet, played by Alan Webb; and the defrocked Reverend T. Lawrence Shannon, by Patrick O'Neal.

Tennessee had written a short story called "The Night of the Iguana," years ago, in the 1940s. Very little of it is left in the play except the title, the old hotel in the mexican rain forest, the poor lizard, tied up without food or water, and the gentle spinster with her watercolors. The two homosexual writers have been dropped, and a whole collection of new characters added. The most wonderful of these is old Nonno, based on Tennessee's grandfather, the ninety-seven-year-old Reverend Mr. Dakin, in gesture and mannerism, with the same invincible spirit, in spite of being nearly blind and deaf and close to death.

Nonno's granddaughter, Hannah, travels with him much as Tennessee traveled with old Gramps. Hannah, who has seen everything, and is both gentle and unconquerable, speaks Tennessee's own moral code: "Nothing human disgusts me unless it's unkind, violent."

The object was to take this traveling circus all over the country and let it shake itself down. Tennessee said it was his longest and most appalling tour. For a while the whole operation seemed doomed.

Bette Davis, then the reigning queen of Hollywood, was making her return to the stage. She was tremendous as Maxine—and also an autocratic and temperamental prima donna. She did not like the young director, Frank Corsaro.

The first rehearsals were at the Algonquin Hotel, in a suite, with big tables set up for the cast. Margaret Leighton told Mike Steen that everybody was "sitting around drinking coffee and trying to pretend it was all very social—and shivering with horror and fright." She herself was, as usual, very nervous, but Tennessee was "even more nervous than the cast." And he was working right with them the whole time, there and on the road. Leighton said:

> With the amount of his writing that was rewritten, altered, replaced, taken out, or put in again, you could have made another play. Tennessee rewrote something every day. He started very early in the morning and the new pages were usually given to us at a kind of preluncheon meeting, perhaps eleven-thirty, twelve o'clock, maybe even earlier. Tennessee, in those days, I think I'm right in saying, used to work from something like six to ten or from seven to eleven in the morning. Then we got the material. We used to go to the theatre in the afternoon and work on it, and it went in at that night's performance. And this went on for eight weeks, and he was there every minute of the day. All the time.

They started out, rather tentatively, in Rochester, New York. Before they reached Detroit, Tennessee was getting lonesome, and asked Frank to have their dog, Satan, sent up from Florida. The dog was a huge black Belgian shepherd. He seemed so nice, even though he may have looked terrifying to some. He would look into Tennessee's eyes with his own lovely yellow eyes, and lick his hand. Tennessee had an idea this indicated affection, but as it worked out, he may simply have been tasting the meat. It was Frank whom Satan really loved.

One morning, Satan had watched, jealously, while Tennessee climbed into bed with Frankie. Satan growled, angrily, but that didn't stop Tennessee.

The same evening the hotel doctor came up to their room to treat Tennessee for a head cold, and while he and Frank were in the bathroom discussing the problem, Satan leaped onto Tennessee's bed and bit him on each ankle, to the bone. Tennessee believed Satan would have have killed him if Frank had not pulled him off. The dog had to be taken to a vet and put to sleep.

And so began another of Tennessee's great feuds with the medical profession. The dog bites, neglected for about a week, became badly infected, and his ankles swelled to about twice their normal size. He had to have a massive dose of antibiotics, which nearly knocked him out, and he was rushed to a hospital, prepared to stage another dying. A dog bite (no rabies involved) was becoming a "close shave with death."

He went to the emergency ward, and teetered excitingly between life and death behind white canvas curtains, with Frank keeping a three-hour vigil. He was then taken upstairs to—disaster. He didn't have any Seconals or "pinkies." The nurse would only give him half of one. And Frank had left. He put through an emergency call to Frank, who groped sleepily out of bed, staggered back to the hospital with a bottle and left quickly, still not completely awake.

Disaster again. It was the wrong bottle; these were diuretic pills, which he was taking, too, but no Seconal.

He jumped out of bed and dressed. He couldn't put on his shoes, his ankles were too big. He started to run out without shoes. A nurse stopped him, and told him he couldn't leave. After all, he had been dying just a few hours before. She said it was not like a hotel, you couldn't just check out.

He said he could, and went whooping down in his bare feet and hailed a cab to the Book Cadillac hotel. He said that when Frank saw him hobble into the room, he just moved over in the bed.

It may have been the quickest turnaround in history, from deathbed to domestic bliss. And after that he was okay, he just had to wear bedroom slippers to rehearsals. And he didn't die again for quite a while.

Bette Davis finally blew up in Chicago and fired the director. She was really not his kind of actress. There are two kinds, or have been, since the Actors Studio. The Studio actors have to *feel* the emotion, in their guts, each time. The other kind think all this gut-acting is childish. They believe in technique. Get it right, and then do it the same way each time.

Brando and Kazan, of course, are Studio, or gut, people. Davis, and many of the older actors, like Laurence Olivier and Vivien Leigh, believed in technique. Corsaro was a Studio-type director, and Davis had had enough. She fired him personally. Not only that, she issued orders barring him from the theater. And finally, she insisted, according to Tennessee, that she could *feel* him if he was even in Chicago, and said to get him back to New York and that goddamn Actors Studio! And she made it stick.

The directing would now be done by Chuck Bowden, the producer, and Tennessee, in bedroom slippers.

Dakin arrived in Chicago in time for the opening night, and went straight to the Blackstone Hotel. There he found his brother in bed, with both legs heavily bandaged, propped up on pillows. He was still working.

They were hoping to have the play in first-class condition for Chicago, home base for Claudia Cassidy, by this time the most influential critic in the country outside of New York. After all, Claudia had written his first great review, for *Menagerie*. Claudia would love *Iguana*.

Dakin loved it. Bette Davis had settled down to a fine performance, and he thought that Margaret Leighton, as Hannah, gave the most luminous and graceful performance he had seen since Jessica Tandy's Blanche in *Streetcar*. Hannah is the one who really speaks with Tennessee's voice in this play, and has some of the most beautiful lines he has written.

Cassidy, always independent and never predictable, wrote in the Chicago *Tribune* the next morning that "Tennessee Williams has written a bankrupt play." She didn't like it at all.

Nevertheless, the play stayed several weeks in Chicago, and then moved on to New York for opening night at the Royale Theater on December 28. They all feared that the New York critics, usually the toughest of all, might be even more damning than Cassidy.

After the final curtain, Leighton came back sadly to her dressing room. She said, "Alan Webb, who played the grandfather, came into my room after everybody had gone and we were cleaning up, and said, 'Well, Mag, what do you think?' I said, 'I don't think there's a prayer. It's down the spout.'"

Tennessee, too, was prepared to be savaged by the critics—but he was not. They liked it very much, and a few months later gave it the New York Drama Critics' Circle Award, with twelve out of the eighteen votes cast. It was his fourth Critics' Circle Award. Time magazine put him on their cover, and in the long cover story called him "the greatest living playwright in the English speaking world."

Two years later John Huston directed the film version and Tennessee went down to Mexico for part of the shooting. Ava Gardner was Maxine, Deborah Kerr was Hannah and Richard Burton the renegade priest.

Tennessee was edged out of the 1962 Pulitzer by a musical, awarded best musical by seventeen out of eighteen of the New York drama critics and given the Pulitzer. Something about succeeding in business; two characters named Abe Burrows and Frank Loesser were skillfully involved. But Tennessee had two Pulitzers already.

Walter Kerr did an essay about *Iguana* in his book *The Theatre in Spite of Itself*. It is full of praise for the play and concludes: "We go to the theatre month after month and become accustomed to plays that are put together; then Mr. Williams returns and reminds us what it is to watch poetry in the process of finding itself."

CHAPTER 24

After *Iguana* Tennessee was once again on a mountaintop, so once again he was restless and uncomfortable.

A few years before he had written a short story, "Man Bring This up Road," which had been published in Mademoiselle. By the time he returned to his Key West workroom it was already on the way to becoming a play, *The Milk Train Doesn't Stop Here Anymore.*

But almost certainly the most important event of 1962 was the break with Frank Merlo and the resulting great change in his personal life, a change surely for the worse.

For all these years their relationship had been happy and almost (though not entirely) monogamous. And the consequent housekeeping-order of his life had contributed to better, more stable conditions of work. In that way Frank had really added to the excellence of the plays.

But Frank was losing vitality, becoming moody and less enthusiastic about sex. Tennessee thought it might be drugs. He knew that Frank had been dipping into his many bottles of pills, and suspected he might be going farther, even into heroin, where Tennessee had never been. Frank was also smoking about four packs of cigarettes every day.

Finally Frank went up to New York for a medical checkup. Tennessee, feeling lonesome, found a blond twenty-two-year-old from New Orleans with nice skin and shapely rear quarters, known as "the Dixie Doxy."

When Frank came back he found Tennessee in a big hotel on Key Biscayne, near Miami, working hard on *Milk Train*. And the Dixie Doxy was parading around the swimming pool in crimson nylon trunks.

Frank moved Tennessee back to Key West, and that was the end of the Doxy, the end of round one in the bout.

Round two: A young man who had played in the Spoleto Festival version of *Iguana* visited Key West, and it was nip and tuck whether Tennessee or Frank would have *him.*

Round three: Three "queens" from Miami visited Key West and Tennessee admits there was a big afternoon and evening at a local motel. (Work,

241

needless to say, went on as usual in the morning.) Considerable alcohol was consumed and his recollection was that he may have been intimate with all three of them. Naturally, after all that, he was hungry and came home to dinner.

Round four: Frank was waiting for him. Tennessee sat down to the dinner table in the patio, expecting food. It arrived. The meat loaf, he recalled, just missed his head, and so did a bowl of succotash and the salad. He sat down beside the meat loaf on the floor of the patio and found it delicious. By this time, Frank had zoomed off in the car.

Round five: While Frank was off again, on another medical examination, Tennessee invited a painter friend, whom he'd met in Tangier, to visit him. They did some painting together. A friend of Frank's caught them one evening rather well on the way toward *flagrante delicto*, and put in an emergency call to Frank. Shortly after arriving, Frank sprang at the painter and seized him by the throat. Tennessee called the police. Frank let go. The police, who liked Frank (everyone on Key West did) took him off to a friend's house for the night. Frank came back to find Tennessee and the painter ready to take off in the car. Frank suggested that, after fourteen years together, they should at least shake hands. They did.

Tennessee and the painter drove up to Miami, where they checked into a motel for a wild night. They had lunch at Marion Vaccaro's, and then went back to the motel. The sexual demands of the artist (who remains anonymous) were too great, even for Tennessee, so he was sent off to San Francisco with a pocketful of money. (He had painted Tennessee's portrait.) Tennessee went on to his New York apartment on East Sixty-fifth Street.

And so began life without Frank Merlo.

They were to see each other again many times during the last year and a half of Frank's life, but it was the end of their living together, and the day-to-day competence of Frank was gone.

Paul Bigelow, who knew them both intimately for many years, and was fond of them both, understood their relationship perhaps better than anyone else. He made a number of shrewd observations on tape:

SM: What did you think of Merlo?
PB: I was fond of Frank.
SM: And you think he was good for Tennessee, basically?
PB: Well, I think he would have been, if it had been possible for Tennessee to accept his virtues. Unfortunately, you see, that's the last thing Tennessee can accept in anyone, his virtues.
SM: Well Frank had problems, too. Wasn't he taking heroin, and things

like that? [This was asked because of Tennessee's statements that he thought Frank might have been taking heroin.]

PB: Well, he may have been at some point, but I don't think so at all. I think if he had been I would have known it. [But in a long discussion, Paul hedged that statement; at least one person he'd known almost that well was found to be a drug addict, and Paul was not aware of it.] Frank believed in romantic love.

SM: You mean he was really, romantically in love with Tennessee?

PB: Yes, he was, there was no doubt of that, and this was not acceptable to Tennessee.

SM: It sometimes seemed to me that in the very early stages, with several characters, one of them named Kip, he certainly seemed to have romantic love. That was before you knew him?

PB: Oh, no. But there was a feeling Tennessee was not reciprocating.

SM: He doesn't really reciprocate romantic love?

PB: If he did he was very careful to keep things like that from me.

SM: You said Tennessee couldn't accept virtues, that Frank was unacceptable to Tennessee because he was virtuous, but what were the virtues?

PB: What Frank wanted was domesticity, a domestic life, an organized life. He wanted the meals at the time they were supposed to be served. He did not want raffish people wandering around. He was after all, a lower-middle-class Italian with very strong feelings about what consitutes respectability.

SM: He wanted a respectable family?

PB: Exactly. Tennessee, whose approach to life was that of an aristocrat, was having none of it. The last thing he wanted was a middle-class existence. He spent his life running as hard as he could to get away from it. [Paul was reminded of the time, during the Diana Barrymore period, when Frank threw everybody out of the apartment at about two A.M.] That was right. Frank was against Tennessee's drinking too much, getting too tired, knowing his work pattern. He put his foot down and told people to go home.

A sad and lonely period was beginning. In February 1962 he wrote his mother that he thought he needed to be in a rest home for "at least a month" and in the same letter said that he hoped Dakin could arrange to work and live in New York. He suggested that perhaps Miss Edwina might come to New York, too. These moves were not possible at the time.

He continued to work on *The Milk Train Doesn't Stop Here Anymore*. It would be his main preoccupation for nearly two years. *Milk Train* is the story of Sissy Goforth, the aged, omnipotent empress of a private island, connected to Italy by a goat path, along which comes Chris Flanders. There is in him a bit of Val Xavier, Tennessee's wandering, fugitive minstrel, here a poet and sculptor of metal mobiles—and partly a symbolic angel of death cum gigolo, who has often managed to be present at the deaths of various other rich old crones. The writing is often poetically beautiful, especially in the speeches of Chris, and also witty, notably in the scenes between Sissy and an ancient marchesa known as the Witch of Capri, played onstage by women, and on film by Noel Coward.

In the stage version, Tennessee uses a device from the Japanese Kabuki theater: black-costumed stage assistants, invisible to the characters, who shift screens and other props. This is functional, to eliminate scene changes, and it also serves to emphasize the fact that we are one step away from reality. The play, Tennessee says in his introduction, is an allegory, a "sophisticated fairy tale."

Frank Merlo wanted to see Tennessee again. He came up to New York to the Hotel Dover. He was all right financially, since he owned 10 percent of *Cat* and *Camino* and *Tattoo*, and was still receiving a salary of about $150 a week. Tennessee said he would see him only with Audrey Wood, and they arranged a meeting at Tennessee's Sixty-fifth Street apartment.

Tennessee reported that Frank was well behaved and calm but puzzled.

They decided that the separation would be final, and that Frank was to continue to draw his salary, and of course the royalties from his share of the plays. It was, in effect, a divorce, with alimony.

Though Frank left with Audrey, he telephoned to say that he wanted to see Tennessee alone. Tennessee agreed to see him only at a bar. They met, but there was no reconciliation. Tennessee reported that he told Frank he wanted to get his goodness back.

Tennessee, still struggling with *Milk Train*, flew to Tangier with a young poet he called "Angel." In Tangier he could see Paul and Jane Bowles. He and Angel stayed in a rented cottage near the beach, where Angel proved to be a great comfort to him.

He could write, and did so. But he had trouble talking.

His old friend, Gian-Carlo Menotti, agreed to do the world premiere (a tryout) of *Milk Train*, and Hermione Baddeley consented to play Sissy Goforth. Hermione, full of wit and bounce, must have cheered him up enormously. Another old friend, Herbert Machiz, was directing, and Tennessee was giving him rewrites all the way through the rehearsals. Most of them, Hermione told Mike Steen, were a great improvement.

Hermione added that *Milk Train* was "the most successful of that year," at Spoleto. "We received the sort of applause rather like the opera. Ten, twelve, fifteen curtains. It was ecstatic. Claudia Cassidy came over from Chicago and she just went all out about the play. You know, she really loved it."

Tennessee said that Hermione gave a tremendous performance. He was sharing a box with Anna Magnani, who had driven over from Rome. Anna kept saying, "*Come magnifica!*" which, Tennessee thought modestly, was referring to Hermione's performance, not the play.

Elizabeth Taylor and Richard Burton came to Spoleto to see it, "but they came the only night we were off," Hermione said. Menotti gave them a big party, all the same.

Frank Merlo had gone down to Key West, where he had many friends. People down there said he could have been elected mayor. One day he was sitting at an outdoor cafe with Dan Stirrup, the architect, and others. He leaned over the table and a stream of blood came out. A doctor took X rays. Frank, the four-pack-a-day man, had lung cancer.

When Tennessee arrived back in New York in the fall, he heard from Marion Vaccaro that Frank was in Memorial Hospital for Cancer and Allied Diseases. Tennessee visited him before the operation, and every day afterward, he said, until Frank was released. He wrote that he loved the Little Horse as much as ever, and was distressed to hear from the doctors that nothing really could be done. The operation had not been successful. The tumor was too close to his heart to be removed. The doctor said Frank had only six months to live.

Frank went back to Key West alone and rented a small house. Tennessee bought him a TV and sent over their dog, Gigi, and a monkey named Creature, for companions. A few weeks later, Frank moved back to Tennessee's house to the upstairs bedroom. Tennessee and Angel were downstairs, in the other one.

All that winter Frank grew weaker.

Edwina's book, *Remember Me to Tom*, was published in the spring of 1963. Tennessee was angry about it. On March 26 he wrote a disturbed letter to Dakin. He felt it was a great mistake for her to say so many frightful things about their father after his death. And he was angry about tasteless references to Rose and Diana and others on the book jacket. In fact, he was especially enraged about Lucy Freeman, the coauthor, for taking advantage of his mother's "senility."

Lucy Freeman had admitted to Mead, in a meeting in 1979, that the book was quickly researched, based on conversations with Edwina that lasted only a few weeks at her house in Clayton. The book appeared at the time of the New York newspaper strike, and did not do very well. But she insisted that there was no attempt to hurt the family, and that she had modified Edwina's criticisms of Cornelius.

Tennessee was pleased, however, that Miss Edwina had settled in happily at Gatesworth Manor, an apartment-hotel bought by the Episcopal church for aging members of the church. It is on Union Boulevard in midtown St. Louis. The atmosphere is not that of a typical old peoples' home. Bridge and cocktail parties seem to be going on continuously. Mead's first cousin, Minnoe Woodward, was living there at the time, and they became close friends.

This was the first time that Miss Edwina had not run her own household. She was now seventy-eight years old.

Tennessee also noted in his letter that he was trying to negotiate better terms with Audrey Wood through the Dramatists Guild.

When Key West became too hot, Tennessee brought both Frank and Angel to Nantucket, but the mixture did not work, and everyone was unhappy. Finally Tennessee and Frank came back to the New York apartment and Angel was sent down to Key West. Frank slept in the main bedroom and Tennessee stayed on the couch in the study. Frank bolted the door every night, which Tennessee assumed could only have been against him.

He wrote to Dakin that Frank was becoming desperately worse. The disease was spreading to his pancreas and liver. He had to go back to Memorial for cobalt treatment, and finally had to stay there. He was as thin as a skeleton and had to be taken to his room in a wheelchair.

Throughout all this, Tennessee had been doing more rewriting on *Milk Train*, a play that he said he had worked on longer than any other. The next trial run was at the Barter Theater, a lovely old colonial playhouse in Abington, Virginia, the second oldest in the United States. Tennessee went down there for rehearsals.

Claire Luce was playing Sissy Goforth and she reported that Tennessee was continuously and massively rewriting during the rehearsals. She remembered asking him about the ending. What was wrong with Sissy? What disease was killing her? He told her, "I don't know, baby. Maybe she had a death wish, like me." But a few days later, when rehearsals were going better, he said he didn't have it anymore.

Tennessee thought Donald Madden was "brilliant" in this version, but he preferred Hermione's Spoleto version of Sissy to Claire Luce's. Adrian Hall was directing the Abington production and Audrey Wood was there. But Tennessee felt that the audience was "apathetic."

Tennessee was obviously disturbed at this time by Frank's condition.

There are many contradictions here. In an interview with Jay Garon in New York, in March, 1979 Mead was told that Tennessee had probably never gone to Memorial to see Frank at all. Garon, a writer-agent and a neighbor of Tennessee's in Key West (who also lives part-time in New York) had heard that Tennessee had "washed his hands of Frank." This is hearsay, since Garon did not meet Tennessee until about 1976.

The Tom Buckley interview in the November 1970 Atlantic quoted unnamed "friends" as saying that "Tom ran away from him [Frank] during his final illness. He paid all the hospital bills, of course, but he didn't go to see him." This did not necessarily indicate indifference. Tennessee had a horror of illness and hospitals.

In Tennessee's account, in Memoirs, Frank died right after the Abington production, yet Hermione, in her interview with Mike Steen, said that Frank was still alive during the later Milk Train run.

However, there is no proof that Tennessee abandoned Frank at the end, even if he made mistakes of memory in the recollection of the episode. As he recalled, he flew back to New York from Abington, not even waiting for the reviews, as soon as he heard that Frank was dying. He said he was so upset he had to have a sedative shot from his doctor. Then he went out and got drunk, and by the time he returned home, he had a call from the hospital saying that Frank was dead. He wrote Dakin saying that Frank had returned to his Catholic faith and had received the last sacrament just before he died, and that the death was sudden.

He also said that he went into a seven-year depression.

But the Milk Train rumbled on. Roger Stevens wanted to do it with Tallulah as Sissy. Tennessee held out for Hermione. Paul Roebling, who had played Chris at Spoleto, was signed on again.

It opened in New Haven. Mildred Dunnock, who was delighted to play the Witch of Capri, so different from the mournful roles she was too often given, told Mike Steen a story about the final rehearsal before the New Haven opening. Just as they were being given their last notes, Tennessee's cousin, Sidney Lanier, an Episcopal priest, walked down the aisle. "Tennessee saw him coming and suddenly rushed across the stage to him, laughingly and jokingly, yet seriously, and said, 'Bless me, Father! Bless me!' And then, right there, as Tennessee knelt, Sidney Lanier put his hand on his head and gave him a blessing. It was a curious, curious thing."

But it didn't help much in New Haven. Tennessee said that the opening was "somewhat disastrous" in spite of a fine performance by Hermione. Afterward, when a crowd of people not connected with the production swarmed backstage, he threw one of his tantrums and ordered them out, saying the play was in trouble, and they needed to work.

Tennessee did more writing and they moved on to Boston, where Hermione was better than ever, in spite of an opening-night disaster. Her red wig fell off. She pretended not to notice, continued to hustle about and when she came back to the fallen wig, popped it on backwards. It was in character, and the audience loved it.

The Boston reviews were mixed. Elliot Norton called it "an exploratory but important stage work." Hermione, euphoric and riding on a glorious wave of applause, felt that both Boston and Philadelphia were "great hits," and said that during these runs there was little rewriting.

But Tennessee, understandably depressed, and perhaps more realistic, reported that the Philadelphia notices were poorer than Boston's, and that business was not very good. In Philadelphia he stalked out of a party given by the Roeblings for the cast because he was not seated at the main table.

The Broadway opening coincided with another of New York's recurrent newspaper strikes, so there were no printed reviews, only written ones, privately circulated. These were fabulously in favor of Hermione, in fact, the greatest, Tennessee thought, of those for any actress in any of his plays since Laurette Taylor's in *The Glass Menagerie*. But the reviews were, he thought, cool.

Roger Stevens decided to close the play.

However, *Milk Train* came tooting back almost immediately. Tony Richardson, the young English director (then famous for his *Tom Jones* film,) saw the script, liked it and David Merrick agreed to do a new production. Tennessee wanted Hermione again, but by this time she had a Hollywood commitment. They decided on Tallulah and, in fact, Tennessee told her he had written the play for her in the first place. This was true, but Hermione's performances in Spoleto had simply been irresistible.

Tallulah agreed but Richardson didn't, and finally consented to her only if Tennessee would accept Tab Hunter as Chris. Hunter, the handsome Hollywood star, had never played a major part on Broadway. Tennessee was shattered. He wanted Donald Madden, who was available. He asked Dakin if he could think of some way to get Hunter out of it, but no one could.

Tallulah in her prime would have been a truly magnificent Sissy Goforth, but in the fall of 1963 she was in bad shape. She did try to get fit. As Lee Israel wrote, she "changed gears to prepare to perform. She modified all her habits considerably and, for beauty and vigor, even tried eating regularly." But it didn't work. She was even having trouble remembering her lines.

She and Tab Hunter did not hit it off. In the first discussions, Lee Israel stated that he seemed to be most concerned "about the problems involved in having his horses shipped from one part of the country to another."

This paragraph from Tallulah's biography is a good account of the Tab Hunter–Tallulah conflict:

> Rehearsals began on November 19. The hassling started soon there-after. Tab and Tallulah stood center stage one afternoon as he wound up a long, long speech written to end: "The man held out the money to me. And I . . . And I," to which Tallulah was to say, "You took it. You took it, didn't you?" He neglected to say the second "And I." Tallulah said gently, "Dahling, you have another line." Tab jumped up in the air and screamed, "What the *fuck* difference does it make?" Tallulah looked out into the darkened theater at David Merrick, Tennessee Williams, and Tony Richardson and simply shrugged stoically. She said to her caddy that night, "If I were ever going to be the temperamental Tallulah Bankhead, it would have been right there."

Tennessee thought that the pills and liquor Sissy kept taking onstage were real.

At the beginning Tennessee and Richardson had a good working relationship. But when the out-of-town tryouts went badly, Richardson seemed to lose interest. When Tennessee criticized him one day, Richardson told him he was a "chronic hysteric." Tennessee admitted this might have been true at the time. Finally Richardson left the production in Baltimore to try to make peace with his wife, Vanessa Redgrave.

But Tallulah had the most problems, "delivering those lines which she managed to remember as rapid, peakless explosions of breath. People walked out of the theater disgusted with her unintelligibility."

They considered closing the play out of town, but finally decided to bring it into New York. At the first preview Tallulah's claque gave her a huge ovation, even if they didn't hear every word she said. Tennessee wrote that she was so weak she couldn't project beyond the front of the theater.

The opening-night audience did not like it, and Tennessee wrote that the critics "demolished it."

Miss Edwina had come on for the opening, but as Tennessee wrote to Dakin, he was so depressed that he flew off to Key West before she even left for St. Louis.

Milk Train closed in New York after five performances.

When he reached Key West he found that his house had been opened to the public as a tourist attraction. He had to hide from the mob in his studio.

CHAPTER 25

This was the beginning of a really dreadful time for Tennessee. For a while he became almost a recluse. Miserable in Key West, he went back to his apartment in New York. He said that he ate very little except plain spaghetti, which he boiled up and ate without sauce.

He wrote to Dakin that he was trying to practice the Chinese *mei yoo guan chi*, or "no sweat" philosophy, but it wasn't easy.

Nan Lanier, the wife of his cousin Sidney, dropped in occasionally to help him. She would ring the downstairs bell until someone would let her in with the buzzer, then knock on his door until he finally opened it.

Once, when he told Nan that he couldn't sleep at all, she sent him to a psychiatrist, who gave him an injection to raise his blood pressure and a prescription for Doriden and Mellaril tablets to get him to sleep. He said that one Doriden and a five-hundred-milligram Mellaril really knocked him out.

Sometimes he had Angel with him, mainly when he was in Key West, and the young poet tried to console him. But this did not help much, partly because Angel was (or Tennessee thought he was) seeing a handsome pilot on the side. In any case, Angel was dismissed that spring. Angel told him, with tears in his eyes, that he thought he had found a home. Tennessee, who had several houses, couldn't find a home either. He said he was having no sex at all.

He felt he simply had to travel, not so much to be anywhere in particular, only to be somewhere else. At times like this he often turned to his old drinking and traveling companion Marion Vaccaro, the banana heiress who lived in Miami. She agreed to join him.

Before leaving he wrote to Dakin asking him to assume powers of attorney while he was gone. He also said he had tried some psychiatric treatments in Florida, but they were a "bore."

He and Marion flew to Spain and wandered around, drinking freely. But in those days nobody, not even the banana queen, was perfect for him. She was tremendously rich, and he was certainly not poor at this point,

251

but she irritated him continually by (he thought) cheating on their bills. He once wrote to Paul Bigelow that when they traveled together his bill always managed to be twice as big as hers. (They were usually, if not always, in separate rooms; they were not lovers.) She would charge her bottles of scotch to his bill. Rich people, he told Bigelow, were infinitely more acquisitive.

They spent some time in Barcelona, a city he liked a great deal, and later went down to Tangier to see Jane and Paul Bowles.

While in Tangier he received a letter from Audrey Wood telling him that his New York apartment had been robbed again, for the second time in a month. Audrey suggested that he have everything stored, but Tennessee was not sure he wanted people going through his private papers— that is, if any were left.

They sailed back, his first ocean crossing in a long time. He thought it would be good for his nerves. But apparently that didn't help either.

His memory of this period is confused, but he did go back briefly to his small and looted New York apartment, and it is probable that this is the time he was visited by the "tall and stately" woman whose name he couldn't remember and referred to in his *Memoirs* as "Eleanor of Aquitaine." She was really Nancy Venable, a Baltimore society woman he had met on board ship. She finally got through to him by buzzing and knocking interminably, as Nan Lanier had done; he told her he couldn't talk. She said there was no need to, and sat quietly beside him on his apricot-colored love seat and massaged his head.

He knew he would have to leave his little apartment, so vulnerable to burglars. It was the beginning of the period in which New Yorkers had begun to retreat behind fortifications, triple locks, iron-barred windows and even armed doormen and closed-circuit television, because the police could no longer cope with crime. He rented a duplex apartment in a building on West Fifty-fifth Steet. He needed more room to accommodate his young cousin, Jim Adams, who came to look after him. Jim was actually Grandmother Dakin's great-nephew, and had come to New York to study ballet and theater arts.

In a long and almost confessional letter written from West Fifty-fifth Street to Paul Bowles, Tennessee said that he and Jim saw little of each other, communicating mainly by notes left on the alcove dining table, with information like "getting groceries," or "sent suit to cleaners." He was seeing a psychiatrist seven days a week, "occasionally skipping a Sunday."

He said nothing about his writing, though he must have been working on a revision of *Summer and Smoke*, retitled *The Eccentricities of a Nightingale*. It is much simpler, with four characters eliminated (Doc, Rosa, Gonzales and Nellie) and some of the melodrama (like the murder of Doc) removed. There was at least one experimental production of *Eccentricities* that year, but it would not be produced on Broadway for another twelve years.

His previous working schedule must have changed, because he wrote to Bowles that he was going to bed at ten and reading until 5:00 A.M. He did not say what he was reading. Then he would take the "little yellow pills" that were supposed to bring him out of his depression. He also mentioned that the "Queen of Bananas," Marion, was staying in his Key West house. He was not too happy about it, as she was a "lifter," and a "collector."

Something psychologically violent must have happened between that letter and a second letter, undated, but obviously written soon after from the Fifty-fifth Street duplex. The "yellow pills" in the first letter were probably amphetamine, most likely Dexedrine, which came then in yellow pills, usually embossed with the letters *SKF*, for SmithKline and French.

What probably happened, in those few weeks, was the aftermath of a visit to "Doctor Feelgood," and the beginning of "speed" or amphetamine injected directly into the veins, perhaps the most potent mind-jolter ever concocted, and perhaps even the most insidious mind-wrecker.

By his own account, it happened in the following way, but his memory of the period is confused and often chronologically mixed up. He wrote that he had reached such a state of depression that "somebody who cared about me," not named, but a professional acquaintance, who was one of "Dr. Feelgood's" patients, suggested that Tennessee go to him. This friend had been helped out of alcoholism by the doctor. Tennessee never mentions the doctor's name, but it has since been printed often, even on front pages: Dr. Max Jacobson.

Tennessee said the doctor had about him "a magical atmosphere of understanding and compassion." He remembered no examination, nor even having his pulse or blood pressure checked; the doctor just looked at him and "concocted a shot" that he made up from several bottles. (So it evidently was not *all* amphetamine. Apparently no one except the doctor knew what went into the mixture.)

Then he injected it into Tennessee's hip, "and within about a minute a miracle took place. It felt as if a concrete sarcophagus about me had sprung open and I was released as a bird on wing."

His friend drove him back to the empty Fifty-fifth Street apartment (this dates it as the time of the move to the duplex). He felt marvelous and asked his friend how long the feeling would last. His friend told him not to think about that.

There was nothing illegal about this—assuming it was amphetamine, which was at this time a legal drug and could be bought by anyone in pill form for about five cents a pill at any drugstore, with a prescription. Many doctors would prescribe them freely, if only for weight reduction. They reduced appetite. Students, businessmen, housewives all took amphetamine then, usually as Dexedrine. But when the "speed freaks," mostly the "hippy" dropouts, started melting down the pills and injecting them, they would sometimes put as many as a hundred pills into one shot—the alcohol equivalent of drinking a case of whiskey at one gulp. The effect was explosive and destructive.

Tennessee admitted things might not have gone so badly if he had just taken the injections and not mixed them with alcohol, Doriden, Mellaril and his morning barbiturate that he took at the same time as the shot. He had never mainlined any drug before, had never used the needle himself.

As in all things except writing, he was led almost innocently down a garden path by others. And if the writing seemed to improve, for the moment, he would go along with it.

In his second letter of this period, to Paul Bowles, he mentioned for the first time his *piccures*, or injections, that he was giving himself. (After the first injections, Dr. Max sent him vials of the liquid.) He was worried that an air bubble might kill him, but then quoted William Burroughs, who said that if a bubble killed you "there wouldn't be a living junkie on earth." Tennessee wrote that he had lost interest in both television and sex. (The sex part is odd; amphetamine usually acts as an aphrodisiac.)

He said he was going every weekday to a psychiatrist, who telephoned him on weekends to make sure he had taken his Elevil, his Unicaps and his Flovil (for his liver) and asking if he was taking his walks in Central Park and his swims at the Y. Incredibly, there was no mention of speed in connection with this doctor. Evidently he didn't tell one doctor what the other one was doing. The psychiatrist (he wrote to Bowles) wanted him to resume some kind of sex life.

One might suppose that these letters to Paul Bowles, written at a time of mental crisis, almost as a kind of outcry, would be chaotic, a mess, scarcely readable. They are not at all. The typing, certainly done with his own hands, is, as always, almost letter perfect, the spelling and grammar practically impeccable. He simply couldn't write badly, even when it didn't count.

Something explosive certainly began to happen to his playmaking. He admitted that writing became easier and much quicker. It is plainly quite different. Whether it is better than it would have been otherwise no one can say. To some writers amphetamine gives a great surge of euphoria, a reduction of inhibitions and great enthusiasm—until it wears off. Whether this helps or hurts the writing depends on the writer, and the kind of thing he is writing.

Tennessee wrote that *Slapstick Tragedy* was written with speed. Previous to this autumn there is no mention of the play. (Actually they are two short plays, *The Mutilated* and *The Gnädiges Fräulein*.) In a letter to his mother, dated October 9, 1964, he wrote that he had found a new psychiatrist who was helping him out of his depression, and that even though he had not planned to have a new play this year, he had now written *Two Slapstick Tragedies* (he later dropped the *Two*) and that Chuck Bowden (who had produced *Iguana*) wanted to produce them. Bowden was on the West Coast trying to sign Margaret Leighton for them.

The two *Slapstick* plays must have been written almost instantly, and unlike so much of the writing he had been doing previously, it had few if any roots in previous short stories or other writing.

The Mutilated takes place in the French Quarter of New Orleans, and is about a woman, presumably a whore, named Trinket, whose breast has probably (we are never told exactly) been removed, and who is being black-mailed by a shoplifter named Celeste, who threatens to tell that Trinket is mutilated. It is done to a background of Christmas carols and ends with a prayer to Our Lady. It may be Tennessee's worst play. Somehow it has the hallmark of a deeply depressed writer, as though it were done, or at least conceived, before the speed.

The other one, *The Gnädiges Fräulein* (the gracious young lady) has the wild, uninhibited feel of an amphetamine high, very high. It is an almost surrealistic farce-fantasy, partly self-mocking. It happens on Cocalooney Key; the main character is the Fräulein, whose eye has just been pecked out. The Greek chorus is composed of a society editor and her friend, both dressed in gray and white (that is, colorless). The Fräulein, very colorful, competes with the cocalooney birds, who look like Big Bird in "Sesame Street," for the waste fish at the fishermen's dock, and they eventually peck out her other eye. Grisly as this sounds, it is all done in whooping good humor. In his *World of Tennessee Williams*, Richard Leavitt says it deals with "the dualities of life-death and flesh-spirit." But it is speed all the way through, and the trouble with speed is the letdown.

There is other evidence that Tennessee was coming out of his depression, at least temporarily. In the same letter he told Dakin and his mother that he had been up to Ossining to see Rose on the previous weekend, and planned to go again the following Sunday. He was pleased with her. When they went into the drugstore she didn't ask for twelve cakes of soap, as she sometimes did.

He spent Christmas in New York with Rose. They had a Christmas tree and a fire in the fireplace. He took her to dinner at the Plaza, where she told the waiter she wanted only a Coke and a bowl of chili. The waiters at the Plaza knew her well, and were not dismayed.

CHAPTER 26

By February, Chuck Bowden was ready to go on *Slapstick Tragedy*. He had a cast, director, designer and composer—in fact, just about everything except the money. Tennessee's nerves were on edge.

It was at this time that he wrote the last letter that Donald Windham published in his 1940–65 series, and the first one he had written him in more than a year. The occasion was receiving and reading (twice) Windham's new novel, *Two People*. He told Windham it was his best book. Tennessee also told him that he and his cousin Jim had gone out to dinner, and from there to a party at Edward Albee's house, given for some Russians who never arrived. Albee's *Tiny Alice* was playing on Broadway at the time.

Bowden scraped together enough money to do some previews of *Slapstick*. He signed up Leueen MacGrath and Kate Reid, and the Broadway opening was scheduled for March. In a letter to Miss Edwina on February 16, Tennessee said they were in their second week of previews. But once again investors were afraid of fantasy, and of a bill with two short plays. The money ran out and the opening was postponed. When he was interviewed in September by John Gruen, there still wasn't enough.

So once again he was depressed, and into the midst of this new depression came the man he called "Ryan" in his *Memoirs*, and whose real name is Bill Glavin.

Like so many of the events in Tennessee's life, the entry of Bill Glavin into it was the result of a coincidence. It just happened. And Bill became, after Merlo, his intimate companion for longer than anyone else.

We located Bill in Nutley, New Jersey, across the river from Manhattan. He was living in a neat basement room in a friend's house. Bill is thin, healthy and handsome, a bit taller than Tennessee, with brown hair and a mustache, affable, intelligent and well spoken. He was wearing casual clothes, a jacket over a clean white turtleneck sweater, and was willing to be taped.

Bill said he had met Tennessee briefly years before, but had not seen him for a long time. Then—

257

BG: I ran into Mike Steen in a bar in New York. He'd moved to California. I was delighted to see him. I was living in my family's house in New Jersey, little town called Arlington, about twenty-five minutes from Manhattan, and I invited Mike to come back and stay with me that night. He was leaving for California the next day. He stayed over. I went back with him to the city the next day. There was somebody he wanted to say good-bye to. "Would you like to come up with me?" And I said, "Certainly," so we went up and we were knocking on the door, and a few minutes went by and finally the door opened and it was Tennessee, of all people. So Mike introduced me to Tennessee. I didn't say we'd met before. We went in and we had cocktails with Tennessee, and the whole situation seemed kind of strange. Tennessee was very tense.

SM: He didn't have anybody to take care of him at this time?

BG: He had a very nice young man, Jim.

DW: Jim Adams. A cousin.

BG: Jim was staying with him at the apartment. [The Fifty-fifth-Street duplex.] It struck me that Tennessee was very lonely, something struck me as wrong. And I was going through a very heavy trip in New Jersey. My mother had just died, and my father was in the process of dying of cancer. There was some empathy I picked up, it must have been, with Tennessee... I saw Mike off at the airport, and I went back to New Jersey.

[*Bill had a few beers with a friend that evening and told him:*]

"You know, there's something very sad about that man, and no one seems to be doing anything about it," and I still remember to this day his saying, "Glav, are you sure you know what you're getting into?" And I said, "It doesn't matter, I'm going to see if I can't do something." Over the next month or so I would go to Tennessee, knock on the door and wait, sometimes a very long time and he would finally answer it and I would go in.

SM: Was he on some kind of drugs?

BG: Well, he talked very well, of course, but there was something radically wrong. I think he was in great fear of everything. The telephone would ring and we'd both just sit there. Of course I couldn't answer, it wasn't my phone, and Tennessee wouldn't answer. Then I'd go back again.

SM: And nobody else was around?

BG: Jim would be in and out, you know, Jim was busy, taking classes. So gradually the phone would ring and Tennessee would say, "Bill, would you get that?" And I would get it. We would never go out to dinner. Jim would cook us something. Gradually he would say, "Would you like to go out to dinner?" And I said, "Yes." So after dinner, then we'd come home and have a drink and then I'd go back to New Jersey. I was working on the house, tearing it apart and rebuilding it. And gradually we got to know one another very well, and Jim, he had things to do, and I guess he felt the time had come to go out on his own.

[Tennessee's opinions of Glavin, as recalled years later, are that he was the handsomest of his companions, and that his greatest virtue was his managerial ability, his way of organizing the nonwriting parts of his life. That was more important than any emotional attachment. He liked his "rollicking" nature, and said they laughed a good deal together. He thought Bill had been "ruthless" in getting Jim Adams out of the apartment.]

BG: Tennessee had to go out to California for a play, and Tennessee said— he never asked me what I did or anything, I wasn't working at the time and I was too much at home—and he said, "Would you come to California with me? I really should go. I don't want to go alone." So I said, "Yes, all right," so that's how our relationship evolved. When we got back from California he asked me if I'd like to stay at the apartment. And I said yes.

SM: And you sort of did the cooking, and things like that?

BG: Well, we went out. I'd cook a hamburger for lunch if he didn't feel like going out, but eventually we started going out, and we went out from there on in. We'd go out for lunch and go out for dinner, and finally we started seeing people like Maureen Stapleton, who I knew was a dear friend. She was a very safe person and would be very kind and understanding to what Tennessee was going through. And I found out later that Maureen certainly was the one because she certainly had gone through an awful lot.

SM: And you went down to Key West?

BG: Yes, and we would go to St. Thomas . . . But we never stayed longer than two weeks at any place.

Tennessee wrote that he didn't even remember the first time they had met. Evidently it had been in the fifties, when Bill had come into his place with friends. Bill said that Tennessee had praised the beauty of his behind. However, his memory of Bill was always mixed up with his recollections of that frightful period of the 1960s, which he wanted to forget. He felt, later, that Bill was the Chance Wayne, the gigolo, of his own *Sweet Bird of Youth*, with himself as the aging, ailing star. Chance of course could not have been based on Bill because *Sweet Bird* was written before their relationship.

Tennessee said that they did not have sex together frequently, and that only at Bill's initiative, "only three or four times." And with no one else. Tennessee also stated that Bill was bisexual, and very attractive to ladies, even, apparently, to Elizabeth Taylor, whom he "embraced" during the shooting of *BOOM!* on Sardinia.

Like everyone else who knew Tennessee well, Bill was impressed by the continual work, every day.

BG: I think in the years that I knew Tennessee, I can say there were possibly three days out of those years that he didn't get up and start work immediately...and for at least two, three or four hours...and those three days that I can think of he was absolutely impossible, not unkind, but very jumpy and they weren't good days for him at all.

The speed injections had been going on for some time when Bill started living with Tennessee. Bill didn't like the idea:

BG: I certainly never approved of that witch doctor, that Dr. Feelgood...I thought he was a frightening man. I used to go to the office with Tennessee and it was such a frightening experience. His office was a very sad office, but there were many, many poor people, and no way could they have been paying, so I give that to his credit, he wasn't after money, though he was probably getting enough money from some of the other people I saw. I met him a couple of times. And a couple of times Tennessee would say, "Why don't you try this?" and I'd say, "No way!"
SM: This was basically speed?
BG: That's what it turned out to be, from what I've heard. No one will ever know, Max never said what was in it.

Bill told this story to illustrate how important the injections had become:

BG: We flew to Barcelona for a few weeks' vacation...Tennessee would get a couple of vials of brownish liquid to shoot himself up in the hips. We flew to Barcelona. Tennessee liked to stay at El Colon. So I unpacked for Tennessee, which I usually did, and hung things up, and I said, "I'll meet you downstairs and we'll have lunch." So I went upstairs, and pretty soon Tennessee walked into the restaurant. I'd got to know the man so well that I could feel his moods. The restaurant just chilled, it was like a butcher's refrigerator. And Tennessee came up to the table and he had his sunglasses on, and he sat down, and I said, "Oh, God!" I was exhausted from flying already, and he said, as only Tennessee can say, "How nice of you to have unpacked for me." And I said, "Tom, I always unpack for you." And he said, "Yes, you do, don't you?" And I said, "Oh, God, what's the matter?" And he said, "The witch doctor's brew is missing." And I said, "Tennessee, the maid would never take your medicine." Naive me! And he said, "Why of course she wouldn't." And I said, "Well, you don't think I took it!" And he said, "I know you don't approve of the witch doctor." And I said, "No, I don't, but I certainly would never take any medicine from you." So he said, "Well, we must fly back *immediately* to New York!" I said, "You mean *now?*" And he said, "Immediately!" I said, "Okay, Tom." So I got up, and I could not get [tickets] out of Barcelona—there were conventions, it was summertime—so I called the American Embassy, and they got us tickets. And being the kind of person I am, all of this was inside me, but I was really torn up, no sleep or anything, flying back to New York, neither of us saying anything. He was just staring straight ahead, with his sunglasses on. And I said, "You know, when we get back to the apartment you're going to find that stuff on your dresser." And he said, "No, I'm not!" And I said, "I'm not going back into that apartment first!" And he said, "You certainly aren't!" So we got back to New York, and I opened the door and he went in and marched into his bedroom and I marched into my bedroom and slammed the door so hard all the plaster came down, and I just fell into bed, and pretty soon there was a little tap-tapping on my door, and I said, "Ye-es?" And he said, "I found my medicine," and I said, "Oh, that's good, Tom. I'm going to go to sleep now, we'll have dinner later."

SM: And it was on his dresser?

BG: It was on his dresser.

And on another occasion:

BG: One time I didn't go to the doctor's office, and Tennessee came back into the apartment and I heard the door slam, and I saw him go rushing into his bedroom, holding the top of his head, and he said, "The doctor told me to go home immediately and work for at least four hours." He disappeared into his bedroom and hacked away for four hours and we went out to dinner afterwards, and I said, "How'd the work go?" And he said, "Oh, it wasn't worth a damn. I had to tear it all up."

It was during the first summer with Glavin that they moved to the thirty-third-floor apartment on Central Park West at Seventy-second Street.

He wrote to his mother that it had a lovely view, and would be so high that there would be no traffic noise.

During the summer of 1965 he had his last meeting with Tallulah. As Mike Steen remembered they were at a dinner party, and at the end of it Tallulah embraced Tennessee to say good-bye. They had both been drinking, and were both quite mellow. Tallulah, always witty, said to him, "Tennessee, you and I are the only constantly High Episcopalians I know."

The real turmoil going on inside him during this period must have been almost unimaginable. Only he knows about that, and he tried so desperately to forget the whole time that he did probably force most of it out of his conscious mind. In a much-quoted story, he is said to have told Gore Vidal that he slept through the sixties, and Gore replied, "Well, you didn't miss a thing, baby." Tennessee left out the accompanying caveat: "If you missed the sixties, Bird, God knows what you are going to do with the seventies."

Tennessee was willing to do anything, anything at all, to make the writing go. He would even be, as he called it, a zombie for most of the day in order to have his explosive burst of creativity, based on speed, for the three or four hours of his morning work stint. Whether or not it was wise to lash his brain this way, he had only one motive—to make the writing better.

He was struggling to drive himself into a new dimension, to go beyond the relative realism of his first great plays, and into a free flight of the imagination. He had tried this first in *Camino Real*, and he was moving toward the lovely, far-out poetry of *Out Cry*. The poet-playwright always has a problem. He cannot, like Val Xavier's bird, live forever on the wind. Unlike that bird, his actors do need feet, and food as well. His audience sits in real chairs, and sometimes coughs; his angels have no wings, only checkbooks. His bird can live only fitfully on the wind; he has to give it feet so that it could land on boards.

When he was blocked on one piece of writing, he would switch to another. At about this time he gave a long interview to John Gruen, for his book, *Close-Up*.

> I write as soon as I get up in the morning—facing that terrible question as soon as possible: Will I be able to write today? And how will I write? I begin with two cups of coffee, rather strong coffee. And then I go to my bedroom and I give myself an injection to pick me up. At first I was terrified of taking the injections—giving them to myself. But I've gradually learned to do it. And I give myself one c.c. of whatever the thing is, the formula—I don't know what it is. I just know that immediately after it I feel like a living being! Then I can go to my table and work.

In the same interview he told Gruen he had been working on a novella called *The Knightly Quest*. He was at the moment of the interview having a problem; he had taken it out of an envelope and the pages had spilled onto the floor, and two-thirds of them were not numbered. He was not sure he could ever get them back in the right order.

This is entirely believable; many of the original manuscripts in the University of Texas archives are still not numbered; some have been shuffled and are therefore almost unintelligible.

The marriage between his good friend Nan Lanier and his cousin the Episcopal priest, Sidney Lanier, was breaking up. The Reverend Mr. Lanier had fallen in love with a wealthy widow, and while this conflict was in a state of lively discussion, Nan and Sidney came to visit Tennessee and Bill. Tennessee wrote to his mother reminding her that Nan was part Cherokee Indian, and on this evening had managed to consume much firewater. She then lit into Sidney—or, as Tennessee put it, "blessed him out."

But Tennessee, in spite of his problems, still had his wits about him. Nan had got to the point of phoning the Episcopal bishop, asking him to come over to Tennessee's. Bill Glavin said that Tennessee was becoming more and more disturbed. Then Bill noted that Tennessee had disappeared altogether.

After fifteen minutes or so, during which time the situation had become even more frantic, Tennessee appeared in the living room, wearing a tuxedo. He said, "Bill, aren't you ready yet?"

Bill ran out, put on his black tie and dinner jacket and appeared in the living room. Tennessee told the others, "We have to go now!" And the two of them loped out.

"Where are we going, Tom?" asked Bill, when they reached the elevators.

"I don't know," Tennessee said. "It was the only way I could think of to get out of the apartment."

Tennessee was continuing to visit Rose. He wrote to his mother that the drives to Ossining were lovely that fall, the leaves beautifully colored. He took Rose to a restaurant, and when she had finished she told the waitress to give the rest to the hog. The waitress said they didn't have a hog, so she told her to give it to the dog. She had just changed the name of her parakeet from Ella to Rose, and then to Rosella. Though Tennessee was always sad about her, he felt she was as content and as well adjusted as she could be.

Chuck Bowden's production (with Lester Persky) of *Slapstick Tragedy* was held up for a year because of money. Leueen MacGrath had stood by for all this time. And still no money.

Tennessee continued to be worried about the plays. He knew they were in the same vein of fantasy as *Camino Real*, and it had never really succeeded. He said he was beginning to feel old, he had to work harder, he was getting tired. He needed to have his shots of speed.

Unfortunately for the patient Ms. MacGrath, Margaret Leighton became available for *Slapstick*, and only then were the investors willing to pay money. Tennessee was delighted to have Leighton, who had played Hannah so beautifully in *Iguana*. He thought she could do absolutely anything.

Leighton said to Mike Steen that during rehearsals Tennessee was "curiously placid and sanguine, for him, not for anybody else, but for him. He wasn't doing pages of rewrites."

But the atmosphere at the theater was strange. Margaret's husband, Michael Wilding, visited the theater during two weeks of previews and said, "There wasn't a mass of people flying around backstage, saying, 'Darling, this is marvelous.' Ominous silence went on. People didn't come round back, which I felt had to mean they were reserving very much their judgment and weren't entirely delighted with the plays . . . so I felt it was sort of dying as it went along. But Tennessee sat there in his box and he laughed at the jokes, which were very funny."

Slapstick Tragedy opened at the Longacre Theater in New York on February 22, 1966, directed by Alan Schneider.

Even before the curtain rose, Margaret Leighton had dire forebodings. For one thing, she could hardly move. Every performance she had to crash through a fence carrying a fish bucket, and on the night before the opening she had cracked a shoulder blade, and had to open with her arm in a sling. She had lost her voice, too, and could speak only in what she described as "a sort of little old lady's voice."

It was a disaster. Tennessee, in his *Memoirs*, put some of the blame on the director, Alan Schneider, who remained in his memory as a grin and a red baseball cap. The reviews were bad. A more considered, later opinion, was written for the Nation by Harold Clurman, who, of course, knew Tennessee well:

> However we interpret this nightmare it is written in an odd but effective mixture of gallows humor and Rabelaisian zest. On opening night the audience laughed uproariously at the broad-stroked slapdash language, but though I was able to appreciate the style I could not bring myself to smile. I was too conscious that its author was in pain. . . .
>
> Both plays are sure to be seen and acclaimed in future productions at universities, community theatres and on foreign stages.

In spite of the poor reception of the play, Tennessee took Leighton and Wilding to Sardi's the night after the opening. Tennessee said he overheard her saying to Wilding, about him, "Poor thing, it's pitiful, he doesn't know what hit him." Yet in her interview with Mike Steen, Leighton was sure she never said it. "He has invented the whole thing," she said, twice.

In any case, Tennessee was sure something had hit him, and he didn't blame Leighton at all. He said he would never forget her superb performance in *Fräulein*.

The work went everlastingly on. There was film interest in *Milk Train*, and Tennessee knew that the highly stylized Kabuki stage production would have to be changed entirely for pictures. He wrote a screenplay himself.

Bill Inge saw a copy of this screenplay before it was filmed. Someone connected with the production had shown it to him. *Milk Train* was the only play of Tennessee's that he had not seen, so it was all new to him. He told Mike Steen:

> I was living at the Algonquin Hotel for a few weeks, so I took it back to my hotel room that night and read it, and I read some of the most beautiful writing that Tennessee had ever done! I read a beautiful, flawless, deeply moving film script... And I was so deeply moved by that screenplay when I finished it, I'll admit, tears came to my eyes...

So, it is possible to write well for the screen, but the writing doesn't always find its way through the whole process. The film was called *Boom!* and Tennessee admits, himself, that from a script standpoint, *Milk Train* was successful only as the film *Boom!*

The negotiations for making it into a film were carried out in England by producer Lester Persky. He wanted Sean Connery to play Chris, but he couldn't do it; he hired Joseph Losey, whom Tennessee admired a great deal, as director. Then Persky told Tennessee that if he invested $30,000 of his own money, he thought they could get Liz Taylor and Richard Burton, and it would make him a million. Tennessee had grave doubts, mainly because of their ages.

But no one knew whether Taylor and Burton would play the parts. Bill Glavin told the "Sardinia story" to us:

BG: Tennessee and I were vacationing in Rome, and they were trying to find out who was going to play *Boom!* We wanted Elizabeth Taylor. The rest of the picture was not cast. And the Burtons were going to be in Sardinia.

SM: Yet Tennessee said that Elizabeth was too young and Burton was too old.

BG: Yes he did, but the picture hinged on Elizabeth Taylor. Taylor would have been box office... He was interested in seeing *BOOM!* done, or *Milk Train* being done, as he always called it, and if it was to be done as a movie, and the only way was with Elizabeth Taylor, then he would settle with Liz Taylor. So we went off to Sardinia. Neither one of us had ever been there before. I remember landing at the airport, and driving to the hotel, which was not on the chic part of Sardinia. The water was lovely, and everything, you know, and we were expecting the Burtons. One day we got a telephone call that the Burtons had just docked, so we went out on our balcony and we saw their yacht, they'd just bought it, it was a German yacht, ugly thing on the outside, and it steamed in, and we got a telephone call that Elizabeth would see us, so we went down to meet them. We were standing on the dockside, and, I'll never forget it, the speedboat came roaring up, and as it was a little distance away I spotted Elizabeth Taylor in the speedboat with her hair flying back, and she jumped out of the speedboat, threw her arms around Tennessee. She had white ducks on, and she said, "Look what's happened to me, just because I insisted on meeting you at the dock." And one pant leg was all wet. In stepping off their yacht into the speedboat the waves had shifted and her leg got caught between the speedboat and the yacht... So then we went out onto the yacht and there was Richard Burton and Rex Harrison and his wife and a couple of other people. We had cocktails. Elizabeth had two little dogs, so she brought them down and said, "Guess what, my babies have made love for the first time." And I thought that was kind of charming, and they were talking about the picture, and I went in to mix a drink. [*They all had dinner on the yacht, and Tennessee and Bill finally went back to their hotel.*]

BG: The next day we still had no idea whether the Burtons were going to play the parts or not. All of a sudden we saw their yacht pull out. The Burtons were leaving, and it turned out they went up to the next cove. They finally telephoned, so we got the car and went out on their yacht again. Richard was there, and Elizabeth was in bed. Tennessee and Richard were talking on the deck and I went in to see Elizabeth, and she said, "You know, Bill, I really hurt myself yesterday!" And she had a terrible bruise on her leg. And Richard came in and said, "Watcha up to, Love?" And we just laughed, and when we went out Elizabeth said she would do the picture, and Richard announced that he would do it, too. I remember Elizabeth saying, "Don't you think you're a little overweight, Richard?" And—Burton and I got along great—he looked over at me and he said, "By the time we're about to shoot I'll be as gaunt as Glavin." And Elizabeth said, "Don't push your luck, Richard!"

And that is how, in the upper reaches of jet-set cinematics, big agreements are made. They shot the picture in Sardinia in a location of extraordinary beauty.

Tennessee still thought that Elizabeth was too young and Burton too old, but he liked the direction and the script and he loved the sets. He thought the film was an artistic success in spite of the miscasting.

But Bill Inge, who had thought the script was so very beautiful, went to see the movie:

> I think I spent about twenty-five minutes at that movie. It took me about that long to find out that the people who had produced that movie had understood nothing of it. They had not seen or felt its poetry. They had seen none of the beauty in the script that I had read. The flawless, flawless film script had been changed and had been destroyed. And then it was so disheartening to hear on television and read in the newspapers and magazines the critical reactions to it. Of course it is always easy to blame the writer, and I think I heard Miss Judith Crist on television tell what a lousy script Mr. Williams had given this great director, Mr. Joe Losey, to work with. That was the attitude that all the critics took...

Tennessee's assumption that Glavin was bisexual sometimes created considerable friction in their relationship, and several times seemed close to destroying it. Bill's interest in Elizabeth Taylor is clear, and Tennessee was even more worried about Bill's affection for Nan Lanier, who by this time was divorced from Tennessee's cousin Sidney. Nan (called "Anne" by Bill) was with them part of the time in Italy.

Tennessee remembered an incident in Positano, when the three of them were in a cab. They were in the back seat, and Bill had an arm around Nan's shoulders. Bill said, as a joke, that Tennessee should go and sit in the front seat. But Tennessee said he got angry and told Bill to get out of the cab. And he did.

Glavin told another story of the Positano trio, showing his side of the coin.

BG: We were staying in a very lovely place. The apartments kind of dripped over this beautiful cliff. We were all situated every which way. Anne was in one apartment at one level... About twelve of us went out to dinner. [Among them were Maggie Smith and Bob Stevens.] Ten-

nessee loved to eat, nothing interrupted him, he had a voracious appetite—for everything, it seems. And all of a sudden, we were all eating
and having a marvelous time, I thought, and Tennessee looked at Anne
and said, "I know what you're up to!" And of course everyone kind of
stopped eating, with their forks half raised to their mouths, and he of
course kept shoveling in the pasta, and Anne said, "What do you mean?"
And Tennessee said, "I know, you're running off to London with Glavin!"
And that I did not expect to hear. Anne said, "What do you mean?"
And he said, "I saw you both sitting on that balcony with the flowers
spilling over, and geraniums as big as footballs, holding hands and having
cocktails, last night." I said, "Tom, we were having an after-dinner drink,
which you were invited to, and you didn't want to come." And Anne
burst into tears and fled up the hill. And that was the last we saw of
Anne. End of a lovely dinner. Tennessee finished his dinner. Nobody
else did.

These were things that happened in the afternoons and the evenings,
but the work went on, seven mornings a week. During much of this time
he was writing *The Two-Character Play*, which would later evolve into *Out
Cry*.

Tennessee and Glavin went back in the autumn to New York, to the
apartment on Central Park West.

CHAPTER 27

He wrote to Dakin that he was looking forward to the New York City Center revival of *The Rose Tattoo*, with Maureen Stapleton, who had created the part. He was worried about Maureen because her husband had recently left her. But she was getting back into shape physically, trimming down, and weighed less than when she played Serafina fifteen years before.

Tennessee was also concerned about the recent Florida hurricane, which had damaged his property, and also about his colored cook, Leoncia, who had to have one eye removed and a glass one put in. He was paying for the operation.

Shortly afterward, he wrote to Miss Edwina that she must think of Rose as being as happy as they could possibly make her. He would be bringing her to New York to shop for a new winter coat. He would take her to dinner at the Plaza with their friend Jo Healy.

He said, too, that he had seen a relative, Joseph Lanier Williams, who sold clothing, and also owned the plantation called Panther Creek, which had come down through the family, bought by the first Williamses in America.

He was still writing and at this time seemed to be swinging back and forth between his *Two-Character Play*, an early draft of *Confessional*, which would later evolve into *Small Craft Warnings*, and a third play, *Kingdom of Earth*.

And he was still using injections of speed. Dakin was beginning to notice personality changes in his brother. During the next summer he and Joyce and Edwina went out to the West Coast again, to stay at the Beverly Hills Hotel, while Tennessee was conferring with the film moguls. While he was in Tennessee's room a special delivery package arrived, containing vials of the brown syrupy liquid. Tennessee was becoming obsessed with unfounded fears that even his closest friends were conspiring against him.

Tennessee was most concerned at this time about revising and polishing *The Two-Character Play* for its tryout in England by the Hampstead Theatre Club, the London equivalent of a first-class Off-Broadway theater.

Though he said he worked longer on *Milk Train* than on any other play, he seems to have felt more protective, almost obsessive about *The Two-Character Play*, and its later version, *Out Cry*. As much a long dramatic poem as a play, it is unlikely to have, in this age, the popular appeal of dramas like *Menagerie* and *Streetcar* and *Cat*, but is considered by many to be his most sensitive and beautiful work. Beethoven once said about his extraordinary last quartets, when told that they were "not music": "No, not for our time." Perhaps *Out Cry* is still ahead of our time; it has almost no conventional plot, and no copybook conflicts.

It seems to have grown, by a kind of accretion, from a beautiful short play that takes place in the South. There is no realistic setting, the sets are all built out of words. A brother and sister, Felice and Clare, are living, like recluses, in their family's house. Their mother and father have been killed, perhaps, as the sister says, by a housebreaker (we assume this is not true), or that "father killed mother and himself" (possibly true), or even conceivably (we're never sure) the two of them may have done it, or perhaps they only *thought* they might have.

Their relationship is—incestuous? Well, perhaps not physically—or is it? They are insane? Well, they know all about State Haven, the local asylum; they have surely been inmates there. They have no money, and no way of making it, and now almost no food, and are terrified to go out, and they will probably just stay in the house and starve.

This short play could certainly stand on its own, but it isn't long enough for an "evening." Around it, Tennessee has constructed a play-around-the-play, which then makes it a play-within-a-play, and the characters are actors, also brother and sister, and also named Felice and Clare, who are discovered at the very beginning, on a kind of stage-within-a-stage, in an unnamed country, abandoned by the rest of their company. They want to, and yet are terrified to, act out "the two-character play."

It is too easy to assume that the incestuous, or near-incestuous relationship stands for Tennessee's love for his sister. It is more likely that Felice and Clare are two facets of Tennessee himself, full of all the inner terror that did indeed haunt him at the time. The characters, like Tennessee himself in the sixties, are gentle, sensitive, vulnerable, fearful and dreadfully alone. If there is such a thing as symbolic or abstract autobiography, this is it, beautiful, haunting and terrifying, possibly more so than some audiences can stand.

One of the people who read the script early was Hume Cronyn, husband of Jessica Tandy, the original Blanche of *Streetcar*. The two of them had done (and done superbly) *The Four Poster*, one of the longest-running two-character plays in history. In his talk with Mike Steen, Cronyn gave his reaction after reading the play, which he thought was something that "Jess and I might attempt."

Cronyn thought it was "terribly difficult to do but I thought it was impressive and that there was some marvelous writing in it. And that, in a fashion, there was more revelation of Tennessee in that play than in anything of his that I have ever read."

It was produced in December 1967, in Hampstead, in northeast London, far from the West End theater district. But it wasn't too far to go for the London critics. They were not greatly impressed, though the London *Times* reported, "Mr. Williams succeeds quite brilliantly in sustaining the idea that nothing whatever is to be relied upon and if we get through one veil there is another just beyond."

Hume Cronyn and Jessica went to London to see it. Cronyn thought the production was disappointing, and that it should be done again, and differently. Cronyn telephoned Audrey Wood and Tennessee. Williams told him:

> "I'm not at all well, Hume, I'm not at all well. I'm feeling miserable."
>
> And I think [Hume continued] that part of the problem recently is that current success has escaped him. It's as though he were writing on a different plane, on a different level, and somehow the form and pressure of this time is escaping him and he is seeking desperately to find some way of expressing himself to the world of today, particularly to the young people of today. In *The Two-Character Play* that quality came over very, very strongly. I mean that terrible effort to reach out to say what had to be said. The whole setting, the dark theatre, the sense of being locked in, the quality of alienship, if there is such a word. There was only one person in the world with whom he had any kind of relationship at all, or either character had. And even that was half fantasy. If was a dream world in which somehow two people were baying at the moon.

It was a shrewd analysis. But Cronyn and Tandy, unfortunately, never did the play. Tennessee wanted Margaret Leighton for it and tried to persuade her. So did Audrey Wood, but it wasn't to be. That was not, however, the end of *The Two-Character Play*. He would continue to work at it, off and on, for another five years.

By this time, early in 1968, he had finished another play, *Kingdom of Earth*, perhaps the most underestimated of all his plays.

Its period of gestation was long, even for Tennessee. He believes the idea first came to him back in 1940, when a whore was sitting on his bed, in Mexico. The girl was American and the bride of a wealthy young Mexican, who had married her in New York, and then driven Tennessee (who had met him through a car-sharing ad) to Mexico City. The young man seemed to be having problems consummating the marriage, and Tennessee was explaining to the disappointed bride that he, Tennessee, was scarcely in a position to do much better.

The idea lay dormant for a long time. What would happen if a man, not especially *macho*, brought a whore back home as his bride?

Years later he wrote a short story about it, one which, in those days, would have been considered much too sexually explicit to be published in most magazines. It appeared in a limited edition of the *Hard Candy* collection, published by New Directions in 1954; and is no longer in that collection, but now in *The Knightly Quest* volume.

It is in the final paragraph of the story that the title appears. (The story is written in the first person, as told by the character named Chicken.) Chicken didn't know about the Kingdom of Heaven. Did anyone? He was full of lust. It was earth he was after.

In the story there is no flood, and the other male, named Lot, is not a transvestite, as he would become in the play.

The story later became a one-act play, which was published in Esquire with the same *Kingdom of Earth* title. The action in both story and play had been brought back to Williams country, the Mississippi Delta.

As the play grew into full length, the weaker of the two males, Lot, becomes more effeminate, with bleached blond hair. The girl, Myrtle, is a small-time carnival showgirl, and sometime prostitute. (The original story is much more specific about this. She was actually in a brothel in Memphis.)

The third character, Chicken, has become, in the play, half black, the bastard son of a white father and a black woman. The main reason Lot marries the whore is to cheat Chicken out of the family farm. There are only these three people, and the Mississippi River, whose flood waters are rising.

Even in the expanded, full-length version, the play retains its simple story, with little added except a flood. It is strong, and inevitable, and has much of the power and poetry of *Streetcar* and *Cat*. Tennessee seems to be back home again. The very first line, describing the set, makes this clear: "It should have the mood of a blues song about loneliness."

Hollywood offered him $400,000, cash on the barrel, in a preproduction deal, with bonus clauses hiking it up to more than a million dollars if the play became a big success on Broadway. As finally produced, on film, it was called *The Last of the Mobile Hot-Shots*, made by Sidney Lumet.

David Merrick agreed to produce the stage version and José Quintero was signed to direct. Tennessee wanted Maureen Stapleton to play Myrtle. He had written it, he said, with her in mind. But the producers wanted Estelle Parsons, who had just become a big name because of her fine job in the film *Bonnie and Clyde*. She would later win an Academy Award for it.

Tennessee, almost desperate for success after the last terrible years, was especially nervous, and Parsons, who liked him immediately, noticed this. Both she and Mike Steen were at some of the early rehearsals. Parsons said:

> I remember feeling that maybe he was laughing out of some nervousness of his own. Sometimes it would be nice to hear him laugh and other times I would wonder what he was laughing it, because he has such a big laugh you couldn't miss it. I felt that he seemed very naked, and I suppose naturally that goes without saying that a playwright is naked when his play is read. But you seem to really feel it from Tennessee. You feel things from him and that's very unusual, because you meet few people even in the theater who are not awfully well covered up in social circumstances. But Tennessee doesn't seem to be. He just puts his heart right out on the line the whole time.

And there was an important change in the way Tennessee acted. He did not, as usual, hover over all the rehearsals and make vast revisions. Steen said, "He wasn't at the rehearsals...as often as any of us would have liked him to be."

There were many problems. As Dakin wrote, in an article in the St. Louis *Globe-Democrat*, Tennessee and David Merrick had a quarrel about the title, which he said Merrick considered "too biblical." Merrick wanted to call it *The Seven Descents of Myrtle*, referring to the seven descents into Dante's *Inferno*, but Broadway wags said it was because Myrtle came downstairs seven times during the play. Others thought it was about The Seventy Cents of Myrtle, presumably reduced from two bucks.

Tennessee hated the new title. The argument almost escalated into legal action, and he finally gave in. Myrtle's seven descents went up in lights, but the printed version is now called *Kingdom of Earth*, with Myrtle's descents in parentheses and small letters.

There were arguments over direction, too. Tennessee wrote that Merrick wanted to fire José Quintero, but Tennessee wanted him to stay, and stay he did. José was having drinking problems, which he later overcame.

Parsons happened to meet Kazan and told him she was scared about doing the play. He gave her excellent advice:

> Get with Tennessee every hour of the day and night. Whenever you can sneak out to be by Tennessee's side you be there, because he knows more about his work than anyone and he'll tell you. So I did try to do that.

She had to admit that at this time Tennessee wasn't talking a whole lot to anyone. But something must have rubbed off, because Tennessee thought her performance was "superb." He thought Brian Bedford, who played Lot, was superb, too. There was some criticism of the casting of Harry Guardino, usually fine in Italian parts, as Chicken, who was supposed to be half black. Parsons thought the part should have been played by a black.

The Philadelphia tryout went reasonably well. Harry Murdock, the *Inquirer*'s man, wrote that the play "contains the acid humor, the alleviating passion and the earthy conversation that has characterized all the works of Tennessee Williams." He was respectful, but not ecstatic. He may have been a bit weary, too. The Philadelphia version ran for three hours. Tennessee finally cut forty-five minutes during the two weeks before the Broadway opening on March 27, at the Ethel Barrymore Theater.

Dakin was there, covering the opening for the *Globe-Democrat*. He joined Tennessee after the show.

> Sardi's restaurant was the scene of the last act of Tennessee's *Seven Descents*. Dante's Inferno had been the inspiration for the show's final title and Tennessee looked as though he had been through the torments of hell as I met him on the steps of the famous restaurant.
>
> The crowded room burst into applause for Tennessee as I followed my brother into the room that he dreaded to enter to await the reviews. It was almost like a condemned man entering a chamber of execution. Somehow he sensed that Barnes' review would be bad.
>
> "I will stay only fifteen minutes," he said, "and will withdraw to my apartment before the reviews come in."
>
> Photographers edged their way to our table and celebrities of show business appeared to be photographed with my brother. He permitted this to take place without relish. He seemed to be beyond protest, utterly exhausted by what he had been through.

José Ferrer came up, resplendent in a red vest, but looking much like a king of hell in his beard and his dark features. . . .

True to his word, Tennessee took his departure, pausing to speak or wave to members of the cast, and to Angela Lansbury of *Mame*, celebrities like Ed Sullivan and former Mayor Robert Wagner, movie stars such as Joanne Woodward—and disappeared into the enshrouding night.

Dakin stayed long enough to discover that the *Times* "had failed to appreciate the show." And no one else was very enthusiastic. Only Walter Kerr, writing later in his Sunday review in the *Times*, said that it had excellent and funny characterizations, and hoped that Tennessee would rewrite it. He did, of course, cutting it still more.

Kingdom of Earth was helped at the box office slightly when Estelle Parsons won her Academy Award for her role in *Bonnie and Clyde*, about two weeks after the New York opening, but nothing could save it. The play closed, having run only about a month.

There were, however, many later productions. For example, in March 1975, it had a fine production at the McCarter Theater in Princeton, using its original *Kingdom* title. It was revised by Tennessee and slightly shortened. It was also labeled "a comedy." Clive Barnes was there, and reported that the "writing can be seen as possessing a great deal of humor and strength." However, he thought the construction was "flimsy." But he said there was "still a power and sweetness to the play."

But Tennessee was very disappointed. He began a period of slightly more than a year that was to be the strangest and probably the most painful of his life and would end by his being committed to a mental institution for three months, and breaking with Dakin, Glavin, Audrey Wood, in fact, almost all of his former friends and associates.

Meanwhile there was a period of considerable sound and fury, not all of it signifying anything.

On the morning of June 23, 1968, the world was awakened with the news that Tennessee Williams was missing, and possibly murdered.

Dakin, in Collinsville, Illinois, had received a letter from Tennessee, mailed in New York and unquestionably in his brother's handwriting, saying:

> If anything of a violent nature happens to me, ending my life abruptly,
> it will not be a case of suicide, as it would be made to appear. I am

not happy, it is true, in a net of con men, but I am hard at work, which is my love, you know.

That was written in ink. Above it was a headline written in pencil:

MELODRAMATIC BUT TRUE.

All of this was scrawled on the stationery of L'Escargot, which may sound like a den of thieves, but was actually a fashionable French restaurant on Third Avenue between Fifty-eighth and Fifty-ninth streets.

Dakin was alarmed and told the press, "I believe he is in quite imminent danger. I'm inclined to believe he's packed up and gone into hiding."

The New York police sped to Tennessee's apartment on West Seventy-second Street. No one was there, and there was no indication where Tennessee had gone. Telephone calls to his agent, Audrey Wood, and his lawyer, Allan Schwartz, revealed nothing. Tennessee Williams was missing.

And he was certainly not at L'Escargot, eating snails, anymore. The headwaiter merely shrugged. He had no idea where Monsieur Williams was.

The Collinsville, Illinois, telephone switchboard received its first (and probably last) call from *Pravda*, in Moscow, for Dakin Williams. Moscow wanted to know: had Tennessee Williams really been murdered? Moscow knew that he lived in a violent capitalistic society, where people were murdered all the time. Dakin told *Pravda* he didn't know. No one knew whether his brother was alive—or dead.

In order to get to the bottom of all this, we shall have to go back to the beginning. It all started, as we can read in *Memoirs*, with a lady friend who was looking for some pills. She telephoned saying she needed money to get home, and Tennessee said to come up, he would give her cab fare. She came up to the thirty-third-floor apartment, and it was clear that she really wanted some of Tennessee's pills, the *strong* pills, like Seconal. He offered her some Miltowns.

At that point Bill Glavin returned. The woman looked at Bill, then pulled Tennessee out to the main concrete balcony. How could he, she asked, live on the thirty-third floor with a man with eyes like Glavin's, and a balcony like this?

Tennessee wrote that he called up the moving company, and the next morning all the furniture was removed.

Bill Glavin's taped version goes like this:

BG: I don't know the lady in question, but the telephone rang. She was from New Jersey, and Tennessee hadn't seen her in a long time. Tennessee said, "She's an old friend, coming to visit, a lovely creature, you're just going to love her." I said, "Fine," and the doorbell rang and Tennessee jumped up and said, "I'll get it," and he flung open the door and here was this poor creature leaning up against the doorjamb, poor thing, she was a wreck . . . She came in and she sat on the couch and Tennessee and I sat on the other couch. I mixed them a drink and she asked Tennessee if he had any pills and Tennessee said, "I have some Librium," and of course she wouldn't talk about Librium, she wanted Seconals, or Doriden or something, so she tried to lock in on me, and she said, "Tennessee, where do you get the nerve to live on the thirty-third floor with somebody who has eyes like that?" And believe it or not, I think it was shortly after that that we moved out of the place.

SM: According to the *Memoirs*, he moved out the next day.

BG: No, that's not true, and everyone knew where we were. We went to, I can't think of the name of the hotel, awful place, and it was the hotel where Tennessee sent that letter off to Dakin.

SM: What letter was that?

BG: Well, if I should be found dead, it won't be an accident.

SM: Presumably you were going to kill him.

BG: That's a funny story. There was a marvelous little French restaurant we used to go to, L'Escargot, and we were there having lunch. We'd just visited [a woman who later died of cancer]. We had walked into this [hospital] room and you could smell death all around you. So, I was having lunch with Tennessee, and he said, "There was nothing wrong with that lady," and I said, "How can you say that when we just left the room, stinking of death." And he started to scream at me and I started to scream at him, and he said, "You're as queer as a two-dollar bill," and I started to laugh, and I said, "The expression is 'three-dollar bill,'" and he said, "You must leave immediately," and I said, "You mean the restaurant, or you mean for good, or what?" And he said, "Leave immediately!" And I got up and as I was going out the door, I heard him call the waiter for a pen and paper, and I thought, "Oh, God, what's he up to now?" So I went back to the hotel and went to sleep. And next day the telephone rang and it was either Bob Simons or Allan Schwartz, the lawyer, and he said, "Where's Tennessee?" and I said, "What time is it?" and he said it was eight o'clock in the morning, and I said, "Well, I'm sure he's in his room." And he said, "Well, have you heard the radio?" And I said, "At eight o'clock in the morning?" And he said, "Well, this letter was sent off, and now in London, and Tokyo, and Berlin—" And I said, "Well, he's perfectly okay." Of course we'd just moved out of the apartment to this hotel. So I waited for Tom to call me and he finally called me, and he said, "Shall we have some lunch?" "Marvelous idea," I said. "Have you written to your brother lately?" And he said [Bill went into a deep Mississippi drawl], "Why should ah write to mah brothuh?" and I said, "Have you had the TV on, or anything?" He said, "No." And I said, "Well, that letter you wrote to Dakin said if you should be found dead, it wouldn't be an accident." "Oh," he said. I said, "Listen, I'm picking you up, like every five minutes, scared to death you're going to fall and hurt yourself when I'm not with you, and I'm not going to go to prison or be sent to the electric chair because you fall down and I'm not next to you." And he said, "Let's go down and have some lunch." And I said, "Oh, Christ!" So we went down, and we were sitting at the bar and Tennessee said, "I don't think I'm giving you enough money," and I said, "You're giving me plenty of money."

SM: How much was he paying you, or do you want to answer that?

BG: I don't know. Two hundred a week? Something like that. But, I said, "You can do something, show me a little consideration, a little kindness." He said, "No, I'm not paying you enough money, you're going to get three hundred a week." And I said, "I don't need three hundred a week." And he said, "Shall we have some lunch?" And I went up the next day to see the packers. We'd both moved out of the apartment, and moved into this one on Fifth Avenue and Central Park South. No big to-do about it—but the papers had gone to the [thirty-third floor] apartment, and we weren't there.

SM: Dake, this was the time you got the call from Moscow?

DW: Yes. I thought there was a genuine threat to his life, so I gave [the story] to Walter Orthwein and he put it on the front page of the [St. Louis] *Globe-Democrat* and all the news services picked it up from there.

It should be added that, in spite of the statement in *Memoirs*, Tennessee had suddenly, and in terror, called the moving company to get all the furniture out the next day—well, the New York *Times* reported that the lease on the thirty-third-floor apartment was up the next day, anyway.

So, as Tennessee wrote, it *was* melodramatic—but was it true?

Tennessee did telephone Dakin to let him know he was all right, so that his mother wouldn't worry. Miss Edwina, questioned by reporters, said she hadn't worried much anyway. "My son," she said, "has done such things before."

But Tennessee's real problem was that he was terribly depressed over the reception of *Kingdom of Earth*, a play that he felt, with reason, deserved better treatment.

*   *   *

That autumn he and Glavin spent several months in the Los Angeles area, partly because of the production of *Camino Real* at the Mark Taper Forum. He was having a love affair with California, which might have resulted in a permanent move there if it had not been for some very strange, and also highly melodramatic, happenings, even more so than the New York flurry, and involving considerable quantities of blood, real blood, on the floor.

In October he wrote two letters to Dakin, urging him to bring their mother out to California, even suggesting that she might want to rent the Clayton house and move there permanently. He suggested that Dakin and Joyce and their daughters move out there, too, so they could all "be close together in such a lovely part of the country."

Dakin and Miss Edwina did come out for a short visit, but Tennessee was unable to uproot them from the St. Louis area. He was still thinking about staying in California himself and was talking with a real estate dealer about a house with a swimming pool. He was prepared to negotiate, planning "to find many defects in the property before an offer."

Tennessee had been to see that Hollywood monument, Mae West, whom he found "so egocentric that she talked entirely about herself." He found her "boring but touching," and noted that Glavin was not allowed to smoke "in the presence."

He was also conferring with Mike Steen, who was interested in making a film of one of Tennessee's short stories, "One Arm," the title story of one of his collections. It is about a one-armed male prostitute and a strange murder.

He wrote to Dakin that he was already making more friends in California than he had in either Key West or New York. It looked as though he might abandon Florida and become a Californian.

But this was all changed by the weird and disputed "kidnapping of Tennessee Williams." There is no question that *something* happened—but exactly what?

Tennessee himself, in his *Memoirs*, barely hints at all that went on during a "fantastic" night, but then, as he admits, he had only a dim view of it, since it happened while he was lying in his bedroom, drugged. He stated that there had been a fight between a man he calls "Pat," not his real name, and Ryan, not Glavin's real name either, and that the floor was stained with blood.

One fact seems to be agreed upon, that the blood was Glavin's, so he has a right to tell his version of the story.

Both Tennessee and Glavin had known Pat for many years, and during that visit to California, where Pat lived, he occasionally drove them around. Listening to the conversation of Pat and his friends, Glavin thought, "My God, these guys are fascists!"

Since *fascist* is a semantically loaded word, Glavin was asked:

SM: What kind of things were they saying?
BG: I wish I could—[remember]—I can't.
SM: Against Jews, things like that?
BG: Everything they said was in a fascist tone.

[So, nothing specific. But whether they were "fascist" or not, Pat and his friends were probably talking to Tennessee about Glavin, who they thought was a bad influence on Tennessee.]

BG: I don't know what happened between Tennessee and me. Pat finally got to him, I guess.

[They were at the Hollywood-Roosevelt Hotel, and while Glavin was sitting by the pool . . .]

BG: Tennessee came down to the pool.
SM: Did you have any idea that Tennessee had any feeling about this fascist stuff, too, or was he conscious of it?
BG: I don't think he was. He came down to the pool and he said, "You'll find the ticket at the front desk. We're not to see each other anymore." At the time I was totally exhausted by all these goings-on, and I said, "All right," and he said, "You're to leave tomorrow. Look up Bob Simon—" that was his accountant—"and there'll be some money for you in New York." I said, "That's nice, but I'm not leaving tomorrow. No one tells me to leave for anywhere." And I got up from the table, and I left a couple of days later. And in the meantime Maureen Stapleton called me at the Hollywood-Roosevelt and said, "I hear you're in trouble out there," and I said, "How did you know?" "Never mind how I know, you get back here." I went back [to New York] having no idea what was going on, and I got a call from Audrey, and she said, "Bill, what's going on out there? I just got a telephone call from Tennessee saying he was surrounded by fascists and would you come out and get him?" And I said, "Well, if Tom is in trouble, of course I'll go out." I left the next

day, and I got to the airport—I don't remember if I telegraphed him I was coming, or told Audrey to tell him I was coming—anyway, when I got to the airport in Los Angeles, I was being paged, it was Tennessee, and I said I had made a reservation at the Hollywood-Roosevelt, and he said, "There is no need for you to stay there, I have this big house in the canyon, come right there." So I asked him the address.

SM: He'd rented a house in the canyon?

BG: Pat had probably rented it for him. So I took a taxi, and I had my suitcase, and I got out of the cab, and I walked through the kitchen, and there was Pat's friend, and to say he was surprised to see me is putting it mildly, and he said, "What are you doing here?" And I said, "Where's Tennessee?" And he said, "He's resting." So we were sitting there, and this friend, he was all right, he offered me a drink, and I was sitting there drinking—and Pat came in through the sliding glass doors, his arms full of groceries, and he dropped them, turned white as a ghost and looked at his friend and said, "What is he doing here?" He still wasn't quite upset yet... And he turned to me and he said, "What the hell are you doin' here?" And I said, "Ask Tennessee." He turned to his friend and he said, "Has Tennessee made any phone calls?" and the guy said, "No." Pat went over to the other side of the kitchen to the chair—and I was getting a little nervous, and then all of a sudden—it seemed like a flash, like a bolt of lightning—he was off of that chair, and he was on me and had a hammerlock, and he had me down on the floor, and he had one arm around my neck, the hammerlock, and the other around my throat, and my face pushed onto the rug, and I started to black out. I said, well I guess this is it... and luckily enough he let up, he still had the hammerlock, he got me outside and bent me over a car that was in the driveway, and he was twisting my arm, and saying, "I'd like to rip this arm right out of your socket," and he told his friend to go and call the police, and those were the dearest words I ever heard, and I just stayed over the hood of the car until the cops arrived. And of course there was blood all over the rug, from my nose. And the cops arrived and Pat said, "We caught this man trying to break into the house." And I said, to the officer, "This is ridiculous, Mr. Williams, who lives here, invited me here." And the cop said to Pat and his friend, "What about this?" and they said, "Mr. Williams is under a doctor's care and cannot be disturbed." So the police went through my bags and everything and said, "Well, we're going to take you downtown," and I said, "Great! Get me out of here before these guys kill me." So they took me down to the police station.

* * *

Meanwhile, back in the canyon, a somewhat drugged Tennessee awakened in the bedroom and walked out to the kitchen to find the floor stained with blood. And there was a man, unknown to him, and "formidable," who began to give him a "piercing inquisition." And his temporary secretary, hired to take the place of Glavin, was washing the dishes and not helping him.

The "formidable" man was actually a psychiatrist, sent by his friend Bill Inge. He was allowed to telephone Inge, but Inge said he was having a party. So, before they could stop him, Tennessee quickly dialed the operator and shouted to her to get the police to come to Hermit's Glen, that people were invading his house and there was blood on the floor.

The psychiatrist ran out, Pat started mopping the bloody floor and Tennessee phoned Audrey Wood in New York. Audrey, who, according to Tennessee, "hated Pat and was fond of Ryan," said that Ryan—that is, Bill—was trying to get bailed out of jail, where he had been sent by Pat as a housebreaker.

Back to the Los Angeles police station: Ryan—Bill—had a police record—an unpaid traffic ticket. He owed sixty-eight dollars and he didn't have that much with him, so he was frantically calling friends to get the money, among them Audrey Wood, in New York, who thought he was joking. But at least she told him to meet Tennessee at the Hollywood-Roosevelt Hotel.

The police were still not sure that Glavin was not a burglar or a kidnapper, and telephoned Dakin in Collinsville. Dakin told them that Bill was okay.

The police arrived at Hermit's Glen and escorted Tennessee to the hotel. There he found Bill, who had managed to pay his fine. As Bill said:

BG: He came to the hotel and he said, "What happened?" and I told him and he said, "Well, we must fly out of here immediately. These people are trying to kill me."

SM: You think he was being paranoid about this?

BG: No, and he told me they'd pulled out all the telephone wires out of the house and there was only one phone working.

SM: Was that true?

BG: Yes, I don't think Tennessee made that up.

So they did fly back to New York and the California migration was over.

Of course "Pat" should have known better. He is neither a fascist nor a gangster, and though he seems from Glavin's account to come out of this as the bad guy, his intentions, however misguided (or however his plan misfired) were to help, even rescue Tennessee.

Pat, who has been quoted in this book under his real name, wrote the authors a letter saying, "I still can't resist being protective of TW. I am not worried that 'Pat' may come across as a 'bad guy' in TW's *Memoirs*. One doesn't help people they love and wonder what others will think of them."

Pat's motive was to protect Tennessee, to free him from what he regarded as the dangerous influence of Bill Glavin, even to force him into what Pat regarded as almost emergency psychiatric care.

One of Tennessee's problems is that he inspires in all who know him, and love him, this exaggerated impulse to protect him and, if necessary, even to capture him, for his own good, and nobody likes to be captured for any reason.

It is not only that they believe he is a valuable national resource; they feel they have to protect him because they love him, and because he can't, or won't, protect himself.

Tennessee's backlash against all this possessive cosseting is a desperate don't-fence-me-in phobia, a kind of rage for freedom. Once he hears the benevolently closed gate clang behind him he becomes a caged lion, roaring that he has the right *not* to be protected, even from himself.

Bill Glavin was, arguably, at this time, a bad influence on Tennessee, but he was no deliberate villain. In the autumn of 1968 Bill probably knew Tennessee better than anyone else, possibly better than anyone except Frank Merlo had *ever* known him. He also wanted to protect Tennessee, but within the framework of Tennessee's own desires and life-style.

Bill was enough of a pragmatist to know that Tennessee would rebel against any restraint, would in fact throw him out, and Bill did not want to be thrown out. Bill's life with Tennessee was not an easy one, but it was fascinating and well paid. He wanted to hang onto the job.

There is no doubt that Bill was, and still is, very fond of Tennessee. His lingering feeling is one of affection, even though he was so often frustrated, exasperated and mind-boggled in the relationship. Bill understood Tennessee's real but dangerous belief that it was his way of life that was an important ingredient in his method of writing; that Tennessee meant it when he said, "If I got rid of my demons, I'd lose my angels."

Neither Bill nor Pat nor Dakin—and no doubt not even Tennessee himself—knew the answer to the dilemma: how to save Tennessee from himself without destroying him, as well as the playwright, in the process.

The "kidnapping" affair, then, was a kind of rehearsal, a dire prediction, of the dreadful crack-up that was only a few months away.

CHAPTER 28

In January 1969 Dakin persuaded Tennessee to be baptized into the Roman Catholic church. Tennessee had said he would be willing to do this on his deathbed, if only to please Dakin. And at this moment, and not for the first time, it looked as though the deathbed might not be far away.

"Don't you think," Dakin asked, "it is time to call a priest?" He was quite surprised when Tennessee agreed.

They were in Key West. A priest was called and a baptismal ceremony was held on Epiphany at St. Mary's Star of the Sea Catholic Church. Tennessee quoted Father Le Roy's teaching about life after death as something that had to be taken on faith. "Jesus Christ taught it (the doctrine), so it must be true," he said. And he later added, to *Time* magazine, that he was converting to "get my goodness back."

Bill Glavin was there and in honor of the occasion Bill (already baptized in the church) confessed and returned to the church.

The only other people present were Dakin, Tennessee's black cook Leoncia and Margaret Foresman, then editor of the local paper, the Key West *Citizen*.

Foresman, who is now part of the local government of Key West, in an interview said that she and Leoncia, who were down in the front of the church, didn't know what they were supposed to do; neither one was a Catholic. Foresman said that Tennessee's prebaptismal confession was probably "the shortest confession in history." After the ceremony they all went back to Tennessee's house.

Margaret Foresman has known Tennessee for more than twenty years, long before the death of Frank Merlo. She often visited the Duncan Street compound, invited as often by Frank as by Tennessee. Like almost everyone, she was very fond of Frank.

However, the conversion to Catholicism seems to have had little effect on Tennessee's life. He rarely goes near a church, and seemed embarrassed when the priest came to his Key West house to visit.

His psychological storm continued, but he was still writing, and a new playscript was ready for production early that year—*In a Bar of a Tokyo Hotel*.

Richard Lee Marks and Henry Jaffee signed contracts to produce this, and reserved the Eastside Playhouse, an Off-Broadway theater in uptown Manhattan. The producers traveled down to Key West and conferred with Tennessee "daily for about a week," yet he said he had no recollection of their visit.

In some ways, *Tokyo Bar* is the most terrifying of his plays because it is about himself, thinly disguised, as he was in the period immediately before his confinement. He spares nothing, and no one, neither himself nor the audience. The protagonist, named Mark, is an artist who seems to be willing to destroy himself if his art requires it. He has been painting in his hotel room, above the bar, and he apparently paints in a business suit, because he comes down to the bar with it covered in paint. He falls down continually; Tennessee said that during this period he was "always falling down" and nobody ever caught him. Mark is so shaky he can't raise a drink to his lips.

In *Tokyo Bar* Tennessee was true to his own code, to look as deeply as possible inside himself, and then put down what he saw, no matter what it was. Mark believed that an artist had to lay his life on the line. He was terrified of stopping work for even a moment because he might lose momentum, especially when he was exploring a whole new style of work— as Tennessee then considered that he was doing. And exploring new, forbidden country terrified Mark just as, we must assume, it terrified Tennessee.

And it terrifies those who have a protective, mother-hen feeling about him, as almost all the people who know him have. He is a tireless progenitor, by immaculate conception, of mother hens.

For the audience, the people who don't know him that well, it may not be enough. The tragic center of the action is the playwright himself, a shattered self, and the play may not create enough empathy in a spectator who has not been walking hand in hand with the author through his private inferno. If the audience cannot cry for the author, it may laugh at the play, or even worse, may feel sick. A play can totter when its only feet are the playwright's. Those who don't know the wounded playwright may think Mark is a wounded monster.

Tennessee's attitude toward the other characters is cooler and more rational. Mark's wife, Miriam, the ultimate bitch, and his agent and the Japanese barman are lucid, and some of their dialogue is brilliant.

Many, including Dakin, believe that Miriam, the bitch-wife, is another facet of Tennessee's character, the erotic, materialistic side, just as Mark is the spiritual and artistic side. If so, it is exaggerated. Tennessee's bad side is really not that bad.

The barman won't go near Miriam because she always puts her hand on his crotch. She has a warehouseful of Mark's valuable pictures, and she hopes he'll die soon. When he does, she speaks a closing line that could almost be Tennessee's epitaph: "He thought he could create his own circle of light."

It was rehearsed in early spring, with the best people. Herbert Machiz directed and Anne Meacham was, Tennessee said, a "superb" Miriam. Donald Madden was marvelous as Mark. Madden, he wrote in *Memoirs*, was one of three actors for whom he wrote plays, or parts of plays, more than once. The others are Brando and Michael York. At this time, he wrote, he was in love with Madden, but he kept it to himself.

Glavin was there during rehearsals, and the main thing Bill remembers is a dead canary. One day during rehearsals, probably a Sunday, he and Tennessee drove up to Ossining to see Rose. She told them her canary had died a few days before. Bill said, "Rose wasn't upset as much as Tennessee was."

They went back to New York and the next day bought a new canary and took it to their hotel room, still in the box-cage from the pet shop. During rehearsals Tennessee worried. He wanted to get Rose's canary a *nice* cage, "one of those marvelous Victorian bamboo cages." As Bill recounted: "I walked down Third Avenue from the theater down to Fifty-ninth Street, going in all those antique stores, but in all the cages the spaces were too big, they were for parrots."

Back at the theater, Tennessee was busy making revisions for *Tokyo Bar*. Finally Bill had to tell him there was no cage.

"That's all right," said Tennessee. "I talked to Rose on the phone. She doesn't want another canary anyway."

When Bill came back to the hotel suite the canary was gone.

"Where is it?" Bill asked.

Tennessee said, "Don't ask me about the canary." So there is probably one more free canary in Central Park.

If that story has any point, it is that Mark, the artist in the *Tokyo Bar*, was too far gone to worry about a cage for a canary for a lady in a cottage in the woods near Ossining, New York. But Tennessee wasn't.

However, as the rehearsals went on, conflicts developed, and finally there was a showdown between Tennessee and the director, Herbert Machiz. Tennessee himself took over the direction.

Dakin arrived in New York in time for the last preview, on the Saturday before the opening. He sat with his brother while he was making last-minute notes on a scratch pad, and adding a few lines.

The play opened on a Sunday evening, May 11. In spite of fine performances by Anne Meacham and Donald Madden, the reviews were not good. Tennessee's old admirer, *Time*, said it was more worthy of a coroner's report than a review.

Clive Barnes's review in the New York *Times* wasn't all bad. Barnes wrote:

> This is Mr. Williams' sad bird of loneliness, and although the play repelled me with its self-pity as much as it fascinated me with the author's occasional sudden resurgence of skill—there are plaintive notes of poetry recalling Williams at his very best. A simple phrase such as "a diaphanous afternoon in August floats across like summer smoke," or "an artist has to lay his life on the line." There are more flashes of genius here than in any of his later plays.
>
> Like *Camino Real*, *Tokyo Bar* is avant garde and will be appreciated and applauded in the theater of the future.

The audiences were having trouble with it. The play may have been too much for strangers, and audiences are made up of strangers. But some who knew Tennessee surely cried.

After the opening Dakin and their mother were having lunch in Tennessee's hotel room. Tennessee had ordered a beautiful sealskin coat for his mother from Bergdorf-Goodman. She had already been taken to the store for measurements.

Miss Edwina said, "I must admit, Tom, that I did not like the play. I think you should take up some other kind of work!" She did not, however, suggest what other work it might be.

Tennessee was so shattered by this remark that he telephoned Bergdorf's and cancelled the fur coat.

By this time Glavin was ill in New Orleans. Tennessee took Anne Meacham with him on a ship to Tokyo. This had nothing to do with the *Tokyo Bar* play. The Japanese had invited him to see a new production of *Streetcar*.

On the way he did another public dying, and as usual it was only partly his fault. He had had a swelling under his left nipple. A doctor in New Orleans had made some remarks about breast cancer as being rare in men, without any formal diagnosis that Tennessee had it.

Tennessee speculated to a reporter that he might be having cancer of the breast. The press, which hadn't had a Williams crisis for weeks, spread the word: Tennessee Williams was dying of cancer.

In Bangkok, the king of Siam's own surgeon removed a bit of something, not malignant, from his chest, using a local anesthetic. It was painful, Tennessee said, but not fatal.

They proceeded to Japan. In Yokohama he had his last meeting with Yukio Mishima, who drove out to the port to have dinner with him. Tennessee felt that Mishima looked tense and grave, and wondered whether he had, at that time, already decided on his dramatic act of hara-kiri, committed a month or two later.

Tennessee and Anne Meacham had scarcely arrived in Japan when Anne telephoned Dakin. She said, "Dakin, I positively cannot cope with your brother one moment longer. You must come to Japan at once."

There are no exact details of what was happening. Several years later, when he was interviewed by Playboy, Tennessee said of the Japanese trip: "I began washing the pills down with liquor and I just went out of my mind. I took sedation every night, and every morning I took something related to speed, so that I could still write."

He told Rex Reed that he ran away to Japan "to escape the brutality of the press, and my agent Audrey Wood never sends me anything good about me. My poor little dog Gigi landed in quarantine. We left in such haste I didn't look into her vaccination papers, so I had to rent a Japanese house and hire Japanese servants at great personal expense because that was the only way they would let my dog out of quarantine. Oh, it was a dreadful mess. That was the beginning of my breakdown. I had been disintegrating for years, but that was the final culmination of events. I went out of my mind."

Mead spoke to Anne Meacham in New York about all this. She was charming and obviously still very fond of Tennessee. And she felt, like all his friends, protective about him. She said she would not say anything about what happened in Japan.

After receiving Meacham's phone call, Dakin prepared to fly to Tokyo from Lambert Field, in St. Louis. Before boarding the plane, however, he phoned Western Union and discovered that there was an undelivered cable for him at their East St. Louis office, saying that Tennessee was arriving in San Francisco that afternoon.

Bill Glavin also received a wire saying that Tennessee would be in San Francisco. Bill was already there with Tennessee when Dakin arrived. The three of them moved into the Mark Hopkins Hotel. Tennessee said he would like to stay in San Francisco for a while, and Dakin went around for several days looking for apartments in the Nob Hill area.

During this time Tennessee slept as long as seventeen hours a day, knocked out by the strong Doriden sleeping tablets, and would take speed injections for his writing stint. Dakin went out looking for needles, fearing that old needles might cause hepatitis.

Tennessee was able to go out with Dakin and Bill to dinner, sometimes taking a further evening speed injection before going out. Tennessee had trouble walking, but they went by cab all over the San Francisco area, Chinatown, Sausalito, wherever.

Glavin and Dakin helped Tennessee back to Key West and almost immediately afterward Tennessee broke with Glavin.

So, for a painful period of some weeks, he was alone and in bad condition. As his friend, the novelist David Loomis, said later: "He never knew where he was most of the time. He staggered. His hands shook. He was incoherent. He'd get paranoic and scream and shout and cry."

Would it have been better if Glavin could have been brought back? Margaret Foresman wasn't so sure about that. She said that Bill was "a likable guy," though she considered him "weak, like a reed in the wind." She felt that Tennessee had become tired of Bill's independence, his way of wandering off alone to the Key West bars. She felt he "could have been a lot kinder to Tennessee."

Tennessee's closest friend then was his old drinking companion Marion Vaccaro, the "Banana Queen," who would occasionally make the drive down the causeway from her home in Miami.

Margaret Foresman used to come over to Tennessee's compound from time to time to check up on him and see if he was all right. He had Leoncia, the cook, there during the day, but after she left he was all alone.

One evening, while Foresman was there, Marion arrived and Tennessee invited both of them to go out to dinner. He and Marion first went through a rather heroic number of drinks. Foresman declined the dinner invitation, but began to be more and more concerned about how they would make it to the restaurant, a few blocks away. So when they started out—she believes Marion was driving—Foresman decided to stay half a block behind in her car to make sure they got there.

They wandered a bit over the road, but they did reach the restaurant. Then there was a long pause until they both stood up, more or less, on either side of the car, not sure whether they could navigate to the entrance. Leaning heavily on each other, they finally reached the door. "Somebody helped them in," said Foresman, "and then I whizzed off and went home."

Tennessee often telephoned Foresman, asking for help of one kind or another, and she always tried to do what she could. One evening while she was at the office, trying to put the newspaper to bed, Tennessee called her and told her he thought somebody was in his house. She went right over and, as she said to the authors:

Here was poor Tennessee. He'd had himself locked in his bedroom. There wasn't a soul there. His idea seemed to be that Glavin had gotten somebody in there, hiding, to kill him, or something . . . it was all kind of a mixed-up thing. Well, I couldn't stay there and protect him all night, but I couldn't leave the poor man alone. I called the police to send an off-duty man. The deputy came and went through the house thoroughly. There wasn't anybody there. He locked the doors again. Tennessee was really kind of spaced out, but (I knew) he ought to have somebody, because of course he fell.

And he did fall, badly. A new kitchen was being built under the direction of Dan Stirrup, the Key West architect. The stove had been moved out onto the patio, so that Tennessee could make his Silex of coffee. Early in the morning, as he moved the Silexful of boiling coffee from the stove, he fell on the patio tiles and scalded his bare shoulder with boiling coffee. He said he was so "spaced out" that he noticed no pain, and began work.

His shoulder had to be bandaged by a doctor. Margaret Foresman heard about this and decided to telephone Dakin in Collinsville. She was not worried that anyone else would hurt him, but she feared he might manage to kill himself accidentally. She said, "You know what kind of doses people give themselves when they get far gone." She told Dakin about the scalding, and said he ought to come down to Key West. (Neither she nor Dakin feared he would deliberately kill himself.)

After Foresman's call, Dakin had another, from Audrey Wood, who had been alerted by Marion Vacarro, urging Dakin to help Tennessee. Finally Dakin had a call from Tennessee himself. "Dakin, an attempt will be made on my life tonight."

Dakin was already preparing to leave for Key West. He was not worried about the "attempt," but he knew that his brother was in danger. He said, "Tom, I can't do anything about it tonight. Will it be okay if I fly down tomorrow?"

Tennessee said it would be all right.

And yet, as Margaret Foresman said:

Tennessee has never forgiven him [Dakin] for it [for the whole subsequent episode] . . . he's never forgiven me [for calling Dakin]. He somehow had the idea I had a crush on Bill Glavin. That's the last thing in the world!

Dakin flew from St. Louis the first thing in the morning. As he remembers: "Arriving in Key West the next morning, I found my brother in dreadful shape. His arm had been badly burned by the scalding water. In the back of my mind I wanted to get him into Barnes Hospital in St. Louis where a cousin of ours [Dr. Carl Harford] was a member of the staff, but I couldn't do anything without TW's permission.

"Tennessee was definitely on his last legs and badly panic-stricken. Seizing on this opportunity, I suggested to Tom: 'Don't you think we better get you to a hospital?' I'd hoped to spend a couple of days in Key West myself, but he said, 'Yes, tonight.' Striking while the iron was hot—it was now or never—I immediately made reservations and we flew to St. Louis.

"He acted very badly on the plane because they'd serve only two drinks to a customer. It was Sunday and we couldn't get anything in St. Louis either. He was furious, but fortunately I had a bottle of whiskey at my mother's home in Clayton, where we spent the night."

Tennessee told Playboy that Dakin had brought him a typewriter that evening at Miss Edwina's house, but he "couldn't hit any of the right keys, and I told him the typewriter was no good, and he said, 'Tom, you really must check into the hospital now.'"

Tennessee said he wanted to go back to Key West. But after a long discussion he finally agreed to enter Barnes Hospital the next day.

Dakin said, "Through my cousin, I got him into the most expensive and luxurious place available, the Queeny Tower. With a bottle of booze in one hand and his little blue bag of pills in the other, he looked like he had the world by the tail. But the hospital was just making routine tests."

To Playboy Tennessee said, "I spent one day there in a very deluxe ward watching television programs. I was so demented that all the programs seemed to be directed personally at me—isn't that fantastic? Even Shirley Booth's little program, 'Hazel.' I thought Shirley was making veiled innuendos about me."

Meanwhile the doctors concluded that he had "acute toxic poisoning from drug intake."

Dakin said, "They took away the booze and the pills, and Tennessee did what he had done on many occasions in the past—he started to walk out.

"I'd sent him a big bouquet of flowers (along with cute drawings by my two small daughters) in hope of getting a friendly welcome, but he was furious with me. Dr. Berg, the neurologist whom Tennessee called 'Ice Berg,' was there, and he was going to let him walk out. Having gotten him this far, and knowing that he was incapable of making a decision for himself, I determined that to save his life I must intervene and keep him in the hospital, by force if necessary.

"I called Dr. Douglas Lilly, a trusted general practitioner, into the case, who advised me that if I chose to take the responsibility I could sign him in for ten days."

Tennessee began to realize that he was being surrounded. He later recalled all this in the most outraged passage in his *Memoirs* and years before he gave Robert Jennings, of Playboy, an equally hopping-mad account: "...all of a sudden my brother came in grinning with a bunch of flowers and some crayon pictures drawn by his children, and in came Momma, and I said, 'I'm leaving here at once.' And they said, 'Oh, no, Tom. In fact, you're being transferred to another section.' And I said, 'Oh, no, I'm not.' So I rushed into the closet and somehow got into my clothes and I rushed down into an elevator and noticed a horrible intern—sort of an albino creature you know—towering over me, and every time I pressed the DOWN button, he would shove the doors open with this great arm of his. I just couldn't escape and so I finally ran back to my room and I said, 'You must get me out of this nuthouse.' His mother was in there, threatening to faint, and crying out for smelling salts. He was about to make a dash for a fire escape and freedom when a "goon squad," as he called it, rushed in with a wheel chair. "I had my little flight bag containing my pills and my liquor, with me, and the last thing I remember is their snatching it from me as I was wheeled into the violent ward..." In *Memoirs* he called it "Friggins Violent Ward," but the real name is the Renard psychiatric division of Barnes Hospital.

Dakin's account of the episode is as follows:

"By this time Tennessee had dressed and staggered toward the elevator. Bob Arteaga, a friend and local photographer famous for his pictures of the St. Louis arch, but the ugliest man I ever knew, was with me and he attempted in vain to pacify my brother.

"'Who are you?' asked Tennessee coldly in response to Bob's friendly gesture of placing an arm around my brother's shoulder.

"'I'm a friend of Dakin's,' said Bob.

"'I wouldn't brag about that,' said Tennessee. He was at the elevator, thinking he was going to the airport, en route to New York—to his certain death—when an intern got behind him and injected him with something in his arm that put him to sleep."

Dakin says that when he woke up, Tennessee said, "Where am I, at the Plaza?"

Tennessee hotly denies he said any such thing, and that Dakin made it up.

Whatever he said, he woke up in the Renard psychiatric division of Barnes, the only place in the hospital where people can be forced to stay.

By any account, Tennessee must truly have gone through hell for a number of days. He says they took him off the Doriden "cold turkey," and that it gave him three convulsions and a heart attack. Dakin confirms that the doctors told him Tennessee had the convulsions, and that he did nearly die.

Was the treatment rougher than necessary? Tennessee certainly thinks so. He remembers clearly the "stabbing pains" of what he called a "silent coronary," and made the flat statement in *Memoirs* that the resident physician intended to commit "legalized murder" on his person, and almost succeeded.

He had vivid dreams or hallucinations, including one rather Freudian one in which, shortly after the birth of Dakin, he watched him sucking the breast of his mother in a St. Louis hospital. He thought it represented a "never-before-spoken sibling rivalry." Perhaps never spoken before, but one that always existed strongly, in both directions, and still does.

Tennessee wrote a poem about his ordeal called "What's Next on the Agenda, Mr. Williams?" which he sometimes reads aloud, and did for Tom Buckley in his Atlantic interview. In it the Renard ward is called "Brigance Division of Barnacle Hospital in the city of St. Pollution." He was sure they were "sewing a winding sheet" for him.

For several days he was in such delirium that he didn't know where he was. Part of the time he was kept in a bed with barred sides, like a child's crib. And though he was in a ward for "violent" cases, he swears that *he* never was. (If he was, it would have been the first time in his life.) But some of the others were. He remembered that a big Irish truck driver knocked out the front teeth of a homosexual queen, and was concerned that it might be his turn next.

One woman tore out all her hair by the roots. And on one occasion his electric shaver was confiscated, on the ground that he could somehow have committed suicide with it. They even took his watch because it had a glass crystal. They needn't have worried. He has never been suicidal.

Dakin remembers that he didn't see Tennessee for the first three days because his brother was so angry, but after that visited every day except when Tennessee became infuriated again. The conversations would go like this:

"Dakin, when in hell can I get out of this damn place?"

"When your doctors, Levy and Berg, say you can," was always my reply.

Then he would ask the doctors, "When can I get out?"

"When your brother Dakin says you can," was their usual answer.

He would beg Dakin to smuggle liquor in for him and then get angry when Dakin failed to do so. Then Dakin would stay away for two or three days to let him cool off. "After a while he became very friendly and very much his old self. I hadn't seen him that way in several years, and had almost forgotten what it was like."

One of the doctors, Dr. Levy, told Tennessee a very clever thing, motivating him to cooperate with the treatment: "Tennessee, if you play ball with us you'll write better than you ever wrote before in your life when you get out of here."

Even in the violent ward, Tennessee had occupational therapy; he chose painting in watercolors. He did a portrait of his left hand, with an outsize little finger, something a Freudian might blow up into a major psychosis.

Andy Brown of the Gotham Book Mart, in New York, sent Tennessee boxes of books, which he read. (Andreas Brown is the most knowledgeable bibliographer of Tennessee's works, and books about him. He runs the West Forty-Seventh Street store and simultaneously carries on a witty and erudite conversation about Tennessee. This handsome, humorous and pleasant character spent years helping to organize the Williams Archives at the University of Texas, and was most helpful in the writing of this book.)

After a month of being nonviolent in the violent ward, Tennessee was transferred to an open ward where he stayed, Dakin says, voluntarily. There he played bridge every night for about four hours. One of the players was an older woman who had an absolute dread of electric shock treatments, and yet he said she was given them regularly.

One day Dakin found him alone in the ward and very sad. Dakin asked where the other patients were; he said they had all gone to a film showing. Didn't he want to go? Yes, he did, but they wouldn't let him. Why not? He had written something dirty on the wall, about one of the nurses, and they were going to have to paint it all white.

Bill Glavin had moved back into the Key West house, to take care of Gigi, the bull terrier. He wrote a number of letters to Tennessee. Bill had been seeing Margaret Foresman and Danny Stirrup. He told about the new kitchen, still under construction. The letters are almost effusive in their statements of affection for Tennessee. Bill wrote that he missed Tennessee very much. Glavin, who had already been fired at least twice, plainly wanted to stay on.

Audrey Wood wrote about preparations for the New York revival of *Camino Real*. Al Pacino had done an excellent reading as Kilroy. She was sending Tennessee a biography of the young Eugene O'Neill.

As Tennessee's condition improved, the usual storms began to blow in the usual teacups: shirts, for instance. Were the dirty shirts that Dakin said

Joyce had personally washed and ironed for Tennessee *really* clean? Tennessee said, "No!" Dakin bought some new ones. Ah, but they were Hong Kong shirts, said Tennessee, *cheap* shirts with threads coming out of the seams!

So, if this were a biographical movie, the music would swell. The crisis is over! Dawn breaks! Close-up of the tough old nurse smiling through tears. Shirts! Shirts! Music up to crescendo! He'll come through!

He was becoming popular in the open ward. In fact, several women wanted to marry him. And if anyone doubts his own statements about this, Dakin said he heard a woman proposing to Tennessee during one of his visits. "Oh, that's just a put-on!" Tennessee said, but Dakin could see the look in her eyes. "Very serious." She meant it.

"On the surface," Dakin added, "he seemed friendly toward me, but underneath he was secretly seething with hostility because I had interfered so dramatically with his freedom. Once he blew up in rage when an intern insisted upon opening a package delivered to him in my presence. It was humiliating for him to be subjected to searches of this sort, which the hospital deemed necessary for his protection."

In the last month he was allowed to walk around the block but he was, he said, followed by someone in a car to make sure he didn't "escape." And toward the end he was allowed to take a cab to Clayton. His main purchase was a bottle of nonprescription sleeping pills, which only blurred his vision. On his final foray, he visited a doctor who didn't know him, gave a false name and conned him into three Seconals. When he returned to Barnes he was told he would be released the next day.

He went back to Miss Edwina's house in Clayton for the Christmas holidays. There he watched, on television, the film made from his novel, *The Roman Spring of Mrs. Stone*, starring Vivien Leigh and directed by his old friend José Quintero. He loved the film, which he called "a poem." The only problem about the film was that Miss Edwina was talking so much he could barely hear the sound track.

Whether the three months' stay at Barnes Hospital was the best possible solution, there seems to be no question that *something* had to be done for his well-being.

Margaret Foresman was asked this direct question: "It's your opinion, isn't it, that if the two of you [Dakin and Foresman] hadn't done something about it, something very bad might have happened to him?" She replied: "Oh, yes, he was in very bad condition." She also added that when he returned to Key West he was very much better.

In a letter to Dakin dated November 20, 1970, James Laughlin wrote: "I think you [Dakin] did absolutely the right thing that had to be done in the matter of hospitalization. It may have been very rough for Tennessee, but my impression is that he is a great deal better since he had that treatment."

Tennessee's point is not that nothing should have been done, but that what was done was done brutally, beyond what was necessary. He wrote to Dakin on November 11, 1970, saying he had talked to his doctor in New York, who had told him it was unnecessary, and he told of a friend (named in the letter) who had been in a "much worse" condition than his own, who went to a private psychiatric hospital in New York. He was gently withdrawn from his alcoholism by sedation, in a lovely private room.

So, perhaps it could have been done more pleasantly.

Dakin is sure that he saved his brother's life, and if he had not done it, no one else would have.

To this day Tennessee has never completely forgiven Dakin for committing him to Barnes. Tennessee was not particularly monstrous or villainous in this respect. It was not an unusual reaction. Many people, perhaps *most* people, who are committed to mental institutions never completely forgive those who did it. It is not difficult to understand why. If it could be done once, when it was justifiable, perhaps (they fear) it could be done again when it might be merely profitable, or otherwise advantageous. It is a very tricky thing.

Tennessee left Clayton before the end of the holidays and went to New York for the January opening of the *Camino Real* revival. From there, on New Year's Eve, he sent a telegram to Dakin in Collinsville, advising his brother to go to Chicago if he wanted to see a Williams play. They were doing a good revival of *Cat*. But Dakin must "definitely not" come to the New York *Camino*, because—

I AM NOT YET READY TO SEE YOU STOP TRUST YOU UNDERSTAND.

Tennessee expected to see Rose over the weekend.

Margaret Foresman and Bill Glavin were both there when he arrived in Key West. Foresman recalls:

I don't think Bill lasted very long after Tennessee came back from the hospital, because the first night he came back, you know, when everybody was happy that he was going to be all right—what does Glavin do? "Bye!"—and goes off downtown, cruising, and left Tennessee alone the very first night, and I thought that was pretty rotten.

Tennessee was irritated at Glavin for several other reasons. He felt that Bill had authorized unnecessary work on the Duncan Street compound, putting a stained glass window into the kitchen, and ordering a completely new patio à la Beverly Hills.

Foresman described the first time she went over to Tennessee's place on Duncan Street after his return from the hospital. A group of people, including Dan Stirrup, were going over there for dinner, and one of them called her and asked her to join them. She said, "I got there and Tennessee went into his bedroom and said he would not come out until I left. I left, and that's when I learned that he thought I was in love with Bill Glavin."

Apparently that was her punishment for her part in the Barnes Hospital episode. And though she saw Tennessee around Key West after that, "he never called me again when he had any problems."

Tennessee's story is that Glavin had invited "a lady of profligate habits" (not named) to dinner one night, and he, Tennessee, had "slammed into the bedroom." There is no proof that the "ladies" are the same lady, but if Margaret Foresman, now a member of the Key West government, was then a lady "of profligate habits," she has now changed her ways.

Glavin's sins, in Tennessee's eyes, were multiplying. Bill invited a large number of people to a party at an expensive restaurant. Tennessee said he hadn't invited them, and refused to play host.

That night, Bill's last at the compound, he came in "drunk and evil," according to Tennessee, and "taunted" him. Tennessee was at the time with Mary Louise Manning, Alec Wilder the composer, and John Young. Mary Louise felt Tennessee's pulse, told Glavin that he was dangerously disturbed and ordered him out of the house. He went and John Young stayed, and the palace revolution was over. Margaret Foresman continued to be *persona non grata*.

John Young, Tennessee's new secretary, was then in his late thirties, a former YMCA secretary and assistant film director. He doubled as a cook when Leoncia wasn't there and as chauffeur and general household manager. He was paid $200 a week and certainly must have earned it. Among those in the new in-group were David Loovis, the novelist, and Andrew Lyndon, who had been an old friend.

With Glavin out, the word spread that Bill had been a bad influence, or at least had acted like a presidential-appointments secretary, keeping some of Tennessee's friends away and even, some said, encouraging Tennessee to take drugs. Glavin denied this. The truth is probably that Glavin did not encourage the taking of drugs, merely that, being malleable and easygoing, he did little if anything to steer Tennessee away from drugs, and certainly must have helped him to obtain them when asked to do so.

Bill was paid a reported $300 a week "to stay out of Key West."

Tennessee was looking and feeling a great deal better. He was working again, making more revisions in *The Two-Character Play*, which would become *Out Cry*, and for the first time in years gave a public reading, this time at Duke University. The students gave him a standing ovation. He read a whole one-act play to them, *I Never Get Dressed 'Til After Dark on Sunday*, and they loved it.

During this period a kind of time bomb was being prepared, and set to explode in October. No one suspected that a pleasant journalist named Tom Buckley was setting the fuse.

Buckley visited Tennessee and noted how much better he looked. No longer was he "puffy-faced and pasty-white." He was tanned, in better trim, having lost about twenty pounds, and was swimming twenty laps a day. He was "calm, indubitably lucid, and mildly amused at himself and the world."

Tennessee told Buckley that he was hoping to have *Out Cry* produced on Broadway, but that Audrey Wood did not share his enthusiasm for it and wanted to have it done at some little theater. Buckley, noting a possible crack in the Williams-Wood alliance, went straight to Audrey, who told him, "Of course I want to see him produced on Broadway. That's just Tennessee's 'normal' paranoia." And that was not surprising, since an agent makes a great deal more from a successful Broadway production than from an Off-Broadway one.

But that was not Buckley's time bomb.

Meanwhile Tennessee continued to work. He was thinking about a short play called *Confessional*, which would later be expanded to become *Small Craft Warnings*.

And then, in October, the Buckley bomb burst, when his interview and profile appreared in the November Atlantic. There were really two bombs. One was for Dakin. It was the first time he had heard the story that Tennessee had cut him out of his will. He had been almost the sole heir. It was supposed to be a punishment for committing Tennessee to Barnes Hospital. In the interview with Buckley, Tennessee described how he had cut Dakin out of all the inheritance except for $25,000, which would be paid after Rose's death—*if* Dakin had not removed her from her pleasantly wooded sanitarium and put her into some frightful snake pit. The main estate would go to the Rose Isabelle Williams Foundation for Creative Writers.

The amount of money involved was indeed large. Including the real estate and the royalty value of the works, which were then being performed all over the world (as they still are), the total value amounted to several million dollars. Dakin estimated that at this time it may have been about three million. But Dakin was especially upset by the implication that he had to be bribed to keep his sister in a pleasant sanitarium. The whole operation, Dakin felt, was rather severe punishment for, as he believed, helping to save his brother's life.

But to most people, the real time bomb in the article was not the part about the will. This was the first public and reputable statement that Tennessee was homosexual. He had never made a secret of this fact with his friends, and it had been known and accepted by them for many years. But in those days, before gay liberation, the concept of homosexuality was simply unspeakable to many ordinary citizens.

Actually, the references to it in Buckley's article were very mild, such as the fact that Tennessee's psychiatrist, Dr. Kubie, had "tried unsuccessfully to change his sexual orientation," and a statement about "a sexual preference that he shares with kings." There were no embarrassing or erotic details. Compared with the revelations Tennessee himself was to make in his *Memoirs*, and the later ones from the Windham letters, this was scarcely more than a partly raised eyebrow.

But the commotion at the time was downright giddy. Dakin wanted to blast the Atlantic immediately, perhaps even sue them. Audrey Wood wrote to Dakin about "Mr. Buckley's disastrous piece in the November *Atlantic*"— but advised Dakin not to send his letter.

Dakin wrote to his brother: "We are just going to try to ignore the whole thing and pretend it never happened."

James Laughlin wrote to Dakin, saying, "That article about Tennessee in the *Atlantic* was extremely painful, and I'm rather surprised that a magazine of that reputation would print anything which was, in a sense, an invasion of privacy."

Symptomatic of the change in the public attitude is Dakin's handwritten comment, scrawled on an old Xerox of this article in 1978: "It isn't nearly as offensive as I first thought."

In 1970 New Directions published Tennessee's most recent plays in a volume titled *Dragon Country*. It includes the *Tokyo Bar*, the two *Slapstick Tragedy* plays, *The Mutilated* and *The Gnädiges Fräulein*; his play about the death of D. H. Lawrence, *I Rise in Flame, Cried the Phoenix*; *Confessional*; and three short ones, *I Can't Imagine Tomorrow*, *The Frosted Glass Coffin* and *A Perfect Analysis Given by a Parrot*.

The *Tomorrow* play is probably Tennessee's closest to the Beckett type of bare-bones nothing-drama, and is the one that contains the *Dragon Country* quote. (There is no play called *Dragon Country*.)

"Dragon Country, the country of pain, is an uninhabitable country which is inhabited." In *Tomorrow* there are only two characters, called "One" (female) and "Two" (male), and "each is the only friend of the other." The male, a teacher, is now almost totally unable to speak. The two meet every evening to play cards and watch television. Everything is reduced to nothing, and there is nothing left but death. It is a reflection of Tennessee's mood at his lowest point during the crack-up.

The Frosted Glass Coffin is a kind of geriatric vignette, very short, and in very black humor. Old people are watching some of Miami's many others of great age, standing in line at a cheap cafeteria.

A Perfect Analysis Given by a Parrot is a short play about two aging whores during an American Legion convention in St. Louis. (Here they are called "the Sons of Mars.") One whore has her fortune told by a printed slip, selected by a parrot, saying she has "a sensitive nature." The humor is very black, too, and some of it is very funny.

Except for *Confessional*, which was the nucleus of the commercially successful *Small Craft Warnings*, none of these plays was a commercial success. Yet any writer of books would consider the volume itself practically a best-seller. There have been at least five printings, and there are bound to be more. Probably not one book in two hundred goes into five printings. These far-out experimental plays are popular with readers and with avant-garde theater groups.

For a whole year Dakin had no word at all from his brother. Just before Thanksgiving he sent a letter to Tennessee, which included these paragraphs about the "saving" of Tennessee's life:

> I am very sorry the "saving" was such a traumatic thing, and I know that you really must somewhere deep down realize that it is not just to blame me for the type of procedure used by the professional doctors in effecting the cure. I did not prescribe "cold turkey" any more than I will cook the same for our Thanksgiving dinner this week. Susy is in charge of that and we are going to eat it at Mother's Wydown establishment!

He added:

> The last thing I will *ever* say to you about the recent unpleasantness (I think it is high time for you and me to achieve a really good relationship) is this: When you think of my part in your recent "cure" also think of yourself trying to stagger up the stairs of a restaurant in Key West, New York, or San Francisco in the several *years* prior to your two months at Barnes Hospital. You once told me you would rather

not be alive than to exist in the physical, mental and emotional fog that enveloped you.

Tennessee was continuing, as always, to work. He was polishing *The Two-Character Play* for its first appearance under its new title, *Out Cry*, in a production planned for the summer of 1971 in Chicago.

Dakin arrived unannounced at the Key West compound in February, to try to see his brother for the first time since Barnes Hospital:

> It was eleven A.M. when I knocked furiously at his garden gate. No one answered, but the light was on in his living room. I climbed over the gate and peered through the window of his living room. I could see the door to his bedroom open in response to the furious knocking on the front door.
>
> Like a vision in a dream, a beautiful young man emerged, clad in a blue velvet robe, with blond shoulder-length hair and wide blue eyes.
>
> "Who are you?" he asked suspiciously through a crack secured by a chain on the door.
>
> "I am Dakin, Tennessee's brother," I replied. "Who are you?"
>
> "I am Victor Herbert!" was the amazing reply. "Wait here and I'll tell Mr. Williams you are here."

Victor soon returned to say that Mr. Williams suggested Dakin go to the Hotel La Concha. He would phone him in the morning. The call came through about noon. Tennessee said, "Victor and I are having supper at Le Mistral at seven this evening. We would be pleased to have you join us." Dakin remembers:

> Obediently at the appointed hour I arrived at this small, narrow French restaurant near the foot of Duval Street to find Tennessee and Victor seated in a booth, happily chatting away. I could hardly believe my eyes at the costumes they were wearing. Young Victor was clad in bright red velvet with white lace collar and cuffs. My brother was sporting a somewhat similar outfit in royal blue velvet, but fortunately minus the lace borders.

In a later account, in the September 1971 Esquire, Rex Reed noted that Tennessee had finally had enough of Victor's flamboyant costumes, and was buying him a conservative blue suit. As he said, "These red Santa Claus suits you wear are fine for Key West, but they don't go over at the Edwardian Room of the Plaza Hotel" (in New York).

In spite of the previous alarms and confrontations, the evening at Le Mistral passed pleasantly. Tennessee told Dakin he had discovered Victor in Miami, where he had been a telephone operator. He had not been, however, innocent in the ways of the world, even that subdivision of it.

Tennessee took Victor down to New Orleans, where they had a suite at the Royal Orleans, and where he continued to work on *Out Cry*.

Rex Reed interviewed him there for the Esquire profile. He told Reed he was "off the booze" (though he was drinking a bit of white wine) and took only two Miltowns and half a Nembutal a day.

He was already beginning to worry about the proposed tryout for *Out Cry*, and feared the Chicago critics, especially Claudia Cassidy, who had been so rough with *Iguana*.

Then he sailed for Rome on the *Michelangelo*, with his portable, the script and plenty of paper.

CHAPTER 29

The summer of 1971 was notable for two events that were closely related. One was probably the best production of one of his current plays in the last ten years, and the other the final break with Audrey Wood.

Ever since the production of *The Two-Character Play* in London in 1967, Tennessee had been revising it. Paul Bigelow, who was reading plays for Cheryl Crawford, saw a script brought back from London by Michael Redgrave, who hoped to do it in New York. Paul said that he was simply overwhelmed by it, but wondered who in the world was capable of doing it justice. He thought perhaps only Maggie Smith could do the woman's part. He knew it could never be done on a shoestring—by which he meant a shoestring of talent. Physically, it did not require a complicated or unusually expensive production.

Bigelow said (and he added that Audrey Wood agreed) that he thought it was possibly Tennessee's greatest play, though neither of them expected it would be his most popular one. He thought of it as "a complete artistic expression, the way you think of the great Chekhov plays."

Tennessee called the revised version *Out Cry* because, as he said to Robert Jennings in the Playboy interview, "I had to cry out, and I did." At one point the actress exclaims, "Out, out, human out cry."

George Keathley directed the first American production at the Ivanhoe Theater in Chicago in the summer of 1971. He chose one of Tennessee's favorite actors, Donald Madden, for Felice, and a lesser-known actress, Eileen Herlie, as Clare. Madden, though a bit too old for the part, was nevertheless superb, and the choice of Herlie was an inspiration.

The first preview, given to a young audience, was well done. Keathley's direction had been excellent. And Bigelow thought Herlie was reading the lines with great sensitivity and beauty. The production was simple, much simpler than the later New York one, and the play seemed to come through sharply and clearly. The young audience liked it.

305

The second preview was given to a society of theatergoers, mostly matrons, probably what the English would call an "Aunt Edna" audience, intelligent but conservative, and not quite ready for anything as adventurous as *Out Cry*. They were relatively cool toward the play.

So the stage was set for the final breakup with Audrey Wood, ending the relationship that began in 1939. This was not really the cause, it was just the spark that set off the explosion. The gunpowder had been accumulating for years. Both Dakin and Paul Bigelow believe that the underlying cause was the same one that had broken all the other relationships, with Glavin, with Allan Schwartz (his lawyer), with Margaret Foresman, with Dakin, with almost everyone he knew before the Barnes Hospital commitment. He must have felt that those who didn't help to get him in at least didn't get him out. The reason was that they all had affection and concern for him, and thought he needed treatment. Audrey had lasted longer than any of the others, but had begun to be in disfavor at least a year before, as the Buckley interview showed.

After the performance for the "Aunt Edna" audience, Tennessee felt somehow that Audrey had agreed with them. No one else, especially Audrey, thought this was so, and even Tennessee admitted that his anxieties may have led him astray.

They were in Donald Madden's dressing room with several witnesses. Tennessee says he "became a sort of madman," and said to Audrey, "You must have been pleased by the audience reaction tonight. You've wanted me dead for ten years. But I'm not going to die."

There was nothing Audrey could say to this, so she said nothing. She didn't stay for the opening night and flew back to New York. She never acted as his agent again.

There were stories that Tennessee had used violence against her. He denies them, and such a thing is so completely out of character for him that it is not credible. There has never been a confirmed incident in which he used violence toward anyone, at any time.

Paul Bigelow said that Audrey loved *Out Cry*. He believes that part of the tension between Tennessee and Audrey was caused by Maria Britneva, now the Lady St. Just, and that the rupture was at least partly caused by "a quarrel between Maria Britneva and Audrey." In answer to the question, "In other words, it was really Maria who broke up Audrey and Tennessee?" Bigelow replied, "Yes."

When Audrey Wood was questioned about this in New York (March 1979) she was understandably reluctant to give away too much copy—she was writing a book herself.

Later, in answer to a letter asking specific questions, Audrey wrote:

I think you can safely say I disagree with any statement which would indicate I had no admiration for a play called *Out Cry*, that was originally called *The Two-Character Play*. It remains one of my favorite Tennessee Williams plays. Actually, Paul Bigelow, a friend I admire greatly, I don't think is accurate in saying I had quarreled with Maria Britneva or she had quarreled with me. There was, to my knowledge, no quarrel. I have known Maria for many years. I am not aware of any contretemps with Maria. I think she simply favored Tennessee and he remains one of her oldest friends.

So it is probably true that there was no actual confrontation or hair-pulling between Maria and Audrey at the time. But Maria, always fiercely loyal to Tennessee, probably believed, rightly or wrongly, that Audrey was bad for him, and may have tried to persuade him to change agents.

Audrey was also asked if it could be stated that she "disagreed violently" with the Bigelow statement (that Maria caused the break-up). Audrey wrote, "If you want to use the quote from Bigelow, I would ask that you remove 'disagrees violently' from the text."

If it is true that the Lady St. Just thought Audrey Wood was bad for Tennessee, she is the only one of all the people interviewed who felt this way. Everyone else thought she had been very good for him. Audrey always spoke of Tennessee with affection. And he, in his *Memoirs*, declared she is "a truly remarkable woman."

With Audrey Wood not in the audience, *Out Cry* had its Chicago opening night—in fact, its American premiere, as the Chicago *Tribune* put it, celebrating the fact by printing a color photograph of Eileen Herlie and Donald Madden on the front page.

Dakin was there, happy to have been *invited* this time by Tennessee, but somewhat startled to read in the newspaper interviews that he had committed his brother to "a state insane asylum . . . a cut-rate place." Barnes wasn't either "state" or "cut-rate"—but it may have seemed so to Tennessee at the time.

The audience was apparently puzzled by the play, and when Tennessee and Dakin walked into the Keep Room of the Ivanhoe Theater for the after-play party, they were braced for some rough Chicago reviews.

Glenna Syse of the *Sun-Times* gave them one. "What you want to know," she wrote, "is whether or not Tennessee Williams has made a successful comeback. And the answer for the moment will have to be no."

But Claudia Cassidy, the dowager queen of Chicago critics, whom Tennessee had feared the most, came out of her semiretirement to do a beautiful review in the Sunday *Tribune*. She wrote, "Something extraordinary happened at the Ivanhoe Thursday night. There, on a poetic little rat's nest of a stage, Tennessee Williams came back." The whole review was a rave, ending:

> There is in *Out Cry* the terrible, wrenching impact of the compas-
> sionate and the implacable so often found in Tennessee Williams' best
> plays. He said in *The Glass Menagerie*, "This is a memory play." Well,
> in a sense so is *Out Cry*.
>   The atavistic memory the true writer senses, adapts, draws on and
> develops in his own image. It is part of him, and the stamp of the coin
> is authentic. I found at the Ivanhoe an extraordinary play staged and
> acted, I should think, about as well as it can or will be. And I found
> Tennessee Williams, who can do something not many men can do. He
> can write a powerful, implacable, compassionate and mesmeric play.

The Chicago run was assured, but the momentum was not great enough to carry it on to Broadway. That would not happen for almost two years, with a different production.

That same summer, William Hunt produced Tennessee's short play *Confessional* in the summer theater at Bar Harbor, Maine. Tennessee was too busy in Chicago to go there, but he was pleased to hear that it was well received.

By this time he had appointed Bill Barnes as his new agent. Barnes, a handsome and pleasant young man, was a member of the same large service group as Audrey Wood, then called IFA (for International Famous Agency) and now called ICM (International Creative Management). Barnes talked with Hunt and discovered he was interested in doing an Off-Broadway production. They received copies of the Bar Harbor reviews, which Tennessee declared, in a letter to Hunt, were the best he had had in ten years.

During this correspondence, in the fall of 1971, Tennessee moved to New Orleans for the months of November and December. He was looking for an apartment and he was working hard, transforming *Confessional*, a long one-act play in two scenes, into *Small Craft Warnings*, about half again as long, also in two parts, promoted to acts one and two.

It is a comparatively realistic play that takes place in a waterfront bar in southern California. The characters are Monk, the owner-bartender, who lives upstairs alone; Leona, the main female character, an itinerant "beau-tician" who is mourning her dead, gay violinist brother; she has been sharing her trailer with Bill, a stud, whose sole asset, his penis, is named Junior; Violet, a drifter who lives above an amusement parlor and likes to feel men's crotches, especially Bill's; Steve, a short-order cook who sleeps with her; Quentin, a homosexual scriptwriter; Bobby, a cyclist from Iowa, picked up by Quentin; and Doc, an alcoholic doctor who has lost his license. The play was originally called *Confessional* because each character gives a kind of Chekhovian monologue of confession to the audience.

Though the homosexuality of characters has played important parts in several of his plays, notably *Cat* and *Suddenly Last Summer*, this is the first in which it is openly discussed as a way of life. Tennessee's late-in-life feelings about it here are sad, disillusioned and bitter. Leona, mourning her gay brother, talks about the "sickness and sadness in the heart of a gay boy." And Quentin agrees that the boy may be better off dead.

Later, in his own confession, Quentin talks bitterly about "the deadening coarseness" of homosexual experience, "quick and hard and brutal," and of a monotonous pattern. Compare that with the lyricism of a night with Kip, in Provincetown, thirty years before.

Even Monk, the proprietor, talks about how dreadful it is if your place becomes a gay bar and "it sounds like a bird cage."

One of the important changes, from the short play to the longer one, is in the monologue of Bobby, the young cyclist. In *Confessional* he indicates he has had intercourse with Quentin, which he said was an "initiation," which frightened him because he liked it. In *Small Craft* there is almost an about-face. He has a different story. He had lain under a blanket with both a girl and a boy and both of them had said "love"—and he was bewildered. When he leaves, he is apparently not yet "initiated," and the author seems to hope that he will never be.

Tennessee said later, when he was actually playing the part of Doc, that Quentin was far closer to his own character. And the whole play is more of a sad lament about homosexuality than it is an attack against it. There is sorrowful commiseration with the people caught up in it.

The contrast between this lament and the seductive accounts of homosexual love in his *Memoirs* is striking; yet the paradox is that the two were written at almost the same time. The *Memoirs* were being worked on in 1972, during the revision of *Small Craft Warnings*. However, the revelations of the *Memoirs* are mild compared with the lusty, Rabelaisian accounts written at the time and preserved in the letters to Don Windham. There is very little sadness in the early letters, just whooping, erotic enthusiasm.

Tennessee entered the *Small Craft* affair scared and hurt. He had been savaged by critics so many times in the past few years. In a letter to Bill Barnes from New Orleans he wrote that he expected that he, personally, would be reviewed more than the play. But he kept moving along, and a week later sent Bill a batch of rewrites. He said he was trying to bring the character of Leona more into focus.

By this time Barnes had signed up three young producers to do the play in New York: Robert Currie, Mario de Maria and William Orton. Tennessee returned to Key West in January, and by then they had rented the Truck and Warehouse Theater, far off Broadway. He liked the sound of that name. The producers were happy with the script and moving toward an April 2 opening.

Then, about a week before opening night, he flew to Chicago. It was the day before the Illinois primaries. Dakin was running for Democratic nomination for senator, against Representative Roman Pucinski, sometimes called Pooch. The Tennessee-Dakin feud had cooled considerably and he was there to give Dakin a hand.

They called a press conference and Tennessee appeared, wearing a full beard, a green plaid sport jacket and black slacks. Dakin, who had been first assistant United States attorney for the eastern district of Illinois, was at this time in private law practice.

The reporters, however, kept changing the subject to playwriting, and in fact the *Tribune* wrote a play:

D: If we can just get twenty percent of the Chicago vote, we can win it.
T: But you're not going to.
D: I think I'm going to get sixty to seventy percent of the downstate vote, because nobody there knows who Pooch is, and I'll get a lot of the Chicago suburban vote because they do know who Pooch is.
T: I don't think you can win this primary, you are too decent a person.
D: If we can just get on television tonight . . .
T: But we're not.
REPORTER: I say it would make a great play.
T: I'll stick with my plays, the human area. Politics is unhuman.
     (Curtain)

The *Sun-Times* added this remark from Tennessee: "Dakin is a serious man. He's a man of stature and clarity."

But in spite of the fraternal aid Dakin lost the primary, and Tennessee headed for New York and the Truck and Warehouse Theater.

Small Craft Warnings did open as scheduled on April 2, and it was, as he wrote to his three producers afterward, "a very lovely production." The experience had been pleasant. He told Mario, Bob and Bill that he had "never had producers with whom it was happier for me to work, nor a cast . . . that I felt more affection toward . . ."

All this says a good deal about Tennessee's improved frame of mind and his condition generally. He expected the worst in the reviews. Gore Vidal had told him, "Your personal publicity had been so terrible that you can never get good reviews again in your life in America."

But the notices were not that bad. They were "mixed." As William Glover's Associated Press story put it, "Many reviewers found the play's characters were ghosts from dramas past." When Glover said this to Tennessee, he replied, "What do they want, blood? At sixty-one, I don't have blood to give. I gave them good writing. I achieved my purpose, which was to write a play that corresponded to a short story."

Tennessee was most pleased about the scene with Quentin, the elderly homosexual, though he added that Quentin was not his own kind of homosexual. And he said that writing was still the greatest satisfaction of his life. In the interview he seemed anxious to set the record straight about himself. And he had, probably, that very morning, written a page or two of his *Memoirs*.

He was still, three weeks after the opening of *Small Craft*, sending rewrites to Bill Barnes.

He had not had a commercially successful play since *Iguana*, eleven years before, and he was determined to make *Small Craft* a success. He was doing lots of interviews and talk shows, and he was trying to persuade his producers to find a theater farther uptown.

He was really doing three things at once: pushing *Small Craft*, doing readings all around the country and writing hard on his *Memoirs*. For example, in the month of the *Small Craft* opening, he was also touring his one-man show, "my fan dance with falling feathers and a kangaroo partner," as he described it to his producers, at the universities of Indiana and Minnesota. He certainly seemed healthy and full of gumption.

Doubleday had advanced him $50,000 to write his *Memoirs*. He certainly didn't need eating money, with his plays being performed everywhere, but he said at first he was doing it for the money. Then he became fully absorbed in this form of confession, and boomed along happily in a chatty style, breaking off his remembrances every few pages to chat about what he did the night before, and how *Small Craft* and *Out Cry* were progressing. His chronology is as imaginative as *Alice in Wonderland*—or as Tennessee himself—a delight to a reader and a giddy ride on a roller coaster for a biographer. The rule has to be: Take nothing for granted, and everything with a grain of salt.

His own barefaced revelations make all the previous profiles, taped interviews and other allegedly shocking accounts, like those in the Atlantic, Esquire and Playboy, seem like mimeographed releases from the Salvation Army.

The original manuscript must have been truly enormous. As printed it's a sizable book, but Doubleday published only about half of the material he submitted. Yet a great many of the plays are not even mentioned. He felt that talking about the plays would be "boring" to the reader.

Then, suddenly, he decided to become an actor. He pumped up the character of Doc, in *Small Craft*, and with a shrewd showman's eye on the box office, decided to play the part himself. His trio of producers found a better house, the New Theater, and the author came onstage for the opening night at the new location.

He played the part for five performances, and the consensus was that he was pretty good. He played the alcoholic old doctor quite convincingly, and he didn't even change his clothes. He came to the theater in a white linen suit with a white panama hat and a gold cross on his chest, played the part and went home just that way. If anything spotted the suit it would be in character for Doc anyhow.

He says in *Memoirs*, probably written the next morning, that he made a few fluffs and sometimes ran out of breath, but he got a big hand. He admits he made some outrageous ad libs, appreciated more by the audience than by his fellow actors.

In addition to performing as Doc he would sometimes conduct a symposium after the performance with the audience. Tiring of this solo act one evening, he called up his old friend Maureen Stapleton. She joined him on stage and they read his short play *A Perfect Analysis Given by a Parrot*. She did the part of Bessie, at sight, and he read the part of the other whore, Flora. She did her part beautifully, of course, and he sent her a bouquet of roses the next day.

Another time he read his strange geriatric play *The Frosted Glass Coffin*, and he said that many people walked out. It isn't a play for everybody.

In *Memoirs* he tells of the wildest night of all in his *Small Craft* personal appearances. He had planned to read his latest short story, "The Inventory of Fontana Bella," to the audience after the first Saturday-night performance, at about 9:00 P.M. After a picnic with friends on Billy Barnes's terrace, he tripped over a garden hose and came up bloody. By the time he arrived, bandaged, at the theater, a few minutes late, the audience had left. There were various outcries, pleadings and recriminations. Tennessee went sulking to his Hotel Elysee suite, was massaged, soothed and then propelled forth to read "Fontana" to the audience before the midnight show. "Fontana" is about a 102-year-old *principessa* who manages to get raped, more or less, by a stork while wandering around her palazzo naked. It's a "tour de farce," and about as black as black humor can get. He said that the audience reaction was "perfunctory," and was sad that no one laughed at his "jokes on paper anymore."

There was method in all this madness. Tennessee thought that if *Small*

Craft could become a solid commercial success, he would have a better chance to arrange a first-rate production for *Out Cry*, the play that was closest of all to his heart.

It worked. The word-of-mouth was that almost anything could happen at the New Theater, and the audience kept on coming. *Small Craft* had a healthy run of almost six months and finished well in the black.

Two different producers, Chuck Bowden and David Merrick, were both considering major productions of *Out Cry*. Bowden was thinking of casting Paul Scofield as Felice. Scofield, however, had other commitments. Merrick swept in, signed a contract and began planning for a long tryout tour followed by a Broadway production.

Peter Glenville was signed to direct and Tennessee began working with him on the latest revisions of this infinitely rewritten script.

Then Tennessee took off for New Orleans, back to Dumaine Street and an apartment where he had just sent a load of furniture from New York. The van load included his wonderful big brass bed, which was a kind of memorial to Frank Merlo.

A few weeks later, still restless, he flew to Venice with a planeload of "beautiful people," including Andy Warhol, Sylvia Miles, Billy Barnes and Rex Reed, all heading for the film festival.

Michael York, by this time a famous film star, was in Italy too, and Tennessee hoped he could be persuaded to do *Out Cry*. Tennessee sent him a script. York had been looking for a play to do on Broadway and had turned down many. He read *Out Cry*, thought it was excellent and knew that the role of Felice would be a marvelous one for him.

Both parts are equally difficult, and the problem was to find someone to play Clare. David Merrick favored a young actress named Cara Duff-MacCormick. It was no secret that he was fond of her personally, but Duff-MacCormick was no "starlet." She had just won the Clarence Derwent acting award and was very talented.

Tennessee, now back in New York, went to Glenville's "opulent quarters" to hear her read the part. He felt that she was indeed gifted, but he knew this was a role that demanded the stature and the presence of a major star. No decision was yet made. Meanwhile, Tennessee said that Glenville was putting back some of the cuts Tennessee had made in Chicago. But he said he would cut them once again whether Glenville liked it or not.

Tennessee hoped they could get Genevieve Bujold. Bill Barnes talked with her, she came to New York and Tennessee met her at Bill's apartment. He thought she was "an incredibly perfect Clare" and told her, "You're beautiful! And slightly mad!" But Glenville said that she had done a "terrible reading." Finally Bujold went back to Montreal and called from there, saying she was doubtful about having to move to New York. Tennessee thought she was a bit frightened by the play.

They finally settled on Duff-MacCormick and rehearsals began in mid-December. Jo Mielziner, not in the best of health, designed a strange, abstract and rather ponderous set.

The first shakedown was at New Haven, and while they were there Tennessee had a symposium with about fifty students from the Yale Drama School. It is hard to believe his statement that the most interested member of the group was a large black dog.

New Haven and Yale were relatively noncommittal about *Out Cry* and the company moved on to Philadelphia. According to Paul Bigelow, the Philadelphia production was close to a disaster.

Paul was convinced after reading it and seeing Keathley's simple but excellent Chicago production that *Out Cry* was one of Tennessee's greatest plays.

Bigelow decided to slip into Philadelphia privately, to see it alone, at a Wednesday matinee, without alerting Tennessee. He bought his ticket and went in—and there was Tennessee in the lobby. They had, as usual, a big reunion meeting and Bigelow settled down to watch the play.

He was shocked. The set was poorly lit; Mielziner was ill, and no one had the authority to light it properly. Bigelow thought this was one of Mielziner's more cumbersome designs. When little Cara made her entrance, he could hardly see her, and he heard "this piping little voice. It was not a commanding voice...and after a while out came this sweet little girl..." Bigelow was desolate, because he thought that Tennessee's entrances usually showed genius. Michael York's interpretation, he thought, was "marvelous" and "brilliant." But he felt that Cara was not yet ready for this very difficult role.

Bigelow went back to Tennessee's hotel after the matinee to talk with him and Michael York. Tennessee was worried because "in Chicago we got laughs where we were supposed to, and in Philadelphia we're not getting any." Bigelow told him, "You cannot play comedy in the dark, and you haven't got any lights. Michael is making a speech at the top of the ladder and you can't see anything but his feet. You can't see Michael."

Michael said that Mielziner was ill and wouldn't allow anyone else to light the set. Bigelow told him, "Michael, you're a star. You go over to that theater tonight and tell that stage manager if that set isn't lighted you're not playing. You'll get some lights."

Paul saw it again that evening and it was lighted. "And it worked, it got the laughs."

But Bigelow was still unhappy about the production. He much preferred George Keathley's direction in Chicago. Tennessee asked him to come down to Washington with the production, but he declined, saying he had not been invited by the director.

At the Kennedy Center, Tennessee was still making revisions. But at that point he said that Glenville refused to insert any more changes. The play was performed much as it was in Philadelphia and was politely received. Richard Coe of the Washington *Post* praised it highly.

Then they all came in to New York for the March 1 opening at the Lyceum Theater, his first on Broadway since 1968. Tennessee was so pessimistic about the reception of the play that he arranged for a limousine to pick him up at the theater half an hour before the final curtain, to go directly to La Guardia airport for a flight to Miami.

Tennessee saw the first act from the balcony. On his way down, during the intermission, he heard someone say that the play had been better at the tryout in Chicago, the Keathley production. Tennessee told him, "Thanks, I agree."

And soon after that he left, so he missed the ovation that Michael York and Cara received after the final curtain. He conceded finally that she had loved and understood the play better than anyone else except himself. But he still felt it might have had a better chance of success with Genevieve Bujold.

The reviews were not enthusiastic. Clive Barnes was, he said, "cautiously respectful," but not enough to bring crowds to the Lyceum. After twelve performances Merrick decided to close the play.

Tennessee said that it took him a full year to recover from this, but he was certainly not sitting in a darkened room wringing his hands. Actually this was a period of enormous and fruitful work in many directions, many of them far from the theater.

In Key West he finished writing his *Memoirs* and was putting together his volume of short stories, *Eight Mortal Ladies Possessed*, writing a short semiautobiographical novel, *Moise and the World of Reason*, and a television play, *Stopped Rocking*, for Maureen Stapleton. He was rewriting *Kingdom of Earth* for a production at Princeton, and beginning work on his next play, *The Red Devil Battery Sign*. It sounds bewildering, but he liked to work that way. If he was stuck on one project, he could switch to another.

Recalling these days to Richard Coe of the Washington *Post*, he said that his typewriter began clacking at 6:00 A.M. and often continued until noon. And it was a "push" machine, too. He never liked electrics, saying they were "too quick on the touch."

He was joined at this time by a young veteran of the Vietnam war,

Robert Carroll, then twenty-five years old, redheaded and pleasant looking, and a writer. Tennessee wrote in an article for Travel Bazaar that Carroll was "the most talented young writer I have met in half a lifetime." He moved into the guesthouse and remained a close companion until 1978.

One of the last of Tennessee's *Eight Mortal Ladies Possessed* stories to be written was "Sabbatha and Solitude" and it should be read, at least twice, by everyone who thinks of Tennessee in his stereotyped public image as a gloomy manufacturer of tragic and tortured ladies. Sabbatha is hilarious and full of slightly veiled self-mockery. Sabbatha, a potty poetess and once the crowned queen of sonnet sequences, is in decline and living in a drift-wood shack on the New England coast with an Italian gigolo-painter half her age. She dreams of her once numerous horde of lovers, chills her veins in spring water, while Giovanni is off forging her checks, only to return, in his fashion, to her arms. Sabbatha thinks there can be a "certain elation" in going mad if you don't fight it. By a kind of reverse *Catch-22*, a person who can write like that about madness can't possibly be all mad.

"Miss Coynte of Greene," another mortal lady, celebrates the death of her bed-dirtying old grandma by going off the rails, sexually speaking, even with gentlemen of dark complexions. This is Rabelaisian and very funny. Miss C feels that we all go easily from birth to death. It isn't a problem unless we make it one.

"Happy August the Tenth," a devastating study of two lesbians, and the leading story of the volume, was chosen by Martha Foley for her *Best American Short Stories of 1973*.

He was also writing his second short novel, *Moise and the World of Reason*. He instructs us to pronounce Moise this way: "Say *mo*. And then say *ease*, with the accent placed (ironically) on the *ease*." Like *Mrs. Stone*, it is about the same length as a play, or about half as long or less as an average novel. They were either transposed from plays, or from ideas for plays, and both could be recycled into plays. (Of course *Mrs. Stone* became a successful film.) But it would seem that both are more workable as novels, largely because so much of their content is subjective, thought rather than spoken. *Moise* particularly is like a game of chess in that the physical action is almost nil, but the subjective activity is violent.

Moise is so frankly, barefaced homosexual (literally bare-assed explicit) that it would be virtually impossible to do on any stage. Here there is no transference, as in *Mrs. Stone*, and possibly *Sweet Bird*, from aging homosexual male to aging heterosexual female. *Moise* calls a spade a damned shovel. "I" is a thirty-year-old homosexual writer. Moise, of the title, is a woman, but she is a secondary character.

Tennessee is there in the flesh in two characters, young and old, as "I" and as an old playwright, written in the third person, a cruel self-portrait with warts, as he saw himself at the time he wrote the book. "I" lives in an abandoned warehouse on the outskirts of Greenwich Village, near the Manhattan docks, forever writing in Blue Jay notebooks on an old Bon Ami crate. He is still in love with Lance, a black skater now dead, and is in the process of losing his young lover, Charlie.

He is propositioned by "a freakish old playwright" who is working in the Bowery at the Truck and Warehouse Theater. The older man is short, southern and partly blind, with weaknesses for speed and wine and poetry. He is haunted by ghosts who closely resemble Tennessee's grandfather, grandmother, Frank Merlo and Marion Vaccaro.

It is a cruel caricature of himself, showing all the bad and none of the good. "I" refuses the advances of this dirty old man. Moise herself, a penniless artist who starts but rarely finishes pictures, appears mainly at her own bare-bones party in the beginning of the book, and again toward the end. She acts as a catalyst, bringing together the young Tennessee and the old one. The book is close to masochistic flagellation, trying so hard to be cruely honest that it shows only one side of the truth. It is lewd, brutal and often very funny, and it is beautifully written. But his two self-portraits, especially the older one, are scarred by the marks of his own whip.

Moise was published in March 1975 by Simon & Schuster, his first with this house. So he was dealing, almost simultaneiously, with three publishers, Simon & Schuster, Doubleday and New Directions.

He was also conferring with Jule Styne and Leslie Bricusse, who were adapting *The Rose Tattoo* into a musical. A Broadway musical is always the longest of long shots. At this time it would have cost about a million dollars to put one on stage. So far, nothing has yet come of this one.

By the spring of 1975 he seems to have recovered from his *Out Cry* depression, at least outwardly. In March, Richard Coe of the Washington *Post* found him bland, soft-spoken, hardworking and healthy, and delighted that *Cat* was having a triumphant revival at the Kennedy Center. After talking with him for two hours, Coe reflected that in all this time Tennessee had not once said an unkind thing about a living soul. Nor, in fact, a dead one.

Red Devil Battery Sign was taking final shape and David Merrick was ready to try another production. It would be elaborate and expensive, with a large cast and complicated sets. The final cost, in fact, would be about $360,000. Merrick allied himself with three other producers, Doris Cole Abrahams, Robert Colby and—because Claire Bloom was to play the leading lady—Hillard Elkins, her husband. Anthony Quinn agreed to play the male lead.

An elaborate tryout tour was planned, to start in Boston and move on to the Kennedy Center in Washington, before arriving on Broadway. Edwin Sherin would be directing.

Red Devil takes place in Dallas, soon after the Kennedy assassination. The female lead, called only the Woman Downtown, is the estranged wife of an evil, multinational tycoon, owner of the Red Devil Company. She is in love with a man named King, the leader of a Mexican mariachi band, who is dying of a brain tumor. There are projected images of wars and assassinations and a pulsating red light, which one might say is the title role. After the death of her lover the Woman joins a sort of urban guerilla group, attacking what she feels is a corrupt civilization.

At about the time Tennessee was getting ready to leave New York for the Boston opening, Marian Christy of the Boston *Globe* found him to be jaunty, in fighting trim, wearing "an impeccable grey Cardin suit." He said he was laughing more these days. In fact, a few days before, he had laughed so hard at Sardi's that he fell off his chair and sprained his hand. Even laughter, with the world champion hypochondriac, could be dangerous.

There were many problems in the complicated production. But it did manage to open at the Shubert Theater in Boston on June 18. Anthony Quinn was fine in a difficult part. Claire Bloom was strikingly beautiful as the Woman Downtown, and was strong and frightening in the melodramatic portions. But some in the rear seats didn't think her voice was strong enough. They had trouble hearing her lines.

Elliot Norton of the Boston *Herald-American* thought it was a "presently unfocussed play that teeters and totters eerily between true tragedy and mawkish melodrama." He gave it a long and serious review, however, found fine characterization and writing in it, and thought it was good enough to be rewritten.

Kevin Kelly of the *Globe* blasted it, calling it "a mess." Thor Eckert of the *Christian Science Monitor* liked it, saying it was a "haunting theatre piece" and "cause for rejoicing." He felt it showed that Tennessee had not lost his touch.

The audiences were big. In the first week they bought $67,000 worth of tickets. Yet it closed on the second Saturday night, for complicated reasons, even though some $140,000 had already gone into the box office. The four producers disagreed about casting and production and lawsuits were threatened. The Washington and New York openings were canceled.

Tennessee said he was "devastated" and offered to give up all his royalties to date to help pay for the move to Washington. The offer was refused, so he bought two first-class plane tickets to Italy, one for himself and one for his dog, Madame Sophia, and flew away.

Merrick mourned the fact that it could not have been tried out more simply, with more time for revisions. Once a juggernaut of this size started rolling, it was difficult to slow it down for repairs. What Tennessee really needed was a leisurely month or so working with an experimental group, the way he had done in Miami, slowly building *Sweet Bird*.

Paul Bigelow said of this period of Tennessee's life that there was always a tendency for other people to rush his plays into production prematurely, without allowing him that long period of gestation and revision that he had needed in the preparation of his early great plays, and probably needed even more at this time.

Anthony Quinn, who could have made much more money doing a film, was unrepentant. Time quoted him: "I'd rather be in a flop by Tennessee Williams, whom I consider to be the world's greatest living playwright, than in a hit by a shit."

In any case, Tennessee was already rewriting *Red Devil*. It would appear the following year in, of all places, Vienna, at the English Theater. Tennessee referred to this as the "official world premiere," when, after several weeks of tryout performances and revisions, it had its formal opening on January 17, 1976. He flew there and, as usual, made revisions in the script. There were big audiences and the play was well received.

Sy Kahn, the drama professor of the University of the Pacific, saw it there. He thought the production was uneven, with some of the accents closer to London than Dallas. He felt that although the script needed more revision it still generated power and, as he wrote, it "sent at least one Vienna lady howling from the theatre into the night."

But immediately before that, Tennessee had what was certainly his biggest public success since *The Night of the Iguana*. The *Memoirs* that he had been writing, off and on, for three years were finally published by Doubleday in the fall of 1975, and created a sensation.

After all the profiles and interviews the basic patterns of Tennessee's personal life were generally known, but there were scores of new revelations in the *Memoirs*, even though Doubleday had cut out dozens of them, many for legal reasons. Some reviewers were shocked, but the notices were big, with many pictures, and hints of unspeakable secrets now revealed.

There was much genuine praise like Dennis Brown's: "... an extraordinary and historical memoir... a major artistic addition to the prolific output of an astoundingly resilient life..." Rex Reed said there was "candor and wit and a peculiar vitality..."

The public was intrigued and the book climbed onto the bestseller list. The climax came in the Great Fifth Avenue Bookstore Riot, just before Christmas. Dennis Brown was there.

A small ad in the New York *Times* announced that Tennessee would be at the Doubleday Fifth Avenue bookstore between noon and 2:00 P.M., to autograph copies of his *Memoirs*. By 11:45 the store was so jammed that no other business could be transacted and people kept crowding in until the police were called. Crowds were beginning to gather on the sidewalk, too, and police had to close the store and set up police lines for customers. The queue soon stretched more than a block along Fifth Avenue.

Tennessee arrived at 12:27, "impeccably dressed in a blue bow tie and a three-piece gray suit that almost perfectly matched the color of his salt and pepper hair." He began autographing. Panic struck Doubleday. They were running out of books. They sent out red alerts to all their other stores and to the warehouse. Messengers began to arrive in cabs with books in cartons, in shopping bags, in stacks.

Two o'clock came and went. The crowds grew. Until 4:00 P.M. Tennessee kept on, finally autographing more than eight hundred books. Doubleday said he had broken their record.

"You mean," he said, "I drew more people than Jacqueline Susann?" Yes, they told him, he had.

He said his hand wasn't tired, only his head, and he went off to have a late lunch at the Russian Tea Room.

The book continued to sell. To the many who criticized him for being so frank, especially about his sex life, he replied, "When you write your life, there's no way to do it but honestly. You either do it honestly or you don't do it at all. Now that it's done I think I'll find myself leading an increasingly private life."

But he would never be allowed to live a really private life again. As he was making that statement, the volume of his letters, written to Donald Windham, was already in the hands of its publisher, Holt, Rinehart & Winston. These revelations would be even more sensational, and often more accurate, since they were written at the time and not distorted by memory.

At this moment, in New York alone, three of his plays were running. Irene Worth was playing the Princess in *Sweet Bird of Youth* at the Harkness, Maureen Stapleton was Amanda in *The Glass Menagerie* at the Circle in the Square and *27 Wagons Full of Cotton* was at the Phoenix.

As always, he was most concerned with work in progress. Less than a month after the Doubleday riot, another new play, opened at the American Conservatory Theater, often called just ACT, in San Francisco. It had the strange title *This Is (An Entertainment)*. The action takes place in a hotel in a mythical European country. The main character is another of his monster-women, a countess who has three different personalities, and three men, a husband and two lovers, all of whom she is managing to destroy. There is also her mother's ghost, an invading revolutionary army and—it *is* confusing. The San Francisco critics were puzzled and doubtful.

Tennessee was spending a good deal of time in Key West. One friend and neighbor was the literary agent Jay Garon. He reported, in an interview in New York, that Tennessee was far from being the recluse he had been in the late sixties.

At one dinner party at a neighbor's house, Tennessee stood up spontaneously and began doing one of his favorite recitations, the speech of Mother God Damn, owner of the largest brothel in Shanghai, from the play *Shanghai Gesture*, by John Colton:

> "Yes—yes—yes—all—all I survived—whippings with hippo hide when I was stubborn—hot dung thrust into my nostrils and stinging leeches in my ears so I could not sleep—I survived!—sulphur burned on my naked back to make my tired body gay . . . Hate helped me—black gods helped me—hell and the devil helped me—I lived! I lived!

Then, said Garon, he trembled violently and keeled over. Garon and others, terrified, put wet towels over his face, trying to revive him. When they were almost convinced he was dying, or dead, Tennessee winked and said, "You thought it was for real!"

He was the biggest tourist attraction on Key West, even bigger than the Hemingway house. The powers that were on the island decided to call a new wing of the library the Tennessee Williams Wing, perhaps hoping for a large cash donation. Tennessee gave them a tape of himself, reading his poetry, and told them they could use it to raise money for the library. Garon finally negotiated a contract with a recording company, Free Sounds, to produce a record album from the tape. Tennessee got cold feet about this and, Garon said, ended up by canceling permission to use the tape as a record.

Another facet of the Tennessee Williams Key West tourist industry was the formation of a Tennessee Williams repertory company. In April 1976 *Suddenly Last Summer* was produced at the Greene Street Theater. The players were startled and delighted when he drove up with seven new lines of dialogue, and stage directions for a new ending. Mrs. Venable would henceforth collapse onstage rather than offstage. He then attended the opening performance and led the applause.

The major production that year, 1976, was *The Eccentricities of a Nightingale*. He wrote a story about this, accompanied by one of Hirschfeld's cartoons, for the Sunday New York *Times* drama section of November 21.

He said it all started in Rome in the summer of 1951. He was "working against time" to rewrite *Summer and Smoke* for H. M. Tennant's production in London. He was mainly trying to cut excessive or distracting material, but was also making important improvements.

He arrived in London with "a practically new work"—and there began the strangest mix-up of scripts in his life. Or, how to have a hit play with the wrong playscript.

He was met in London by Maria Britneva, who told him they were already in the midst of rehearsals for *Summer and Smoke*, the old version. So it was too late to change scripts. He gave the new version to Maria, who said she would put it away.

When he saw her, as he wrote, ten or fifteen years later, she produced the new script and stuffed it into his overcoat pocket, so that he would be sure not to forget it. He read it through that night and worked on it some more. It had a summer tryout in 1964.

According to this account, Tennessee, no academic stickler for dates, had made a mistake, he had got it wrong. He couldn't possibly have re-written the play in 1951, because José Quintero and Geraldine Page did that magnificent version in 1952, at the Circle in the Square, a big success, and they had used the old version. If there had been a new, better version, surely it would have been used then, meaning that the 1951 story had to be wrongly dated, it had to be *after* 1952. There was no way they would use an old version for a big production. So the date was checked out in the London *Times* files—and Tennessee had been right. *Summer and Smoke* did indeed open at the Lyric Theater, Hammersmith (then probably the greatest of Off–West End theaters and since rebuilt) on November 22, 1951, with Margaret Johnstone as Alma, and was reviewed, not too favorably, by the *Times*.

So, with the much better version in Maria's drawer, in England, José Quintero made a smash hit in New York out of the old one!

Clive Barnes, who knew *Summer and Smoke* well, thought that *Nightingale* would be merely a revision of that play, and was surprised and pleased to note that it was "a different play with different characters and even a different theme." He thought it a major improvement and declared it "effectively knocks *Summer and Smoke* off the map as a literary curiosity." He recognized the fact that the conflict had changed from the more general one of soul against body (as symbolized by the minister's house and the doctor's house) to a conflict between two people, as Barnes put it, one hot and one cold, the warmhearted girl and the reserved mother's boy. It was more credible than the first version. It was "a warm, rich play" and "Mr. Williams at his shining, gentle best." Betsy Palmer played Alma, Shepperd

Strudwick played her father and David Selby the boy. Edwin Sherin directed.

Tennessee felt a great deal better. It was the best Broadway reaction he had received in a long time.

He then moved even farther back, to that winter of 1938–39 that he had spent in New Orleans, right after leaving Iowa University. He had put it all down years before in his almost completely autobiographical story "The Angel in the Alcove." He called the play *Vieux Carré*, after the old French Quarter.

Back in his studio in Key West he settled down to make *Vieux Carré* ready for Broadway. He was not in the best of moods. As he wrote, he was even an old bear to the poor little Greene Street players in Key West, where he was highly displeased with many details in the *Nightingale* production, including the feather in Miss Alma's hat. But he was sorry later, and was extra nice to the leading lady the next day.

He was working hard, in preparation for the May 10 opening of *Vieux Carré* on Broadway. A few weeks beforehand, he was being interviewed in his Key West patio by Anna Quindlen of the New York *Times*, who was impressed that this was his twenty-ninth major play. She asked if he was running dry for new themes and ideas, presumably not realizing that this was an old theme and idea.

Tennessee told her it was not as easy to write now as when he was young. "The wells of emotion that spring spontaneously from the mind and spirit do not flow with the power that produced *The Glass Menagerie* and *A Streetcar Named Desire*."

And when he wrote his preopening essay for the Sunday drama section of the New York *Times*, he seemed depressed, and in fact never even referred to *Vieux Carré*. "I am widely regarded," he wrote, "as the ghost of a writer...remembered mostly for works which were staged between 1944 and 1961." And toward the end of the essay he wrote, "In my heart an inscrutable bird of dark feather seems to have built a nest which I can never quite dislodge, no matter how loudly I cackle or widely I grin."

The play had a number of New York previews, one of which Dakin attended; he wrote a favorable review for his hometown paper. It opened at the St. James Theater on May 10, with Sylvia Sidney playing the tough old landlady, Mrs. Wire. The other reviews were less favorable than Dakin's and it closed after a short run.

Perhaps some of his trouble was simply jet lag. *The Red Devil Battery Sign* was rehearsing and opening in London at almost exactly the same time that *Vieux Carré* was opening in New York, and he was dashing back and forth. The new supersonic plane the Concorde was in service, allowing westbound travelers to arrive two hours before they started, and he was on it so much that he claimed a record for the number of Concorde transatlantic flights.

Red Devil opened on May 9, with Maria Britneva in the cast. It had a moderate success and managed to hold out until late July. The London *Times* interviewed him the day after it closed, on July 24, in the lobby of a Knightsbridge hotel where he was drinking iced tea with Maria. They seemed mellow and content, and talked of their friendship of nearly thirty years.

That year New Directions published his second major book of poetry, *Androgyne, Mon Amour*, which has a great deal more of his curious mixture of French and English than he used in his earlier volume, *In the Winter of Cities*. In his light verse, as in "Little Horse," or in "Which is my little boy, which is he, *Jean qui pleure ou Jean qui rit*?" both from the earlier volume, there is a simple charm; but in *Androgyne* the poems are more serious, and emphasize the fact that his English is much more vivid than his French.

He was doing quite a lot of painting at this time and was even selling a number of his paintings, some for as high as $2,500. One of them appears on the color jacket of the *Androgyne* book, and several can usually be seen in the art galleries of Key West, along with those of a professional Key West artist, Henry Faulkner. (Both Tennessee and Dakin have bought Faulkner paintings.)

A Williams could be, for instance, in "pencil and oil" or "pencil and acrylic." They often have a pale, almost etiolated look. One of them for sale (price $2,000) at the time the authors were in Key West, was a 1978 portrait of Robert Carroll, titled *Esprit de Robert*; another, with an almost Gauguin-look and lots of tropical foliage, was called *Au Jardin des Palmes*, and another was a self-portrait of Tennessee with Robert Carroll.

He was busy writing *Crève Coeur*, another memory play, this one about a lake, once considered far out in the country from St. Louis. A streetcar line went all the way there, and in summer there were open-air cars.

This was another idea that started many years before. In the Texas archives there is a short one-act play called *Crève Coeur*, not dated. (There are no manuscripts at the University of Texas written after 1969.) It is a dialogue between two old spinsters about to take the streetcar out to the lake.

Tennessee expanded the cast to four women, who are "making an adjustment to a realistic acceptance of life on the terms offered," as he told Victor Volland of the St. Louis *Post-Dispatch*. He also expanded the title to *A Lovely Sunday for Crève Coeur*.

The play had its premiere at the Charleston, South Carolina, division of the Spoleto Festival, and there are plans for further, larger-scale productions.

In August he visited St. Louis to see Miss Edwina, then in good form at the Gatesworth Manor. St. Louis is at its hellish, sizzling worst in August; he amazed Victor Volland by saying he liked St. Louis, even though he admitted it "is about the hottest place I've ever been, except maybe Singapore." But he was mellow and full of smiles and said the city he had called "the city of St. Pollution" had its own charm. A headline across five columns shouted, "Mellowed Tennessee Williams Revisits St. Louis." He had just been to see Rose in her Ossining cottage, and had brought back a pretty sketch he had done of her.

There was a bit of joshing with Dakin, who had, that summer, been acting in Thomas Del Vecchio's play *The Trial and Trials of Oscar Wilde*. Had Dakin been the playwright who was put in jail for his sexual quirks? Not at all. He had acted the role of the Marquis of Queensberry, who sent him there.

Tennessee also flew to London that summer for the production of *Vieux Carré* at the Piccadilly Theatre, one of the largest in the West End. The play succeeded much better than it had in New York, with good reviews and a run of several months.

That winter in Key West he made all the news services again, with headlines of violence and murder. There were always large numbers of teenage dropouts and drifters on the island, a sizable gay population and a considerable group of drug smugglers, dealing mainly in marijuana and cocaine. The mixture of all these characters sometimes caused explosions.

One evening Tennessee's house was besieged by young men who threw beer cans on his porch and shouted, "Come on out, faggot!" and set off firecrackers. Dotson Rader, the writer and a former editor of Esquire, who was the only person at home at the time, thought they were attacking with guns.

Shortly afterward real guns were used. Tennessee's gardener, Frank Fontis, was killed. Fontis, a tall, burly, forty-nine-year-old eccentric, also acted as curator of the Key West Railroad Museum, and looked after Tennessee's compound when he was away. On the night of January 5, 1979, Fontis was shot dead, and both his house and Tennessee's were ransacked. It is still a mystery; no one knows who did it, or why, and the most likely guess is that there was some connection with drug smuggling.

The most valuable treasure in Fontis's house had not been taken—a large stack of Tennessee's manuscripts, which Tennessee had not realized were missing.

A few weeks later Tennessee and Rader were mugged. At about one in the morning they were walking down Key West's main drag, Duval Street, having had a drink or two apiece, and singing hymns, when they were confronted by four or five young men and attacked.

News was flashed all over the world, as though there had been an assassination attempt. The truth, as recorded on the blotter of the Key West police station, was: "Mr. Williams and friend, Mr. Dotson Rader, were accosted by four or five white males in the 500 block of Duval Street. The attackers advised they knew who Mr. Williams was. At this point the attackers punched Mr. Rader in the jaw. Mr. Williams advised that he was thrown to the ground. Mr. Dotson Rader and Mr. Williams were then kicked by the attackers. I could not see any evident injury to Mr. Rader or Mr. Williams. Neither wanted to get any medical treatment...Mr. Williams and Mr. Rader took a cab and went to Mr. Williams' house."

Tennessee admitted that the assassination had been exaggerated somewhat by Rader.

However, the Key West police ordered a general cleanup of the area around Duval Street. Even the little Cuban restaurant, El Cacique, was requiring customers to wear both shirts and shoes. Pants, trunks or loincloths had always been taken for granted.

About a month later, Tennessee was again attacked, if that is the right word, by two other invaders, the two biographers. Mead had flown from London to Miami to meet Dakin, who had driven down from Collinsville in a Volkswagen minibus with Joyce and an Illinois dentist friend of Dakin's, Dr. Jim Gover, and his wife, Yvonne. It was the first time Dakin and Mead had met, though they had been corresponding for many months. By this time Mead had been researching for a year, and had written a first draft. All five drove down the long causeway to Key West in the bus.

Meanwhile, Tennessee had just returned from Los Angeles, where *The Eccentricities of a Nightingale* was being transposed into a television play. He was sitting in his brightly lighted patio, wearing a linen jacket and an open-necked shirt, surrounded by palm trees, luxuriant jungle plants and several young men in white T-shirts, one of whom was Dotson Rader, and another Richard Zoerink. They were calmly and soberly playing penny-ante poker.

At about 10:30 P.M., the telephone rang. It was Dakin, calling from a motel in Key West, asking if he could come over. Tennessee said he could.

Dakin arrived shortly afterward, bringing the dentist, the two wives and a tall, graying man with thick glasses named Mead, whom Tennessee had never met, though he had read some of the newspaper stories planted by Dakin saying that the two of them were doing his biography. No one had told Tennessee that this crowd would descend upon him at eleven o'clock at night.

Tennessee said there was no alcohol in the house, and none was evident. He sent Richard out for some white wine. Dakin brought in some cans of beer from the minibus.

They talked for an hour or so about many things, but not about a biography. Tennessee was angry about a newspaper article that had just appeared, an interview with Miss Edwina, then in a St. Louis nursing home. The interview made her sound like Mr. Bones in a minstrel show. Tennessee tried to discourage talk about his plays, and when Richard made the extraordinary statement that *The Glass Menagerie* was "as surrealistic as *Camino Real*," Tennessee said that Richard was boring him. Richard, squelched, stopped talking.

As the invading group left, about midnight, they paused in Tennessee's small living room in front of his portrait of Frank Merlo. Frank's long, honest face, painted even longer in the picture, looked almost like one of Modigliani's. His eyes were staring straight ahead.

Mead asked Tennessee if they could get together during the next few days and talk. Tennessee said only that "a lot of biographies are being written about me." That was the total conversation between them. The five people climbed into the minibus and left for the motel.

The next evening Dakin and Joyce were invited by Tennessee to have dinner with him. Mead and Dr. Jim and Yvonne ate at El Cacique, all of them wearing the required shirts and shoes. Dakin and Joyce played bridge with Tennessee, and returned about 1:00 A.M., to report that Tennessee had already authorized a biography, and that this one, if written, would be unauthorized.

The following morning Dakin telephoned Tennessee's house. Someone, possibly Dotson Rader, answered, then went away. The phone was left off the hook. Dakin was told later by one of the young men that Mead was not to be allowed "to climb over the wall of the compound," something it had not occurred to Mead to do. At this moment Mead would have abandoned the whole project if he had not already spent a year on it.

The biographical team conducted investigations around Key West, then drove back to the mainland, to continue working in an "unauthorized" manner.

Tennessee had been—unknown at the time to the biographers—unusually preoccupied. He was engaged in a large project that would keep him in turmoil for the next two years, and it was quite unlike anything he had ever done before. The episode had almost the shape and the mood of one of his tragedies.

It began after he read two books, Nancy Mitford's *Zelda*, a biography of Scott Fitzgerald's tragic wife, and Zelda's novel, *Save Me the Waltz*, which is close to being autobiographical. Zelda died in a mental hospital in 1947. Tennessee was fascinated. The parallels were so close, his and Scott's crack-ups, as were the dreadful psychological problems of these two women they loved the most.

He started writing a play about real people, nominally at least, the first time he had ever done that in a full-length play. The only other one was the one-act play about the death of D.H. Lawrence, and that had very little connection with reality.

He had read the books, he knew the facts, but he threw most of them out the window and began writing what he called a "ghost play." It took place mostly on the lawn of a mental hospital during the last visit by Scott to see Zelda. Never mind that Scott would really have been in Hollywood with the journalist Sheilah Graham, trying to finish *The Last Tycoon*; never mind that there was talk about the suicide of Hemingway, which happened twenty years after Fitzgerald's death. They were all ghosts, and they were partly Tennessee and Rose, and the ghosts of those American expatriates Gerald and Sara Murphy, possibly the most charming people of the whole jazz age, preserved in aspic by Fitzgerald in *Tender Is the Night* as they were, once upon a time, in the south of France, and not at all the way they seemed to Tennessee.

As was his custom, Tennessee wrote it again and again; he called it *Clothes for a Summer Hotel* because Scott Fitzgerald was dressed for Hollywood, or for dreams.

Several drafts of the script were finished by the time Tennessee and Dakin were invited to a gala reception at the White House in December. President Carter was preoccupied with the Iranian hostage crisis, but the festivities went on, and continued at the Kennedy Center, where Tennessee was given one of the annual Kennedy Center honors, along with Henry Fonda, Ella Fitzgerald, Martha Graham and Aaron Copland.

That was only a pause in the preparations for *Summer Hotel*. José Quintero read the script and agreed to direct. Geraldine Page said she would play Zelda. They all met on New Year's Day, 1980, near Times Square.

Geraldine Page was frightened by the script and wanted more revisions. José Quintero said he felt he was "on trial for murder," but claimed he always felt that way on the first day of rehearsals. He said that he and Tennessee and Geraldine Page were very different people from what they had been back at the Circle in the Square.

It would be a big, expensive production, budgeted at $400,000, of which $20,000 was Tennessee's own money. Almost immediately there were frightening crises. They had planned to open at the Annenberg Center in Philadelphia. Suddenly a booking was available at the Kennedy Center in Washington on January 28, much too soon. They were not ready but they opened anyway, in a hectic scramble. Tennessee was still making changes almost every day. Half an hour before curtain on opening night some of the costumes still hadn't arrived from the airport.

So the play was not at its best and the Washington critics were not enthusiastic. One said it was the worst play Tennessee had written in the last twenty years.

But they soldiered on and Tennessee kept on giving the cast new lines. Page was ill and Kenneth Haigh, who played Scott, was frantic not to be able to rehearse with her. John Handy, the stage manager, was heard to say that "Zelda's asylum is the perfect setting for the play."

They kept on making changes and on February 28 they opened at the Blackstone Theater in Chicago, during a snowstorm. Dakin was there at opening night. They all feared that a savaging by the Chicago critics would make a New York opening virtually impossible.

Opening night was far better than the one in Washington. They went to a cast party at Maxim's de Paris, and even before the critical verdict was in, the Tennessee-Dakin battle began again. Dakin was running for the Democratic nomination for senator from Illinois, and he and Tennessee had agreed to hold a joint press conference. However, Tennessee told Chicago columnist Aaron Gold that Dakin "says he likes the play but didn't understand it. He wouldn't, he's too crazy."

Meanwhile, the reviews arrived; they were not raves but somewhat encouraging. The *Tribune* said that the portrait of Zelda was one of Tennessee's finest.

But the "Dakin is crazy" remark started the war again. Dakin attended a poetry reading by Tennessee, finding his brother in a purple track suit with white piping, and sneakers. Dakin announced that the "crazy" remark had cost him thousands of votes, and canceled the press conference.

Opening night in New York was March 26, Tennessee's sixty-ninth birthday, at the Cort Theater. The reviews were not good. The shrewdest but perhaps the cruelest thumbnail summing-up was by Clive Barnes: "The play—and this is not flippant—should perhaps have happened to two other people." He meant that it was overloaded with history and the ghosts of real people, which kept Tennessee from developing his own "fantasy of gilded, tragic destiny." Brendan Gill of The New Yorker was angry, not

so much at the play itself, but about the fact that the people, some of whom
he had known, were simply not like that.

The play closed after fourteen performances and lost an estimated
$450,000, including Tennessee's $20,000. So, having worked hard for more
than a year, for no wages, only a huge loss, did he then abandon *Clothes
for a Summer Hotel*? He went back to Key West—and rewrote it entirely.
He would not, he simply would *not* give up.

He had recently bought a pleasant house with a swimming pool for Rose,
not far from his own. A cousin, Estelle Adams, Jim's sister, came down to
take care of her. Rose would be living close to him for the first time since
his student days in St. Louis.

He was in New York on June 1 when word reached him that Miss
Edwina had died in St. Louis, at the Bernard West Pine nursing home.
She would have been ninety-six in August. Dakin was there with her, as
he had been almost every day in the year and a half since she had entered
the home. At the end Edwina was thin and frail, but the nearly indes-
tructible old gentlewoman had never really conceded that she was Amanda
of *The Glass Menagerie*, probably the century's best-known stage mother.

Tennessee went to St. Louis immediately for her funeral at Christ Church
Cathedral, and after the burial visited Dakin and Joyce in Collinsville, across
the river. There were stories in the newspapers that the two brothers were
at last reconciled. Previously, numerous newspaper accounts had quoted,
or misquoted, Tennessee to the effect that Dakin was planning, somehow,
to appropriate 50 percent of *Menagerie*'s royalties, still very valuable. As it
worked out, the will (written by Dakin) provided that all the royalties
reverted to Tennessee. Tennessee was pleased and soon afterward wrote
to Dakin that he had never cut Dakin out of his will—"that was just talk."
He also wrote a generous foreword to Dakin's new book, *The Bar Bizarre*,
memoirs of his legal adventures.

They went together, a week after Edwina's funeral, to the White House,
their second visit in six months. This time Rose was with Tennessee.
President Carter presented him with the Presidential Medal of Freedom,
the highest award that the government can give to a civilian. The two other
writers who received medals were Eudora Welty and Robert Penn Warren.

After receiving his award, Tennessee read one of his short poems, which
the newspapers said was about his mother, but actually written many years
before about old Grand, and was a miniature portrait of the old lady,
standing by the stove, spicing meat with cinnamon and cloves.

The president said, in presenting the medal, "Tennessee Williams has
shaped the history of American drama. From passionate tragedy to lyrical
comedy, his masterpieces dramatize the eternal conflict of body and soul,

youth and death, love and despair. Through the unity of reality and poetry Tennessee Williams shows that the truly heroic in life or art in human compassion."

This statement had a fine ring to it, a kind of tolling of the bell, the last rites for Tennessee as a playwright. The funeral was premature. Tennessee was already working on a play that some considered his best in the last twenty years, *A House Not Meant to Stand*, the first in which Dakin was to appear, only slightly disguised.

Yet it might never have happened if it had not been for an extraordinary gentleman, Gregory Mosher, and his Goodman Theatre, a fine experimental playhouse in Tennessee's luckiest city, Chicago.

Tennessee had written a one-act play very quickly, in two weeks, had lost it, rewritten it from memory in one night, as he told Richard Christiansen of the Chicago *Tribune*, then found the first version and used the best lines of both. he called it *Some Problems for the Moose Lodge*, and it was full of ghosts, a disintegrating southern family with an addled mother, and a father named Cornelius, like his own, but also obsessed, like his brother Dakin, with attempts to be elected to public office.

It was first produced in a little theatre in Atlanta along with some of his other one-act plays, and directed by Gary Tucker, once known by his *nom de guerre*, "Eleven," as a director of experimental plays in Chicago since the 1960s.

Tucker brought a copy of the play to Chicago and arranged a meeting with Greg Mosher and Tennessee at the Pump Room. Mosher had not yet read the play but agreed to do so. He liked it and produced it in his small Studio, not his Mainstage, in November 1980, directed by Tucker. It was politely received, and that might have been that, except that Mosher thought it could be expanded into a full-length play.

Tennessee went back to work, and a few months later the long version, then titled *The Dance Money*, was ready. It went into rehearsal, still in the little Studio at the Goodman. Tennessee kept on making revisions during rehearsals. The title was changed to *A House Not Meant to Stand*, and it opened in April 1981. Both he and Mosher agreed it needed more work.

Mosher decided to bring in a new director, Belgian-born André Ernotte, who had done a fine job of directing Harold Pinter's *Betrayal* at the Goodman the previous season.

Ernotte went down to Key West and spent several days with Tennessee, suggesting changes, including the addition of several monologues. Tennessee agreed with some of these and made revisions.

Rehearsals began for a full-scale production on the Goodman Mainstage. Tennessee wanted Maureen Stapleton for the mother but settled for Peg

Murray, and discovered he liked her very much. He stayed in Key West during most of the rehearsals, but came to Chicago for the opening night, April 27.

The audience was pleased and the reviews were the best he had received in a long time. The *Sun-Times* ran a three-column headline: "Tennessee Williams, Goodman have a winner in 'House'" above Glenna Syse's review. She said that Tennessee was "still a major voice in the American theatre," and called him "a canny old hound dog who knows where all the bodies are buried," The play was "a meticulous honeycomb of a story, a complex spiderweb with a gossamer heart and a granite spine,"— a favorable, if mixed metaphor.

Claudia Cassidy liked it, too, saying, "It is shrewd as well as bitter, often sharply, acridly funny as well as sad."

It ran for weeks at the Goodman to well-filled houses. Dakin went there and watched, somewhat mesmerized, to see himself finally in one of Tennessee's plays. True, Cassidy had described Cornelius as "mean-spirited" and Glenna Syse called him a "cantankerous old codger who would pull the plug on his whole family to run for congress and spite his lodge buddies."

No matter. Dakin later told his collaborator in St. Louis that Cornelius was definitely based on himself. "Were you angry?" "No, no!" he said, laughing. "He's used everybody else in the family. It was time he used me."

Tennessee kept on working, like a prima donna who continues to make farewell performances for years. He said that he would write no more plays—well, no more *long* plays—but then added that there was another one almost ready, called *Masks Outrageous*.

He was cornered last August in Sicily, a place he loved, by a British journalist, Nigel Andrews, whom he told between cackles that he was writing a play about exploding volcanoes. One must remember that he would say almost anything to interviewers, often making it up as he went along. And then, a day or an hour later, with his gray beard wagging and his eyes twinkling, he would tell the next reporter something entirely different, even contradictory.

He said he would always continue to write, even on his deathbed, if he had to dictate.

Tennessee Williams died on February 25, 1983, in his two-room suite at the Elysee Hotel in New York. The city's chief medical examiner stated that the playwright choked to death on a plastic cap, the kind used on nasal spray or eyedrops. Only three days before, a close friend, Edmund Perret, reported that he had spoken to Tennessee on the telephone, and that the playwright had said, "I think I might be cashing in." But, "he said that all the time," Perret added. Dakin, when he heard about his brother's death, said that he was not really surprised. "I had known three months before that his health was deteriorating," he told the New York *Times*. He is buried next to his mother in Calvary Cemetery, St. Louis.

On the day following Tennessee's death, the *Times* published a laudatory editorial under the headline; "Remembered Magic," and commented:

> "No one who ever saw it forgot it: a woman with a broken mind taking the arm of the man who is to escort her to an asylum and saying with exquisite courtesy, 'Whoever you are—I have always depended on the kindness of strangers.'"

"Tennessee Williams... left many mourners: strangers who for forty years depended on him for the most magical evenings in American theater."

He was without question the greatest living American playwright, a term he disliked, because he assumed it meant only that he was not yet dead. But he can now stand up to the dead as well as the living. His only real rival as the greatest American dramatist of this century is Eugene O'Neill. The two of them changed the whole shape of American drama. To compare them is difficult. Before O'Neill there was almost no serious American drama at all and Tennessee's writing, word for word, is incomparably better than O'Neill's.

Before *The Glass Menagerie* no one believed that a play of quiet emotion, written in beautiful poetry, could compete in Broadway's commercial marketplace, full of highly polished hit machines. Before *Menagerie* writers like William Inge and Carson McCullers assumed that the Broadway theatre was simply not a medium for which they could write, and plays like *Picnic* and *The Member of the Wedding* might never have been written.

Tennessee was not an intellectual. He read relatively little, his tastes in art and music were naive, and he had almost no sense of politics or even of simple citizenship. In his personal life he could be cruel, though never physically, and hurt many people very deeply. On the other hand he was most generous with his friends, and helped to support many less successful authors.

In *Orpheus Descending* he told about a bird that had no legs, only wings. It spent its whole life in the sky, living on the wind. He was like that. His feet were never on the ground, but in the beauty of his words he was always flying high, and living on the wind.

He imitated no one, he seemed not even to hear the strident babel of Broadway, yet somehow his quiet voice rose piping clear above all the shouts and cries and choruses.

When a lonely crippled girl blew out the candles that lit her menagerie of glass, and the curtain fell on the gentlest and most beautiful play on Broadway, there was an explosion of applause that shook the rialto, and it would never be the same again.

INDEX

Note: In the early part of this book, Tennessee Williams is referred to as "Tom." For consistency, this index will refer to him throughout as "Tennessee."

335